American History through Hollywood Film

American History through Hollywood Film

From the Revolution to the 1960s

MELVYN STOKES

Waubonsee Community College
Aurora Campus
18 S. River Street
Aurora, IL 60506

BLOOMSBURY
LONDON · NEW DELHI · NEW YORK · SYDNEY

Bloomsbury Academic

An imprint of Bloomsbury Publishing Plc

50 Bedford Square	1385 Broadway
London	New York
WC1B 3DP	NY 10018
UK	USA

www.bloomsbury.com

Bloomsbury is a registered trademark of Bloomsbury Publishing Plc

First published 2013

British Library Cataloguing-in-Publication Data
A catalogue record for this book is available from the British Library.

ISBN: HB: 978-1-4411-7429-1
PB: 978-1-4411-7592-2
ePDF: 978-1-4411-7747-6
ePub: 978-1-4411-5349-4

Library of Congress Cataloging-in-Publication Data
A catalog record for this book is available from the Library of Congress.

Typeset by Newgen Knowledge Works (P) Ltd., Chennai, India
Printed and bound in India

CONTENTS

LIST OF ILLUSTRATIONS

ACKNOWLEDGMENTS

I am very grateful for the support of Nahed and Sarah during the months spent writing this book, and for much else besides. The idea for the book was born during a conversation with Claire Lipscomb of Bloomsbury Publishing, who has been a very helpful and encouraging editor. I would also like to express my gratitude to Rhodri Mogford of Bloomsbury Publishing, together with Gillian Pressley and Matthew Jones of UCL. The staff of the Reuben Library of the British Film Institute were, as always, extremely helpful during the process of researching and writing the book. The copyeditor did an exemplary job. I am very grateful to Leigh Priest for compiling the index, quickly and thoroughly as always. Any mistakes that remain are the responsibility of the author.

Introduction

The last few years have seen a dramatic growth in the use of Hollywood feature films dealing with American history in college and school classrooms on both sides of the Atlantic. In an increasingly image-conscious and image-oriented culture, students often engage deeply with such films and discuss with enthusiasm the interpretations they offer of the past. This growing interest has encouraged the publication—in some cases republication—of books debating the intellectual issues arising from using movies in this way. These works have, in the main, fallen into two categories: single-authored works or edited collections. The single-authored works are usually theoretically driven, analyzing a relatively small number of films to illustrate particular issues and problems that arise in bringing American history to the screen.[1] The edited collections are often fairly diffuse, covering an eclectic range of films and topics of interest to a range of contributors and embracing different methodological perspectives.[2]

American History through Hollywood Film differs from both categories. A single-authored work, it focuses on a range of filmic representations of major subjects and themes in American history, arranged in a broadly chronological way. Chapters on the American Revolution, slavery, Lincoln, the Civil War, and legacies of the Civil War (the legend of the "Lost Cause" and the Ku Klux Klan) are followed by chapters on Native Americans, immigration, the Depression of the 1930s, the anti-Communist "inquisition" in Hollywood, and aspects of the crucial decade of the 1960s (civil rights, the Kennedy assassination, and the beginnings of US involvement in Vietnam). The first five chapters are thematic, demonstrating how Hollywood's interpretation of particular subjects changed over time. The chapter on Lincoln, for example, begins with early silent-era movies and concludes with Steven Spielberg's *Lincoln* (2012). The last five chapters closely analyze either a single film or a pair of films on a particular subject.

In structure, if not I hope in style, *American History through Hollywood Film* resembles a history textbook. Like all textbooks, it cannot hope to cover the whole of American history and has to be selective in terms of what is included and what is not. In chronological terms, I decided at an early stage to start with the Revolution, omitting colonial history. Deciding when to finish was a more difficult problem, but it finally seemed to me that it would be enough to cover two centuries of history in a work of this kind and the book consequently ends with the 1960s. Some events (the Revolution, Civil War, and 1930s Depression) and one commanding personality (Lincoln) seemed to call out for inclusion. In deciding what else to include, I was much influenced by the argument that Hollywood's own coverage of history has been highly selective. Its productions, comment Jeremy D. Stoddard and Alan S. Marcus,

> . . . tend to be made for a broad general audience, so the history of the majority of this audience, traditionally white and middle-class, is emphasized . . . The end result is an audience that learns much of what they know about the past from viewing simplified, "whitewashed" . . . historical narratives that generally exclude or minimize the roles of marginalized people in the national story.[3]

Chapter Two, on slavery in American film, and Chapter Six, on Native Americans, are intended as a counter to this inbuilt bias in terms of subject-matter—as is Chapter Seven, on the "new" Jewish and Italian immigrants of the late nineteenth and early twentieth century, who were resented and looked down upon by many white native-born Americans.[4] Finally, it seemed to me that the legacy of the Civil War, the investigation into Hollywood by the House Committee on Un-American Activities (HUAC)—a time in which the history of the film industry itself intersected with national politics—and the crucial decade of the 1960s with its racial and political challenges all merited inclusion. The themes and subjects covered here are all ones I have found, in more than 20 years of teaching American history-on-film courses, to appeal to students from both the United States and Britain.

At the heart of the book is the analysis in some detail of 21 films, released between 1915 and 2012, dealing with aspects of American history.* Some of these (*The Birth of a Nation, Gone With the Wind,* and *Mississippi Burning*) appear in more than one chapter. In the case of each film, I have tried to synthesize what historians and film writers have said about it while analyzing the movie concerned to produce what I hope will be new insights into its treatment of history. The 21 films are not, of course, the only ones to deal with the historical theme or subject concerned. Most belong to a rich tradition of moviemaking representing, for example, the Civil War or Native Americans. I have endeavored to show how and why those traditions

---

* *The Birth of a Nation* (1915); *The Iron Horse* (1924); *Abraham Lincoln* (1930); *Gone With the Wind* (1939); *Young Mr. Lincoln* (1939); *Abe Lincoln in Illinois* (1940); *The Grapes of Wrath* (1940); *The Way We Were* (1973); *The Godfather Part II* (1974); *Hester Street* (1975); *Revolution* (1985); *Mississippi Burning* (1988); *Glory* (1989); *Dances With Wolves* (1990); *JFK* (1991); *Guilty by Suspicion* (1991); *Amistad* (1997); *The Patriot* (2000); *Cold Mountain* (2003); *Lincoln* (2012); *Django Unchained* (2012).

develop, and the place of the key 21 films in them, by analyzing or citing more than 150 other films on the same subjects. *American History through Hollywood Film* also makes considerable use of movie reviews. The work of film critics, while not allowing us to recuperate the reactions of actual movie spectators, does at least allow us to establish—in the words of Janet Staiger, a pioneer of movie reception studies—"not a so-called correct reading of a particular film but the range of possible readings and reading processes at historical moments."[5] Movie reviews can provide us with evidence relating to films that no longer exist or are not easily available. Favorable reviews can suggest why a particular interpretation of history was acceptable at the time of writing, hostile ones indicate the reasons for it being perceived as objectionable. When critics disagree with one another—sometimes bitterly, as over *The Birth of a Nation* and *JFK*, at other times less passionately, as with John Ford's *The Grapes of Wrath* and *Hester Street*—their differences of opinion often revolve around matters of historical interpretation. Reviews, when analyzed diachronically rather than synchronically, can also draw attention to the ways in which filmic representations of a historical event, issue, or individual change over time.

Why study the way US history is shown on film in the first place? In part, because it matters. "Hollywood's interpretations of American history," writes Robert Brent Toplin

> can make a significant impact on the public's thinking about the past. Historical dramas . . . often . . . stimulate wide-ranging debates about their interpretations and lead to the publication of articles and books about the issues they address. . . . Especially since 1915, the year in which [*The*] *Birth of a Nation* excited intense arguments because many thought it presented a racist vision of the Reconstruction era, audiences and critics have been engaged in lively disagreements about the way in which cinematic historians deal with their subjects.[6]

Hollywood for a century now has been a major force in how Americans view their past. Despite the millions of words written about the Civil War and the television programs made about it, for example, it seems likely that most Americans' view of the Civil War and the Reconstruction period is still profoundly shaped by *Gone With the Wind*. When *Gone With the Wind* was premiered on network television over two nights in 1976, NBC claimed a total audience of 110 million. Ninety percent of today's US population is believed to have seen the movie at least once. By comparison, around 40 million Americans watched one or more of the programs in Ken Burns's much-acclaimed television series on the Civil War, first broadcast on PBS in 1990.[7]

As early as the mid-1910s, film director David W. Griffith was arguing that the movie camera was "the instrument with which history is beginning to be written." "The truths of history today," Griffith declared, "are restricted to the limited few attending our colleges and universities; the motion picture can carry these truths to the entire world . . . while at the same time bringing diversion to the masses." He foresaw a time "when the children in the public schools will be taught practically everything by moving pictures. Certainly they will never be obliged to read history again." Griffith also anticipated history being learned in this way in the home: "when one wants to refresh one's mind about a historical incident," he suggested, predicting in many ways today's televisions, computers, I-Pads, cellphones, DVDs, and Blu-Rays, each house would have a "receptacle" for the films concerned and a screen to show them on.[8] Although many more people take history courses in college than a century ago, Griffith's vision of a world in which history on film has replaced—for millions of people—history in books seems much closer to reality. The history viewed in a Hollywood movie, even by college students, may be more real and convincing than the history uncovered within the pages of a history book. "Friends who teach high school and college courses on Vietnam," wrote journalist/historian Stanley Karnow, "tell me that, for most of their students, *JFK* is the truth."[9]

Hollywood feature films approach history in a very different way from scholarly books and articles. With rare exceptions, they are not based on what historians regard as source-materials: archival records. Or, more precisely, they do not use archival records in the same way as historians. The main purpose of most Hollywood "research" is to secure authenticity in the visual "look" of the film—it helps imply that, if so much attention is paid to details (the red earth of Tara, Indian costumes in *Dances With Wolves*, the restaging of the assassination of John F. Kennedy in the same Dallas location) then the story the film tells is probably also true. Few if any Hollywood filmmakers have done research of the kind organized by Jean Renoir in France.[10] Preparing for his film *La Marseillaise* (1938) about the French Revolution, Renoir assigned Mme. Jean-Paul Le Chanois to research the background of the battalion from Marseilles that fought in the revolutionary war. Mme. Le Chanois discovered that the existing historical orthodoxy about the battalion—that it was composed of foreigners, particularly Italians, and "wild-eyed, irrational, criminal type[s] on the fringes of society"—was wrong. Working in the local archives in Marseilles, she found that the members of the battalion were "unquestionably French" and respectable, being "made up of former army officers, city magistrates, stone masons, carpenters and agricultural workers"—insights incorporated by Renoir into his film.[11]

Most historical films tell fictional stories (many are based on novels). Their characters are often fictional or given fictional qualities and experiences. *The Patriot* asks us to accept that Australian star Mel Gibson is "really" Benjamin Martin, a man who never existed but helped win the Revolutionary War. So far as we know, Lincoln never judged a pie-making competition of the kind suggested by *Young Mr. Lincoln*. The settings of movies are themselves fictions. Much of *Revolution* was shot in East Anglia, England, "Ellis Island" in *The Godfather Part II* was the old marketplace in Trieste, Italy, and *Cold Mountain*, a Civil War film about Appalachian North Carolina, was shot for the most part in Romania. As well as inventing "historical settings and people on the screen," it is also necessary to fictionalize events, as Robert A. Rosenstone explains,

> for a variety of reasons—to keep the story moving, to maintain intensity, to create a dramatic structure, and, above all, to allow the history to fit within time constraints (a life, a war, or a revolution, all within two hours). For historical films, different kinds of techniques are involved in this invention, techniques that we can label *Compression* (bringing together actual events that occurred in different times and places), *Alteration* (changing events slightly to highlight their underlying meaning), and *Metaphor* (using an invented image to stand for or sum up events too complex, lengthy, or difficult to depict).[12]

Compressed, altered, made metaphorical—generally fictionalized—as it may be, Hollywood's history has the power to create meaning out of the past. It does so for profit, by entertaining what it hopes will be a mass audience. It does so within the constraints imposed by a particular industry at a particular time and wider trends in American society at large (see Chapters Eight and Nine in particular for discussion of these points). It offers, viewable on a screen, a combination of image, dialogue, music, and sometimes text, creating, in imaginative terms, what appears as living history. We see what it might have been like to live through the American Revolution or the Civil War, arrive as a new immigrant or struggle along route 66 to California in the midst of the Depression. We see Indians hunting buffalo, the Klan ride, HUAC in session, and the Kennedy assassination. We also see how views change over time, as spurious, benign views of slavery give way to the horrors of the "middle passage" and the gallant sacrifice of African American soldiers at Fort Wagner. There is something that is challenging, but also intensely human about Hollywood history. "Through [cinematic] art," declared Steven Spielberg in a Dedication Day speech at Gettysburg in 2012, "we enlist the imagination to bring what is lost back to us, to bring the dead back to life. This resurrection is, of course, just an illusion, it's a fantasy and it's a dream, but dreams matter somehow to us."[13]

While Spielberg was right about the emotional appeal of many films about American history, his attempt in the same speech to draw a clear distinction between historians (who "gather evidence" and create "diligently reconstructed narratives") and filmmakers (who are obliged creatively to go "to the impossible places that other disciplines like history must avoid" in order to reimagine the past) created a false division.[14] For historians who, like myself, study historical films, movies are cultural products reflecting the broader social and cultural context of the time in which they are made and received. They speak to the values and sometimes the anxieties of their period. As argued in Chapter Four, *The Birth of a Nation* (1915) connected with racial and ethnic concerns at the start of the First World War while *Gone With the Wind* (1939) echoed the tensions of the late Depression era. Films such as *The Howards of Virginia* (1940, Chapter One) and *Abe Lincoln in Illinois* (1940, Chapter Three) were seen as comments on the uncertainties of the international situation in the opening months of the Second World War. *Hester Street* (1975) and *The Godfather Part II* (1974), both in Chapter Seven, expressed—and were responses to—the growing focus on questions of ethnicity that emerged in the 1960s and early 1970s. *Lincoln* (2012), by limiting itself to the brief, successful struggle in the House of Representatives over the draft of the Thirteen Amendment abolishing slavery, constructed Lincoln as an adept, bipartisan manager of Congress—an ideal hero for the current era of gridlock in Washington.

Hollywood historical films offer rich materials for study by historians. They are by no means simple subjects for analysis. At times, they can be inconsistent or contradict themselves. *The Birth of a Nation* and *Gone With the Wind*, for example, have traditionally been seen as representing slavery as a benevolent institution, with kindly masters and happy slaves. In reality, as suggested in Chapter Five, there are sequences in both films that draw attention to the brutality and oppression that lay at the roots of slavery. Historical films can foreground major historical issues. *Dances With Wolves* (1990), for example, raises issues to do with the concept of the frontier, the nomadic lifestyle of the Lakota Sioux, racial construction and interracial relationships, the strategy of the US army, and the decline of the buffalo. *The Grapes of Wrath* (1940) deals with the causes of the agricultural depression, the role of the Federal government in matters of relief, the problems of migrant workers, and trends toward unionization and political radicalism. A historical film, argues Robert A. Rosenstone, "must be judged against what we know can be verified, documented, or reasonably argued. In other words, we must judge it against the ongoing discourse of history, the existing body of historical texts, and their data and arguments."[15]

Determining how accurate and original the filmic view of history is can only be done through research in other historical sources. Yet part of the fascination of historical films is also to do with how and why they present the view of history they do at the time they are produced. To understand *The Grapes of Wrath*'s representation of the Great Depression, for example, we need to know about the impact of the Depression on the movie industry itself and the regime of self-regulation embodied in the Production Code Administration. Understanding *Dances With Wolves*' presentation of the history of the Lakota Sioux makes it necessary for us to know, not just about Hollywood's previous treatment of Native Americans, but also about broader changes in the United States, including the rise of modern environmentalism and Indian activism. Exploring American history through Hollywood film can take us in many new and fruitful historical directions.

CHAPTER ONE

The American Revolution

The American Revolution was *the* decisive event in American history. Without it, there would not have been an American history in the sense of the story of an independent country known as the United States of America. One hundred and twenty years after the Declaration of Independence (July 4, 1776), the movie industry was born in the United States. During the next century and more, it would produce many films dealing with people and events in American history or, at least, with historical settings for fictional narratives. In the first years of the movies, a number of films were produced dealing with the American Revolution. This cycle ended abruptly in 1917. After this, what strikes the historian is how *few* films were produced by American filmmakers set against a background of the Revolution. This chapter will explore the development of filmic representations of the American Revolution over time and discuss the reasons for its neglect by moviemakers after 1917.

Between 1908 and 1917, paralleling the vogue for "historical" Civil War pictures, was a similar—if much more limited—tendency to produce films set against the background of the American Revolution. At least 17 such movies appeared.[1] Several were made by important directors (Edwin S. Porter, J. Stuart Blackton, David W. Griffith, and Charles Brabin) and major production companies (including Edison, Kalem, Vitagraph, and Biograph). Ironically, several of the directors were born abroad—Blackton and Brabin in England, Émile Chautaud in France. Since some of these films have not survived and others, including the later *Cardigan* (1922),[2] are difficult to access, it is not possible to comment in detail on their interpretation of the Revolution. The first nine films about the revolution in any case consisted of only one reel, lasting a maximum of around 15 minutes. These initial films can have been little more than a short series of tableaux, relying for audiences' understanding on the scenes they depicted already forming part of the collective cultural memory derived from school books, paintings, monuments, Fourth of July parades, poetry, and political orations.

Two things, however, are clear about this cycle of films. The first is that more than half foregrounded George Washington as a character. Washington was played by Joseph Kilgour in *Washington Under the American Flag* (1909), Ben F. Wilson in *The Battle of Bunker Hill* (1911), Charles Ogle in *How Washington Crossed the Delaware* (1912), Logan Paul in *The Flag of Freedom* (1913), William Worthington in *The Spy* (1914), an unknown actor in *Washington at Valley Forge* (1908) and Pedro Léon in a second film with the same title (1914), George MacQuarrie in *Betsy Ross*, and Noah Beery in *Spirit of '76* (1917). As Barry Schwartz has argued, Washington's reputation had declined in the aftermath of the Civil War: not only had the Civil War made the Revolution appear less significant as a conflict, the decades that followed with their territorial and economic expansion sharply diminished Washington's own stature. Yet by the early twentieth century, his reputation was reviving again, as artists, writers, and historians created a "dualism of commonness and distinction," presenting him simultaneously on the one hand as a symbol of frontier spirit and democratic values and on the other as a genteel aristocrat whose example served as a reproach to the vulgarity and corruption of contemporary businessmen and politicians.[3] The Washington of early twentieth-century movies seems to have echoed this reviving stature. He is a key historical figure: in *Betsy Ross*, for example, *Variety* noted, Betsy's "deftness with the needle attracts the attention of Washington as he is seeking some one to make up the flag he has designed."[4]

If early films about the Revolution paralleled changes in the reputation of George Washington, they also expressed the growing nineteenth-century tendency to create cultural and political myths out of the Revolution itself. The movies entitled *The Boston Tea Party* (1908 and 1915) are a case in point. As Alfred F. Young has argued, the destruction of East India Company tea in Boston harbor on December 16, 1773—a key event in the background to the Revolution—was not commonly known as the "Boston Tea Party" until over 60 years after it took place. It was described in this way for the first time in the titles of two books (1834, 1835) recounting the memories of shoemaker and revolutionary George Robert Twelves Hewes. As Young points out, the term was embraced and disseminated by Boston political conservatives eager to draw the radicalism from what had been a radical act ("the destruction of the tea") by giving it a frivolous name.[5] The title of both films endorsed the change of name. *Midnight Ride of Paul Revere* (1907) and *The Midnight Ride of Paul Revere* (1914) were based less on history than an 1861 epic poem by Henry Wadsworth Longfellow.[6] *Betsy Ross* (1917) was a melodrama focusing on the tangled love-lives during the Revolution of two Philadelphia sisters, one of who supposedly made the first American flag. According to the claim first made by her grandson in 1870, Ross had transformed Washington's plan for a flag containing 13 six-pointed stars into a flag with five-pointed ones, which she then produced. As scholars have pointed out, there is no convincing evidence that this took place: Betsy Ross did exist but her role in the evolution of the American flag was a fiction created by late nineteenth-century conservative nationalists looking for a female heroine who, in the words of Lauren Thatcher Ulrich, would be "patriotic yet safe."[7] Finally, two films about the Revolution released in 1908 and 1917 derived their title from that of the patriotic picture painted by Archibald McNeil Willard for the 1876 centennial revolutionary exposition in Philadelphia: *The Spirit of '76*. The appearance of the second of these films in a United States that had just entered the First World War had strange, unanticipated consequences for a film about the American Revolution.

The United States v. "The Spirit of '76"

Robert Goldstein was a Los Angeles film and theatrical costumier. He produced most of the uniforms and clothes for David W. Griffith's racist epic of the Civil War era, *The Birth of a Nation* (1915). Running out of money, Griffith persuaded Goldstein to accept payment on the basis of a share of the film's profits. The vast commercial success of *The Birth of a Nation* not only made Goldstein wealthy, it also left him ambitious to produce a film that would be as spectacular epic on the same lines as Griffith's. It would be set against the background not of the Civil War, but of the American Revolution.[8] On June 14, 1916, the *Moving Picture World* announced the formation of the Continental Producing Company with Goldstein as the main shareholder and informed its readers that the company hoped to produce a film "perfect as to its historical accuracy and detail, with an entirely original and sensational story closely interwoven."[9] The fictional narrative of the film, described by Anthony Slide as "extraordinarily lurid,"[10] dealt with the unsuccessful efforts of George III's half-Indian mistress, Catherine Montour, to make herself queen of America. It ended with her, unknowingly, about to marry her brother until, at the last possible moment, the relationship was revealed. Interspersed with the melodrama was an ambitious series of historical tableaux: Patrick Henry's speech to the Virginia House of Burgesses, Paul Revere's ride, the battle of Lexington, the signing of the Declaration of Independence, and Washington at Valley Forge.

Shortly before the United States entered the First World War in April 1917, Goldstein finished work on his 14-reel film. During the 18 months of the production, he had had to deal with unscrupulous partners, seemingly endless financial problems, repeated efforts to remove him from the picture and continuous attempts at sabotaging the whole project (which he blamed principally on D. W. Griffith and his agents). The film was scheduled to open in Chicago on May 7, but the chairman of the Chicago Censorship Board, Major Metallus Lucullus Cicero Funkhouser, refused to grant a permit allowing it to be shown. He did so, according to the *Motion Picture News*, on two grounds: "that it might serve to arouse bitterness and sectional feeling against England, now one of the United States' Allies in the present war" and that "[t]he battlefield horrors . . . contained in the picture . . . might militate against recruiting."[11]

The Censorship Board as a whole asked for 16 cuts in the film, but did not give any assurance—once they were made—that a permit would be forthcoming. Goldstein made the requested cuts and tried to show the film without a permit on May 14, but was prevented from doing so by the Chicago police.[12] The next day, he sought an injunction from Judge Jesse A. Baldwin to restrain the city from stopping the film's exhibition. A special showing of the film was organized for the judge and about 200 people, including newspapermen. Although the *Chicago Daily Tribune* subsequently reported that the film was "highly innocuous" and revealed no "pro-German trend," Baldwin finally declined to grant the injunction on the grounds that the case was outside his jurisdiction.[13] Goldstein also asked Judge Kavanaugh for a writ of mandamus forcing Funkhouser to issue the permit. In giving his judgment, Kavanaugh dismissed the idea that the film was anti-British (this, it must be remembered, is a film about the American Revolution) but found it immoral because, in dealing with the relationship between a brother and sister who are unaware of their familial relationship, the film seemed to be suggesting incest. With all the controversial scenes removed (and *The Spirit of '76* now down to 12 reels), Funkhouser finally issued a permit and the film opened to broadly favorable reviews on May 28. Reviewers emphasized that, although the film was patriotic, "no feeling of resentment is aroused against any of our present allies" and that "it contains nothing that would dampen the fervor of America at war."[14]

If Goldstein thought for a brief moment that he was now out of the woods, he was sadly mistaken. So far as he was concerned, everything now depended on the west coast opening. Goldstein continued to edit what was now already a much-edited film and arranged to have the opening at Clune's Auditorium in Los Angeles, where both Griffith's *The Birth of a Nation* and *Intolerance* had premièred, on November 28, 1917. During the morning before the première, the film was shown at Clune's to a special audience that included Assistant US District Attorney Gordon Lawson, several members of the American Protective Association (a strongly nationalistic organization), District Judge Benjamin Franklin Bledsoe—a committed supporter of the war effort—and the British consul in Los Angeles and his family.[15] The preview seemed to have gone well and Goldstein was left to continue with his preparations for the opening. What happened during the next few hours is open to very different interpretations. According to Goldstein himself, he restored some of the short pieces of film that had recently been edited out in order to promote greater continuity. His critics, however, alleged that the scenes he put back in were mainly those showing British atrocities during the Cherry Valley Massacre of 1778: the bayoneting of a baby by a soldier, the stabbing of an elderly Quaker by a Hessian mercenary, British soldiers dragging a woman by the hair, and a British officer forcing a young woman into a bedroom.[16] Assistant US District Attorney Gordon Lawson and Burritt S. Mills of the American Protective League, watching the first two showings of the film, noted these reinsertions and Judge Bledsoe—interrupting his Thanksgiving dinner to do so—issued a warrant for the seizure of the film. Next day, when Goldstein filed a motion demanding the return of the film, Bledsoe not only denied the motion but ordered Goldstein's arrest for violating the Espionage Act passed in June 1917.[17]

On December 4, 1917, a Federal grand jury indicted Goldstein on two counts in relation to the Espionage Act and one under the Selective Service Act. Under the first count, it was charged that he "willfully and unlawfully attempted to cause insubordination, disloyalty, mutiny and refusal of duty on the part of the military and naval forces of the United States" by producing a film "designed and intended to arouse antagonism, hatred and enmity between the American people and the people of Great Britain, at a time when the defendant knew well the government of Great Britain . . . was an ally of the United States in a prosecution of a war against the imperial government of Germany."[18] The second and third counts dealt with the alleged influence of his film in discouraging draftees from reporting for military duty. Since Goldstein was unable to raise the $10,000 required to secure bail, he remained in jail for the four months before his trial started on April 2, 1918. He found it very hard—in the anti-German atmosphere of the time—to find a lawyer willing to defend him. One lawyer, Earl Rogers, in what Anthony Slide calls "an extraordinarily damning statement," announced that—although he was willing to be a defense attorney—he had a son fighting in France and that he would step down if "any pro-German tinge to the acts of Goldstein" was identified. (In the end, Rogers did not appear on Goldstein's behalf.)[19] Anti-German feeling was especially high in California in the spring of 1918, following a recent allegation that German Consul in San Francisco Franz Bopp had earlier conspired to blow up American munition ships. On the first day of the trial, the Los Angeles Times published a picture of an ad promoting The Spirit of '76 which had been damaged by the wind and now read "Spi '76." Superimposed over the picture itself were photographs of Bopp and Goldstein with the headline: "Dynamiter of Munition Ships Goldstein's 'Angel'?"[20]

Once the case—which would become known with deep unintentional irony as The United States v. The Spirit of '76—got underway, it rapidly became clear that Goldstein had very little chance of being acquitted. A procession of witnesses attested to his real or supposed anti-British sentiments and the (in fact nonexistent) financing for his film offered by Germans such as Bopp.[21] Witnesses also alleged that he had circulated a petition against US involvement in the war (which was true, though hardly a crime) and had insisted that the film needed scenes of British atrocities in order to be financially successful.[22] Judge Bledsoe, a rabid supporter of the war, was clearly biased against him. As for the jury, as the *Los Angeles Times* commented: "nearly every member . . . has a relative in the army or navy" or else had themselves been drafted and "were awaiting call to service."[23] On April 15, 1918 Goldstein was convicted on the first two counts of his indictment. Two weeks later, Bledsoe sentenced him to ten years in prison on the first count and two years on the second—the sentences to run concurrently—and fined him $5,000. Although his sentence would later be commuted by President Wilson to just three years, Robert Goldstein remains the only film director ever sent to jail for producing a film on the subject of the American Revolution.[24]

What went wrong? Some part of the intense hatred of Goldstein can no doubt be explained in terms of anti-semitism (Goldstein himself later wrote that if he had "taken a stage name like Reginald Scarborough" everything "might have been all right.")[25] But most of it had to do with his "German" background (his father had emigrated from Germany in the early 1860s and Goldstein had returned there for a visit aged 14). In an atmosphere in which all things German were tarred by association with a distant enemy— and during a period in which teaching the German language was banned in schools and systematic attempts were made to rechristen "German" products, with hamburgers becoming Salisbury steaks and sauerkraut Liberty cabbage—it was all too easy for right-wingers to depict the naive Goldstein as a pro-German propagandist. The combination of the activities of officially encouraged nationalist super-patriots (the American Protective League), diplomatic pressure from Britain, systematic abuse from the *Los Angeles Times*, and a jingoistic pro-war judge in the end produced what Michael Selig has termed "an exemplary case of the suppression of civil liberties."[26]

In the end, what also destroyed Goldstein was timing. If his film had first come out in 1915 or 1916, it would not have been so controversial. If it had been released in 1919 or 1920, the passions excited by the war would have started to fade. Goldstein himself did exhibit his film in the United States in 1921, when, true to form, he was accused not only of being pro-German but also of attempting to aid Sinn Fein (Irish republicans) by producing so anti-British a movie.[27]

Conservative reaction: The 1920s

The next major film with the Revolution as a subject, made by Goldstein's former colleague D. W. Griffith, was born in vastly different circumstances.

In May 1922, the Daughters of the American Revolution (DAR) wrote to Will H. Hays, the former Republican politician who was now head of the Motion Picture Producers and Distributors of America (MPPDA), to ask why no film had been made about the American Revolution.[28] Clearly, the DAR had never heard of the films produced on the subject before the First World War and either were unaware of—or chose diplomatically to ignore—the Goldstein saga. Hays was very conscious that Hollywood was currently the target for much criticism as a center of "immorality." In September 1921, Roscoe "Fatty" Arbuckle had been arrested and charged with the rape and murder of starlet Virginia Rappe at a drunken party (this was supposedly the era of prohibition). In February 1922, actor turned director Desmond Taylor was found murdered in his Hollywood home. In January 1923, Wallace Reid would become the first Hollywood star to die of drug-related problems. Confronting a growing torrent of criticism of the Hollywood community, it is clear why Hays quickly began to push the idea of a movie about the Revolution: having the DAR on his side meant acquiring a powerful ally. In view of his earlier historical epics, Griffith was the obvious man to make such a film. Moreover, he offered the additional attraction of being detached from the Hollywood establishment: in 1919, the director had abandoned the west coast to return to the east, where he founded a studio located on financier Henry Flagler's former estate at Mamaroneck, New York.[29]

Griffith was eager to undertake the film. Before becoming a film director, he had written an unproduced play on the Revolution called *War* (some of the scenes of which would eventually be incorporated in his new project).[30] On numerous occasions, Griffith had expressed the wish to make a truly spectacular motion picture about the Revolution (which was why Goldstein suspected him of trying to sabotage *The Spirit of '76*). The contrast to the situation in which *The Spirit of '76* was made, however, could not have been greater. Griffith's *America*, as it came to be called, was filmed with the approval of the DAR. The US Government even helped with the production: Secretary of War John W. Weeks permitted Griffith to film battle scenes using soldiers from the First Infantry Division and the Third Cavalry.[31] In order to legitimate the film so far as possible as "history," Griffith engaged in historical research, sought the advice of historical consultant John L. E. Pell,[32] and contacted both museums and historical societies. Wherever possible, he persuaded such organizations to loan authentic relics for use in the film. Thus, in the sequence dealing with the fight at Lexington Common, the actor playing the British Major Pitcairn carried the real Pitcairn's silver pistols (which he had lost) and the last drum roll came from the actual drum used in April 1775.[33]

In many ways, *America* (1924) was modeled on Griffith's *The Birth of a Nation*. It claimed to be "history." It had a grandiose title that emphasized "its aspirations to epic status."[34] It was similarly based on a historical novel—in this case, Robert W. Chalmers' *The Reckoning*. It alternated historical set-pieces (Patrick Henry's speeches, Paul Revere's ride, armed clashes at Lexington, Concord, Bunker Hill, Merriman's Corner and Johnson Hall, the Declaration of Independence, Washington at Valley Forge, and Cornwallis' surrender at Yorktown) with more "domestic" or family scenes. *America* also had its "renegade" figure—disloyal American Walter Butler (Lionel Barrymore) who, like mulatto leader Silas Lynch (George Siegmann) in *Birth*, schemed to build an empire of his own.[35] Finally, the conflict between American revolutionaries and anti-revolutionaries ended with a symbolic act of reconciliation: the marriage of Minuteman Nathan Holden (Neil Hamilton) with Nancy Montague (Carol Dempster), the daughter of a Tory judge. Critics were almost unanimous in their praise of the finished film. According to *Photoplay*, it was "one of the greatest thrill pictures ever made." *Variety* heralded it as an "outstanding achievement" that would be "paramount as a box office attraction." A reviewer for *Harrison's Reports* insisted that "it contains every element necessary to success, both financially and entertainingly."[36]

The fact that *America*—in common with *The Spirit of '76*—had Walter Butler as a major character as well as other obvious similarities between the two films prompted Goldstein to claim that Griffith had copied his work. (When the two met for the last time in Germany in 1925, Griffith magisterially told his former investor that "you cannot copyright history.")[37] Unlike Goldstein, however, Griffith was an Anglophile. He bought his suits from English tailors.[38] He had enjoyed his time in England in 1917 making the anti-German propaganda film *Hearts of the World*. He had no desire to offend the British. Consequently, he retitled *America* as *Love and Sacrifice* for its British release and made substantial changes to the film itself to avoid hurting British sensibilities. New titles presented the Revolution essentially as a Civil War between two different groups of Englishmen and blamed George III's scheming advisers, rather than the King himself, for causing the war. The new version further emphasized the villainous Butler's American origins.[39]

Even in its revised version, however, the British Board of Film Censors initially refused to allow the film to be shown because "it was likely to cause 'bad relations' between Britain and the United States." Despite a personal plea from Griffith, the censors continued to resist issuing a certificate permitting the film's release until it was again re-cut.[40] So many changes had been made by the time of the film's final release, concluded the acerbic reviewer for the British trade magazine *Bioscope*, that "appraisement of the scenario is practically impossible" and the film's "historical value . . . negligible."[41] Why did Griffith put so much effort into securing the film's acceptance in Britain? American films, even by 1924, were increasingly coming to rely for their financial success on overseas markets. As Mark Glancy has noted, Hollywood was dependent throughout the studio era on Britain "as the source of the majority of its foreign earnings."⁴² Trying so hard to repackage *America* as *Love and Sacrifice* for the British market, therefore, may have reflected Griffith's recognition of the crucial importance of that exhibition market more than his Anglophilia. His Hollywood successors were equally aware of the importance of Britain as a market, and the difficulty of "selling" the American Revolution to that market may have helped explain why so few films about it were made.

Curiously, *America* was not the only spectacular film about the Revolution to be produced in 1924. Cosmopolitan Productions, established by William Randolph Hearst primarily in order to make spectacles starring his mistress, Marion Davies, released *Janice Meredith*. Again, crucial incidents in the Revolution—the Boston Tea Party, Paul Revere's ride, Lexington, Valley Forge, the battle of Trenton, and the British surrender at Yorktown—were recreated on screen, together with visualizations of the paintings of "Washington Crossing the Delaware" and the marching Minutemen of "The Spirit of '76." "It was almost," wrote one later commentator, "as though American history textbook illustrations came to life with semi-documentary reality."⁴³ Like *America*, *Janice Meredith* was made with "historical accuracy in period costumes, weapons, wigs, uniforms, furnishings and military material." Generally, in fact, since it was a Marion Davies vehicle financed by Hearst, production values were high: the final sequence showing the romantic leads, Davies in the title role and Charles Fownes (Harrison Ford), being entertained by George and Martha Washington (Joseph Kilgour and Mrs. Macklyn Arbuckle) on the lawn at Mount Vernon, was shot in a pioneering two-color version of Technicolor.⁴⁴ Contemporary critics, on the whole, were impressed: a reviewer for the *New York Times* hailed the film as "a brilliant achievement" containing scenes that "will be remembered for years by all those who see it, even if they behold it but once."⁴⁵

According to Cotton Seiler, both *America* and *Janice Meredith* were "extravagant monuments to Americanism."⁴⁶ Neither seems to have been at all influenced by the new and more critical approach to the history of the Revolutionary period pioneered by scholars such as J. Allen Smith, Algie M. Simons, and Charles A. Beard. In Smith's *The Spirit of American Government* (1907), Simons' *Social Forces in American History* (1911) and Beard's *Economic Interpretation of the US Constitution* (1913), the era of the Revolution was reinterpreted primarily in terms of social inequality and class conflict. The Founding Fathers—especially in the period leading to the adoption of the Constitution of 1787—were presented as much more economically self-interested and far less idealistic than they had once appeared.⁴⁷ Not only did the two films ignore this more critical view, but Griffith's *America*, with its themes of class mobility and ultimate social reconciliation, seemed to offer a conservative alternative to it.

In the shadow of the Second World War

After *America* and *Janice Meredith*, there do not seem to have been any important films about the Revolution for 15 years. Styles of filmmaking changed enormously in this period, partly as a result of the innovation of sound. Set-piece historical tableaux were already beginning to look old-fashioned in 1924: they interrupted the fluidity of the action.[48] Intertitles, explaining and contextualizing such set-pieces, virtually disappeared with the move to sound. The "Crash" of 1929 and the economic depression that followed encouraged escapism in movie entertainment. The most characteristic Hollywood products of the 1930s were not films based on historical stories—least of all stories dealing with the American Revolution—but musicals of the Busby Berkeley or Fred Astaire variety. Toward the end of the decade, however, a new interest in films related to American history began to become apparent. The best-publicized of these of course dealt with the Civil War and Reconstruction era: *Gone With the Wind* (1939). But the trend was also obvious in the work of John Ford, who directed one film dealing with the early nineteenth century (*Young Mr. Lincoln*, 1939) and one dealing with the Depression of the Thirties (*The Grapes of Wrath*, 1940). In the middle of this cycle of "historical" films came *Drums Along the Mohawk* (1939).

As "history," *Drums Along the Mohawk* was closer to *The Grapes of Wrath* than *Young Mr. Lincoln*. It made an attempt to show the sufferings and fighting spirit of ordinary Americans living in New York's Mohawk Valley in the revolutionary summer of 1777. Dealing mainly with the experiences of Gilbert Martin (Henry Fonda) and his wife Magdalena (Claudette Colbert), who build and then lose their little frontier farm, it had a considerably narrower focus than the 1936 novel with the same title by Walter D. Edmonds. As historian Anthony Wallace points out, the film concentrates on "the homey details of frontier life" rather than the broader backcloth of the revolutionary war itself. It thus misses the chance to explain "the strategic importance of the Mohawk Valley during the Revolution." The fact that the British commander in the area, St. Leger, badly underestimated the resistance of local colonists—as did "Gentlemanly Johnny" Burgoyne, who led the British attack to the east— meant that the plan to unite three British armies at Albany, cutting off in the process New England from the Southern colonies, was effectively ruined.[49] The film similarly largely ignored the complexities confronting the Mohawk Indians as a result of the Revolution. Led by Joseph Brand, the brother-in-law of Sir William Johnson, the British superintendent of Indian affairs, who had died in 1774, the Mohawks wavered for quite some time before American suspicion and hostility drove them finally to support the British forces by raiding exposed settlements in the Mohawk Valley. The Mohawks in Ford's film were represented as Indians in the traditional Hollywood manner—"as either figures of fun or savage killers"—rather than as members of a minority group making difficult choices in an awkward situation.[50]

With its emphasis on the struggle for economic security and fear of possible war, argues John O'Connor, *Drums Along the Mohawk* reflected both the anxieties of the Depression era and the growing threat posed by the international situation. Looking back at the past, it reassured those watching it that "traditional American ideals" were still alive and that "the nation had overcome hardships before and could do so again."[51] The film also conveyed a strong sense of white supremacy, with Gil Martin managing to ensure the rescue of those imprisoned in the fort by out-running all Indians in the race for help. In reality, as O'Connor points out, the real run was made by a man called Adam Helmer, rather than the fictional Martin. He ran to the fort at German Flats, rather than away from it, and the colonial militia—instead of racing to the rescue—in reality hid behind the walls of the fort watching the Indians rampaging and burning the homes outside. The siege and battle that dominate the final part of the film, therefore, never happened.[52] But the way the film mythologized them—together with the symbolism of victorious Continental soldiers marching into the fort at the end under the Stars and Stripes flag (unlikely in 1777)—suggested that American nationalism could cope with both the rebuilding of America after the Depression and the threat of a new world war.

The next film to deal with a revolutionary theme was *The Howards of Virginia*, released in 1940. Based on Elizabeth Page's best-selling novel of 1939, *The Tree of Liberty*, it was closer in style to *America* and *Janice Meredith* than *Drums Along the Mohawk*. The film combined more intimate moments with epic set-pieces, including the Boston Tea Party and Valley Forge. Yet, while it explained the major reasons for the Revolution, it was also the first talking film revolving around the conflicted loyalties of the period actually to be set in the South. Matt Howard (Cary Grant) comes from a family of poor Virginia farmers. Yet, thanks to the Jefferson clan, he gains an education. Thomas Jefferson himself (Richard Carlson) and Matt grow up together and Jefferson arranges for Matt to survey the plantation of wealthy conservative Fleetwood Peyton (Cedric Hardwicke). He falls in love with Fleetwood's sister, Jane (Martha Scott), and, despite the opposition of her family, the two marry. Matt manages to establish a plantation in the back hills of the Shenandoah, and the couple have three children, two boys and a girl. Encouraged by Jefferson to enter politics, Matt is elected to the Virginia House of Burgesses, where he hears Patrick Henry (Richard Gaines) speak and becomes a firebrand himself. When the Revolution begins, he is among the first to join the army. At first, the War for Independence splits the Howard family: Jane, in common with her brother, is a Tory, and her two sons initially side with her. In the end, however, the boys also enlist in the American army, prefiguring the final reconciliation between Matt and Jane as independence starts to become a reality.

The fact that the film places such great emphasis on the need to fight for freedom—it quotes, for example, Patrick Henry's famous "Give me liberty or give me death" speech—may have been some kind of commentary on the state of the world in 1940.[53] Western democracy appeared in considerable danger from the Fascist threat: France had surrendered to Germany in May and, with German bombs falling on London and other British cities at the time of the film's release in September, it was far from clear that an isolated Britain would be able to resist the Nazi assault.

Films of the 1950s

There had been a gap of 15 years between the 1924 films about the Revolution (*America*, *Janice Meredith*) and *Drums Along the Mohawk*. After *The Howards of Virginia*, there would be no feature films set against the background of the Revolution for a further 15 years. Both the world, and historical understanding of the American Revolution, changed a good deal during that period. The Second World War and the effects of the "Cold War," in particular, encouraged the emergence of the new "consensus" school of historians. While "progressive" historians such as Beard had perceived American history as the result of conflict between selfish, interested groups and the great majority of the population ("the people"), consensus scholars argued that Americans of whatever background were united by certain principles and beliefs. From the consensus point of view, the American Revolution was far from being a real (radical) Revolution on the French or Russian model. Instead, scholars such as Daniel Boorstin and Clinton Rossiter constructed it as the consequence of a conservative reaction on the part of liberty-loving colonists to the growing tyranny of the British government.[54]

Seeing a faraway and repressive British government as mainly responsible for provoking the Revolution opened up the possibility of presenting some British as appealing personal individuals, able despite the war between them to form close friendships with colonists.[55] This was a major theme of *The Scarlet Coat* (1955), a film set in a world of espionage and betrayal. American double agent John Boulton (Cornel Wilde) infiltrates British intelligence. His mission is to uncover the identity of an American traitor with the code-name "Gustavus." Boulton makes friends with British spymaster John Andre (Michael Wilding) and discovers that "Gustavus" is General Benedict Arnold (Robert Douglas), who is planning to surrender West Point to the British. Boulton fails to prevent Arnold's defection. Meanwhile, Andre is caught behind American lines and, in spite of Boulton's efforts to save him, executed as a spy. Reviewers found that the story of the friendship between Boulton and Andre crowded out any claim the film had to represent history. "The story contains little about the reasons for the war," commented one critic. "Considering the 'Now It Can Be Told' claims for this quasi-historical piece," observed another, " we see little of Benedict Arnold or the progress of the war."[56]

The consensus historians themselves offered Americans a view of their past that fitted well with the needs and reality of the Cold War. If not actually derived from consensus history, films about the Revolution in the 1950s tended to parallel its emphasis on American ideological unity and commitment to ideas of political liberty. *Johnny Tremain*, released in 1957 at the peak of the Cold War, referred so frequently to freedom and ideology that—according to one later commentator—it transformed the Revolution into a metaphor "for the struggle against Reds as well as Redcoats."[57] The film, produced by the Disney studio, was set in the period July 1773 to April 1775. Based on a book by Esther Forbes, it tells the story of a young apprentice silversmith (Hal Stalmaster) who is wrongly accused of stealing. Defended by Sons of Liberty members Paul Revere (Walter Sande) and Josiah Quincy (Whit Bissell), he is drawn into the movement for independence and takes part in the Boston Tea Party. After British troops arrive in Boston, he fights with the colonists at Lexington and Concord. It is very much a "Disney" picture, with all the strengths and weaknesses of the brand. A good deal of trouble and expense went into recreating a section of Boston in the 1770s, the British ship *Dartmouth* (one of the three ships involved in the Tea Party), and the early battles of the Revolution.[58] As directed by English-born Robert Stevenson, however—the same Stevenson who seven years later would make *Mary Poppins*—it was a classic children's film of the time: high-minded, sincere, and in places rather tedious.[59]

Like *Johnny Tremain*, *John Paul Jones* (1959) was based on a hero of the Revolution—in this case, a real one. As a "biopic," however, it failed to satisfy most critics. Abner Morison, writing in *Film Comment*, thought that the main difficulty was with the script, which seemed to him "pedestrian and uninspired," lacking those "things that are the essence of good portraiture." "Laborious and incoherent," agreed the reviewer for *Monthly Film Bulletin*, ". . . almost totally unimpressive as a spectacle, and hopelessly unselective, this is less a biography than a conventionally romanticized impression of a famous sailor designed in the form of a recruiting poster."[60] In fact, describing it as a "recruiting poster" was a shrewd thrust. Although the phrase had yet to be invented by Adam Yarmolinsky and used by President Dwight D. Eisenhower, *John Paul Jones* seemed very much an expression of the "military-industrial complex": "dedicated" to Fleet Admiral Chester W. Nimitz, it advertised itself as "sponsored" by Laurence Rockefeller, Charles Dana, Jr., R. Stuyvesant Pierrepont, Jr., and Pierre du Pont III.[61] "I've not yet begun to fight" may have initially been used by Jones during a sea battle during the

Revolutionary War. In 1959, two years after the Russians seemed to have achieved a technological lead over the United States with sputnik, it seems also to have summarized the point of view of the American power elite on the United States' confrontation with the Soviet Union. *John Paul Jones* may not have been a very good film, but it had a certain resonance with some Americans of the time.

Another not very good film about the Revolution that was released in 1959 was *The Devil's Disciple*, based on a play by George Bernard Shaw. The point of the play—that extreme circumstances bring out the true character of people—was almost entirely lost in the filmed version. Instead of Richard Dudgeon (Kirk Douglas) finding out, having begun by pretending to be a minister, that he has the temperament to be a real one, and Pastor Anderson (Burt Lancaster) discovering that he is really a man of action, the film merely "lamely hints" at the possibility of a reversal of this kind and otherwise "is content to exploit the melodrama for its own sake."[62] In a critical review (one of many) of the film, Robert C. Roman blamed this dilution of the play on the fact that the film itself had been jointly made (in England) by the producing companies owned by Douglas and Lancaster. In attempting to turn the play into a vehicle for the two stars, the two companies and (eventually) two directors—Alexander MacKendrick resigned after two weeks of "artistic differences," and was replaced by Guy Hamilton—failed to integrate the film into any kind of coherent order.[63] The character who profited most from this was neither of the revolutionaries but the unlikely figure of British general "Gentlemanly Johnny" Burgoyne, as played by Laurence Olivier. "[P]rojecting the right quality as he wanders through the ruins of Shaw," as one critic admiringly commented, Olivier effectively "stole" the picture. "Not only does he get every value out of some of Shaw's best lines," noted another reviewer, but "he achieves the greater feat of giving a synthetic Shavian sparkle to the additional dialogue, in the process administering such a drubbing to his American co-stars that Burgoyne's military defeats are triumphantly avenged."[64]

Filmmakers and historians: The American Film Institute debate, 1970

The decade of the 1960s—with its political challenges, social radicalism, and growing skepticism of "establishment" values—was not a time when filmmakers showed very much interest in the American Revolution. The only exception to this appears to have been *Lafayette* (1962), a ponderous Franco-Italian "spectacular" chiefly notable for cameo performances by Orson Welles and Vittoria de Sica, which made little impact anywhere. When the decade ended, however, the Bicentennial of the beginning of the

Revolution was starting to prompt a greater awareness of the lack of films dealing with the Revolutionary era.

In 1970 the American Film Institute (AFI) was awarded a grant of up to half a million dollars by the Humanities Endowment to lay the groundwork for a series of up to five films on the events and ideas of the Revolution. An advisory committee was established to help determine how the money should be spent. Besides Richard Kahlenberg, assistant director of the AFI, and two of his colleagues, it included historians Daniel Boorstin of the Smithsonian, Alan Heimert of Harvard University, and Richard Morris from Columbia University. The remainder of the committee represented in some sense the world of film: filmmaker-documentarian James Blue, designer-architect-filmmaker Charles Eames, director John Ford, and screenwriter Daniel Taradash, then president of the Motion Picture Academy of Arts and Sciences. In late June 1970, the committee met in Greystone, California. While the discussion was meant to focus on the production of television programs, in the course of two days it touched on almost all the difficulties that have traditionally confronted—and still confront—attempts to make profitable commercial movies about the American Revolution.

The members of the committee understood from the beginning that there was a strong prejudice in mainstream American cinema against making films about the Revolution. As Daniel Taradash observed, "filmmakers, at least up to now, haven't turned to the Revolution. . . . For the last 15–20 years I think Hollywood has shied away from it like the plague."[65] As the discussion progressed, it became clear that there were a number of reasons that could be advanced to explain this. The American Revolution was a complicated and often confused historical event.[66] It had been endlessly mythologized, becoming in the process a subject, in Daniel Boorstin's words, "full of corn and clichés." Paradoxically, however, while the Revolution remained broadly familiar to most Americans—James Blue remembered learning the outline facts in first grade—it was also curiously distant. The world of late eighteenth-century Americans appeared very remote to their late twentieth-century cousins. It seemed for the most part too WASP, too male, and—as Richard Morris commented—simply too "dandified . . . the tri-cornered hat and so forth" to appeal to modern Americans.[67] Partly because of its "period" flavor and the strength of the myths surrounding it, Hollywood had not so far been tempted to make a movie about the Revolution using the most important elements of its contemporary strategy for appealing to filmgoers—the strategy succinctly summarized by John Ford as "sex and violence."[68]

There was a clear assumption on the part of most members of the advisory committee, however, that the American Revolution itself was *not* something dead and fossilized. Instead, they were clearly viewing the incidents and personalities of the Revolution through the eyes of Americans of 1970—making in the process a series of comparisons of at times dubious historical merit (between modern student unrest and the

Boston Tea Party, between the Sons of Liberty and the Weathermen, and between the Continental Congress's decision to arm the colonists and the Black Panthers.)[69] Overwhelmingly, however, since the committee meeting was held only a few weeks after the shooting of four students by national guardsmen at Kent State University, the comparisons returned to Vietnam. The historians in particular—prefiguring a major change in the historiography of the Revolutionary war—drew attention to the facts that Britain had been disunited over the war, that many of its military and naval forces had been disaffected, that the war had been fought without allies, that it had been fought 3,000 miles away from home, that in a country in which almost everybody spoke the same language it was hard to separate friends from foes, and that to open peace negotiations was actually tantamount to a de facto recognition of American independence. In each case, a parallel could be made with the American involvement in Vietnam.[70]

Other useful comparisons with America in 1970, it was suggested, might include Washington's opposition to the military gaining too much power (demonstrated in his repression of the Newburgh Mutiny) and the collapse of the unity enjoyed by the colonists over the Stamp Act crisis in 1765 in the period leading up to the Declaration of Independence.[71] Finally, members of the committee felt that the projected film or films should reflect the greater racial and gender consciousness promoted by the civil rights and women's movements, although they also underlined the ideological or practical difficulties in the way of this: many blacks, having been promised their freedom by the British, had taken a counterrevolutionary position and the only "kind of a woman's rights type of liberated [woman]" Richard Morris could come up with as an example was Abigail Adams.[72]

At the start of their discussions, the members of the advisory committee seemed overawed by the size and complexity of the Revolution. To cover just one of its many aspects thoroughly, Richard Morris argued, would need a film on the epic scale of *Dr. Zhivago* or *War and Peace*.[73] As the debate continued, however, the group began to refine a set of criteria that would help identify a suitable project: they agreed on the need to challenge the myths surrounding the Revolution rather than reinforce them and they hoped to avoid most of the clichés that had come to be associated with it. They considered various possibilities for an overriding theme, including a film about what Morris termed "a non-cliché type incident that virtually nobody knows anything about" and a muckraking treatment of the Founding Fathers focusing on corruption, especially that associated with land deals.[74] Slowly, however, they began to move toward the idea of centering the project on the doubts and hesitations of one man as he changed from "loyal membership in the British Empire" into a revolutionary. To capture this "existential psychodrama," according to Alain Heimert (who first proposed it), would require a model closer to *Battle for Algiers* or *La Chinoise* than *War and Peace* and *Dr. Zhivago*. There was some desultory conversation over who might be a suitable subject for such a film or film series: Morris suggested Benjamin Franklin, since Franklin's family epitomized the contradictory loyalties of the period (his natural son was the Loyalist governor of New Jersey). Ultimately, however, the members of the committee seem to have reached a consensus that a fictional character should be used.[75]

On several occasions, the AFI people spelt out the kind of project they were aiming for: a series of low-budget films that would attempt to reach the widest possible audience through public broadcasting TV. The series would not be designed to make money, although Richard Kahlenberg clearly hoped that it might succeed in the way *Sesame Street* had done, with commercial television taking up a production "conceived for educational and cultural purposes."[76] Given the budgetary limitations on the series proposed, it was obvious that it would be impossible to film battle sequences. Not only was there no money to hire large numbers of extras, but—as John Ford pointed out—"the costuming alone would be outrageous" and it would be very hard to acquire authentic-looking guns.[77] One or two members of the committee suggested that battles might be simulated. Richard Morris thought that if only a brief vignette was needed "and we really aren't interested in seeing how many times a British soldier stuck a bayonet and disembowelled somebody," it would be possible either to use a chessboard or to follow Charles Eames' example in *Toy Train* by using toy soldiers. Daniel Taradash thought of employing rapid sequences of still photos as in *The History of the United States in One Minute*. But these ideas found little favor with the committee ("That's a very unAmerican movie," commented Heimert on the notion of using stills.)[78] Almost at the end of their two days of deliberations, the committee turned to two final thorny questions: what kind of language should the characters in the series speak and what kind of accent, if any, should they use.[79]

The debates in the committee foregrounded many of the problems that have traditionally faced those making films about the American Revolution and, indeed, have helped ensure that comparatively few such films have ever been made. It is not easy to deal with such a vast and complicated subject or with the mythical (almost mythological) figures it introduced. It is hard to avoid cliché in approaching a subject that, at one and the same time, is so well-known and yet so little understood. It is difficult to make a film about the Revolution that has something "relevant" to say to contemporary audiences. Moreover, in terms of sheer practicalities, it is a subject that seems to call for a massive financial outlay while promising little in the way of profitable return.

Films of the 1970s and 1980s: *1776* (1972), *Revolution* (1985), and *Sweet Liberty* (1986)

On March 15, 1969, a musical called *1776* opened on Broadway. It set out to explain the issues involved in the Declaration of Independence through the eyes of the distinguished figures who debated them—figures who, since this was a musical, danced and sang on the New York stage. Curiously, perhaps, *1776* won a Tony Award and ran for over three years. The fact that the production was a hit intrigued at least one member of the planning committee of the AFI's bicentennial project. "My daughter went to see it last night," admitted director John Ford on July 27, 1970. "She was most enthusiastic. Of course, she's a DAR . . . but I was surprised at her reaction to it because there's never been a [commercially] successful picture about the American Revolution."[80] The great success of *1776* also interested ageing movie mogul Jack L. Warner. Although Warner had never shown much interest in history, he thought he knew a good musical when he saw one (among others, he had produced *Yankee Doodle Dandy* (1942), *My Fair Lady* (1964) and *Camelot* (1967)). He paid over a million dollars for the screen rights to the play's authors and, having already retired from Warner Bros. studio, persuaded Columbia to make the film. Once again, the Revolution proved a difficult subject to bring to the screen. The movie *1776* (1972), notes Thomas Fleming, "was a resounding critical and commercial failure, a most unworthy swan song for Warner, who died in 1978."[81]

Part of the problem was that the film followed very closely the stage production—it focused mainly on Independence Hall and Gardens, making the action very static. Once removed from the more intimate atmosphere of the theater, most of the musical numbers seemed simply inadequate: "the very poor quality of the songs in *1776*," commented critic Alexander Stuart, "in addition to its over-demanding running time of almost 2½ hours, destroys the few attractions it has." The film also tried to spell out the "serious" issues (such as the fate of slavery) involved in the political debates, but these "philosophical set-pieces" lengthened the film and at the same time effectively killed its more "light-hearted" moments. As one reviewer sadly observed, "it takes more than long-winded discussions (sung or spoken) to make an epic, and the Declaration appears to be an unconscionable time a-signing."[82]

The next commercial film to be made about the American Revolution was directed by British director Hugh Hudson and shot in England. *Revolution*, released in 1985, was major-league financial disaster. It was in tenth place on the list of "all-time box office losers" published by *Premiere* magazine in 1992, having cost Goldcrest Productions and Warner Bros. total losses of some $27 million.[83] Critics differed in their view of what the film was actually about: to John Pym it was "a schematic affair" tracing the conversion of Tom Dobb (Al Pacino) to the revolutionary cause; to Alain Garsault, it was an effort to cast light on a historical episode by presenting it through the eyes and experiences of a naive, anonymous figure whom it personally affects; to Derek Elley it was "a story of uncomprehending individuals caught up in the mud, chaos and hysteria of a war waged by politicians and a social class beyond their reach."[84] Certainly, as Elley also pointed out, there was little attempt to follow the actual events of the Revolution.[85] From the beginning of the film, its characters seemed lost in situations that appeared incomprehensible to them (and probably to spectators too). The confusion was compounded by the fact that most scenes were shot, newsreel-fashion with a hand-held camera, which seemed to move round constantly.[86] A majority of sequences were also shot in the rain.[87] In visual terms, then, *Revolution* was very different to Hudson's previous films *Chariots of Fire* and *Greystoke*. Particularly in Britain, moreover, it provoked a firestorm of criticism with its depiction of the British—especially Tom Dobb's principal opponent Sergeant-Major Peasy (Donald Sutherland)—as cruel and vicious oppressors. Such attacks also included below-the-belt jibes at the accents used in the film. "Donald Sutherland," acidly remarked the London periodical *City Limits*, "is Sgt. Mjr. Peasy, a British Schweinhund who likes to torture small boys and mutilate a Yorkshire accent."[88]

In 2009, Hugh Hudson released a "director's cut" of *Revolution* on DVD and Blu-ray that, unusually for rereleases of this kind, was slightly shorter then the original. In the documentaries on the DVD version, including a discussion with Al Pacino, Hudson made it plain that he had conceived the movie as a study of war seen from the perspective of an ordinary soldier. Dobb, that soldier, like most men in his position, knows very little about what is actually going on. Hudson and Pacino planned to add a first-person voice-over to tie together the movie's fragmentary structure and make clearer the broader context. They never had the time to work out who would make the voice-over—Tom or his son Ned (Sid Owen/Dexter Fletcher at different ages)—let alone complete it. Goldcrest was eager to get the film out—it was also working on *Absolute Beginners* and *The Mission* (both 1986) at the same time and wanted to have *Revolution* released in time to qualify for Oscar nominations. In retrospect, Hudson thought this had been "a fatal error, because the film was not finished."[89] He added a voice-over by Pacino to the director's cut. *Revolution* also challenged audiences of the 1980s in a number of ways. As Michael Brooke observed, it deliberately set out to "undermine the stereotypes of both the American patriotic epic and the British heritage film." Tom, its principal character, was at best an unwilling patriot—joining the army only to protect his son—in a Reaganite decade when Sylvester Stallone's "Rambo" was the archetypal action hero.[90] Hudson also believed the movie had been weakened by its implausibly "happy ending," a sequence insisted on by Warner Bros. as the price of their financial investment.[91] To Hudson, the main story of the film was the relationship between Tom and Ned. He removed the accidental reunion of Tom and Daisy McConnahay (Nastassja Kinski) in New York from the 2009 version of the film.

Despite its commercial failure, *Revolution* was the first film to offer an interpretation of the Revolution that brought together several strands of historical analysis. It foregrounded economic and class struggles as Beard and the "progressive" historians had done. *Revolution* did not simply show—in common with earlier films—that both families and communities were divided by the conflict (Daisy, for example, breaks with her Tory family). It also suggested that, at the end of the revolutionary war, workers and farmers had lost out to businessmen, landowners, and speculators: not only is Dobb not compensated for the confiscation of his fishing boat, but the promises of money and land made to ordinary people have been abandoned in favor of a policy of paying off the war debt. As Trevor McCrisken and Andrew Pepper suggest,

> the film challenges a patriotic, benign reading of the American Revolution which posits it as a landmark in human progress and suggests that the revolution, *in spite* of its incendiary rhetoric, was essentially a conservative one . . . Certainly when Dobb arrives back in New York at the end of the film, little or nothing has changed . . . speculators and businessmen have assumed control of the city.[92]

The film also echoes the ideas of scholars who, from the 1960s onward, had begun to write history "from the bottom up," focusing on previously marginalized sections of the community, including the working class, women, and ethnic groups. From its beginnings, Cotton Seiler observes, *Revolution* suggested that the urban poor were involved. Dobb himself is working-class (a trapper/boatman). An early sequence has a New York mob destroying a statue of George III and throwing Tories into the water (Figure 1.1). Seiler suggests that the film shares the sensibilities of historians such as Gordon Wood, Eric Foner, Joan Hoff Wilson, Gary B. Nash, and Ira Berlin who have stressed "the radical democratic ferment of the late eighteenth century," even if it is "not necessarily directly informed" by their work.[93] In practice, however, the initiative of the mob is very unusual. Although the film does include women and ethnic minorities (Dobb's son Ned marries a Jewish woman and Dobb is chased by Iroquois Indians—whom he kills—and taken in by members of the Oneida tribe), none of them with the possible exception of Dobb's wife Daisy is ascribed any agency.[94]

In the wake of *Revolution*, the next year witnessed the release of *Sweet Liberty*, an ironic reflection—written and directed by Alan Alda—on the difficulties involved in turning the American Revolution into a movie. Michael Burgess (Alda), a history professor teaching at a college in the town of Sayeville, North Carolina, has produced *Sweet*

FIGURE 1.1 *A New York mob pulling down George III's statue in* Revolution.

Liberty, a best-selling Pulitzer prize-winning book on the Revolution in the South. A film crew led by director Bo Hodges (Saul Rubinek) arrives in Sayeville to turn the book into a movie. From the moment that hack screenwriter Stanley Gould (Bob Hoskins) shows him the script, Burgess realizes that the scholarly work that has taken him ten years to complete is about to be transformed into a Hollywood comedy. Much of the rest of *Sweet Liberty* is about Burgess's battle for historical accuracy against Hodges's determination to make a film that will be profitable. Hodges argues that 80 per cent of moviegoers are "kids" between the ages of 12 and 22. To be successful, a film has to give them what they want, which Hodges cynically defines in terms of three principles of moviemaking: "One, defy authority. Two, destroy property. Three, take people's clothes off." History as such, Hodges argues, does not matter to this audience: "They don't care if the hats are on wrong or the buttons are on the wrong sleeve. They just want to have fun." Burgess, by contrast, fights for the integrity of his vision of the past, fashioned by detailed study of the letters and diaries of the period. He informs Hodges that the hat of British commander Banastre Tarleton, as worn by screen character Elliot James (Michael Caine), is wrong, as is his red uniform (Tarleton was known as the "green dragoon"), and that the battle of Cowpens—the climax of the "film-within-a film"—was fought in winter (January 17, 1781) rather than summer. He finds a temporary ally in Faith Healy (Michelle Pfeiffer), a "method" actress who gets into the part of Mary Slocum by reading her original diary and requesting lessons in eighteenth-century sewing. He also persuades James that some of the dialogue should be rewritten.

Ultimately, however, Burgess is vanquished. Historical accuracy loses out to the director's view of what will make money. Burgess argues that the film's romantic interest, the love affair between Tarleton and Slocum, the wife of a much-loved American officer, would never have happened. His view is ignored. He also finds himself helping to rewrite Tarleton's part, since Elliot James thinks the suggestion that Tarleton was a rapist and a "bit of a bastard actually" is a threat to his star image. The final confrontation between Hodges and Burgess comes on the day when, aided by local re-enactors who refight the battle of Cowpens (just across the state border in South Carolina) every year, the movie attempts to present the battle as a comedy. Burgess, now dressed as an extra in an American uniform, leads the re-enactors in ignoring Hodges' instructions and attacking and defeating the "British." From Burgess' point of view, he is defending historical accuracy (Cowpens was a major defeat for the British and a turning-point for the revolutionaries in the South). But his own "victory" is illusory: Hodges has used six cameras to shoot the sequence, and when it comes to editing, "I can put it together any way I want." A combination of Hollywood's apparent understanding of its target audience, a mediocre scriptwriter and script, the personal ambitions of two movie stars and the authority of the director serve to undercut any serious attempt to recreate the Revolution in the South. Burgess can only wince after the film's "world premiere" in Sayeville when a television interviewer tells him "it's a great movie . . . American history at its best."

The Patriot (2000)

After the commercial disaster of *Revolution* it was not until 2000 that Hollywood returned to the subject of the American Revolution with *The Patriot*. Released on the Fourth of July weekend, it veered uneasily at times between a heritage picture and what the trade press called "a blood-and-guts actioner," settling down eventually to become what one critic termed a "period vigilante movie."[95] Benjamin Martin (Mel Gibson) is a widower with seven children. He has, the film suggests, been a brave and successful soldier in the French and Indians Wars, but now insists on putting his family first. Even though he disapproves of the principle of taxation without representation, he will not join the Continental Army. His eldest son, Nathan (Heath Ledger), does however enlist. He returns home wounded and at this point the British arrive at the Martin house. The evil Colonel Tavington (Jason Isaacs) seizes Nathan and proposes to hang him for carrying dispatches. When 15-year-old Thomas Martin (Gregory Smith) tries to rescue his older brother, he is shot in the back and killed by Tavington. The Martins' home is burned and wounded Continental soldiers sheltering there shot. At this point, Benjamin Martin recovers his weapons from the chest in which he has kept them and—after first rescuing his eldest son—goes off to fight for independence.

Much of the discourse relating to the film focused on its presentation of "history." It was claimed by publicists for the studio that the Martin character was partially based on Francis Marion, a real revolutionary hero known as "The Swamp Fox."[96] Marion himself was a pioneer of guerilla-style warfare. (One reviewer praised the film for "demonstrating how Gibson's ragtag band of rebels, with their guerilla warfare techniques, were able to carry the day against the Redcoats' academic and outmoded fighting methods.")[97] Spokespersons for the film also claimed that "[e]xperts from the Smithsonian ensured historical accuracy" while "war reenactment groups helped instruct the 600 extras on how to load a musket. . . ." The cinematographer apparently worked very closely with the costume designer to make certain that the clothes, especially in terms of color, conveyed an accurate sense of the period. Gibson himself gave interviews in which he paraded the results of his own "research" into the period.[98]

Despite all of this, however, the film was much-criticized ("chastized to the point of derision," according to one reviewer) for its principal historical inaccuracy: the depiction of the crimes committed by British troops. Like Robert Goldstein and Hugh Hudson before him, German director Roland Emmerich had produced a film accusing the British of atrocities (the killing of young Thomas Martin, the execution of wounded soldiers, and the burning of civilians in a church—the latter apparently based on Nazi conduct at Oradour-sur-Glane in France in June 1944). Yet, for all the furore on both sides of the Atlantic about this issue, the personality of Colonel Tavington is too extreme—indeed, in many ways too cartoonish—to be believable. As Philip Strick argued in *Sight and Sound*, he "is in reality Emmerich's latest Universal Soldier [following on from *Independence Day* and *Godzilla*], a stateless militarist, unchangingly evil throughout."[99]

Many critics compared Mel Gibson's role in *The Patriot* to the one he had played five years earlier in *Braveheart*, as a Scots leader fighting against the English.[100] A much better comparison, however, as one reviewer argued, was with *Saving Private Ryan* (1998).[101] It was, in fact, the screenwriter Robert Rodat and producers Mark Gordon and Gary Lewinsohn, fresh from launching *Saving Private Ryan*, who first decided to develop the film that became *The Patriot*.[102] A major problem, however, was that director Steven Spielberg—in *Saving Private Ryan*—had raised the "acceptable" level of violence that could be shown in war films. *The Patriot* carried on this process (Harrison Ford reportedly turned down the role of Benjamin Martin because he felt the script was too violent for him). At one point, indeed, though mostly off-camera, Gibson's Martin is shown dismembering the corpse of a dead English soldier in front of his three surviving sons. Further refinements of brutality were achieved through the extensive use of Computer-Generated Images, with digital cannonballs shown decapitating Continental soldiers.[103] Probably the most controversial scene in the whole film, however, was the one in which Martin is helped in rescuing his eldest son by his younger sons: the sight of teenage boys firing guns only a few months after the massacre at Columbine high school in Colorado astonished some spectators and probably accounted for the film's "R" rating."[104]

As Trevor McCrisken and Andrew Pepper have pointed out, *The Patriot* was in some ways a more conservative film than *Revolution*: it embodied the traditional myth of the individual as "reluctant hero."[105] It also had a narrower social range: Martin and his family belong to the planter class. Martin's guerrilla band includes a minister (René Auberjonois). Its others members appear substantial citizens, including Dan Scott (Donal Logue). Even one of its rougher illiterate members, John Billings (Leon Rippy) seems to have his own farm. It includes one slave, Occam (Jay Arlen Jones), who is "signed up" by his owner to fight. The film is especially uneasy with Occam and other African American characters. When Colonel Tavington tells Martin's black workers they will be freed if they join the British army, one quickly replies that they are not slaves: "We work the land as free men." (One reviewer noted sardonically that this was "probably the only such labor arrangement in colonial South Carolina."[106]) Occam eventually wins his own freedom—and the respect of initially hostile whites such as Dan Scott—by serving for a year in the Continental army.[107] The final sequence of the film, when Martin arrives home to find Occam and a group of his neighbors rebuilding his plantation house, proved too much for African American director Spike Lee. "How convenient," Lee fumed in a letter of protest to the *Hollywood Reporter*, "to have Mel Gibson's character not be a slaveholder . . . *The Patriot* is . . . a complete whitewashing of history."[108] With the exception of Occam, none of the blacks in the film are given any agency: the depiction of a Gullah village on the coast of South Carolina, peopled by ex-slaves, is included only to provide a backdrop for the marriage of Gabriel and Anne Howard (Lisa Brenner).[109] Anne herself helps Gabriel recruit members of the militia at a church meeting, but is the only female character in the film to become actively involved in the Revolution. In some respects, women in *The Patriot* have less agency than those in *Drums Along the Mohawk* 61 years earlier: Ford's film had women fighting against Indians alongside their menfolk.[110]

There were many superficial historical errors in the film: as in *Sweet Liberty*, Tavington/Tarleton wears a red rather than a more accurate green uniform, since that is expected of British "redcoats." The recreation of the battle of Cowpens (Figure 1.2), as in *Sweet Liberty*, bears little resemblance to the actual battle of January 1781.[111]

FIGURE 1.2 *Benjamin Martin (Mel Gibson) leads the American militia at the battle of Cowpens.*

While the Continental Congress had authorized what would become the "American" flag in June 1777, it is unlikely that it was shown at Cowpens. More crucially, *The Patriot* is weak in sketching out the causes of the Revolution: Martin's comment in the Charleston Assembly of 1776 about opposing "taxation without representation" is a rare articulation of a specific grievance. What the debate in the Assembly does make clear is that there are deep divisions among the colonists on the extent to which—or even whether—they should oppose British policy. *The Patriot* ignored the fact that such differences did not disappear with the beginning of the war. The only American Loyalist in the film is Tavington's subordinate, Captain Wilkins (Adam Baldwin). In reality, according to one historian, "A significant segment of the population of the Carolinas and Georgia remained loyal, and much of the fighting there was a civil war between Tories and Whigs." Half of the "British" army in the South, indeed, was made up of "Loyalist provincial and militia units."[112]

The Patriot was the most financially successful movie ever made about the American Revolution. That success was not attained solely on the basis of the domestic American box office. The film cost an estimated $110 million to make and barely broke even by taking $113 million in the United States. It was the addition of the international box office of $102 million that made the film profitable.[113] In retrospect, downplaying the specifics of the American Revolution seems to have been part of a deliberate strategy on the part of the filmmakers to promote its international success. The use of a major star (Gibson), advertising the film as an "action" epic, and reducing the Revolution essentially to the level of a duel between two men on opposing sides were part of that strategy. So too was the downplaying of race, reflecting a modern urge to be uncontroversial rather than eighteenth-century attitudes. By presenting the Revolution, moreover, as a general struggle for what McCrisken and Pepper term "an amorphous notion of 'freedom,'" they also reconstructed what was a narrow American struggle into "some kind of heroic landmark for human progress—a revolution for all humankind."[114]

Afterword

Will there be a *Patriot II*—or another movie about the Revolution? A big-budget "spectacular" on the lines of *The Patriot* would almost certainly have to follow a similar strategy to enhance its box-office appeal. A less-costly film might be able to grapple more easily with the complexities of the Revolution itself—the ambivalences and contradictions of its supporters, the character of its opponents (including American Loyalists), its social and economic basis, and its ethnic and gendered dimensions. It might even be able to return to the critical view of the revolutionary generation advanced by Beard and other "progressive" historians—a "muckraking" approach suggested by historian Richard Morris in the AFI discussions of 1970. But few films in all have been made set against the backdrop of the American Revolution, and most of these—although they have frequently reflected the outlook and problems of their own time—have paid little attention to historians' interpretations and reinterpretations of the Revolution itself. The film that seemed to have the closest affinity to the historiographical currents of its day (*Revolution*) failed completely at the box-office. If there appears little chance at the moment of a major new Hollywood feature film dealing with the Revolution, the notion that such a movie would extend popular understanding of the American Revolution itself seems even more unlikely.

Filmography

The Spirit of '76 (dir. George Siegmann; Continental Producing Company, 1917).
America (dir. David W. Griffith: D. W. Griffith/United Artists, 1924).
Janice Meredith (dir. E. Mason Hopper; Cosmopolitan/MGM, 1924).
Drums Along the Mohawk (dir. John Ford; Twentieth-Century Fox, 1939).
The Howards of Virginia (dir. Frank Lloyd; Columbia/Frank Lloyd, 1940).
The Scarlet Coat (dir. John Sturges; MGM, 1955).
Johnny Tremain (dir. Robert Stevenson; Walt Disney, 1957).
John Paul Jones (dir. John Farrow; Samuel Bronston/Suevia, 1959).

The Devil's Disciple (dir. Guy Hamilton; Hill-Hecht-Lancaster/Brynaprod, 1959).

Lafayette (dir. Jean Dréville; Cosmos/Films Copernic, 1961 [Europe], 1963 [US]).

1776 (dir. Peter H. Hunt; Columbia, 1972).

Revolution (dir. Hugh Hudson; Goldcrest Films/Viking, 1985).

Sweet Liberty (dir. Alan Alda; Universal, 1986).

The Patriot (dir. Roland Emmerich; Columbia/Centropolis/Mutual, 2000).

CHAPTER TWO

Slavery

In 1997, following the great critical and commercial success of *Schindler's List* (1993), Steven Spielberg released *Amistad*, a film dealing with a historical episode in 1839 in which a case dealing with the legal position of blacks enslaved by the Spanish reached the US Supreme Court, which freed the men and women concerned. For a range of reasons that will be discussed later, Spielberg's film about the treatment of slaves was considerably less successful than his film about the Holocaust. But that he attempted to deal with the issue of black slavery at all was unusual in American cinema. For a variety of reasons connected with guilt, embarrassment, ignorance, apathy, and an accurate assessment of what most moviegoers would actually pay to see, white American filmmakers—that is to say the great majority of filmmakers in the United States—have traditionally fought shy of representing slavery on film in any meaningful sense.

During the first two decades of American film, there were a small number of early films that attempted to convey the brutality of slavery. *The Slave Hunt*, a Vitagraph production from 1907, showed a planter cruelly beating a slave woman with a whip. A young man, presumably her son, rescued her by killing the planter. He fled, pursued by bloodhounds, but was eventually caught and killed. According to the *Variety* critic, the film was "not at all refined or agreeable and leaves a bad taste." The following year, *The Slave's Vengeance* had a slave whipped at the stake on the orders of his master. In revenge, he kidnapped his owner's young daughter and ran away. When he was caught, the little girl pleaded for his life. A reviewer praised this "pathetic finish" to what had otherwise been "a stirring if not happily chosen subject."[1]

Slave stereotypes

On the whole, however, filmmakers were far more likely to portrait slaves who conformed to traditional stereotypes derived from literature and/or the theater. One of the first of these was the noble, loyal, ultimately victimized "Uncle Tom" figure based on the novel first published by Harriet Beecher Stowe in 1852. Not only did this book enjoy extremely long-lived popularity as a literary work—as late as 1899, it was still the book most borrowed from the New York Public Library[2]—but it had also been turned into a play that, by the end of the nineteenth century, was being performed across America by nearly 500 specialist bands of "Tommer" companies. One 1902 reviewer estimated that, in that year alone, the play would be seen by one in every 35 Americans.[3] Given the importance of *Uncle Tom's Cabin* in American popular culture, it is hardly surprising that it was quickly transferred to the screen. In 1903, Edwin S. Porter released a 14-shot film of *Uncle Tom's Cabin*[4] and this was followed by six further versions before the First World War. "Uncle Tom" in these films was usually played by a white man wearing minstrel make-up: the first *black* Uncle Tom was Sam Lucas in 1914.[5]

Before the First World War, other slave stereotypes—again borrowed from literature and the theater—had found their way into American films. Donald Bogle has typified these together as the faithful "tom," the happy-go-lucky "coon," the light-skinned tragic mulatto, and the loyal "mammy."[6] All fitted with the notion that slavery itself was a benign system of labor. In 1915, in *The Birth of a Nation*, D. W. Griffith took this argument a stage further. The main sequence involving slavery itself occurs when Phil, the eldest son of the Northern Stoneman family, and Ben Cameron, the eldest Cameron son, together with his sisters Margaret and Flora, set off to visit the slave quarters. Black workers are shown picking cotton in the background and respectfully doffing their caps to the Camerons and their guests. This pastoral idyll is followed by a shot of the space in front of the slaves' cabins. An intertitle emphasizes that the slaves are well-treated, speaking of "the two-hour interval given for dinner, out of their working day from six till six." The (male) slaves are so little tired by their work in the fields, indeed, that they put on an impromptu dance show to entertain the Camerons and their Northern visitors. Finally, as the group of whites begin to leave, two old slaves approach Ben Cameron: he shakes hands with one and rests his other hand on the second man's shoulder. Obviously, slaves are well-treated by white "massa" and his son, and respond with affection to such benign care. Once slavery has been abolished, however, these amicable relationships endure only between the whites and *some* blacks (the "faithful souls"). Another black stereotype emerges onto the screen: the once-contented slave (represented by Gus) whom freedom and the doctrine of social equality have transformed into an aggressive pursuer of white women. With the emergence of what Donald Bogle calls the "black buck," the full range of African American stereotypes had now finally appeared on screen.[7]

In the first four decades of the twentieth century, there were very few attempts by Hollywood to suggest that slavery itself was not a benign and benevolent institution.[8] This fitted well with the dominant school of historical writing associated in particular with Georgia-born and educated Ulrich B. Phillips[9] and the popular kind of Southern literature represented by the "plantation school" of novelists, especially Thomas Nelson Page.[10] These writers created a nostalgic picture of the "Old South" of slavery and great plantations. Gracious and cultivated, the white society of the antebellum South had been served (willingly) by black slaves who, as Bruce Chadwick notes, "were typically shown as helpful mammies, obliging butlers, smiling carriage-drivers, joyful cotton-pickers and tap-dancing entertainers."[11]

This heavily romanticized view of slavery inscribed in literature and buttressed by history was destined to be spread even further by Hollywood during the late 1920s and 1930s. There were two main reasons for this. The first was the introduction of sound from 1927. This made it possible, for the first time, to incorporate some features of what was constructed—rightly or wrongly—as "black" music into film. Movies such as *Hearts in Dixie* and *Hallelujah!* (both released in 1929), although themselves actually set after the Civil War, seemed to suggest that blacks had carried on living freely on plantations even after emancipation. "Ringing with banjos and brimming with high-kicking, happy darky stereotypes," remarks Jack T. Kirby, "the[se] films conveyed an interpretation of slavery basically the same as Thomas Nelson Page's."[12] Other films in what might be called a "plantation musical" genre included *Dixiana* (1930), *Mississippi* (1935), *Swanee River* (1939), *Way Down South* (1939), *Dixie* (1943), and *Song of the South* (1946). Perhaps the most popular of all these motion pictures were the Shirley Temple "southerns," such as *The Little Colonel* and *The Littlest Rebel* (both 1935).

The second reason for the salience of films dealing with great plantations was the impact of the economic depression beginning in 1929. Hard times and high levels of industrial unemployment made the stability and seemingly timeless rural way of life of the antebellum South seem especially appealing. "Audiences could marvel," observed Edward D. C. Campbell, Jr., "at a culture so reliant on the land and the seasons rather than on the city and business trends."[13] As the 1930s went on, the plantations themselves became grander: Hollywood's representation of the way of the life of the "Old South" became a complex negotiation between filmmakers' desires and ambitions, previous productions, and what spectators now had been led to expect. The relatively small and intimate plantations in *Carolina* (1934) and *So Red the Rose* (1935) gave way to the far more impressive Halcyon of *Jezebel* (1938) and Tara/Twelve Oaks in *Gone With the Wind* (1939). Consistently, however, whether plantation musicals or plantation melodramas, these films depicted happy slaves loyally supporting their masters and mistresses. The one film of this kind that, at first glance, might seem to contradict this portrayal was *So Red the Rose*. Unusually, this showed plantation blacks—told that freedom is about to be achieved—stopping working for their master and his family and, encouraged by their leader, Cato (Clarence Muse), starting to seize the livestock of their owners. But this "slave revolt" is easily put down by the daughter of the plantation family (Margaret Sullavan) who confronts Cato and reduces him to silence by evoking memories of the strong interracial bonds that had (supposedly) existed under slavery. In the end, therefore, this brief moment of black agency fails to undermine the perception of slavery as intrinsically benign.

Films on slavery after the Second World War

A few of these plantation films had a long after-life. Disney's *Song of the South*—described by Jack Kirby as "the ultimate expression of plantation harmony"—carried on being shown in some movie theaters until the mid-1970s.[14] *Gone With the Wind* has periodically been rereleased and, after its first showing on US network television in 1976, became a staple of mass television entertainment.[15] The Hollywood view of slavery as a benign system consequently continued to be the dominant one for a very long time. In the aftermath of the Second World War, however, two mainstream American movies displayed considerably more ambivalence over the institution of slavery. *The Foxes of Harrow* (1947), loosely based on the best-selling novel by black writer Frank Yerby (1946), undercut the perception of slavery as benign by showing a slave woman (an uncredited Suzette Harbin) who would prefer to die rather than have her child brought up in slavery. The *Variety* critic shrewdly observed that this sequence "is likely to run into difficulties in many Southern states."[16]

Band of Angels (1957), the film version of Robert Penn Warren's 1955 novel, had Hamish Bond (Clark Gable) as a former slave trader ashamed of his earlier occupation. The movie also included a beautiful, apparently white girl, Amantha Starr (Yvonne De Carlo), who returns from finishing school in Cincinnati, Ohio, to attend her father's funeral. She quickly discovers both that he died heavily in debt and her mother was a slave. Sold off herself on the auction-block, she is bought by Bond. Hating her new master at first, she eventually escapes with him from approaching Union soldiers in the Civil War, and the film ends on a note of what Jack Kirby describes as "prospective miscegenation."[17] The movie also made it clear that Bond's black overseer Rau-Ru (Sidney Poitier) deeply resented his own status as a slave, although he would later—having fought in the Union Army to free his own people—reach the conclusion that his sometime master had been relatively liberal and unprejudiced. As several reviewers noted, the film was reminiscent of Gable's role as Rhett Butler in *Gone With the Wind*, yet the institution of slavery in *Band of Angels* was perceptibly much harsher than in the earlier film. *Band of Angels*, noted the *New York Times* critic, featured "brutal slave-traders, . . . the heroine cowers on the slave-block piteously . . . and bloodhounds chase slaves across fields."[18]

After 1957, however, as the civil rights movement gained momentum, few new films on the "Old South" and the institution of slavery with which it was associated were made. One that was, *Slaves* (1969), was written and directed by Herbert J. Biberman, a member of the "Hollywood Ten," the group of Hollywood employees who had unsuccessfully confronted the House Committee on Un-American Activities in 1947 and eventually gone to jail. In a radical rewrite of the "benign" view of slavery, this film showed it as a system of exploitation that eventually drove slaves themselves to revolt. The film focused on the story of a black Christian slave, Luke (Ossie Davis), who is sold by his Kentucky master to save his few remaining slaves. He passes into the hands of MacKay (Stephen Boyd), a brutal Mississippi planter. MacKay's mistress is a black woman, Cassy (Dionne Warwick). Luke and Cassy plan to escape together, but the plan fails and Luke—rather than accept MacKay's offer of freedom in exchange for betraying other blacks—dies fighting. The film was curiously balanced in places: the reviewer for *Variety* observed that "sympathetic slave owners are shown as well as hard driving profiteers . . . some white men cared for keeping [black] families together while others—usually because of economic gain—chose to break the family unit and actually breed slaves."[19] Yet it ultimately showed the dark side of slavery, including the exploitation of black women by white masters, and seems to have had little appeal beyond big-city African American audiences.[20]

Miscegenation

A small number of other films later developed much further the highly sensational theme hinted at in *Band of Angels*: miscegenation.[21] After *The Birth of a Nation* in 1915, and the controversy that greeted Griffith's film, sexual relationships across race lines seemed, quite simply, too hot to handle. In 1927, the Motion Picture Producers and Distributors of America adopted a set of guidelines for filmmakers known as the "Don'ts and Be Carefuls." One of the themes that could not be exploited in films was miscegenation, specifically defined as "sex relationships between the white and black races." The Production Code of 1930, commonly known as the Hays Code, repeated the ban in exactly the same terms and this remained "official" Hollywood policy until 1956. When the Production Code was revised in that year, the prohibition on miscegenation was finally dropped.[22] Yet filmmakers did not rush to make films about a highly controversial type of relationship that was still illegal in some American states.[23] (The restrained treatment of the subject in *Band of Angels* may have reflected this). 1967, however, saw the US Supreme Court—in *Loving v. Virginia*—finally ruling such laws unconstitutional. That same year saw the first black and white kiss in a mainstream Hollywood film for over half a century: Sidney Poitier and Katherine Houghton are seen embracing in the back seat of a taxi in *Guess Who's Coming to Dinner*.[24] This movie was set in contemporary times: it took several years for a number of filmmakers to exploit the salacious possibilities of interracial relationships against a backcloth of slavery.

In 1957, Kyle Onstott, a 70-year-old bachelor living in California, published a novel called *Mandingo* about a slave-breeding plantation in Alabama. Bizarrely, although Onstott was an experienced writer, all his work before this had been dedicated to the subject of dog-breeding. Five years later, he published a second novel, *Drum*, which was a sequel to the first.[25] In the early 1970s, Onstott's novels came to interest Italian film producer Dino de Laurentiis, then attempting with some success (*Death Wish*, 1974) to break into the American movie market. In 1975, *Mandingo* was released as a film. With its portrait of a sexually hyperactive black man (Mede, played by boxer Ken Norton), it blended with the popular "blaxploitation" genre of the time.[26] *New York Times* critic Vincent Canby commented that the film had been "handsomely photographed in a number of impressively decaying old Southern houses." The ads for the film, indeed, were reminiscent of those for *Gone With the Wind* "with the old plantation house in the background, the suggestion of crowds caught up in great events, flames, lovers pictured in tempestuous embrace." The difference was that the *Mandingo* ads showed two pairs of interracial lovers. According to Canby it offered "steamily melodramatic nonsense" that conveyed no impression of "what life on the old plantation was really like" because of its "erotic interest in the techniques of humiliation, mostly with sex and violence." Other reviewers were equally caustic: according to one, *Mandingo* was an "embarrassing and crude film" that wallowed "in every cliché" associated with "the slave-based . . . pre-Civil War South."[27]

Clearly designed as an "exploitation" film (and given an "R" for restricted rating), *Mandingo* reached a large audience mainly for its prurience in dealing with the theme of miscegenation.[28] Hammond Maxwell (Percy King), son of plantation owner Warren Maxwell (James Mason), prefers slave Ellen (Brenda Sykes) to his wife Blanche (Susan George). Blanche takes revenge by blackmailing slave Mede into an affair. When she gives birth to a mulatto baby, Hammond kills both his wife and Mede. In spite of its many faults, *Mandingo* did foreground the sexual politics of slavery, undercutting earlier perceptions of it as a benign institution. Robin Wood, indeed, would later (and controversially) describe *Mandingo* as "the greatest Hollywood film on race" for its highly critical view of white Southern patriarchy.[29]

A year later, the same team produced *Drum*, a sequel set on the same Louisiana plantation. The reviewer for *Variety* described it as "a grubby followup" to *Mandingo*, and speculated that part of the financial success of the latter had been due to "the fact that audiences considered it a comedy."[30] *Drum* had its baffling aspects as a sequel. Brenda Sykes reappeared in a different role and Ken Norton was mysteriously reincarnated as the character Drum. The film was just as brutal in representing slavery as its predecessor. "Not since *Mandingo*," observed Vincent Canby, "have I seen a film so concerned with such methods of humiliation as beating, shooting and castration." In the end, Canby dismissed it as "exploitation junk." "Life on the old plantation was horrendous," he frankly admitted, ". . . but movies like this are less interested in information than titillation, which, in turn, reflects contemporary obsessions rather more than historical truths."[31]

Roots

For a more serious look at the history and reality of slavery, it was necessary in the 1970s to look to television more than the cinema. In January 1977, American Broadcasting Company (ABC) broadcast an adaptation of Alex Haley's epic novel *Roots*, an account of a black family's struggle to survive over several generations. Shown over eight nights, it attracted a total audience of 130 million.[32] The mini-series recounted the fictionalized history of Haley's own family from their African roots to freedom in America. It incorporated some "traditional" Hollywood elements: the slave-ship captain (Ed Asner), overcome with guilt, in some ways resembled Hamish Bond and the sexual abuse of black women under slavery was shown in a "downright salacious" manner that to a degree echoed *Mandingo* and *Drum*. On the other hand, it also showed in some detail the experience of the middle passage (the transport of countless Africans by sea to the Americas) and, for the first time, a shipboard slave rebellion. It broke with the clichéd image of the "Old South" of great plantations by viewing slavery against the backcloth of an ordinary North Carolina farm.[33] Indeed, as Bruce Chadwick points out, it fatally undercut many of the myths that had previously surrounded slavery: slaves in *Roots* did nothing "to help their owners keep them enslaved. They did not cakewalk and tap-dance to 'Dixie.' They were not all Mammies and Sambos."[34]

Executives for the ABC network were highly aware that they were making a program about blacks for what was predominantly a white television audience. Initially, they took refuge in "whitening" Haley's narrative: the script by William Blinn introduced many new, albeit often minor, Caucasian characters "to give the miniseries a whiter look." In advertising and promoting the series, ABC foregrounded as many whites as possible. It also distributed many study guides to teachers and students across the United States emphasizing that Haley's story was essentially "history."[35] No doubt these tactics succeeded—to a point. What accounted for the astonishing success of *Roots* in attracting a huge audience, however, probably in the end had more to do with its intrinsic optimism (family members *do* love each other and believe that they will one day be free), the underlying theme of racial integration (the redneck white and the black man in the end become partners), and—rather paradoxically—the idea that it was a universal human story of survival and liberation rather than simply a study in black-white relations.

Coverage of slavery in mainstream Hollywood films, at least until the end of the Second World War, had treated it as a benign and benevolent institution. The idea that slaves were happy with their status was conveyed by many films, including the two great Civil War epics, *The Birth of a Nation* and *Gone With the Wind*. Hollywood formulas encouraged this traditional view of slavery: the plantation musicals and melodramas of the late 1920s and 1930s focused on happy-go-lucky "faithful souls." After 1945, however, there began to be hints—as in *The Foxes of Harrow* and *Band of Angels*—that slavery itself had been a much darker and more oppressive system than Hollywood had previously recognized. By the 1960s and 1970s, the modern civil rights movement and growing black consciousness made it impossible to treat slavery in traditional ways on screen. It could either be shown as brutal (as in *Slaves*) or as a background for steamy tales of interracial lust (as in *Mandingo* and *Drum*). But for most white mainstream Hollywood filmmakers, slavery had by this time—as limits on the representation of sex and violence tumbled—become one of the last remaining taboos. It was much easier, as suggested by French film scholar Anne Crémieux, to comment *indirectly* on slavery in such science fiction films as *Planet of the Apes* (1968).[36] Yet the success of *Roots* seemed to suggest that there might perhaps be a mass audience waiting for the right film to deal with the subject.

Spielberg's *Amistad*

In the closing months of 1997, it appeared that that film was at last about to be released. Material started to arrive in the mail-boxes of educators across the United States that was expressly intended to "sell" a film by the new DreamWorks SKG studio. The publicity material was ostensibly directed toward high school and college students. It included suggested activities for such students that were supposed—as the blurb stated—to "encourage critical thinking about the value of history in light of the long-faded chapter restored to American history in the film *Amistad*."[37] On the one hand, therefore, there was a clear claim by the makers of *Amistad* that their film represented "history"—though a history that had up to this point been largely unknown. But the new movie was also subjected to an alternative and (from its makers' point of view) infinitely less desirable form of prerelease publicity. In mid-October 1997, Barbara Chase-Riboud filed a $10 million claim against DreamWorks claiming that major parts of her 1989 novel *Echo of Lions*—itself loosely based on the *Amistad* incident—had been plagiarized by the studio. Her lawyer, Pierce O'Donnell, listed 13 distinct parallels between Chase-Riboud's fiction and the script of *Amistad*. In response, lawyers acting on behalf of DreamWorks argued that the film itself was "entirely based on history" and that no one individual could copyright "mere fact."[38] Even before the film's release in December 1997, therefore, *Amistad* was the focus of public and legal debate. Was it history or was it fiction? And if it *was* history, what kind of history was it?

The story of the making of the film effectively began in 1978, when African American dancer and choreographer Debbie Allen came across a book on the Amistad mutiny at the Howard University Bookstore. Although that book itself, William Owen's *Black Mutiny* (1953), was a novel, it dealt with a real historical incident: the revolt of black Africans being carried into slavery on a Spanish boat, the *Amistad*, in 1839. Having slaughtered all but two of the crew, they tried to sail the boat back to Africa but were outwitted by the two surviving crew sailors and ended up off the coast of Connecticut where they were stopped and taken into harbor by an American naval vessel. There then followed three separate trials, in each of which the final verdict was that the blacks involved were *not* slaves but free Africans who had been illegally seized. The man who argued the last case, which resulted in their being freed and offered the chance of returning to Africa by the US Supreme Court, was former President John Quincy Adams. By all accounts, Debbie Allen responded to the book in an intensely emotional way. She decided that it was "a true story that the world needed to hear" and in 1984 optioned the rights to the Owen novel. Thereafter, for a decade, Allen became absorbed in a fruitless quest to have her idea produced as a movie.[39]

There were numerous reasons for her failure. Allen herself starred as Lydia Grant in the successful television series *Fame* (1982–7), but she lacked experience and credentials as a producer. Despite the runaway success of the mini-series *Roots* on television,[40] it was not obvious that a movie dealing with the black experience was a commercially viable proposition. Even African American directors fought shy of the project. "Look at

Glory," observed Keenen Ivory Wyatts of the 1989 film about blacks in the Union army. "It barely made its money back. As a black director, you can't afford that."[41] Although Allen's initial attempts to make the film would parallel the early films directed by Spike Lee with the specific intention of packaging black experience to appeal to crossover audiences, Lee's movies were set either in the contemporary period or, like *Malcolm X* (1992), in the recent American experience. And *Malcolm X*, whatever its faults as a movie, was at least dealing with a major character in American history rather than with an almost unknown episode in the distant past.

Allen's luck apparently changed, however, in 1994 when she saw *Schindler's List* and concluded that Steven Spielberg was the man to make the film. Finally, after pursuing various DreamWorks executives, she had a long meeting with Spielberg and seems to have persuaded him of the viability of the whole project. (African American reviewer Thomas Pinnock, who attacked the eventual film as a "Hollywood enterprise" putting "Black people in the background of their own history," dismissed Allen's original fervent pitch to Spielberg as "a modern day parody of 'chucking and dancing for the massa boss.'")[42] Both Allen and Spielberg, however, had clear reasons for wanting to make the film. The black instigator of the mutiny, Cinque, seemed to encapsulate for Allen the history of African Americans. "When I look at him," she explained, "I think about my grandfather, the men of my family—Five generations back, my family disappears into the plantation. Cinque embodies the spirit of millions of Africans who were stolen . . ."[43] While Allen may not have been aware of it, moreover, her take on Cinque followed trends in the historical interpretation of slavery in the last quarter of the twentieth century, with scholars such as Ira Berlin emphasizing the fact that slaves played an active part in molding their world and that they resisted slavery itself in a large variety of ways.[44] For Allen, depicting Cinque as a defiant and ultimately successful leader of a black refusal to accept slave status was a powerful means of destroying the older view of blacks as sambo figures who acquiesced in their own enslavement.[45] Spielberg, too, had personal reasons for his interest in the *Amistad* story. He had already made one commercially successful film set in the past (*Schindler's List*) and was planning to make another (*Saving Private Ryan*) when he approved the notion of a film about the *Amistad* mutiny. He and his wife, moreover, had recently adopted two African American children—his decision to give the green light to Allen's project almost certainly had personal as well as commercial implications. Spielberg himself would later claim that, while listening to Allen's initial pitch, he had been struck by the thought "that this would be something I would be pretty proud to make, simply to say to my son, 'Look this is about you.'"[46]

Both Allen and Spielberg, therefore, set off making their movie—Spielberg as director and Allen as co-producer—with high ambitions. Spielberg, indeed, stated that he wanted his *Amistad* film to accomplish "for the American experience of slavery what *Schindler's List* did for the Holocaust."[47] As a result, African American expectations of the film were initially high. Henry Louis Gates, Jr., who served as a consultant on the project, declared enthusiastically that "It's rare when you see black people participate in violence to defend themselves, be vindicated by the American legal system, and be recognized as the true patriots they are, like Patrick Henry."[48] Certainly, by presenting the story predominantly from the African perspective, *Amistad* involved a major shift in Hollywood moviemaking.[49] It also featured African actors—most notably, of course, Djimon Hounsou from Benin as Cinque—in major roles[50] and had them speak an accurate version of the Mende language in what is now Sierra Leone (the area from which the *Amistad* captives came).[51] The film as a whole can be seen as an attempt to revise the codes surrounding the notion of black armed revolt as represented in American cinema. With the creation of a fictional, native-born American black Theodore Joadson (Morgan Freeman), it also attracted attention to the role played by free blacks in the abolitionist movement.[52]

The Joadson role, however, also demonstrated from the beginning the weaknesses of the film. There are, at times, good reasons for introducing fictional characters into broadly historical films. Representations of this kind can be used, as Robert A. Rosenstone has argued, to present a metaphoric or symbolic historical truth.[53] Indeed, it is necessary almost always to engage in a good deal of invention—of scenes, dialogue, and characters—when bringing "history" to the screen.[54] But Joadson is an anachronism—indeed, almost as glaring an anachronism as the bicycle the Africans from the *Amistad* see being ridden after they first land in Connecticut looking for water. He promotes the illusion that there were many rich blacks in the United States in 1839.[55] He also seems to move with complete freedom in white society, including a highly unlikely meeting with ex-President John Quincy Adams (Anthony Hopkins) at the Adams family home in Massachusetts.

When the film was released, it rapidly became clear that *Amistad* was not going to become the African American *Schindler's List*. Black audiences themselves appear to have reacted in a negative way to it. They seem to have disliked the attempt to make them confront their own past. "Only a masochist," observed Warrington Hudlin, president of the Black Filmmakers foundation, "would want to spend two hours watching themselves be degraded and dehumanized."[56] In an early showing of the film, an African American woman became hysterical during the middle passage sequence and rushed out of the theater. "I felt like I was on the ship," she later explained, "and it was too much. I just really couldn't take it anymore."[57]

The middle passage sequence in *Amistad* is actually, in filmic terms, a flashback showing how Cinque came to be captured and turned into a slave. *Tecora*, the boat shown, is the one that first carried him from Africa to Havana, Cuba, where he was sold and placed aboard the *Amistad*. It is probably the most honest—and the most brutal—treatment of the experience of Africans on a slave ship in the middle passage in American cinema. Far more even than *Roots*, it shows the terrible conditions on the slave-ships, the chaining and poor food, the vicious punishments of the slaves themselves, hints at the high mortality rate, and also at the exploitation of slave women by Spanish sailors (the shot of dancing to music). Most graphically of all, it shows the disposal of 50 slaves when the Spanish realize that they have insufficient provisions to feed everyone aboard.[58]

If African Americans disliked the film, what of the white response? The white characters in the film fall into one of three categories. They are simply ridiculous (like the Christians shown praying and singing) or unscrupulous and ineffective (like abolitionist Lewis Tappan (Stellan Skarsgård) and, ultimately, President Martin van Buren (Nigel Hawthorne)) or they have their character molded and elevated through contact with Cinque. When we first meet Roger Baldwin (Matthew McConaughey), who defends the *Amistad* mutineers in the first trials, he is little more than an ambulance-chaser offering his services to make a profit out of others' misfortune. John Quincy Adams, their eventual counsel before the Supreme Court, is first shown as sleeping during a debate in the House of Representatives. It is suggested that he is a frustrated and bitter old man, jealous of the reputation of his father, John Adams, second president of the United States. But both Baldwin and Adams are ennobled by the end of the film through Cinque's influence.[59]

Amistad also seemed to be part of an effort on Spielberg's part to extend the frontier of acceptable violence in the movies. One month after *Amistad* was completed, the director and much of the same team began shooting *Saving Private Ryan*. But the violence of *Amistad* had the potential to be even more controversial than the later film since it was in essence racial violence. In fact, the release of the film marked the return of an image largely abandoned since *The Birth of a Nation*: that of the black male beast. The violence with which the Africans kill all but two of the Spanish crew right at the start of the film is shockingly bloody. Then Cinque kills the ship's captain with a sword, spearing him through the deck, and standing over him with obvious pleasure as he writhes in agony. The actual justification for the mutiny and its violence (the middle passage sequence) does not actually come until almost half-way through the film.

The straightforward binary position the film offers—blacks are good, whites are bad—may well have reduced the appeal of Spielberg's movie to a predominantly white audience. But it was not the only problem the film faced in attracting a large audience. The film was biased in gender (as well as racial) terms. Although women appear in the film, it is not in any of the major roles. Moreover, as a writer for film magazine *Sight and Sound* pointed out, the film has no happy resolution: "the hard facts of history" preclude Spielberg's "trademark scenes of reunion and reconciliation."[60] While the American legal system is vindicated by finally declaring the *Amistad* rebels free, they sail back to Africa and the slave fort from which they have sailed to the Americas is destroyed by the British navy, Cinque returns home to find that his wife and family have disappeared, and his homeland is being torn apart by civil war. Unlike the television series *Roots*, therefore, *Amistad* is not a hopeful tale, does not foreshadow the eventual integration of blacks with whites in American society, and makes no attempt to elevate the story into a universal one revolving around human liberation.

Amistad was not a great commercial success[61] and, eventually, Spielberg convinced himself that this had been because it was too didactic and "too much of a history lesson."[62] This may have been the case. On the other hand, there are very specific reasons why audiences disliked the film and—no doubt—passed on their word-of-mouth opinion to others. With Cinque, Spielberg and Allen offered moviegoers a kind of hero/villain. He is plainly a man with a commanding presence and forceful character. But he also represents the return of the dark, bestial other, haunting the imagination of whites with the constant specter of violence.[63] "As slave epics go," commented Christopher Hemblade in *Empire*, "and, let's be honest, there ain't much demand for them, this is about the most visceral and unclichéd version you could hope for."[64] Hemblade clearly missed the duality of the Cinque character, with the black beast as a cliché at least since *The Birth of a Nation*. But he also underlined the fact that, albeit for different reasons, black and white Americans responded negatively to the film. "Race screws up Americans," observed Armond White, and—with *Amistad*—Allen and Spielberg tried to tell a story that most Americans—whether black or white—had no real desire to hear.[65]

Without Spielberg, indeed, *Amistad* would probably never have been made. Allen's project had been "stonewalled" for more than a decade,[66] reflecting Hollywood's ambivalence over its theme. In the aftermath of the civil rights movement, it appeared that the traditional ways of handling slavery on screen had outlived their usefulness. The noble, victimized "Uncle Tom," the simple-minded coon, the tragic mulatto, and the mammy were no longer acceptable as racial stereotypes. With the brief exception of the blaxploitation dramas of the 1970s revolving around miscegenation, the Southern plantation had fallen out of favor as a background and theme for filmmakers. *Roots* succeeded on television in 1977 because it subsumed the slavery experiences of African Americans in what Trevor McCrisken and Andrew Pepper term "the context of the ubiquitous rags-to-riches immigrant 'success' story."[67] Not only is *Amistad* different from earlier films about slavery (it is set geographically in the North), but—far from becoming part of American society—at the end of the film, the former captives return to face an uncertain future in Africa.

In many ways, indeed, it is an *African* rather than an African American story. It had almost nothing to say that was of relevance to Americans, whether white or black, other than seemingly demonstrating that the judicial system designed by the Founding Fathers ultimately worked. Yet American slavery survived legally for 26 years after the *Amistad* decision, and it was destroyed in the end not in the courts but through civil war. In 1839, the Supreme Court freed—on a technicality—the African *Amistad* captives; 18 years later, the same court determined in the Dred Scott case that African American slaves were merely property, with no civil rights.

Tarantino's *Django Unchained*

The commercial failure of *Amistad* helped discourage further attempts to represent slavery on the big screen. If Steven Spielberg could not succeed, then who could?[68] In December 2012, Quentin Tarantino released *Django Unchained*, the story of Django (Jamie Foxx), a slave who first secures his freedom with the help of German bounty hunter Dr. King Schultz (Christoph Waltz) before the two set off on a long mission to free Django's wife Broomhilda von Shaft (Kerry Washington), who has been sold to Calvin J. Candie (Leonardo DiCaprio), a charming but highly unscrupulous plantation owner in Mississippi.

From the opening sequence of Tarantino's film, showing a small group of shackled African Americans walking grimly to the accompaniment of jaunty, jangly, Western-style music, it is instantly clear that this is not going to be a serious analysis of slavery. The title of the film and the name of the main black character come not from black history or the history of the American South, but from Sergio Corbucci's violent spaghetti Western *Django* (1966). Franco Nero, the star of Corbucci's film, makes a cameo appearance in *Django Unchained* (Tarantino, in the opening credits, pays tribute to "the friendly participation of Franco Nero"). The original *Django* inspired a series of spaghetti Westerns with similar titles (*Django Spara per Primo/He Who Shoots First*, 1966; *Sei Sei Vivo, Spara!/Django, Kill!*, 1967; *Django Sfida Sartana/Django against Sartana*, 1970).

In addition to the original *Django*, two other films—both released in 1975—appear to have had a major influence on *Django Unchained*. One was the blaxploitation movie *Boss Nigger* (1975), with Fred Williamson as one of a pair of black bounty hunters who essentially take over for a time and run a white town.[69] The second was *Mandingo*. Tarantino had been interested in Richard Fleischer's film for years, commenting in an interview during the 1990s that it was one of only two instances "in the last twenty years [that] a major studio [Paramount] made a full-on, gigantic, big-budget exploitation film."[70] *Mandingo* launched the notion of bare-knuckled blacks fighting each other to the death for whites' profit (with

Ken Norton as Mede killing his opponent by biting through his jugular). *Django Unchained*'s "mandingo fighting" and the killing of one fighter by another are clearly taken from the earlier film.

Django Unchained is a part spaghetti Western, part blaxploitation film, and part exploitation movie. Yet it incorporates elements from many other genres, making it a true pastiche. It is a black Western, in the tradition of *Posse* (1993), which also had blacks fighting an anachronistic Ku Klux Klan. It is a "Southern" or plantation film with a lineage going back at least as far as *The Birth of a Nation*. It is a revenge/rescue drama that echoes certain aspects of *The Searchers* (1956). It is a buddy movie (the sequence in which Schultz and Django are in a saloon with virtually the whole population of the town surrounding and aiming guns at them is reminiscent of *Butch Cassidy and the Sundance Kid* (1969)). It is also the story of a quest, modeled in some respects—as Schultz makes plain to Django—on *Siegfried*, the third opera of Richard Wagner's Ring cycle, itself the result of a blending of Norse mythology and old German legend.

The fact that nearly all the later sequences of the film take place on plantations is a tribute to the enduring cinematic power of the plantation myth. Familiar cultural stereotypes appear: the Southern lady, Calvin Candie's sister Lara (Laura Cayouette), stands up for (white) Southern manners in the way Ellen O'Hara had once done (and while Ellen died of typhoid, Lara is literally blown away). Plantation owners "Big Daddy" and Candie himself are recognizable types, although they owe more to Warren and Hammond Maxwell than Dr. Cameron and Gerald O'Hara. Similarly, Stephen (Samuel L. Jackson) has evolved from the "faithful souls" of Griffith into an "Uncle Tom" figure of surpassing malevolence and power. In the real antebellum South, only 12 percent of slave-owners in 1860 owned 20 or more slaves, although more than half of all slaves lived on the plantations of such owners.[71] Plantation life, the commonest experience for slaves, was proportionally much less common among white slave-owners. But the beauty of the plantation setting (part of the film was shot at the Evergreen Plantation in Louisiana) still seduces filmmakers like Tarantino. The brutal manner in which Tarantino depicts plantation slavery, however, is much closer to how it was conceived in the lurid fantasies of many abolitionists (few of whom had visited the South) than it may have been to antebellum reality.

Brutality was itself a frequent but unquantifiable aspect of plantation life. The plantation was an economic unit and owners developed their own techniques for managing their slave workforce as efficiently and profitably as possible. In most cases, observes Russell R. Menard, these involved a mixture "of incentives and physical punishments," although there is no way of knowing in what proportion. Whipping was comparatively common. Of former slaves interviewed in the 1930s, half of those from the upper South and three-quarters of those from the lower South reported that they had been whipped.[72] Yet, sadistic as some masters and overseers undoubtedly were, and with few laws to constrain them, to kill or injure a slave meant damaging one's own property and "many planters preferred nonviolent over violent means to attain their ends."[73] Those planters do not include Big Daddy (Don Johnson) or Calvin Candie. On Big Daddy's plantation in Tennessee, one of the Brittle brothers is about to use a bullwhip on a slave for breaking eggs. Django and his wife, Broomhilda, have been punished for running away from their original owner by flogging and branding. They have then been separated by being sold to different owners. On Candie's Gothic plantation in Mississippi, with its sweetly deceptive name of "Candyland," the brutalities include attack dogs killing a runaway slave, "mandingo" fighters wrestling with each other to the death, and the hot, airless box on the lawn in which a thirsty, naked Broomhilda is being punished for her latest escape attempt. Castration is obviously a common punishment: Stephen, Candie's shrewd and loyal African American major-domo, knows exactly how long—seven minutes—it takes a castrated black man to bleed to death. But he prefers more imaginative punishments, such as condemning Django to work for the rest of his life down a mine.

The one major difference between *Django Unchained* and earlier exploitation films set on plantations is that sex is not an issue. Django is loyally uxorious and, throughout the film, is determined to find and rescue Broomhilda. Unlike Fred Washington in *Boss Nigger*, he does not chase white women. And unlike Ken Norton in *Mandingo*, he is not chased by a white woman. Miscegenation is present in the film—Candie has a light-skinned mulatto mistress, Sheba (Nichole Galicia) and, when Schultz and Django arrive at Candyland, seems to be offering Broomhilda to Schultz— but is not a major theme. Broomhilda herself, while flogged, branded, sold, and imprisoned in a punishment box, does not appear to have been sexually exploited.

In comparison to *Amistad*, which principally dealt with enslaved Africans in the North of the United States, *Django Unchained* focuses on African American slaves in the South. For a white director to do this has itself been a source of controversy, with black director Spike Lee (who refused to see it) describing Tarantino's film as "disrespectful to my ancestors."[74] Django himself appears to progress "from beaten slave to cool gun-toting cowboy in fancy duds . . . He's John Shaft on a horse, Superfly with a sixgun."[75] He is also coolly ironic ("Kill white folks and get paid for it, what's not to like?" is his response to Schultz's suggestion that he become a bounty hunter). Yet his instincts are not always hip: his blue "Little Lord Fauntleroy" valet outfit provokes incredulity from a female slave. Far more seriously, he plays second fiddle for much of the movie to Schultz. It is Schultz who liberates him from the Speck brothers, proposes that the two spend the winter bounty hunting together, and promises after this to help find and free Django's wife. It is Schultz who teaches him how to use weapons and plans the strategy they hope to use in buying Broomhilda back from Calvin Candie. Finally, it is Schultz who kills Candie, triggering his own death after which Django finally becomes a lead character. In what up to this point has been (among many other things) a buddy movie, Django for the first two hours has been very much the junior partner.

Candie, speaking as a member of the minority of whites on large plantations, at one point asks a deceptively simple question: "why don't they [the black slaves] kill us?" He uses pseudo-science (phrenology) to answer his own question: because the skulls of African Americans show them to be fundamentally passive.[76] The film, at some moments, seems to justify Candie's insane argument. Schultz, for example, having freed Django, has to explain to the other members of the black chain-gang just what the options facing them are with respect to the sole surviving Speck brother: they can either save him and carry him to the nearest town or kill him, bury the two brothers and escape. (Once a white man has spelt out their choices, they opt for the second alternative.) The film's main attempts to undercut the notion of black passivity come from the characters of Stephen and Django. In the movie's final stages, Stephen is revealed as the real power on Candie's plantation and Django, by virtue of three massacres, secures freedom for himself and Broomhilda (though how will they subsequently escape Mississippi slave patrols?). The violence used by Django offers a kind of redemption from the evils of slavery: it is a fantasy of what might have happened rather than what did. With its traditional clichés and stereotypes of plantation life, and its cathartic if imaginary vengeance, Tarantino's movie has little to do with the former realities of slavery.

Filmography

Uncle Tom's Cabin (dir. Edwin S. Porter; Edison, 1903) (many subsequent versions).
The Slave Hunt (Vitagraph, 1907).
The Slave's Vengeance (Pathé, 1908).
The Birth of a Nation (dir. D. W. Griffith; Epoch, 1915).
The Slaver (dir. Harry Revier; Morris R. Schlank Productions, 1927).
Hearts in Dixie (dir. Paul Sloane; Fox, 1929).
Hallelujah! (dir. King Vidor; MGM, 1929).
Dixiana (dir. Luther Reed; RKO, 1930).
Carolina (dir. Henry King; Fox, 1934).
So Red the Rose (dir. King Vidor; Paramount, 1935).
Mississippi (dir. A. Edward Sutherland; Paramount, 1935).
The Little Colonel (dir. David Butler; Fox, 1935).
The Littlest Rebel (dir. David Butler; Twentieth-Century Fox, 1935).
Slave Ship (dir. Tay Garnett; Twentieth-Century Fox, 1937).
Jezebel (dir. William Wyler; Warner Bros., 1938).
Swanee River (dir. Sidney Lanfield; Twentieth-Century Fox, 1939).

Way Down South (dir. Leslie Goodwins/Bernard Vorhaus; Sol Lesser Productions, 1939).

Gone With the Wind (dir. Victor Fleming; Selznick International/MGM, 1939).

Dixie (dir. A. Edward Sutherland; Paramount, 1943).

Song of the South (dir. Harve Foster/Wilfred Jackson, Disney, 1946).

The Foxes of Harrow (dir. John M. Stahl; Twentieth-Century Fox, 1947).

Band of Angels (dir. Raoul Walsh; Warner Bros., 1957).

Planet of the Apes (dir. Franklin J. Schaffner; APJAC/Twentieth-Century Fox, 1968).

Slaves (dir. Herbert J. Biberman; Slaves Company/Theatre Guild, 1969).

Mandingo (dir. Richard Fleischer; Dino de Laurentiis/Paramount, 1975).

Drum (dir. Steve Carver; Dino de Laurentiis/United Artists, 1976).

Amistad (dir. Steven Spielberg; DreamWorks SKG, 1997).

Django Unchained (dir. Quentin Tarantino; Weinstein Company/Columbia, 2012).

CHAPTER THREE*

Abraham Lincoln

In the last two decades, there have been a number of books analyzing how Abraham Lincoln, the dominant politician of the Civil War era, has come to be remembered. In 1994, Merrill D. Peterson's *Lincoln in American Memory* appeared. Peterson demonstrated how various groups in American society sought to reshape Lincoln's life and character to fit their own agendas. His image, constantly reconstructed, echoed wider changes in American politics and society.[1] Barry Schwartz extended Peterson's work in two volumes. The first, *Abraham Lincoln and the Forge of National Memory* (2000), described how Lincoln's reputation grew in the United States between his death and the First World War. Schwartz looked particularly at representations of Lincoln in painting and sculpture, popular magazines, school textbooks, public oratory, and newspapers. The second book, *Abraham Lincoln in the Post-Heroic Age* (2008), traced the decline of Lincoln's reputation from its peak in the 1920s. In this work, a different range of source materials, including cartoons, surveys, advertisements, visits to shrines, and public commemorations was explored.[2] Curiously, both Peterson and Schwartz paid little attention to perhaps the most powerful mass agency in forging the way Lincoln came to be collectively remembered by Americans: the movies.[3]

In his comprehensive guide to popular portraits of Lincoln, Frank Thompson lists 155 films featuring Lincoln produced between 1903 and 1999.[4] Only two scholars have attempted to analyze a wide chronological range of these productions. In 1961, Robert C. Roman published a largely anecdotal essay that recounted the narrative of selected "Lincoln" films up to the mid-1950s. Martin A. Jackson, in a contribution to the *Columbia Companion to American History on Film* (2004), endeavored to cover

*An earlier version of this chapter appeared in *American Nineteenth Century History*, vol. 12, no. 2 (June 2011). The material is published here with permission.

print biographies of Lincoln, his importance in American culture, and movies and television programs about him in a little over four pages.[5] A number of scholars have written about "biographical" films of Lincoln released between 1930 and 1940. As part of a fine essay on the "interpretative framework" within which Lincoln had been understood in American popular culture, David Turley analyzed *Young Mr. Lincoln* (1939) and *Abe Lincoln in Illinois* (1940), emphasizing the manner in which early episodes from Lincoln's life were used to reveal aspects of his character and provide a foretaste of his destiny. Mark E. Neely, Jr., examining the same two films, dismissed *Young Mr. Lincoln* as "corny fiction" and saw *Abe Lincoln in Illinois*, in spite of its errors, as better history. Tony Pipolo, adding D. W. Griffith's *Abraham Lincoln* (United Artists, 1930) to *Young Mr. Lincoln* and *Abe Lincoln in Illinois*, explored all three through the prism of Lincoln's polarized reputation: as the "great divider" who was also the "great reconciler."[6] There have been two main further studies of the representation of Lincoln on film. Bryan Rommel-Ruiz compares the treatment of Lincoln in D. W. Griffith's *The Birth of a Nation* (Epoch, 1915) and other early movies with that by historians of the same era. Andrew Piasecki analyzes the portrayal of Lincoln in John Ford's *The Iron Horse* (Fox, 1924) as a visionary who supported the building of a transcontinental railroad to aid the creation of a modern, unified nation.[7]

This chapter builds upon previous writing about Lincoln on film. It is in part at least a work of synthesis. Yet it differs from earlier analyses in a number of ways. It looks at "Lincoln" movies over a much longer timescale than any writer has done so far. It endeavors to show how—and suggest why—the filmic representation of Lincoln has changed over time. It offers a new and more detailed analysis of many of the key films of the genre. It also seeks to identify, where possible, the critical and popular response to the portrayal of Lincoln in such films.

Lincoln and early film

Lincoln had been a figure of great controversy during his lifetime. Many Americans—by no means confined to the South—distrusted or opposed him. More than 60 percent of the electorate voted against him for the presidency in 1860 and he was only saved from probable defeat in 1864 by the news of Sherman's capture of Atlanta. "Although the object [at the time of his death] of a great deal of immediate sentimentality," commented Eric F. Goldman, "[he] did not become the unassailable Abraham Lincoln of the schoolbooks until two decades after his murder."[8] In fact, Goldman underestimated the time it took for Lincoln to secure his place in history as perhaps the greatest of all American presidents. From 1865 to 1900, argues Barry Schwartz, hundreds of literary works—both prose and poetry—attempted to construct Lincoln as "a demigod," modeled on what David Donald had called the "ideal hero in classical mythology."[9] None of these attempts to mythologize Lincoln sold very well. The most ambitious of them all was the monumental biography produced by Lincoln's former secretaries, John Nicolay and John Hay. Initially published in abridged form by *The Century Magazine* over two and a half years at the end of the 1880s, it was republished as a ten-volume biography in 1890. Yet, as Merrill Peterson notes, the work was "too ponderous" for a magazine such as *The Century* (which lost subscribers while the series was being published) and sales of the multivolume book were small.[10]

What set the scene for the emergence of Lincoln as a major character in the movies (between 1908 and the end of 1915, some 39 films featuring him appeared[11]) was not the attempt to mythologize him but the way in which he came to be constructed in American popular culture. In November 1897, *McClure's Magazine* began to serialize a new life of Lincoln by Ida M. Tarbell. Within three months of the publication of this first installment, *McClure's* had signed up another 100,000 subscribers.[12] Unlike the Nicolay and Hay biography, therefore, Tarbell's portrait of Lincoln clearly touched a chord with readers. Her approach differed in many ways from Nicolay and Hay. It was closer in some respects to the three-volume life published in 1889 by Lincoln's friend and former law partner, William Henry Herndon. But Herndon's attempt to present Lincoln as a characteristic— and often highly crude—product of the western frontier had either been reviled or ignored.[13] Tarbell's genius was to repackage Herndon's Lincoln into a sellable product: like Herndon, she focused on projecting an idea of Lincoln as a Westerner. Unlike Herndon, she presented Lincoln as a great man not so much *despite* his background as *because* of it. Tarbell created a folk myth of Lincoln as a "common man" with democratic values, a typical descendant of generations of pioneering Westerners.[14]

To Tarbell's portrayal of Lincoln as a characteristic Westerner and "man of the people," popular magazines, newspapers, and live theater during the closing years of the nineteenth century added another view: that of Lincoln the merciful. In May 1898, for example, actor David W. Griffith had a major success in Chicago with his depiction of Lincoln in William Haworth's play *The Ensign*.[15] Based on a real incident in November 1861— the seizure of two Confederate emissaries to Europe, James M. Mason and John Sliddell, on the high seas by Captain Charles Wilkes of the USS *San Jacinto*—the play revolved around the attempts of two British officers to pick a quarrel with Wilkes in order to prevent him from sailing to intercept the *Trent*, the British ship bearing the two Confederates. Convicted of the killing of one of these officers, Wilkes escaped execution only through the direct intervention of President Lincoln himself.

Many of the initial films featuring Lincoln similarly focused on his merciful qualities. The story of *Abraham Lincoln's Clemency* (1910), remarked a reviewer for *Variety*, was that "of the soldier boy, who, fatigued and worn out, was found aslep [sic] on duty and sentenced to be shot for breach of discipline, and was granted clemency by President Lincoln."[16] Like *The Reprieve* (1908) and *The Sleeping Sentinel* (1910), *Abraham Lincoln's Clemency* was loosely based on the story of William Scott, a young Union soldier who had been condemned to death for falling asleep on guard duty in 1861, and pardoned at Lincoln's request. A heavily romanticized poem about this incident, written by Francis De Haes Janvier in 1863, provided the real basis for the film.[17] *The Seventh Son* (1912) took its inspiration more directly from the moving letter of condolence sent by Lincoln in 1864 to Boston widow Lydia Bixby, whom he erroneously believed to have lost five sons killed while serving in the Union army.[18]

"Any picture which has Lincoln in it appeals to a large number of people," commented an anonymous writer for *The Moving Picture World* in 1911. The film that provoked this comment was "a war story . . . designed to exhibit the kindness of President Lincoln." What made this movie—*Lieutenant Grey of the Confederacy* (1911)—different from films such as *Abraham Lincoln's Clemency* was that it portrayed Lincoln as merciful to Southerners as well as Northerners. In *Lieutenant Grey of the Confederacy*, he was shown pardoning "a Confederate spy upon the request of his sweetheart."[19] By the second decade of the twentieth century, Lincoln was emerging on film as a champion of sectional reconciliation. In *One Flag at Last* (1911), he was persuaded by Captain Jack Myers (Earle Williams) of the Union Army to release Fred (Harry Benham), the Confederate brother of his sweetheart Bettie (Rose E. Tapley), from prison. The most fanciful of all these films dealing with convicted spies and young female rebels was *The Toll of War* (1913), in which Lincoln freed a Southern girl (Ethel Grandin) sentenced to death for spying against the North. After her release, she witnessed the shooting of Lincoln at Ford's Theatre. The mortally wounded president was carried to her room nearby and died improbably in her bed while she knelt beside him in prayer.[20]

The Birth of a Nation

The growing salience of films about Lincoln in the early 1910s reflected both the impact of the celebration of his 1909 centennial and growing popular awareness, spurred by occasions such as the great Gettysburg reunion of 1913, that the events of the Civil War were now a half-century in the past. In 1915, as the greatest of these commemorative celebrations—that of the ending of the war—loomed, D. W. Griffith released *The Clansman*. Griffith, born in Kentucky in 1875 to slave-holding parents (his father fought as a lieutenant-colonel in the

Confederate Army), had abandoned his career as a stage actor in 1908 to become principal movie director for the Biograph Company. He left Biography in 1913, frustrated at the company's refusal to allow him to make longer films. His new contract with Harry S. Aitken of the Reliance-Majestic syndicate allowed him to make two such longer films each year. *The Clansman*, quickly renamed *The Birth of a Nation*, was closer to the multireel epics that were now being made by French and Italian directors. A three-hour "spectacular," set against the backcloth of the Civil War era and featuring Lincoln as one of the characters, it probably had a greater impact on how the sixteenth president was popularly perceived than all its predecessors combined. Newspapers made estimates toward the end of the movie's initial run in particular cities of the vast audiences that had seen it: 200,000 in Baltimore, 185,000 in Boston, 100,000 in Kansas City and New Orleans. Over the 15 years after its first release, suggested Carl E. Milliken, secretary of the Motion Picture Producers' Association, it was "probably" viewed by 50 million people.[21]

In some respects, *The Birth of a Nation* offered the now-conventional filmic view of a humane and merciful Lincoln. After Lincoln (Joseph E. Henabery) signs the call for 75,000 volunteers that will effectively begin the Civil War, he is shown wiping away tears with a handkerchief. When the Southern "hero" of the film, Confederate Colonel Ben Cameron (Henry B. Walthall), is unjustly condemned to death as a guerrilla, his mother (Josephine Crowell) and Elsie Stoneman (Lillian Gish), the daughter of Radical Northern politician Austin Stoneman (Ralph Lewis), visit Lincoln to plead for a presidential pardon. After some hesitation, the compassionate Lincoln—described as "Great Heart" in an intertitle—agrees. Mrs. Cameron, having barely resisted the urge to embrace the president in gratitude, goes to see her son in hospital and informs him that "Mr. Lincoln has given back your life to me."

Richard Schickel, Griffith's biographer, points out that the director's admiration for Lincoln "dated back to boyhood, when he was imbued with . . . reverence for the magnanimity and wisdom of the man who had defeated the Confederacy."[22] If Lincoln had not been murdered, Griffith believed, Reconstruction generally (and specifically the "Radical" Reconstruction from March 1867) would not have happened. He consequently included in his film a scene displaying a confrontation between Lincoln and the leader of the Radical Republicans, Austin Stoneman, modeled on congressman Thaddeus Stevens of Pennsylvania. Stoneman protests at Lincoln's policy of clemency for the defeated South, insisting that "their leaders must be hanged and their states treated as conquered provinces."[23] Lincoln, however, stays true to the position outlined in his second inaugural (March 4, 1865) in terms of how he proposes to treat the defeated South: "with malice toward none and charity for all." Encouraged by this liberal attitude on the part of the president, the South promptly begins rebuilding itself—a process interrupted by Lincoln's assassination. These sequences leave a false impression. As Eric Foner observes, "Lincoln died without having established a coherent plan for Reconstruction." In his final speech, he even suggested that the Louisiana plan he had earlier favored—that when ten percent of a state's 1860 voters took an oath of allegiance to the United States, they would be able to elect their own government—might have to be modified. The Civil War effectively ended on April 9, with Lee's surrender at Appomattox, and Lincoln was assassinated just five days later, leaving "Reconstruction policy . . . in flux."[24] The South had very little of Lincoln's "fostering hand" to encourage it and the reported reaction of the Southern Cameron family a little later in the film to the news of Lincoln's assassination ("Our best friend is gone") is deeply unrealistic.[25]

What Griffith offered in these sequences was a further development and refinement of the Lincoln legend on film: the martyred president was constructed as a *political* symbol of sectional reconciliation and national unity. This construction was clear in Lincoln's confrontational meeting with Stoneman. It was *visually* suggested in the second half of the film when Union veterans and ex-Confederates take refuge together against marauding blacks in perhaps the most famous icon associated with the Lincoln legend: a log cabin.[26] But neither widespread Southern esteem for Lincoln nor the reconciliation of North and South developed as quickly as the film suggested. For many Southerners to change their mind about Lincoln first needed a growing rapprochement between the sections. *The Birth of a Nation* was wrong in suggesting that this occurred in any significant way during the Reconstruction period. A small number of joint Union and Confederate parades began in the mid-1870s and the tradition grew in the 1880s (one observer identified 24 such reunions between 1881 and 1887). When Union commander and former president Ulysses S. Grant died in 1885, two Confederate generals were among his pallbearers.[27] But it was the 1890s, and especially the Spanish-American War of 1898, that set the seal on this renewed sense of intersectional amity: it was commonplace for newspapers at the time to observe that "the blue and the gray" were marching together for the first time in decades against a common foe.[28] The regional reconciliation set the scene for the emergence of Lincoln as a new symbol of American nationalism. His centennial in 1909 was celebrated in the South as well as the North. It was during the centennial that the Lincoln Memorial in Washington began to be planned as an explicit symbol of reunification.[29] Griffith's *The Birth of a Nation* wrongly extended this early twentieth-century view of Lincoln as an icon of national unity back to the closing stages of the Civil War.

In focusing primarily on Lincoln as an advocate of sectional reconciliation, Griffith carefully avoided what might have been an alternative representation: Lincoln as emancipator of the slaves. *The Birth of a Nation* begins with two scenes that seemingly suggest this will be the main focus of the film. The first, introduced by the intertitle "The bringing of the African to America planted the first seed of disunion," implies that the Civil War was made inevitable by the introduction of Africans into what until then had apparently been an Edenic paradise for whites.[30] It features a minister praying over manacled slaves who are about to be auctioned. The second shot is of "Abolitionists of the Nineteenth Century demanding the freeing of the slaves." Spectators, at this point, may have thought they were about to see a film *about* emancipation. But the focus of the film suddenly switches to two white families: the Northern Stonemans and the Southern Camerons. When slaves on the Cameron plantation finally appear, they are well-treated and happy, putting on a dancing show for the Camerons and their visiting friends, Phil and Tod Stoneman (who, despite being the sons of a Radical Republican politician, seem not at all disturbed by slavery). At no stage in the film is there any reference to the Proclamation of Emancipation or the Thirteenth Amendment. The only slender evidence that both have happened comes shortly after the start of the second half of the film, when real-life Radical Republican Senator Charles Sumner (Sam de Grasse) is shown visiting Stoneman to urge (implausibly) "a less dangerous policy in the extension of power to the freed race."

   The Birth of a Nation was a film that played a crucial role in the transformation of the American movie audience.[31] In large American cities, the biggest and most profitable market for the movies, nickelodeon audiences were mainly working-class and often immigrant. Much of the audience for *The Birth of a Nation*—which was presented in live theaters, with full orchestral accompaniment, and admission prices of up to $2—came from the native-born white American middle class. By 1915, many of these people were becoming increasingly conscious of the racial and ethnic divisions in their own society. The outbreak of the First World War in 1914 further underlined America's ethnic disunity: one-third of all US residents were either immigrants or the children of immigrants, and many retained residual loyalties—or antipathies—to the country from which they or their parents had come.[32] To anxious middle-class moviegoers of 1915, *The Birth of a Nation*—with its story of a new white nation born (at the expense of blacks) through the reconciliation of Northerners and Southerners—clearly struck a responsive chord. They cheered to the echo the riders of the Ku Klux Klan who fought for that white nation.[33] They also accepted without question Griffith's Lincoln as its iconic, unifying hero. The original version of *The Birth of a Nation* developed this role even further by emphasizing Lincoln's preference for racial separation and his support for the idea of "colonizing" blacks back to Africa.[34] One of its final sequences, preceded by the intertitle "Lincoln's Solution," showed African Americans at the dockside waiting to be shipped to Liberia.[35]

Lincoln in 1920s movies

"By 1920," observes Barry Schwartz, Lincoln "had become a demigod."[36] One symbol of this was the erection of the Lincoln Memorial in Washington, DC. Congress had finally agreed in 1910 to build a national monument to Lincoln in Potomac Park. Lincoln's quasi-sacred status was reflected both in the geographical isolation of the monument dedicated to his memory and the style of its construction. Building began in March 1914, just over three months before Griffith started shooting *The Birth of a Nation*, and the Memorial was opened in 1922. Designed by architect Henry Bacon, it resembled a Greek temple (echoing "the ancient Greek practice of placing statues of gods in enclosed temples to secure their separation from the mortal world").[37] From the point of view of filmmakers, however, the most visually significant part of the memorial was the huge statue of Lincoln by Daniel Chester French. This would become a key feature in most subsequent filmic treatments of Lincoln.

1924 saw the first attempt to make a full-length feature film covering the whole of Lincoln's life.[38] Produced by Lincoln enthusiasts Al and Ray Rockett, directed by Phil Rosen, and featuring a man (George A. Billings) who had a strong resemblance to the president but no prior experience of movie acting, *The Dramatic Life of Abraham Lincoln* had a running time of just over two hours. Since the film has been lost, only the comments of reviewers offer any guide to what it contained. In common with earlier Lincoln movies, it included the story of Lincoln's pardoning of William Scott, the "sleeping sentinel." In his early life, Lincoln was presented as eager for self-improvement: learning while other boys played, and walking five miles to acquire a copy of John Bunyan's *Pilgrim's Progress*. But, paradoxically, it was suggested that Lincoln was unambitious for himself: it was Mary Todd (Nell Craig), his wife, who pushed him for the presidency. Although a man of peace, Lincoln was depicted as an implacable opponent of slavery: an intertitle had him uttering the words he had written in his April 1864 letter to Albert G. Hodges ("If slavery is not wrong, nothing is wrong").[39] The critics for *The New York Times* and *Variety* both enthused about the film, but worried that watching what often seemed "like reading a long, long biography of Lincoln" would not appeal to movie audiences as entertainment. Their doubts were amply justified: the film failed at the box office. "It was made with love . . .," reflected a rueful Frances Marion, the author of the screenplay, but "the public looked upon it as an educational film and avoided it."[40]

The most commercially successful picture of the 1920s featuring Lincoln was John Ford's *The Iron House* (1924).[41] Extending further the emphasis placed by Herndon and Tarbell on Lincoln's Western background, Ford set out to associate him with the conventions that were beginning to define Western movies. Not only had Ford himself already made 40 Westerns, but the growing popularity of the genre had been demonstrated by the runaway success of *The Covered Wagon* a year earlier. *The Iron Horse*, as Andrew Piasecki points out, has what would soon come to be regarded as classic aspects of Westerns: "an Indian attack, a cattle drive, a saloon brawl, and the appearance of mythical figures, such as Buffalo Bill and Wild Bill Hickock."[42] Much of the movie is about ordinary people—construction workers and engineers—as they fight Indians, nature, and corrupt landowners to finish the first transcontinental railroad. But Ford makes it plain that it is the vision of Lincoln (Charles E. Bull) that underpins all their efforts.[43] The President appears as a major character in the storyline of the film—first in his hometown of Springfield, as a man believing in the future possibility of a transcontinental railroad, and subsequently when, as President, he resists criticism to sign the Pacific Railroad bill of 1862 into law. An intertitle praises "the far-seeing wisdom of the great rail splitter President" who had tied the American East more closely with the West.

As Piasecki argues, Lincoln was not just a rail splitter: he was a railroad attorney who, in defending the right of Illinois companies to build bridges across the Missouri River, helped secure a northern rather than southern route for the proposed transcontinental railroad.[44] What Piasecki does not explain is why this aspect of Lincoln's career is excluded from the film. It would, in fact, have undercut his representation as a unifying national figure. It is not merely East and West that are brought together in the film by Lincoln's vision of a transcontinental railroad. Ford, following the earlier cinematic tradition that culminated in *The Birth of a Nation*, also presented Lincoln as an agent of sectional reconciliation: an intertitle stresses that the Union Pacific construction crews were "chiefly ex-soldiers of the North and South working peacefully side by side."

It is not only in sectional terms that Lincoln in *The Iron Horse* functions as a unifier. "The basic unit of emotional value in John Ford's films—which is threatened and which must be affirmed through some process during the course of the film," writes Janey Place, "is some version of the family."[45] Lincoln is first seen benignly watching little Davy Brandon (Winston Miller) and his sweetheart Miriam Marsh (Peggy Cartwright) playing in the snow. Davy's father (James Gordon) is a surveyor who believes in the idea of a transcontinental railroad; Miriam's father (Will Walling) is a local contractor who does not. Initially, the railroad as an issue separates the two small families (no mothers are shown). Davy and his father set off for the West, where the father is killed by a white renegade, Deroux (Fred Kohler), who pretends to be an Indian. After Lincoln signs the Pacific Railway bill, however, the grown-up David Brandon (George O'Brien) becomes involved in the railroad's construction as a scout. Deroux tries to murder him but, taking revenge for his father's death, Davy kills him. At the end of the film, he is reunited with Miriam (Madge Bellamy). With Lincoln's vision fulfilled, and the railroad he planned completed, a new family is born.

Making a film about the first continental railroad was, in some ways, a curious choice for Ford and his studio (Fox) to have made. The building of the railroad was accompanied by vast corruption, culminating in the Crédit Mobilier scandal of 1873.[46] Thanks to their high freight rates, railroads such as the Union Pacific/Central Pacific soon became deeply unpopular with American farmers, as the Granger movement of the 1870s and the Populist protests of the 1890s demonstrated. By the 1920s, in any case, the railroads were in steep decline, confronted with the growing volume of road transportation (one symbol of this perhaps was the readiness of railroad companies to loan locomotives for Ford's production).[47] Yet, originally, they had tied the nation together and laid the foundations for the economic growth of the next half-century and its culmination in the consumer boom of the 1920s. The film began and ended with a shot of Lincoln's bust ("His truth is marching on") and was dedicated "to the ever-living memory of Abraham Lincoln, the Builder—and of those countless engineers and toilers who fulfilled his dream of a greater nation." By disseminating a heroic myth about the building of the first transcontinental railroad—and associating Lincoln closely with that myth—*The Iron Horse* offered the "business civilization" of the 1920s a new symbol for its own belief in technological innovation and the unifying effects of material progress. This was, after all, the first decade in which Americans would elect a former engineer (Herbert Hoover) to the presidency.

Lincoln's popularity was already high in the mid-1920s: a *New York Times* reviewer commented that "the mere sight" of Lincoln in *The Iron Horse* "brought volleys of applause from the spectators."[48] Two years before *The Iron Horse* was released, the inauguration of the Lincoln Memorial had drawn attention to the quasi-divine attributes of Lincoln's greatness. Two years after *The Iron Horse*, another event—the publication of the first two volumes of Chicago poet Carl Sandburg's biography of Lincoln—furthered the alternative side of his historical reputation: as a common man. In *The Prairie Years*, Sandburg advanced a view of Lincoln as a folksy Westerner that was very similar to the one originally put forward by Tarbell.[49] He greatly expanded it, however, to include many mythical and fictional features. Sandburg, notes David Turley, "expressed a profound empathy with Lincoln such that he felt licensed to make use of folkloric and legendary material in pursuit of 'the spirit of Lincoln.'" Lincoln was portrayed as a true product of the Western frontier, a "man of the people" who was at the same time conscious of the United States' historic, divinely sanctioned role as the world's foremost champion of freedom and democracy.[50]

Griffith's *Abraham Lincoln* (1930)

In 1930, when D. W. Griffith reengaged with Lincoln as the subject of what would be the first full-length bio-pic of the sound era, his film (*Abraham*

Lincoln), was shaped by the existence of both the Lincoln Memorial and Sandburg's work. At the end of the assassination sequence, the film cuts from the mortally wounded Lincoln (Walter Huston) to a stormy, wintry shot of the log cabin in which he was born. It then segues directly into a shot of the Lincoln Memorial in which the camera slowly tracks forward to pass through the Greek columns to focus on French's statue (to which the lighting gives a pronounced halo effect) as a choir sings "The Battle Hymn of the Republic." Griffith had apparently read Sandburg's volumes in the summer of 1928. He was so impressed that he later tried to hire Sandburg to write the script for his film, but negotiations broke down when Sandburg demanded a $30,000 fee.[51] In the end, the script was written by another poet, Stephen Vincent Benét.

Griffith's Lincoln of 1930 strongly resembles, at times, the Lincoln of *The Birth of a Nation*. He is once again shown as humane and compassionate: he pardons a young soldier convicted of cowardice and, as in *Birth of a Nation*, uses his handkerchief to wipe away the tears after signing the proclamation calling for 75,000 volunteers. His assassination is covered in one of the film's longest sequences. But the fact that the film tries—like Phil Rosen's 1924 production—to cover the whole of Lincoln's life means that some sequences are abbreviated to the point of semi-comedy. The epic Lincoln-Douglas debates of 1858 are summarized in a series of one-sentence exchanges.[52] The Civil War is reduced to the first battle of Bull Run, the subsequent attempts to defend Washington, and Phil Sheridan's ride during the Shenandoah campaign of 1864. Lincoln's women are not shown in a very flattering light: Ann Rutledge (Una Merkel) is irritatingly flirtatious, Mary Todd (Kay Hammond) pushy and obsessed by the need to find good servants. Lincoln spends much of the film muttering "The union must be preserved" to various audiences. Arriving at Ford's Theatre, he is asked to make a speech. Beginning with the useful phrase "Again I say," he repeats disconnected phrases from his second inaugural and the Gettysburg Address.

Griffith's new Lincoln is also a folksy Sandburgian hero: he wrestles with one of his neighbors, is physically strong (one character calls him "the best rail-splitter in the country"), has a fund of stories to meet all occasions, wears a stove-pipe hat and, as played by Huston, has a suitably rangy look. He is instinctively a peaceful man, but he resists the town bully in New Salem—beating him in a fair fight—and later bluntly refuses to countenance any further extension of slavery.

Like *The Birth of a Nation*, *Abraham Lincoln* begins with a sequence dealing with African enslavement. In a very early representation of the horrors of the middle passage, a ship is shown at sea, full of chained blacks. One who has died is unceremoniously thrown overboard. Later, in a major change from *The Birth of a Nation*, slaves themselves are given a degree of agency. A chain-gang of African Americans is shown pulling ropes at a dockside and, despite the presence of a white overseer, singing a song demanding freedom.[53] This is immediately followed by a shot of Lincoln reading a draft of the provisional Proclamation of Emancipation to his cabinet. *Abraham Lincoln*, therefore, unlike *The Birth of a Nation*, did embrace a discourse of emancipation. But that discourse was still subordinated to the foregrounding of the themes of union and sectional reconciliation.

Abraham Lincoln is consciously more balanced in its treatment of North and South than *The Birth of a Nation*: it shows that the Civil War really began when the Confederates fired on Fort Sumter on April 12, 1861. This sequence now precedes Lincoln's call for volunteers to suppress the rebellion. Also unlike *Birth of a Nation*, both Confederate and Union troops are shown marching off to war (in *Birth*, only Confederates are shown). Lincoln pardons a young Union soldier; equally, Southern commander Robert E. Lee saves a Northern spy who is about to be hanged. Yet when a sleepless Lincoln paces the White House at night, it is not slavery he is really thinking about but "the blood it takes to hold this Union together." As his thoughts begin to shift toward the end of the conflict, he is principally concerned not with the plight of freed blacks but with the need for reconciliation between whites: he will not agree to have Lee shot, vetoes the idea of confiscating Southerners' horses since they will need them for spring plowing, and suggests allowing Confederate president Jefferson Davis to escape. He also outlines a magnanimous policy toward the defeated Southern states, declaring—in exactly the same words as in *The Birth of a Nation*—that he plans to take them back "as though they had never been away."

Unlike *The Birth of a Nation*, Griffith's *Abraham Lincoln* did not reach a mass audience. The reviews were mainly good: *Variety* saw it as a "startling superlative accomplishment" demonstrating a rejuvenated Griffith, though it also criticized the romance with Ann Rutledge as "unconvincing in parts." *The New York Times* praised the war scenes ("Mr. Griffith is in his element") but found other sequences too "tinctured with old-fashioned melodrama." There was a general consensus among reviewers that the film was too "episodic in its structure" (Richard Schickel would later observe that it might accurately have been called "Beloved Moments with Mr. Lincoln").[54] Griffith himself commented that, despite favorable reviews, "customers stayed away in multitudes." Confessing that he would "probably never know" why the film failed, he speculated that it was simply "too large a dose of textbook" to be easily assimilated by young moviegoers.[55] The failure of the film was an especially hard blow for Griffith, since he had such high hopes for it—and had put up with a good deal while making it. It is possible that the studio (United Artists) had already decided to get rid of Griffith before production started and deliberately sabotaged the film as a means to that end. In contrast to his close supervision of the editing and scoring of *The Birth of a Nation*, Griffith virtually washed his hands of the final stages of the project. The final editing was done by producer John Considine, Jr., and lacked the seamless skill of many of Griffith's earlier productions (the assassination sequence, for example, while the same length as that in *The Birth of a Nation*, is clearly inferior in terms of dramatic intensity).[56] It may also be that Griffith, facing the challenge of his first talking picture, was no longer the master he once had been.

There were, however, two issues that ran deeper. Griffith's major problem in his epic films, Vlada Petric argues, "was to integrate the individual storyline (usually a love conflict) with the historical or social events and environments that he wanted to be more than mere background."[57] In *The Birth of a Nation*, the character of Lincoln had been successfully linked to the intertwined fictional stories of the Cameron and Stoneman families (Mrs Cameron visits the President—accompanied by Elsie Stoneman—to plead for her son's life; congressman Stoneman and the president argue over plans for the postwar; Elsie and Phil Stoneman are in the audience at Ford's Theatre when Lincoln is shot). Griffith and Benét had, indeed, originally thought of doing something on these lines in *Abraham Lincoln*. They considered having in the foreground of the film two fictional lovers whose story would parallel that of Lincoln. In the end, the young man would be revealed as the sentry Lincoln famously pardoned when he was sentenced to death for being asleep at his post. Either because Griffith and Benét never managed to make the idea work or it was vetoed by Considine, the characters were absent from *Abraham Lincoln*. In retrospect, Griffith felt this had been a mistake: it would have created a human perspective on Lincoln's career and given the film a degree of suspense that a simple biography (everybody knew how the story ended) could never do.[58] Finally, while Griffith in *The Birth of a Nation* had successfully constructed Lincoln as a symbol of unity for a nation uneasy over the ethnic divisions it confronted, his 1930 picture had no similar resonance among American moviegoers as they sought to come to terms with the consequences of the "Great Crash" of 1929.

Lincoln during the 1930s Depression

During the Depression years of the 1930s, Lincoln's spirit was mobilized by other filmmakers in a variety of ways. Many of the political movies of the era made incidental use of him as a means of uniting and encouraging a people who, because of the Depression, appeared to be losing faith in the American democratic experiment. The parallel between the crisis of the 1860s and that of the 1930s was often hinted at in these films. Lincoln brought the two together because he provided an example of strong executive leadership and had helped preserve the American republic at a time of great upheaval. In Gregory La Cava's 1933 film *Gabriel Over the*

White House—a film that in economic terms anticipated aspects of the New Deal but suggested the political solution was to make the president a virtual dictator—Lincoln's presence is constantly evoked: by the bust of the sixteenth president in the Oval Office, by the use of the quill pen with which Lincoln freed the slaves to bring about world peace, and by the frequent playing of the Battle Hymn of the Republic. In other 1930s films, it is Lincoln's words that are cited—as in Leo McCarey's *Ruggles of Red Gap* (1935). For most reviewers, the highlight of the film was the shot in which English butler Marmaduke Ruggles (Charles Laughton) "recites the Gettysburg Address in the saloon [of a frontier town] to a hushed audience of barflies and maverick cow hands."[59]

The Lincoln Memorial became an increasingly obvious filmic symbol of the continuing relevance of democratic values during the 1930s. In Frank Capra's *Mr Smith Goes to Washington* (1939), the monument and Daniel Chester French's sculpture were used to contrast Lincoln's words with the sordid realities of modern politics and to suggest that Lincoln's spirit still lives on as a source of inspiration. Jefferson Smith (James Stewart) is appointed to fill the remainder of the term of a US senator who has died: he is young and deeply idealistic (the governor nominating him describes him as knowing "Lincoln and Washington by heart"). Immediately after he arrives in Washington, Smith wanders off on a tour of national monuments that climaxes with the Lincoln Memorial. He sees the words of Lincoln's second inaugural on the wall and hears the Gettysburg Address come alive as a small white boy—watched by an elderly African American—reads them out to his grandfather. (Capra is making the non-too-subtle point that Lincoln offers inspiration to all generations and races.) Later, after Smith has proposed his first, much-cherished bill for a boy's camp in his home state, he tells his secretary Clarissa Saunders (Jean Arthur) that "I even went down to see Mr. Lincoln again." The location he has chosen for the camp, however, undercuts a scheme run by grafting politicians. "Enamored of the Lincoln precedent," remarked a reviewer in the *Motion Picture Herald*, "the youngster stumbles upon the truth . . . and is ridden down by the [state political] machine when he attempts to expose the steal."[60] But before quitting Washington in disillusionment, Smith makes a final visit to the Lincoln Memorial, where Saunders finds him and convinces him that Lincoln was not merely an idealist but a practical politician who also had to deal with corrupt politicians. Saunders finishes by representing Lincoln as a living presence on the political scene, a man waiting for someone to carry on his principles and struggle to save American democracy ("I think he's waiting for you, Jeff"). Convinced by Saunders, Smith salutes French's statue of Lincoln and goes back to the Senate to launch the filibuster he hopes will save his reputation.

During the course of the decade, and principally as a result of the Depression, Hollywood's representation of Lincoln changed. There were still films released that emphasized his traditional humanitarian qualities. In *The Littlest Rebel* (1935), Virgie Cary (Shirley Temple) persuades the president (Frank McGlynn, Sr.) to spare her Confederate father, who is about to be shot as a spy.[61] In *Of Human Hearts* (1938), Lincoln (John Carradine) recalls a young doctor (Gene Reynolds) from his battlefield duties to upbraid him for his neglect of his widowed mother (Beulah Bondi).[62] Yet there was also an increasing tendency to reinscribe his life in terms of virtues such as self-reliance in adversity, independence, and determination. Many of these films were clearly influenced by Sandburg's biography. The fact that this initially concentrated on Lincoln's youth made Sandburg's Lincoln a convenient symbol for the years after 1929.[63] Lincoln's early struggles could be identified with the difficulties confronting ordinary Americans of the Depression period. Since he had demonstrated great self-reliance and used his energy and talent to surmount adversity, his youthful example could be used as an inspiration for moviegoers of the Depression era. Sandburg's influence was particularly obvious in John Ford's *Young Mr. Lincoln* and John Cromwell's *Abe Lincoln in Illinois*. As David Turley notes, Ford "was an ardent consumer of Lincolniana and brought something of the spirit of Sandburg's early volumes into the film." *Abe Lincoln in Illinois* was written by Robert E. Sherwood, based on his own Pulitzer prize-winning stage play. Both play and film script, Turley remarks, "drew substantially from Sherwood's good friend Sandburg's volumes."[64]

Young Mr. Lincoln

Young Mr. Lincoln depicted the future president (Henry Fonda) as a country lawyer who takes on the defense of two brothers accused of a murder that most of the community (including their mother) believes one of them committed. With the aid of a farmer's almanac, Lincoln proves that their main accuser—who has testified he saw the murder because the night was "moon bright"—could not have done so because of the state of the moon. Then, with a sharp crossexamination, he forces the accuser into a Perry-Mason style courtroom confession that it was he who had really committed the murder. Everything ends happily for Lincoln and his clients. He pockets the fee they offer (he is, after all, a lawyer) and watches as the whole family head off back to their farm. In the final sequence of the film, Lincoln tells a friend he is not going back to Springfield but plans to "go on a piece. Maybe to the top of that hill." As he strides away, the last sequence links Lincoln to his future: the Battle Hymn of the Republic begins to play, there is a storm sequence, and the camera cuts from Fonda's stove-pipe-hatted Lincoln to the face of French's statue.

The film was very loosely based on the trial of William "Duff" Armstrong for the murder of James Preston Metzker in Beardstown,

Illinois, in May 1858. The Armstrong case had been the subject of a novel by nineteenth-century writer Edward Eggleston and many of the scenes in the film were derived from Sandburg's biography.[65] As in real life (Armstrong's mother had known Lincoln when he lived in New Salem[66]), there is a prior relationship between the family at the heart of the story and Lincoln. The Clays first meet Lincoln when they want to buy flannel from his store to make shirts. Since they have no money, he trades the fabric for a barrel of books. One of the books is *Blackstone's Commentaries*—the text, the film suggests, that inspires Lincoln with the idea of becoming a lawyer. Many years later, when the family is in trouble, they turn to Lincoln for help.

After Matt (Richard Cromwell) and Adam Clay (Eddie Quillan) are accused of the murder of "Scrub" White (Fred Kohler, Jr.), *Young Mr. Lincoln* becomes a family melodrama (and a much more developed one than Ford's earlier *The Iron Horse*). At its heart is the role of Abigail Clay (Alice Brady), the mother, agonizing over the fact that she cannot condemn one of her sons to death by identifying him as the murderer but that, if she does *not* do so, both may hang. As the dominant force in her family (her husband has by this stage died), Abigail resembles other strong Ford heroines, including Ma Joad (Jane Darwell) in *The Grapes of Wrath* (Twentieth-Century Fox, 1940).[67] The travails of the family, as Richard Abel points out, allow Lincoln "to begin paying the debt he incurred from them" at the start of the film by creating his original interest in law.[68] The film suggests that he both adopts the family and is adopted by it. Their farm reminds him of his Kentucky roots, and he suggests that Abigail Clay is like his own mother and Hannah Clay (Arleen Whelan) like his sister. He tells Carrie Sue (Dorris Bowdon) she resembles his lost love, Ann Rutledge.

Ford's screenwriter, Lamar Trotti, focused on Lincoln's down-to-earth qualities, including his folksiness and fund of stories. He also followed closely in the footsteps of Carl Sandburg by including in the script a range of humorous but mythical incidents: a pie-judging contest, a wrestling match, and a tug-of-war. The picture Trotti painted of Lincoln was essentially that of a shrewd, self-educated young man intent on achieving his personal ambitions. One crucial incident in the film, however, reflected wider trends in Hollywood rather than anything in Sandburg's volumes. The latter part of the 1930s saw the appearance of a cycle of films about lynching, including Fritz Lang's *Fury* (1936) and Mervyn Leroy's *They Won't Forget* (1937). *Young Mr. Lincoln* followed this trend. It had Lincoln himself—through a mixture of physical strength ("I can lick any man here hands down"), homespun humor, and moral suasion ("when men start taking the law into their own hands, they're just as apt . . . to start hanging somebody who's not a murderer")—preventing a mob from hanging his clients (Figure 3.1).[69]

Although he confronts a lynch mob to protect the rule of law, Ford's Lincoln seems unconcerned with the details of law itself. It seems to him

FIGURE 3.1 *Lincoln (Henry Fonda) disperses the lynch mob in* Young Mr. Lincoln.

at bottom simply a matter of morality. "Right and wrong, that's all there is to it!" he exclaims on reading Blackstone. "I may not know much about the law," he tells the prosecutor at the trial, "but I know what's right and what's wrong." During the trial of Matt and Adam Clay, he displays little respect for the jury: he uses flattery to select them and attempts to prejudice them against the main prosecution witness, John P. Cass (Ward Bond), by ridiculing him as "Jack-Ass." Ultimately, indeed, as Virginia Wright Wexman points out, he uses his "charismatic authority" to force a confession out of Cass, thereby removing any need for the jury to decide the case.[70] There is one aspect of Ford's Lincoln, however, that points to the experience of Lincoln the president: he is prepared to use physical force to defend a moral position. His first case as a lawyer sees two irate farmers quarrelling over the debts they owe each other. Lincoln suggests an equitable, common-sense solution but, when they baulk at this, obliquely threatens them with violence by telling a story of how, during the Black Hawk War of 1832, he "butted two men's heads together." He also subdues the lynch mob by, among other tactics, threatening to use violence.

The *New York Times* critic saw the picture as a representation of Lincoln's "happy years, before he got into politics." In reality, politics is present at a number of points in the film. In the very first sequence, Lincoln is introduced by a pompous politician to a small crowd as a fellow-candidate for the legislature. Lincoln's speech ("I'm plain Abraham Lincoln") is much less florid. His politics, he says, are "short and sweet," amounting to the traditional Whig platform: "I'm in favour of a national bank, the internal improvement system and a high protective tariff." "These," he declares, "are my sentiments and political principles." Later, he endorses the idea of free—as opposed to slave—labor, a distinction Eric Foner places at the core of 1850s Republican ideology.[71] His family left Kentucky, he explains, because "with all the slaves coming in, white folks had a hard time making a living." Ford's Lincoln needs no slaves to do his work for him: he competes in the rail-splitting contest at the fair, chops wood at the Clay farm, and cleans his shoes—and cuts his own hair—before going to the party at the home of Ninian Edwards, the brother-in-law of Mary Todd (Marjorie Weaver). The rivalry between Lincoln and Stephen A. Douglas is also constantly hinted at in the film. Lincoln first meets Douglas at the Edwards's party. ("Not even his enemies," Douglas tells Todd, "deny he [Lincoln] has a certain political talent.") Improbably, Douglas is present in court throughout the trial of the Clay brothers (he appears to be advising the prosecution, though at one point the judge suggests he effectively take over the defense in order to save at least one of the brothers). When Lincoln wins the case, Douglas promises him "never to make the mistake of underrating you again." The stage is set for the 1858 senatorial contest between the two men—and the presidential race two years later.

The *New York Times* critic thought the film "one of the most human and humorous of the Lincoln biographies." The same reviewer praised Fonda's performance in the title role as "one of those once-in-a-blue-moon things." *Harrison's Reports* hailed it as "perhaps his best performance to date." The critic for *Variety* similarly thought Fonda's playing of a young Lincoln "impressively realistic" and praised the film itself as offering "very good entertainment." At the same time, however, he worried that the "leisurely pace" of the film and the lack of a significant "romance interest" (Lincoln's relationship with Ann Rutledge and courtship of Mary Todd are dealt with very superficially) might doom the film at the box office (doubts shared by the reviewer for *Harrison's*).[72] The *Variety* reviewer, probably referring to the war clouds gathering in Europe, also remarked that the "theme is timely and almost topical in its reaffirmance of the democratic principles that govern American civil liberties," but no other commentator seems to have taken up this point.[73] The success or otherwise of the film appears to have been determined by the energy that went into promoting it (the manager of a theater in Hibbing, Minnesota, who arranged to show it around Lincoln's Birthday and made deals with local grade schools, reported "outstanding business for three days") or by the size and region of the community. It did best in small towns in the North: the manager of a cinema in Milan, Indiana, wrote of "packed houses" and three days of "dandy business." In Drew, Mississippi, by contrast, the manager noted that "the folks just don't go for pictures of this kind." The manager of a Detroit cinema similarly underlined the film's lack of appeal to his big-city clientele. "It seems," he sadly confessed, "that many movie goers just stay away from history pictures."[74]

Abe Lincoln in Illinois

Abe Lincoln in Illinois begins with Lincoln (Raymond Massey) as a self-taught young man with a passion for reading. He and two friends row a flatboat of hogs down the river to New Orleans, stopping briefly in New Salem where the pigs try to escape and he meets Ann Rutledge (Mary Howard). Returning to New Salem, he becomes a not very successful storekeeper. The film has many Sandburgian touches. When a gang of toughs break into the Rutledge tavern, Lincoln fights and beats the leader in a wrestling match. He is also elected a militia captain in the Black Hawk war against the Indians and is shown incompetently (though amusingly) training new recruits.

The film displays little initial interest in Lincoln as a politician. His local popularity leads to his election as a member of the state legislature, but the election is used only as a background to romantic tragedy: Ann Rutledge, Lincoln's sweetheart, is taken ill on the night of the election and dies. Subsequently, there is a cryptic reference to New Englanders wanting to revenge the murder of abolitionist editor Elijah Lovejoy (in Alton, Illinois, in November 1837), but Lincoln himself decides not to run for reelection and comes home to set himself up as a lawyer and meet Mary Todd (Ruth Gordon). Lincoln is represented as a man so humane he could never kill a deer and, though he supports the Whig presidential ticket in 1840, does not want to run for Congress because he might have to vote for war over what he disdainfully calls "a tract of land or a moral principle." Massey's Lincoln, as a reviewer for the *Motion Picture Herald* pointed out, "is a languid, somewhat indolent fellow, gentle and just but not conspicuously noble, brilliant and assertive, whose friends . . . and wife kick him upstairs into the presidency." Other reviewers also commented that it is the "shrewish nagging" of his ambitious wife that pushes him toward the presidency in the film while Lincoln himself is represented as lacking in ambition.[75] In reality, as William Herndon, Lincoln's friend and law partner, would later claim, his ambition was "a little engine that knew no rest."[76] Sherwood and Grover Jones, the man who helped adapt his play for the screen, preferred to show Lincoln as an unwilling target of the "cold ambition" of his wife who is pushed into "the empty triumph of winning an office he did not want" and launched on the path that will lead him to civil war and ultimate martyrdom.[77]

Sherwood's original play had dealt with the origins of Lincoln's destiny in a better way. In a key speech, it had shown Lincoln praying with a family of Oregon-bound pioneers for the survival of their gravely ill son. It was at this moment that Lincoln had been shown beginning to accept his own responsibilities and possible future place in history. But, to the enormous frustration of star Raymond Massey, who played Lincoln both on Broadway and in the movie, this scene disappeared from the film, making it less an evolving personal story than what Massey would describe in his autobiography as "a documentary, a procession of episodes."[78]

Another, more factual weakness of *Abe Lincoln in Illinois* is that, after Lincoln's wedding in November 1842, the story fast-forwards 17 years. An intertitle reads: "And then—years that marked the growth of a man, and of a nation." It is followed by a montage that takes the story up to 1859, ending with the surrender of John Brown at Harper's Ferry. The problem with this as history is what it misses out: the Mexican War, the Compromise of 1850, the Kansas-Nebraska Act, the Appeal of the Independent Democrats, and the emergence of the Republican Party. The film makes indirect reference to the administration of the Fugitive Slave law and direct reference to "Bleeding Kansas," the Dred Scott decision of 1857, and the John Brown raid. But exactly what *Lincoln* is doing in this period—apart from setting up a legal partnership with Herndon, being elected to Congress, and being shown making one speech—and what he thinks about the developments of these crowded years are left unexplored.[79]

With this montage over, the chronology becomes confused. The film has the John Brown raid of 1859 happening *before* Lincoln is nominated to run against Stephen Douglas (Gene Lockhart) for the US Senate in 1858. But unusually, in the Lincoln-Douglas debates, the film shows both men reciting passages from their own speeches—even if, in using an extract from Lincoln's "house divided" speech, it was a speech delivered *before* the debates actually began. Lincoln subsequently wins the Republican nomination for the presidency and then the presidency itself. In the final sequences of the film, Douglas offers him support and Lincoln delivers his farewell address to a crowd at the Springfield railroad station (Figure 3.2). By this point, he has grown a beard and become the Lincoln of the Civil War photographs. At the very end of the film, he sits alone, hunched on the back of the train that is taking him to Washington and his destiny.

David Turley points out that the stance adopted by Lincoln in the Lincoln-Douglas debates "was as applicable, if not more so, to the United States internally and internationally at the end of the 1930s as in the 1850s." Lincoln's endorsement of the notion of "national unity and, by extension, international unity of democratic forces to meet the threat to liberty" was relevant to the rising Fascist threat abroad. Since the film ends before Lincoln's inauguration, it "leaves unresolved" the issue of whether his commitment "not to allow popular government and liberty to pass

FIGURE 3.2 *Lincoln (Raymond Massey) bids farewell to his Springfield neighbors as he leaves for Washington in* Abe Lincoln in Illinois.

from the world" can be achieved without war. The Second World War had broken out four-and-a-half months before the film's Washington première and, even though there was no large-scale fighting in Europe before May 1940, it is clear that some critics of *Abe Lincoln in Illinois* regarded the film as a timely reminder of core American values in a menacing world. Frank Nugent of the *New York Times* saw the film as a "moving and eloquent tribute" to what the United States should "stand for, and must stand for, in these and future times." The reviewer for *Harrison's Reports* went further, interpreting the movie as a possible hint of US involvement in the war: it offered, he wrote, "inspiration to Americans" by passing on "a message that might be heeded today—to preserve and fight for freedom and democracy."[80]

Ominously, the critic for *Variety* cited in his review the "traditions exist[ing] in the trade that a Lincoln picture does not possess big box office appeal." In order to break those traditions—probably derived from the reception of Griffith's bio-pic of 1930 and *Young Mr. Lincoln*—he suggested that the film would need "strong selling, hustling exploitation and showmanly handling." The première of *Abe Lincoln in Illinois* in Washington, attended by First Lady Eleanor Roosevelt as well as writer Sherwood, director Cromwell, and star Massey, was everything this critic recommended. It was preceded by a Lincoln "look-alike" competition. The ushers were all debutantes and the Newspaper Women's Club of Washington, for whose benefit the screening was organized, had been active for weeks in advance publicity and ticket sales. A special edition of a newspaper, the *Times-Herald*, devoted to Lincoln was distributed after the show.[81] Sadly for the picture's producers, the initial success did not last. It may have been, as the *Motion Picture Herald* critic suggested, that the film was more reminiscent of a stage play than a movie.[82] It may also have been that *Abe Lincoln in Illinois* followed too closely on the heels of *Young Mr. Lincoln*, and there was little appetite for a second film on Lincoln's youth.[83] The manager of the theater in Sodus, New York, sent out personal recommendations of the film to his patrons and was rewarded with "above normal" business. Elsewhere in Northern and Western towns, it was a different story. A manager from Granite Falls, Minnesota, considered it "no draw, especially in a small town." It was a "dud" in Clatskanie, Oregon. In St. Clair, Michigan, it led to the "lowest Sunday and Monday business in many a moon." The managers of these theaters regarded the film itself as an excellent production. It had failed, they thought, for reasons to do with general audience tastes—because "patrons want lighter film fare" (Clatskanie) or "historicals don't go here any too well" (St. Clair).[84]

Lincoln after 1940

Merrill Peterson argues that Lincoln's fame reached its zenith in the three decades between 1929 and the sesquicentennial of his birth in 1959.[85] In terms of film, the zenith came earlier—in 1939–40. After that, there was a pronounced move away from depicting him on film. Frank Thompson's comprehensive bibliography of Lincoln films lists 121 in all from 1903 to the end of 1940. Between 1941 and 1999, only 34 more were released.[86] Some of these were short documentaries[87] or films that discussed and reproduced the Gettysburg address.[88] Others referred to Lincoln and his influence rather than portrayed him[89] or featured only a voice reading his words.[90] In fact, Lincoln's relative disappearance from movie screens since 1940 poses a historical problem of its own (though it may in part have been a consequence of the mixed fortunes of *Young Mr. Lincoln* and the commercial failure of *Abe Lincoln in Illinois*). After 1940, no major studio or film director attempted a biopic dealing with any part of Lincoln's life for more than 70 years. Only one movie, *Tennessee Johnson* (1943), dealing with the rise to power of Lincoln's vice-president and eventual successor, Andrew Johnson, painted a sympathetic portrait of Lincoln's difficulties in office. That portrait may have reflected the fact that at the time the film was made, the United States was once again involved in a major war. The other films in which Lincoln featured have fallen into three broad categories: Westerns, movies dealing with conspiracies—successful or not—to assassinate the president, and comedies/satires.

Lincoln featured in a small number of Westerns. In *Rock Island Trail/Transcontinent Express* (1950), Lincoln (Jeff Corey) was again—as in *The Iron Horse*—involved in the westward expansion of the railroad. In *New Mexico* (1951), played by Hans Conreid, he had a part until his assassination in making peace with the Indians. In the second part of *How the West Was Won* (1962), John Ford used Lincoln (played for the last time on screen by Raymond Massey) as the introduction to the sequence he directed on the battle of Shiloh. Including Lincoln in a Western was a way of exploiting his reputation while at the same time avoiding the black/white racial issue. He might, as in *New Mexico*, be involved in the reconciliation of races, but it was Indians and whites who were involved. As the civil rights movement grew from the mid-1950s, as the Western itself began to decline as a genre, and as Lincoln's own reputation faded, displacement of this kind became harder and Lincoln virtually disappeared from Westerns. The single exception to this appears to be *Guardian of the Wilderness* (1976), a movie dealing with the successful efforts of Galen Clark (Denver Pyle) and naturalist John Muir (John Dehner) to persuade Lincoln (Ford Rainey) to sign a 1864 law preserving the Yosemite Valley and the Mariposa Grove of giant sequoia trees from exploitation by lumber companies by ceding them to the state of California. This "ecological" Western, reflecting the growing strength of the environmentalist movement in the 1970s, effectively reconstructed Lincoln as an early supporter of what Peter Coates terms "wilderness preservation."[91]

The second category of Lincoln films was not new. It might be said to have begun with John Ford's *The Prisoner of Shark Island* (1936), which dealt with the story of Dr Samuel Mudd (Warner Baxter), who—without knowing what had taken place—provided medical treatment for John Wilkes Booth (Francis McDonald), the assassin of Lincoln (Frank McGlynn, Sr.). In 1951, Anthony Mann directed *The Tall Target* in which a discredited New York policeman (Dick Powell) foils an attempt to kill Lincoln (Leslie Kimmell) in Baltimore on his way to Washington for his inauguration. *The Prince of Players* (1955) dealt with the life of actor Edwin Booth (Richard Burton). Part of the film covered the assassination of Lincoln (Stanley Hall) by Booth's brother, John Wilkes Booth (John Derek). *The Lincoln Conspiracy* (1977), clearly made in the aftermath of the assassination of John F. Kennedy, the debate on the findings of the Warren Commission (1964), and the Watergate scandal, not only alleged that Lincoln (John Anderson) had been targeted by a conspiracy involving Edwin Stanton (Robert Middleton) and other high government officials but also that assassin John Wilkes Booth (Bradford Dillman) escaped to live in Canada. The latest film of this type, Robert Redford's *The Conspirator* (2011), offers a feminist slant on the assassination by focusing on the story of Mary Surratt (Robin Wright), the only woman co-conspirator to have been charged in relation to the killing of Lincoln (Gerald Bestrom). Defended by war hero Frederick Aiken (James McAvoy) at her trial, Surratt is found guilty and hanged for treason. Critic Richard Corliss argued that the film's account of her persecution by the Andrew Johnson (Dennis Clark) Administration, including secretary of war Edwin Stanton (Kevin Kline), offered a clear parallel with—and critique of—the actions of the Bush Administration in the wake of 9/11.[92] In general terms, assassination films marginalize Lincoln by representing him solely as a victim, a spectral figure whose infrequent appearances are there only to underline his tragic destiny.

The third category of films overlapped to some extent with the second. *The Faking of the President* (1976) was a satire in which Lincoln (William J. Daprato) becomes involved in the Watergate scandal surrounding Richard Nixon (Richard M. Dixon). In the wake of the assassination of JFK, Lyndon Johnson's attempts to manipulate public opinion over the Vietnam War, and Watergate, a growing skepticism manifested itself toward all politicians, including Lincoln. The sixteenth president's reputation also suffered in the final decades of the twentieth century from a declining faith in political leaders and "great men," as well as an increasing tendency to debunk historical figures. By the 1980s, the unquestioning respect for Lincoln had gone, and he was featured in cameo roles in several satirical comedies, including *Two Idiots in Hollywood* (1988), *The Big Picture* (1989), and *Happy Gilmore* (1996).[93] In *Bill and Ted's Excellent Adventure* (1989), Bill (Alex Winter) and Ted (Keanu Reeves) are high-school students about to flunk their history class reports. But a friendly stranger lends them a time machine in which they travel around picking up a miscellaneous group of historical figures: Beethoven, Ghengis Khan, Napoleon, Socrates, Billy the Kid, Freud, Joan of Arc—and Lincoln (Robert V. Barron). No one shows any reverence toward this Lincoln. Appearing on the stage of Bill and Ted's high school, he delivers a parody of his Gettysburg Address, finishing with the deeply un-Lincolnesque line: "Let's be excellent to each other—and party on, dudes." In 2012, perhaps the strangest "Lincoln" film ever was released: *Abraham Lincoln: Vampire Hunter*. Having seen his mother (Robin McLeavy) killed by vampires, Lincoln (Benjamin Walker) grows up with a mission to eliminate them. As president, he is doubly committed to this since he realizes vampires are fighting with the Confederates. A curious combination of historical epic/biopic and horror, the movie lacked the humor to justify the jokiness of its title.

Lincoln's changing reputation

Over a quarter of all the American movies featuring Lincoln that have been made were released between 1903 and the end of 1915. These early films took their cue from popular history and the live stage: they portrayed Lincoln as democratic and approachable, a "man of the people" who was a merciful chief executive. This was, of course, a highly selective approach. While the real Lincoln could show intense compassion for individuals, he was also a political leader who vigorously prosecuted a war in which at least 620,000 men died. Focusing on his compassionate side meant ignoring much of his record as a war president. Additionally, during the early 1910s, Lincoln came increasingly to be represented on screen as a symbol of reconciliation between the sections—a perception that would reach new heights in D. W. Griffith's *The Birth of a Nation*. Once again, there was some evidence in favor of this view, including the leniency implied in Lincoln's initial "ten percent" plan for Southern Reconstruction and the healing words of his second inaugural ("with malice toward none, with charity for all"; "to bind up the nation's wounds"). Yet Lincoln had been implacably committed to the destruction of the Confederacy and his second inaugural can also be read as expressing determination to continue the war until slavery had been utterly destroyed. Portraying Lincoln as a symbol of sectional reconciliation not only required an equally selective interpretation of his record, it also effectively sidelined the whole issue of slavery.

The period between 1920 and 1940 saw the production of many "Lincoln" films. In Griffith's *Abraham Lincoln* (1930), although emancipation is mentioned, it is still seen as less significant than Lincoln's role as the unifier of the nation. As late as 1935, in *The Littlest Rebel*, Lincoln was still being presented as the focus of sectional reconciliation. But the 1920s and 1930s saw other issues come to the fore as filmmakers continued to explore the man whom Eric Foner describes as "infinitely malleable."[94] To John Ford, in *The Iron Horse*, he was a prophet of technological change and postwar material progress. Filmmakers of the Depression era, such as Gregory La Cava in *Gabriel Over the White House*, used Lincoln to suggest that economic problems could be surmounted by wise leadership. Frank Capra, in *Mr. Smith Goes to Washington*, used him as a foil against political corruption. At the end of the 1930s, Ford produced *Young Mr. Lincoln*, in which Lincoln featured as a self-reliant young man able to make his way in the world—a moral for a country still suffering from economic depression. A year later, John Cromwell released *Abe Lincoln in Illinois*, another movie treating Lincoln's early years. Cromwell's Lincoln—like Phil Rosen's in *The Dramatic Life of Abraham Lincoln* 16 years earlier—was an unambitious man driven by his wife to embrace a tragic destiny. But in arguing in the Lincoln-Douglas debates for democratic forces to unite in defense of liberty, he also seemed to some to be insisting that democratic countries—including the United States—adopt a stronger line against Fascism.

After 1940, Lincoln became less popular as a character in movies. The commercial failure of films such as Griffith's *Abraham Lincoln* and Cromwell's *Abe Lincoln in Illinois* discouraged more biopics based on his life. From the mid-point of the twentieth century, as a strong civil rights movement emerged, the dominant discourse of national unity and sectional reconciliation gave place to a new emphasis on freedom and emancipation. This shift made it harder to represent Lincoln on screen. Despite the iconic reference made to him by some civil rights campaigners, some of Lincoln's own views on race were troublesome. As Barry Schwartz points out, "the Great Emancipator had not been the Great Integrator." While accepting that African Americans were entitled to freedom and the right to hold property, he had not believed that they had "the right to vote, petition, or serve on juries—and certainly not to social and cultural equality."[95] In the last decades of the twentieth century, reflecting growing doubts about "Great Men" in history, declining patterns of deference, and increasing cynicism toward politicians generally, the once-potent figure of Lincoln in the movies was sidelined into an occasional appearance in Westerns, assassination dramas, and comedies. Some of the directors of these films, however, demonstrated just as much historical imagination in constructing "their" Lincoln (Lincoln the advocate of reconciliation with Indians, Lincoln the environmentalist) as filmmakers such as Griffith and Ford had once done.

Spielberg's *Lincoln*

In March 2001, it was announced that Steven Spielberg's production company, DreamWorks SKG, had bought the rights to a forthcoming biography of Lincoln by Doris Kearns Goodwin, a former Harvard professor. From first reports, it seemed that the film Spielberg proposed to make would reinterpret Lincoln through the deconstructive prism of modern concerns. Goodwin's book apparently would weave together the personal and the political. It would offer a "Lincoln" informed by the Clinton era: Goodwin apparently had come to believe that "Lincoln and [Mary] Todd were the most dysfunctional first couple in Washington history." The film, it was alleged, directed by Spielberg himself, would depict "the so-called 'Great Emancipator' as a manic depressive racist who nearly lost the American civil war."[96] While Goodwin's biography, published four years later to considerable acclaim, did cover Lincoln's personality and personal life, it was primarily devoted to demonstrating Lincoln's political skills and the self-confident way he managed his cabinet during the Civil War.[97] It was not immediately obvious to Spielberg or, at that stage, anyone else how her 750-page book might be made into a film.

Work on the project began in 2001. It was reported that John Logan, cowriter of *Gladiator*, had been asked to write a script, and, once the screenplay was in existence, Spielberg offered the role of Lincoln to

Daniel Day-Lewis, who turned it down. Two years later, Spielberg told syndicated columnist Cindy Pearlman that a script was "in development" that focused on the relationship between Lincoln and black abolitionist Frederick Douglass. There was speculation that Tom Hanks would play Lincoln and Morgan Freeman Douglass. By 2005, according to *Variety*, Spielberg had hired a new screenwriter, Paul Webb, and was in discussions with Liam Neeson for the role of Lincoln. For the next four years, until he dropped out of the project, Neeson was designated as "Lincoln." In 2009, once Neeson left, Spielberg sent a new script by playwright Tony Kushner to Daniel Day-Lewis, who still did not want the part. By this stage, the screenplay dealt with the final four months of Lincoln's life (it would subsequently, on Spielberg's insistence, cover only two months) and had begun to focus on the struggle to pass the Thirteenth Amendment abolishing slavery through Congress. After Spielberg's long campaign to persuade Day-Lewis to play Lincoln finally succeeded, shooting began in the fall of 2011.[98] While the credits of the film would acknowledge that it was partly based on Goodwin's book, the episode at the heart of the film—dealing with the background to the vote in favor of the Thirteenth Amendment by the House of Representatives—was covered in less than four pages.

Lincoln begins with a sequence showing hand-to-hand fighting at the battle of Jenkins' Ferry, Arkansas, on April 29–30, 1864. This segues into soldiers reminiscing to Lincoln himself about the battle and Lincoln's Gettysburg address (November 19, 1863), which one black soldier can recite fluently. The film then moves on to its real focus: the campaign, masterminded by Lincoln, to persuade congressmen to accept the proposal (already agreed by the Senate) for a Thirteenth Amendment. The debate in the House begins on January 9 and ends with a vote on January 31. The movie could have ended in Capra-esque fashion at this point, with wild celebrations greeting the narrow vote in favor (or perhaps, a little later, with Lincoln setting off for Ford's Theatre). Instead, there is an awkward coda that covers the aftermath of the third battle of Petersburg (April 2, 1865), Lee's surrender to Grant at Appomattox, Lincoln's fatal shooting on April 14 and a flashback to him delivering his second inaugural on March 4, 1865.

Spielberg's film has been criticized on two main fronts. The first focuses on factual errors in how *Lincoln* represents "history." It is unlikely that anyone would have known the words of the Gettysburg address by heart in 1865—the speech did not acquire its iconic significance until several decades later. Despite his earlier political career as a Whig, Lincoln did not have a portrait of William Henry Harrison in his office and it is highly improbable that Alexander Gardner would have loaned his fragile photographic plates to anyone, least of all Lincoln's son, the rambunctious Tad (Gulliver McGrath). There were no coins with Lincoln's image in circulation in 1865. There is a reference in the film to

Confederates wanting to expand black slavery to Latin America, where the Spanish had in fact introduced it more than a century before the first slaves arrived in the British colonies. Mary Todd Lincoln (Sally Field) did not watch the debates in the House from the gallery. Congressmen did not vote by state but alphabetically by name. At various points in the movie, actor Tommy Lee Jones makes Vermonter Thaddeus Stevens sound as if he comes from Jones's native Texas. Lincoln's deathbed sequence is closer to later solemnized, hagiographical portraits and accounts than the grim and confused reality.

The second and more important front concerns the movie's narrow focus. As Eric Foner has pointed out, *Lincoln* offers "a severely truncated view" of the achievement of emancipation. In common with most major social and political changes, it had deep roots. Abolitionists had campaigned for decades to extirpate slavery. The Thirteen Amendment itself, Foner notes, had its origins in a petition campaign of 1864 by a group of women abolitionists. Since the beginning of the war, African American slaves escaping to the Union lines had made what happened to slavery a national issue; by the time the House began its debate, some "were sacking plantation homes and seizing land." Slavery, Foner concludes, "died on the ground, not just in the White House and the House of Representatives."[99] Others, including Kate Masur, have criticized *Lincoln* even more harshly for suggesting that "African-American characters do almost nothing but passively wait for white men to liberate them." Since the civil rights movement, historians have been documenting the role slaves played in their own liberation. The Freedmen and Southern Society Project, founded in 1976, has played a major role in this process. In 1990, Masur argues, Ken Burns's documentary series on the Civil War began to some extent to disseminate the results of such scholarship to a wider public. Spielberg's movie represents a step backward: "it reinforces, even if inadvertently, the outdated assumption that white men are the primary movers of history and main sources of social progress."[100]

Both Foner and Masur are correct: there is no firm evidence in the film that slaves sought their own liberation (or, with the issuance of General William T. Sherman's Special Field Order number 15 on January 16, 1865—a week after the debate in the House on the Thirteenth Amendment began—were settling in 40-acre tracts on confiscated land 30 miles inland from Charleston, South Carolina.[101]) Indeed, the only slaves to be seen in the movie are those in Alexander Gardner's photographs. Masur also takes Spielberg to task for ignoring the "organized and highly politicized community of free African-Americans" in Washington. This is true in a literal sense, but the movie does include Elizabeth Keckley (Gloria Reuben), one of the leaders of this group, who is Mary Lincoln's seamstress and accompanies her to the House debates. Keckley, observes Donald R. Shaffer, is shown "lobbying Lincoln with forceful dignity."[102] She also points to another contribution made by African Americans to what, after the Emancipation Proclamation on January 1, 1863, had become a war to end slavery as well as save the Union: her son has died fighting in the war. *Lincoln* draws attention on many occasions to the presence of black fighting men in the Union army (though the African American corporal in the opening sequence points out to Lincoln that African Americans are paid less than whites and have no similar chance of promotion). One of the most revealing shots in the film—which shows just how much has changed in four years of war—is the evident sense of shock of the Confederate peace commissioners when confronted with an escort of black cavalry.

There are, however, no major black characters in *Lincoln* (the movie might have profited greatly from the presence, as originally intended by Spielberg, of Frederick Douglass). The narrative is not driven by African Americans at any point: Elizabeth Keckley and black soldiers apart, the paradigmatic black figures are those who sit in the balcony of the House to watch—rather than influence—the debates, or Lydia Smith, the partner of Thaddeus Stevens, who is introduced for the first time only after the crucial vote has taken place and dare not appear with him in public lest it create a scandal. What we are left with is history of a very traditional kind, dealing with the doings of one "great white man": the Lincoln who emancipated the slaves. (Harold Holzer, who was a script consultant for the film, also wrote a "young adult companion book" to go with it. Its title: *Lincoln: How Abraham Lincoln Ended Slavery in America*[103]). The twist in the story is that the film is also deconstructive: it shows "Honest Abe" as a skilled practitioner of the blacker arts of politics. He hires three political pros, led by W. N. Bilbo (James Spader), to bribe "lame-duck" Democrats who have been defeated for reelection the previous November to vote for the Amendment. He encourages Thaddeus Stevens to temporize, to hide his belief in full black equality so that the measure will pass (Keckley disapproves and walks out in dismay). He dissimulates, deliberately creating the impression that peace negotiations with Confederate commissioners do not exist (they are about to happen, though not in Washington). He does secret deals, notably with Republican grandee Francis Preston Blair (Hal Holbrook). He also cajoles and personally canvasses wavering congressmen.

By early January 1865, the civil war was clearly in its last stages. Lincoln, as he explains to his cabinet in the film, was unsure of the legality of his Emancipation Proclamation of 1863 (conceived and justified as a war measure) and concerned that peace might come with slavery still in existence in the South. Without a constitutional amendment to abolish it, its status would be decided by state law. Lincoln, reelected for a second term, could either throw his support immediately behind the proposed Thirteenth Amendment abolishing slavery (already passed by the Senate) or wait until the new Congress, with many more Republican members after the 1864 elections, convened. But that would probably also mean having to deal with new senators and congressmen elected by the South once the war was over, who would fight the amendment in Congress. Equally, under Article 5 of the US Constitution, for an amendment to be ratified needed the consent of three-quarters of the states. Though the film does not mention this, Lincoln may also have believed that the best chance of passing the Amendment was while the war still continued and many Northerners continued to blame the "slave power" for causing it. He decided—and that decision forms the basis for the film—to go for an immediate vote in the House.[104]

His decision taken, as the film shows, Lincoln needed the votes of all Republican congressmen. But the party in the House was divided, with a greater range of opinions than Spielberg's movie suggests. *Lincoln* shows the president negotiating between the left-wing including those such as Stevens, who believe in full black equality, and the right-wing, represented in the film by Blair, who regard the Republicans as a "conservative anti-slavery party" and do not necessarily favor abolition. Blair's price for support is the opening of peace negotiations with the Confederacy. Lincoln agrees to this, though he appears to believe (and will make explicit in his second inaugural a few weeks later) that the war should continue until the "offense" of slavery has gone.

By concentrating so much on political process, the movie makes little effort to probe Lincoln's views on race. Lincoln himself confesses that his father had been a racist, his main reason for leaving Kentucky being dislike of blacks. In his debates with Douglas in 1858, Lincoln had firmly denied believing in "perfect social and political equality with the negro," putting him at odds with Stevens and the radicals. His attitudes had changed in some respects during the Civil War: in the film, he declares himself in favor of selectively enfranchising the most intelligent blacks, echoing his final real-life speech after Lee's surrender in which he expressed disappointment that the new state constitution of reconstructed Louisiana had not extended the suffrage to some African Americans—those who were literate and/or "serve our cause as soldiers."[105] Yet in two respects, neither mentioned in the film, it seems that Lincoln's ideas on race had not changed over time. A recent book by Phillip Magness and Sebastian Page suggests that his interest in resettling blacks in colonies outside the United States had not disappeared, as once believed, with the Emancipation Proclamation, and that he may have been attempting to revive the idea in early 1865.[106] Nor had he given up the notion of compensating the slaveowners for the abolition of slavery: he suggested it to the Confederate commissioners at the Hampton Roads conference but abandoned it when his cabinet unanimously disapproved.[107]

Spielberg's Lincoln is reminiscent in some respects of earlier Lincolns on screen. He is the "Great Heart" of early twentieth-century films: he pardons a boy who has lamed his horse to avoid fighting with the cavalry. He is still the accessible and open president, talking regularly with ordinary people in what he calls his "public opinion baths." He is a democratic Lincoln—he cleans his own boots. Like Griffith's Lincoln of 1930, he waits to hear the result of a battle in a telegraph office. Like Griffith's Lincoln of 1915, he meets Thaddeus Stevens (Austin Stoneman in *The Birth of a Nation*) though in Spielberg's film they are allies on the same side rather than opponents arguing for different approaches to Reconstruction. The shot of Spielberg's Lincoln riding through the war-torn landscape after the battle of Petersburg is oddly similar to Griffith's shot, in *The Birth of a Nation*, of "War's Peace," also after Petersburg (though Griffith had no Lincoln in the frame).

Spielberg's Lincoln, as convincingly played by Daniel Day-Lewis, has a relatively high-pitched voice (as did the real Lincoln). He has a seemingly endless reserve of folksy stories, though people react to them in different ways: William Seward (David Strathairn) looks bewildered and uncomprehending, Edwin Stanton (Bruce McGill) listens in barely suppressed frustration. He talks knowledgably about Euclid's theorem while confessing he has not had much formal schooling. He is a family man: one of the strengths of the movie is showing the White House as a home (even if his wife Mary detests it). He has a good relationship with his youngest son, Tad, a much more tense one with his eldest son, Robert (Joseph Gordon-Levitt), who wants to fight in the war, and an even more difficult one with his occasionally hysterical wife. In public life, he is remorseless in pursuit of long-term objectives: meeting the three Confederate peace commissioners, led by Alexander H. Stephens (Jackie Earle Haley), at the Hampton Roads conference, he makes it plain that he is not prepared to accept less than the full restoration of the Union. Above all, Spielberg's Lincoln is a politician of great ability, guile, and resourcefulness. He manages, in an America even more divided than today, to pass a crucial measure through the House that a majority of members initially oppose. Gridlock in Washington, he suggests, is not as inevitable as it may often appear.

Filmography

The Reprieve (Vitagraph, 1908).
The Sleeping Sentinel (Lubin, 1910).
Abraham Lincoln's Clemency (dir. Theodore Wharton; Pathé-Frères, 1910).
Lieutenant Grey of the Confederacy (dir. Francis Boggs; Selig, 1911).
One Flag at Last (Vitagraph, 1911).
The Seventh Son (dir. Hal Reid; Vitagraph, 1912).
The Toll of War (dir. Francis Ford; Bison Motion Pictures, 1913).
The Birth of a Nation (dir. David W. Griffith; Epoch, 1915).
The Dramatic Life of Abraham Lincoln (dir. Phil Rosen; Rockett-Lincoln Film Company)
The Iron Horse (dir. John Ford; Fox, 1924).
Abraham Lincoln (dir. David W. Griffith; United Artists/Art Cinema Corporation, 1930).

Gabriel Over the White House (dir. Gregory La Cava; Cosmopolitan Productions, 1933).
Ruggles of Red Gap (dir. Leo McCarey; Paramount, 1935).
The Littlest Rebel (dir. David Butler; Twentieth-Century Fox, 1935).
Fury (dir. Fritz Lang; MGM, 1936).
The Prisoner of Shark Island (dir. John Ford; Twentieth-Century Fox, 1936).
They Won't Forget (dir. Mervyn LeRoy; First National/Warner Bros., 1937).
Of Human Hearts (dir. Clarence Brown; MGM, 1938).
Mr. Smith Goes to Washington (dir. Frank Capra; Columbia, 1939).
Young Mr. Lincoln (dir. John Ford; Twentieth-Century Fox, 1939).
Abe Lincoln in Illinois (dir. John Cromwell; RKO, 1940).
Tennessee Johnson (dir. William Dieterle; MGM, 1943).
Rock Island Trail/Transcontinent Express (dir. Joseph Kane; Republic, 1950).
New Mexico (dir. Irving Reis; Irving Allen/United Artists, 1951).
The Tall Target (dir. Anthony Mann; MGM, 1951).
The Prince of Players (dir. Philip Dunne; Twentieth-Century Fox, 1955).
How the West Was Won (segment directed by John Ford; MGM, 1962).
Guardian of the Wilderness (dir. David O'Malley; Sunn Classics, 1976).
The Faking of the President (dir. Alan and Jeanne Abel; Spencer Productions, 1976).
The Lincoln Conspiracy (dir. James L. Conway; Sunn Classics, 1977)
Bill and Ted's Excellent Adventure (dir. Stephen Herek; De Laurentiis Entertainment, 1989)
The Conspirator (dir. Robert Redford; American Film Company, 2011).
Abraham Lincoln: Vampire Hunter (dir. Timur Bekmambetov; Abraham/Bazeleves/Tim Burton Productions, 2012).
Lincoln (dir. Steven Spielberg; DreamWorks SKG/Twentieth-Century Fox/Reliance, 2012).

CHAPTER FOUR*

The Civil War

Howard Strickling, studio publicity director of M-G-M, put out a mimeographed booklet outlining a promotion campaign for The Red Badge of Courage. *"It has BIGNESS. It has GREATNESS! First, last and always, it is ENTERTAINMENT in the grand tradition!" the foreword stated . . . Civil War stories, it was asserted in another section, had long made popular movies;* Gone With the Wind *had grossed millions of dollars and* The Birth of a Nation *had been the greatest grosser of all time.*

LILLIAN ROSS, *Picture*[1]

In the spring of 1950 Lillian Ross, a staff writer for the *New Yorker*, decided to follow the making of a John Huston film, *The Red Badge of Courage*, based on Stephen Crane's classic 1895 novel of the Civil War, from its inception to final release. As a result she wrote a series of articles, published in book form in 1952. In creating one of the few full-length studies of the production of an individual film, Ross also shed considerable light on how the Civil War was regarded in Hollywood. Essentially, as the publicity release implies, the war was seen as a source of stories to entertain. Louis B. Mayer and other MGM executives did not regard *The Badge of Red Courage* as having much entertainment value: it did not have a conventional plot, a romance, major female

* Part of this chapter was originally published in Susan-Mary Grant and Peter J. Parish, eds, *Legacy of Disunion: The Enduring Significance of the American Civil War* (Baton Rouge: Louisiana State University Press, 2003). It has been extensively rewritten and is published here by permission.

characters, or (if made as Huston wanted) stars. Huston, by contrast, liked the simple story "of a youth who ran away from his first battle in the Civil War, and then returned to the front and distinguished himself by performing several heroic acts." His interest in the theme may have developed during the Second World War, when he produced a film on the breakdown and treatment of shell-shocked soldiers. Indeed, it was the *psychology* of heroes/cowards that primarily concerned the director in *The Red Badge of Courage*. Having received the go-ahead to do the film, despite Mayer's opposition, Huston insisted on avoiding as much as possible what he referred to—with great unconscious irony—as the "North vs. South" aspects of the Civil War.[2]

The promotional campaign for *The Red Badge of Courage* never happened in the way outlined in Strickling's booklet. The film went $200,000 over budget, and MGM executives were appalled at the indifferent or even hostile response of spectators at preview screenings. They insisted on cutting a number of scenes and introducing a voiceover narration linking it more closely to Stephen Crane's classic novel, all to no avail.[3] Reviewers praised the film's success in capturing the "allegorical mood of all wars" but warned that it would probably have little appeal to a mass market.[4] Audiences displayed little enthusiasm and MGM found it impossible to find bookings for the film, eventually having to sell it internationally as the lower half of a double bill featuring an MGM musical starring Esther Williams.[5] The second part of the publicity release was also characterized by considerable wishful thinking. While it is true that *The Birth of a Nation* (1915) and *Gone With the Wind* (1939) were enormous commercial successes, they were largely aberrations. Indeed, what strikes the historian most is not the popularity of Civil War stories used as a basis for movies but the infrequency with which such stories have been used and their near-constant unpopularity with moviegoing audiences.

In the days of the early silent film, it is true, there had been an important genre of one- or two-reel films based on Civil War stories or settings. Eileen S. Bowser points out that copyright records (which do not constitute an accurate record of all such movies) suggest there were at least 12 "Civil War" films in 1908, 23 in 1909, 32 in 1910, 74 in 1911, 58 in 1912, 98 in 1913, and 29 in 1914.[6] Some were directed by Thomas H. Ince, who came from New England but was a southern-leaning Civil War buff. Kentucky-born David W. Griffith also directed 11 shorter Civil War dramas before his masterpiece, *The Birth of a Nation*. After America's entry into the First World War, however, the Civil War genre largely disappeared. During the 1920s and 1930s, relatively few films with a Civil War background were produced. Among those that did appear were *Hands Up!* (1926), *The General* (1926), *The Heart of Maryland* (1927), *Morgan's Last Raid* (1929), *Only the Brave* (1930), *Secret Service* (1931), *Operator 13* (1934), *So Red the Rose* (1935), *The*

Littlest Rebel (1935), and *Hearts in Bondage* (1936). Nearly all were unsuccessful at the box office. Consequently, when the notion of filming *Gone With the Wind*, Margaret Mitchell's sprawling 1936 novel of the Civil War and Reconstruction, was first raised with Louis B. Mayer of MGM, Irving Thalberg, Mayer's right-hand man, was utterly opposed. "Forget it, Louis," he is reported to have remarked, expressing the conventional Hollywood wisdom, "no Civil War picture ever made a nickel." Independent producer David O. Selznick, who would finally make the film, also probably had this tradition in mind when he, at first, hesitated over whether to buy the screen rights to Mitchell's story.[7]

The enormous popular and commercial success of *Gone With the Wind* did not open the floodgates to a series of other Civil War films. *The Man from Dakota* (1940) and *Tap Roots* (1948) were followed by less than a score of films devoted to Civil War themes: *The Red Badge of Courage* (1951), *Drums in the Deep South* (1951), *The Raid* (1954), *Friendly Persuasion* (1956), *The Great Locomotive Chase* (1956), *Raintree County* (1957), *Band of Angels* (1957), *The Horse Soldiers* (1959), *Advance to the Rear* (1964), *Shenandoah* (1965), *Alvarez Kelly* (1966), *Journey to Shiloh* (1968), *The Beguiled* (1971), *Glory* (1989), *Gettysburg* (1993), *Pharaoh's Army* (1995), *Ride with the Devil* (1999), *Gods and Generals* (2003), and *Cold Mountain* (2003). With these comparatively rare exceptions over almost three-quarters of a century, filmmakers avoided using the Civil War itself as the setting for their movies. There were practical reasons for this. Civil War pictures are costly to make (both *The Birth of a Nation* and *Gone With the Wind* were the most expensive films of their time). They need elaborate sets, many costumes, and large casts (including vast numbers of extras for the hard-to-photograph battlefield shots). *The Birth of a Nation* and *Gone With the Wind*, moreover, had an intimidating effect on Hollywood producers and directors, who realized that such films would be extremely hard to match.

Taking these things into account, however, it is still surprising that so few films in total have been made about the Civil War, which was almost certainly the most dramatic and defining event in American history. Shelby Foote, in Ken Burns' television series on the war, described it as "the crossroads of our being."[8] It killed vast numbers of Americans: a recent estimate, by demographic historian J. David Hacker in *Civil War History* (December 2011), suggests that the death toll was even higher than previously thought and may have reached three-quarters of a million men.[9] It settled the issue of whether the United States would be one or two nations and led directly to the freeing of four million African American slaves, with all the resulting social consequences. Were there, therefore, more complicated reasons than those outlined above for Hollywood's comparative neglect of the war? Why did audiences on the whole not like (or even not see) most of the films that were made? Why, conversely, did moviegoers greet two Civil War movies—*The Birth of a Nation* and *Gone*

With the Wind—so enthusiastically? Finally, what kind of history of the war was recounted in the movies and how did it alter over time?

It is not only filmmakers who have largely ignored the Civil War, for novelists have tended to do the same. Indeed, C. Vann Woodward argued, the fact that the Civil War has also failed to inspire any major literary classic hints at broader, cultural reasons for the resistance of both creative artists and audiences to embrace themes from the period. Some of these, he suggested, might include an "emotional resistance" to the racial aspects of the war, a gendered response by the public, divided loyalties over the conflict itself, and soldiers' natural reluctance to discuss their experiences.[10] The last of these was of rather more relevance to novels than to movies (although several extracts from the diary of Robert Gould Shaw, white commander of the black 54th Massachusetts Infantry Regiment, were used in *Glory*). Questions of gender, divided loyalties, and race, however, have profoundly influenced the manner in which Hollywood approaches the subject of the Civil War.

During the 1920s and 1930s, based on a substantial amount of evidence, the film industry was convinced that women formed the dominant section of the movie audience, either because they had a *numerical* majority or because they were the primary influence on what their menfolk viewed. The existence of this belief influenced the whole course of Hollywood's development. The star system itself was mainly aimed at women (one theater manager would later describe most movie houses as "Valentino traps") as was the discursive apparatus associated with it (fan magazines and stories about stars in newspapers and periodicals). Through advertising associated with "tie-ups" and licensing deals, Hollywood and its business allies also set out to appeal to women as consumers.[11] Apart from anything else, this involved making certain kinds of films: "modern" films offered better opportunities for displaying product lines such as clothes and cosmetics.[12]

In a broader sense, moreover, the movie industry set out to appeal to its dominant female audience by making the kind of films it believed they liked. A high proportion of 1920s films, therefore, were female-centered melodramas or romances. During the 1930s these gave way to a new genre, the "women's film." Conversely, filmmakers increasingly avoided the types of movies thought to have little appeal to girls and women. Prominent among these were war pictures. In a 1926 survey of 10,000 Chicago schoolchildren, Alice Miller Mitchell found that girls consistently listed war movies as the lowest of ten varieties of film. Three years earlier an even larger poll of 37,000 high school students in 76 cities suggested that even *The Birth of a Nation*—almost certainly the biggest grossing film of the period—suffered from this gender bias. Less than half the number of girls than boys named it as the "Best Picture They Had Ever Seen." Even in the South girls preferred *Way Down East* (1920), a D. W. Griffith tearjerker starring Lillian Gish, although boys supported *The Birth of a*

Nation.[13] The perception that women disliked war movies in general may well have discouraged the making of Civil War films during this period and after, while female hostility or indifference possibly accounted for the lack of success of most of those that were made. Equally, it was no accident that *Gone With the Wind*, the most successful Civil War ever made, was demonstrably a "women's film."[14]

Another important influence restricting the number of Civil War movies made was filmmakers' belief in what Thomas R. Cripps has dubbed "The Myth of the Southern Box Office." In the period between 1920 and 1940, it was thought inexpedient by industry insiders to offend the regional market of the South. When *The Man From Dakota* was released in 1940, *Variety* dubiously remarked that it "will find tough going in the southern states, where Union heroes of the Civil War are still unwanted in film form."[15] Hollywood was convinced that "if it would not sell in the South, it might not sell in the North." Even if, moreover, as was the case, profits made in the South were less than those in other regions, they were still large enough to help bring a production "out of the red."[16] Cripps uses the myth to help explain the racial stereotyping in American movies during this period, but the reluctance to offend (white) southern susceptibilities with regard to a violent and controversial period may also have helped account for the dearth of Civil War movies—and the fact that many of those that were made (including *Hands Up!*, *The General*, *Morgan's Last Raid*, *So Red the Rose*, *The Littlest Rebel*, and *Gone With the Wind*) were based on stories told from the southern perspective. One commentator observed of *So Red the Rose* that "for obvious reasons its south of the Mason-Dixon line box-office chances will be superior to the Yankee belt." Another remarked that much of the dialogue of *The Littlest Rebel* would "make the south purr with pride."[17]

In another article, Cripps also addresses the issue of how filmmakers' approach to the Civil War has been affected by the race question. Film historians such as Douglas Gomery, Ethan Mordden, and Thomas Schatz, he maintains, have emphasized the fact that Hollywood was an economic system within which certain studio styles developed. Such styles were the result of the drive to maximize profits. Studios attempted to guarantee a "risk-free product" by varying films only a little within particular styles or genres. War movies, Cripps notes, have been especially prone to this systemization since they have appeared "so bound up in the nation's survival." Most have eventually become standardized as "a small circle of polyethnic warriors . . . seen holding fast under the stress of combat, thereby propagandizing the need for unity." On the face of it the Civil War presented a challenge to this narrative of "eventual unity," being brought about because of the existence of African American slavery. Although it led to the abolition of slavery, the freedom gained by the slaves was at best only nominal. Blacks remained an "unassimilable Other"—a source of continuing problems and friction in American society. How, therefore, could the Civil War be presented as a "unifying epic"? The solution to this problem, Cripps contends, has by and large been for filmmakers to eliminate racial issues—and thus African Americans—from the movies they have made about the war.[18]

While there are comparatively few films about the Civil War itself, the conflict is referred to in innumerable Westerns. Indeed, Kim Newman writes of "the Western's obsession with the Civil War." That obsession is not, of course, with the war itself, since most fighting was east of the Mississippi, but with its consequences. Many of the main characters in Westerns are depicted as war veterans. Arriving in the West, they find a way of moving beyond the conflict by concentrating on the settlement of this new region. Moreover, white Confederates and Federals often purge their sin of fighting between themselves in order to unite against some other adversary or adversaries. Thus, the blue and gray join forces against Indians in *The Outpost* (1940), *Rocky Mountain* (1950), *Winchester 73* (1950), *Run of the Arrow* (1957), *Major Dundee* (1965), and *The Undefeated* (1969). Yankees and Rebs ally together against Mexicans in *Virginia City* (1940) and French soldiers based in Mexico in *Major Dundee*. It often seems as if the drama of national reconciliation, largely impossible to apply as a formula to the Civil War because of the centrality of blacks to the conflict and its effects, as Cripps points out, is instead displaced onto the Western, where African Americans are no longer regarded as a problem and the whites from both North and South can unite against more culturally permissible—or at least less controversial—"others."[19]

If most of the relatively few Civil War movies made were unsuccessful at the box office, this was clearly not the case with respect to *The Birth of a Nation* and *Gone With the Wind*, both of which reached a mass audience and could be counted as the most profitable movies of their time. The success of these two films can be explained in a variety of ways. Each was based on a best-selling novel. Each was a "spectacle" within the meaning of the term for its time: *The Birth of a Nation*, in fact, by attracting large middle-class audiences to the cinema for the first time, helped in bringing about the demise of the nickelodeon. Each combined the talents of a number of highly competent actors and actresses. Each used music to extend the effect of the film itself. *Gone With the Wind* was also preceded by a long and skilful prerelease publicity campaign (the much-hyped search to identify a suitable Scarlett being one expression of this). Yet none of these reasons, either separately or in combination, seems quite sufficient to explain the remarkable success of the two films. There may well have been features of the wider American society at the time they were released that allowed Americans generally to transcend their indifference toward Civil War themes. There also may have been influences that countered the resistance of nonsoutherners to what was, in essence, a southern-oriented view of the Civil War and its consequences.[20]

The Birth of a Nation

In 1992 an 18-member film board added Griffith's *The Birth of a Nation* to the prestigious National Registry of Film. The decision led to a protest—part of a long campaign—by the National Association for the Advancement of Colored People (NAACP). "To honor this film," argued NAACP chairman William Gibson, "is to pay tribute to America's shameful racial history."[21] Hollywood itself has long regarded the film as an embarrassment: a landmark movie for its technical achievement and the size of its audience, but a work profoundly flawed as a consequence of its racist message. The film treats African Americans in either a patronizing or a disdainful manner. In the first part they are principally shown as contented slaves. The exceptions to this general rule are the mulatto housekeeper of northern politician Austin Stoneman (Ralph Lewis), whose passion for his servant is claimed to be the source of his radical policy toward reconstructing the South after the war, and a unit of black Union soldiers who raid the hometown of the Cameron family in South Carolina and seem eager only to destroy. In the second part of the film, Griffith expands on his creation of what Donald Bogle calls "the brutal black buck."[22] Carpetbaggers and aggressive blacks from the North break up the cordial relationships many early twentieth-century southern whites continued to see as characteristic of slavery, which they believed had uplifted blacks, with the consequence that African Americans regress into brutal and primitive behavior. Blacks onscreen are shown to be ignorant and untutored, to force whites off the sidewalk, to be out for revenge on former masters, and—above all—to want to marry white women. Silas Lynch (George Siegmann), mulatto lieutenant-governor of South Carolina, seeks marriage with Elsie Stoneman (Lillian Gish), the daughter of the northern Republican politician. Gus (Walter Long), a black soldier, wants to marry Flora (Mae Marsh), youngest daughter of the southern Camerons. When he pursues her, she throws herself off a cliff rather than surrender to his advances. This persuades the Ku Klux Klan to confront and finally overthrow what is clearly presented as the savagery and debauchery of black rule.

The Birth of a Nation, in common with *Gone With the Wind*, is unusual in dealing with both the Civil War and its consequences during the Reconstruction period. The content of the latter part of the film was largely determined by Thomas Dixon, Jr. In his contemporary review of the film, Francis Hackett remarked that what it offered was basically Dixon's interpretation of the relations between North and South and their effects on African Americans.[23] Dixon, from North Carolina, had studied at Johns Hopkins University under militant defenders of the Anglo-Saxon creed. Successively actor, lawyer, politician, and Baptist minister, he became a novelist in 1902 in angry response to a staging of the play based upon Harriet Beecher Stowe's novel *Uncle Tom's Cabin* (1852), which Dixon

felt dignified African Americans at the expense of southern whites. In
The Leopard's Spots: A Romance of the White Man's Burden (1902)
and *The Clansman: An Historic Romance of the Ku Klux Klan* (1905),
Dixon elaborated his perception that once the institution of slavery was
overthrown, African Americans "could only revert to bestiality." Part of
this reversion found expression in the black male pursuit of innocent white
women. Griffith, in making his film, expanded on Dixon's story in *The
Clansman*, notably by adding an entire preliminary section on the Civil
War itself but otherwise constructed *The Birth of a Nation* around Dixon's
romance and his racial views (with which Griffith, as a southerner and the
son of Colonel Jake Griffith of the Confederate army, probably agreed).[24]

The curious feature of Dixon's ideas on the threat from African
Americans—and their later representation in *The Birth of a Nation*—was,
on the face of it, chronology. The social crisis some had warned against
during the economic depression of 1893–7 had passed. Starting in 1890
but gathering pace after the decline of Populism, African Americans had
been excluded from political voting by a variety of legal stratagems. By
1905, what Joel Williamson perceives as a second wave of segregatory
legislation was approaching its end in the South, separating the races in
restaurants and hotels, on trains and streetcars. Blacks had been rendered
both politically impotent and socially invisible. Racial violence was less
common. Lynching, which reached a peak in the years after 1889, had
begun to decline in the southern states, including Griffith's own Kentucky,
where it had been particularly prevalent. There seemed little threat to the
established racial order. Pierre Sorlin argues that there was no domestic
crisis apparent when *The Birth of a Nation* was made, making the film's
"alarmist tone . . . somewhat surprising," especially in view of the fact that
most Americans were prepared to remain silent on the "central danger"
portrayed in the film: the supposed "black problem."[25]

It has been common to see the era just before the First World War as
a time of buoyant confidence in the United States.[26] In reality, there is a
good deal of evidence of social unrest and anxiety. The economic recession
beginning in 1913, the continuous arrival of large numbers of immigrants—
mostly from eastern and southern Europe, the processes of urbanization,
a growing fear of radicalism and labor militancy, and the hysteria of the
"white slave" panic make up the backdrop of the time. A number of factors
conspired in these years to bring about a pervasive sense of racial threat.
The 41-volume report of the Dillingham Commission in 1911—confirming
popular stereotypes of "new" versus "old" immigration, the rise of the
eugenics movement and its ideas about superior breeds and unalterable
racial characteristics, publicity on the "yellow peril" in California, and the
feelings of ethnic disunity produced by the outbreak of the First World War
all combined to promote a mood of uncertainty and unease.

It is easiest to explain this phenomenon in the South. Many whites
continued to believe blacks were dangerous: it was an unusual southern

newspaper, as Edward L. Ayers points out, that did not include some stories of black wrongdoing. Segregation had failed to bring an end to the problems posed by race relations. Segregated streetcars, for example, were usually supposed to have whites at the front and "coloreds" at the back, but there was no distinct line of demarcation. To journalist Ray Stanard Baker in 1908, this seemed symbolic: the existence of a color line that neither race was able precisely to define provided a major "source of friction and bitterness." The increasing movement of African Americans to towns and cities increased the possibility of racial conflict there and provoked a further wave of segregation legislation that between 1913 and 1915 separated facilities in factories and attempted to impose segregation on urban housing.[27]

The major change that happened before the First World War was the nationalization of insecurities arising from race. The white South's conversion to the idea of restricting immigration, which happened in part at least because new immigrants (particularly Italians) appeared too ready to fraternize with blacks, was paralleled by growing northern white sympathy for the racial outlook of the South. One reason for this may have been the increasing black migration to the North and some of the tensions that resulted (including the race riot at Springfield, Illinois, in 1908). Enduring suspicion of Japanese immigration into California, which led the state legislature in 1913 to pass a law effectively banning Japanese land ownership there, fostered sympathy on the part of Californian whites for southern views on race. By 1913 all sections were united politically on the need to reduce the new immigration, and bills calling for a literacy test passed Congress in 1913 and 1915. This new and pervasive racial consciousness provided an ideal background for the appearance of Griffith's film, with its condemnation of racial intermixture, rampant distaste for blacks, and triumphant evocation of white superiority.

Other aspects of the time are reflected in Griffith's film. One is the crusade against alcohol. At its convention in November 1913, the Anti-Saloon League had first committed itself to pushing for nationwide prohibition. This followed a period of reverses in which, as Jack Blocker has pointed out, eight states voted to reject statewide prohibition. After 1913 this retreat ended, and prohibition resumed its forward march. Some shots in *The Birth of a Nation* can be viewed as propaganda for prohibition. It was a goal congenial to Griffith, who came from a Methodist background, and he had already made at least three films—*A Drunkard's Reformation* (1909), *What Drink Did* (1909), and *Drink's Lure* (1912)—emphasizing the dangers of alcohol. The fact that Griffith was a southerner, however, and the Civil War and Reconstruction film he was then making was about the South, led him to tie alcohol to the issue of race. Southern progressives frequently linked black crime to the effects of alcohol: reformer Alexander J. McKelway, for example, argued that "if drunkenness caused three-fourths of the crimes ascribed to it, whiskey must be taken out of the Negro's hands."[28] What Griffith did in *The Birth of a Nation* was to provide visual confirmation of that linkage: the renegade Gus, having driven the youngest Cameron daughter to suicide, takes refuge in Joe's gin mill. "Drunk with wine and power," the black lieutenant-governor makes up his mind to marry Congressman Stoneman's daughter.

Griffith's film was fortunate in the timing of its appearance. Had it been produced a decade earlier, in the same year as Dixon's novel *The Clansman* was published, it would almost certainly have attracted less attention. The main reason for this was that, in the interval, a new interracial organization had been launched to help protect African Americans: the NAACP. Founded in the aftermath of the race riot at Springfield, Illinois, in August 1908, the NAACP was quick to recognize the threat from *The Birth of a Nation*. In putting across the "southern" view of the black race, Griffith's film damaged the cause of racial equality. The NAACP embarked upon a strategy of protest to stop the film, prompting court hearings and the lobbying of mayors and censorship boards across America. Apart from securing the reediting of a few scenes and in some locations delaying the opening of the film, these efforts invariably failed. What they did, of course, was generate priceless publicity for the movie. There was, in fact, a considerable symbiosis between *The Birth of a Nation* and the NAACP. The controversy launched by the association undoubtedly made more people want to see the film. But *The Birth of a Nation* also provided the NAACP with "an issue just when it needed one," allowing it to put its own case across with maximum publicity. In many ways it was their crusade against the movie that effectively turned the NAACP into a *national* body.[29]

Gone With the Wind

Released 24 years later, *Gone With the Wind* belongs to a different cinematic universe than *The Birth of a Nation*—one that includes sound, colors, and cinematic celebrities. Hollywood, now determined to lose no segment of its potential audience, had learned its lessons from Griffith's movie. There is no Ku Klux Klan, nor are there any more "brutal black bucks." It is not without significance, for example, that when Scarlett O'Hara (Vivien Leigh) is attacked in Shantytown, it is a white man who assaults her, his black accomplice merely holding the horse—and she is rescued by a black, Big Sam (Everett Brown), one of her family's ex-slaves. Both manners and morals had changed in the interim between the two movies, influencing the manner in which the Civil War years could be portrayed. The "white slave" panic was long dead, and it was possible to depict on screen the demimonde—in the form of the brothel keeper Belle Watling (Ona Munson). Prohibition had been repealed in 1933, and alcohol could once again be depicted as part of southern (male) social life—as at the Wilkes' barbecue. With alcohol no longer a moral (or racial) issue, drunkenness could be presented in an amusing light—as when a supposedly inebriated Ashley (Lesley Howard) and Dr. Meade (Harry Davenport) try to outwit the Union soldiers or when a recently widowed (again) Scarlett consoles herself by drinking alone.

Two aspects of the period when *Gone With the Wind* was made may have influenced the view it presented of the Civil War era and also, perhaps, perceptions of the film on the part of female moviegoers. One scholar dates the appearance of contemporary American feminism from shortly before the First World War as radical thinkers began to challenge the idea that women were condemned by their biological natures merely to childrearing and housework. In *The Birth of a Nation* Griffith may indeed have been taking issue with such an approach by presenting an image of women as largely lacking initiative and in need of male protection. The silent films of the 1920s went beyond this view: the characteristic female image of the "flapper" portrayed women subverting social conventions in the cause of self-expression. An echo of this theme is present in *Gone With the Wind* as Scarlett shocks Atlanta society by her behavior while mourning for her first husband, who has died (of disease) while in the service of the Confederacy.[30]

Such frivolity is swiftly abandoned, however, as Scarlett matures into a strong and independent woman. The manner in which she becomes head of the O'Hara family, the retreat to a temporary household economy at Tara after the war, the recycling of curtains as clothes (although there is no suggestion Scarlett has made them), the decision (albeit for selfish reasons) to limit the size of her family, and even the initiative to take a job (her lumber business) outside the home must have resonated with many women in the 1930s. The idea of women acting on their own seemed far less out of place in a decade in which women increasingly came to play an active role in politics and union organization. In one sense, at least, the film also echoes male anger at the new world in which their role as breadwinner was being challenged. Sara Evans couples James Cagney's grinding a grapefruit in Mae Clarke's face in *Public Enemy* (1931) with Rhett Butler (Clark Gable)'s rape of Scarlett in *Gone With the Wind* as expressions of this sentiment.[31]

In the opinion of Marjorie Rosen, Scarlett shows "spunk and self-sufficiency." Indeed, perhaps the greatest message communicated by the film was the hope and possibility of survival. The Great Depression of the 1930s affected almost everybody. Unemployment (or the threat of unemployment) was everywhere. When *Gone With the Wind* was released in 1939, 17.2 percent of the labor force remained out of work. In the worst two years of the depression, 1932 and 1933, the number of totally unemployed never fell below 12 million, and the average unemployment rate was over 24 percent. Yet as one man told oral historian Studs Terkel years later, "In the worst hour of the Depression, if you were aggressive, if you wanted to scrounge . . . you could survive." Scarlett embodies this spirit. To American

audiences who had lived through the Great Depression, the film's message
of physical survival at all costs had tremendous appeal.[32]

Genres and the Civil War movie

If some superproductions (*The Birth of a Nation, Gone With the Wind*)
owed their success, in part at least, to the connections they made with
the American society and culture of their time, other "Civil War" films
were more self-absorbed, reflecting the codes of certain Hollywood
genres and subgenres. Some had their roots in stage melodramas. *The
Heart of Maryland* (1927), as *Harrison's Reports* noted, was based on
a Broadway play by theatrical producer and playwright David Belasco
that had first been performed in 1895.[33] A critic for the *New York Times*
similarly pointed out that *Secret Service* (1931) was a new version of
"[actor/playwright] William Gillette's Civil War melodrama," also
produced for the first time in 1895.[34] Both *The Heart of Maryland* and
Secret Service were, in essence, spy films. The conventions of such films
(including a near-inevitable intersectional romance) had been established
well before the First World War. Other movies based on espionage of the
interwar period included *Hands Up!* (1926), *Morgan's Last Raid* (1929),
Only the Brave (1930), *Secret Service* (1931), *Operator 13* (1934), and
The Littlest Rebel (1935). The genre was about played out by this point:
Variety commented on *Secret Service* that "there have been too many
pictures dealing with the spy thing in various ways."[35] Some of these later
films attempted to move beyond the clichés of the Civil War spy film to
attract a larger audience: *Hands Up!* was a comedy/Western, *Morgan's
Last Raid* a Western (with cowboy star Tim McCoy), *Operator 13* in
part a musical, and *The Littlest Rebel* a picture featuring child star
Shirley Temple.

If espionage movies set against a Civil War backcloth had mainly died
out by the mid-1930s, melodramas themselves continued to appear for
several decades more. *Drums in the Deep South* (1951) dealt with the
conflicted loyalties of three old West Point friends, one fighting for the
Union, two others for the Confederacy. The complicated plot revolved
around an attempt of one of the Confederates, Clay (James Craig) to
mount guns on a mountain in order to slow down Sherman's march to
the sea. But Unionist Will Denning (Guy Madison) blows the mountain
to pieces, killing both Clay and Kathy, the wife of the second Confederate
who has tried to persuade him to surrender. Despite the fact that Kathy
was played by Barbara Payton, an actress then much in the news for her
colorful private life, the film stirred little enthusiasm. *Band of Angels* (1957)
dealt principally with issues of slavery and miscegenation (see Chapter
Two), but the Civil War obliges wealthy Hamish Bond (Clark Gable) to

move from New Orleans to his upper-river plantation as the Union forces advance and then turns him into a fugitive for burning his crops. *Raintree County* (1957) was the story of three people set against the background of the Civil War era. John W. Shawnessy (Montgomery Clift) is an idealistic young man from Indiana waiting to marry Nell Gaither (Eve Marie Saint). Southerner Suzanna Drake (Elizabeth Taylor) woos him away from Nell and the pair marry and relocate to the South. But Shawnessy hates slavery and he and Suzanna return to Indiana, where Suzanna begins to show increasing signs of insanity. When the war breaks out, Suzanna runs back to the South with their son while Shawnessy joins the Union army. He meets his son again in Atlanta once the war is over but Suzanna is in an insane asylum. When she appears to recover, the family return to Indiana but Suzanna dies attempting to find the fabulous rain tree, leaving Shawnessy to be comforted by the ever-faithful Nell. Most critics were unimpressed, with Bosley Crowther in the *New York Times* describing it as a "long, tedious tale" with "vaporous" characters.[36] *The Beguiled* (1971) had Clint Eastwood as John McBurney, a wounded Union soldier recuperating in a school for southern girls, a circumstance that according to one reviewer sparked "jealousies of meller [melodrama] proportions." McBurney loses his leg and is ultimately poisoned "by the vengeful southern belles."[37]

Some "Civil War" pictures, especially after the Second World War, were modeled after Westerns. *The Great Locomotive Chase* (1956) was described by a critic as "a western with trains."[38] According to Bosley Crowther of the *New York Times*, *The Horse Soldiers* (1959), directed by John Ford and starring John Wayne, was principally for fans of the Western. It was full of "'horse opera' clichés" and told "a conventional story involving a cavalry raid." To Crowther, the precise locale [Mississippi behind Confederate lines] was unimportant: "it could be the Western frontier."[39] *Alvarez Kelly* (1966) was the story of a successful Confederate attempt to steal a herd of cattle from the Union forces in order to feed Confederates besieged and running out of food in Petersburg, Virginia. Apart from the blue and grey uniforms, it could have been a picture dealing with cattle-rustling anywhere in the western United States. Yet while Civil War movies often appropriated the plotlines and conventions of other genres, especially melodramas and Westerns, there was one genre in particular they failed to make much use of: comedy. The seriousness of the conflict, the high casualty rate, and the lingering sectional loyalties inspired by the war meant that few comedies were ever made, and—apart from *Hands Up!*—they were greeted with obvious unease and lack of enthusiasm. Mordaunt Hall commented that, in *The General* (1926), "Buster Keaton . . . appears to have bitten off more than he can chew . . . the fun is not exactly plentiful." *Variety*'s critic considered it "overdone" and "far from funny." Almost 40 years later, Howard Thompson of the *New York Times* dismissed *Advance to the Rear* (1964) in a single paragraph as "a warmed-over brew of slapstick and pratfalls as the Blues and Greys bump heads in wild confusion."[40]

Representing the Civil War on screen

The Civil War lasted just over four years. It was fought over a vast area and involved a variety of military actions. Hollywood filmmakers intent on making movies of the war period have consequently been compelled to be selective. Only a relatively small proportion of Civil War movies have attempted to reconstruct battles. *The Birth of a Nation* shows what appears to be the third battle of Petersburg (April 2, 1865) and *Cold Mountain* the earlier battle of the crater at Petersburg (July 30, 1864). Chickamauga (September 19–20, 1863) is depicted in *Raintree County*, Shiloh (April 6–7, 1862) in John Ford's section of *How the West Was Won* (1962) and *Journey to Shiloh*, Antietam (September 7, 1862) and Fort Wagner (July 18, 1863) in *Glory*, and Gettysburg (July 1–3, 1863) in the film of the same name. The first battle of Bull Run (July 21, 1861), Fredericksburg (December 11–15, 1862), and Chancellorsville (May 1–6, 1863) all featured in *Gods and Generals*. *The Birth of a Nation*, *Gone With the Wind*, *Drums in the Deep South*, and *Raintree County* depict in various ways the burning of Atlanta. But *Gone With the Wind*, the most successful of all Civil War movies, has no combat sequences. Apart from the shots of Atlanta burning, the effects of war are conveyed through the scenes dealing with the publication of the casualty list after Gettysburg, the Atlanta hospital where Scarlett and Melanie work, the vast numbers of wounded laid out in the railroad yards, the bodies and military debris on the road to Tara, and the devastation of Twelve Oaks. This indirect approach to representing the war was also adopted in other movies: Sherman's march through Georgia is shown in *The Birth of a Nation* and referred to but not actually shown in *The Beguiled* (as well as *Gone With the Wind*), and *So Red the Rose* contains a moving scene of a mother searching for her dead son on the Shiloh battlefield.

As well as major battles, a number of smaller military engagements have been used as the basis for films. These include the Andrews raid of April 1862 (*The General* and *The Great Locomotive Chase*), the Grierson raid of April/May 1863 (*The Horse Soldiers*), and the raid on the Vermont town of St. Albans by Confederates operating from Canada in October 1864 (*The Raid*). While the raids themselves happened, and some of the incidents in the films are based on fact (notably the old headmaster marching his young military school cadets to face the Union brigade in *The Horse Soldiers*[41]), there are also a number of liberties taken in order to "improve" the filmed story. These include the introduction in *The Raid* and *The Horse Soldiers* of deeply improbable crosssectional romances. Some films featured guerrilla campaigns: Morgan's Raiders (July 1863) were shown in *Friendly Persuasion* while *Ride With the Devil* covered the conflicts between Confederate Bushwackers and abolitionist Jayhawkers along the Missouri-Kansas border culminating in the Lawrence massacre by William Clarke Quantrill on August 21, 1863.[42] *Alvarez Kelly* took its inspiration from the "Beefsteak Raid" of September 1864 by Confederate cavalry intent on providing food to Southern soldiers in the trenches at Petersburg. *Hearts in Bondage* centered on the naval battle of Hampton Roads (March 9, 1862) between the ironclads of the North (*Monitor*) and South (*Merrimac/k*, also known as *Virginia*). Makers of Civil War movies often made claims about the historical accuracy of what they were doing: Buster Keaton insisted that the costumes and actual train used in *The General* should be as authentic as possible and Wilbur G. Kurtz, a Georgia historian, was hired as historical adviser for *Gone With the Wind* and *The Great Locomotive Chase*. The films themselves, however, usually used the Civil War itself only as a background to the stories they told, and—especially once the cameras started rolling—historical accuracy was often discarded in favor of the demands of an entertaining storyline.[43]

Civil War movies also have helped perpetuate a number of myths. One of these is the legend of the Old South as a land of wealthy plantations, gracious ladies, and chivalrous male cavaliers. What Rollin G. Osterweis termed a "story-book Dixie" had its roots in the work of southern writers in the decades immediately after the war, but Hollywood helped develop and publicize the images associated with it.[44] Films such as *The Birth of a Nation*, *Operator 13*, and *So Red the Rose* dealt with plantation life, preparing the way for what would become the culturally dominant view of southern society after the release of *Gone With the Wind*. In Hollywood's portrayal of that society, farmers who owned few or no slaves, the middle class, and the poor were usually eliminated. Movies concentrate on the small minority of families living on great plantations, depicting a world of genial masters, southern belles, loyal black house servants, and contented field hands. In such a world, not only were there no class tensions but also it seemed that support for the Civil War was nigh universal ("I'm a Confederate like everybody else," claims brothel-keeper Belle Watling in *Gone With the Wind*). There are, it is true, a number of temporary rebels in these movies—like Duncan Bedford (Randolph Scott) in *So Red the Rose* and Rhett Butler in *Gone With the Wind*—who at first refuse to fight, but are eventually too caught up in the struggle.

This view of solid support for the war in the South began to be questioned in *Tap Roots* (1948). Based on a 1942 novel by James H. Street, it dealt with the resistance to the Confederacy in Jones County, Mississippi. Hoab Dabney (Ward Bond) is loosely based upon Newton Knight, who deserted the Confederate army in November 1862 and, a year later, was leading a guerrilla band of local men against Confederate forces. The main grievances of the real Jones County protestors were the Mississippi law exempting large planters from fighting and the depredations of corrupt Confederate taxmen. *Tap Roots* undercut the class basis for this opposition by local small farmers to a "rich man's war" they were asked to fight by having Dabney as a Unionist planter, but was still pioneering in its foregrounding of Southern opposition to the war.[45] *Shenandoah* (1965) was the story of Charlie Anderson (James Stewart), a prosperous Virginia farmer who is also a widower with seven children. Until 1863, he refuses to become involved in the war. "Not believing in slavery," commented the *Variety* reviewer, "he wants no part in a war based upon it" and refuses to allow his sons to go off to fight.[46] But when his youngest son is captured by Unionists and accused of being a "Reb," he launches an unsuccessful private war to try and rescue him. Before the film ends, two of his sons have been killed, one by a looter, the other by a nervous, trigger-happy young Confederate sentry. The film ends on a comparatively happy note with the return of the lost son while the surviving members of the family are at church. Although the movie was antiwar rather than antiConfederate, it underlined the fact that some Southerners opposed slavery and had no interest in fighting to preserve it. Both *Tap Roots* and *Shenandoah* either anticipated or reflected the work of historians who have foregrounded Southern divisions over the war and seen the South itself riven by a true civil war, as areas and counties broke with the Confederacy, there was violent class-based resistance to the draft, desertions from the Confederate army reached epidemic proportions, African Americans began to secure their own freedom, and many white Southerners fought for the Union.[47]

Two films, separated by almost half a century, suggested that the North was also not united in its support for the war. *Friendly Persuasion* (1956) told the story of Jess Bidwell (Gary Cooper) and his Quaker family in southern Indiana. Both parents are pacifists, deploring the violence of the Civil War, but when Morgan's Raiders—Confederate cavalrymen led by General John Hunt Morgan—appear, their son Josh (Anthony Perkins) joins the home guard to protect the local community. Josh is wounded in a clash and Jess goes off with his gun to rescue him. He overpowers a bushwacker who has killed a neighbor and tries to kill Jess himself, but his Quaker beliefs persuade him to let the man go.[48] *Gangs of New York* (2002) revolved around a long feud between two lower Manhattan gangs that climaxed during the New York City drafts riots of July 13–16, 1863, when rioters—many of them working-class Irish—attacked both the wealthy (who could pay $300 to avoid the new conscription laws) and African Americans, whom they blamed for the war and regarded as economic competitors.[49]

Missing from nearly all Civil War movies is any sense that blacks resisted slavery or were prepared to fight to gain their own emancipation. After *The Birth of a Nation*, the image of the black soldier with a gun in his hand disappears from films for several decades. It returned, at first, only in piecemeal fashion. Enoch (Joel Fluellen), a free black worker living in the North, asks for a gun with which to fight Morgan's raiders in *Friendly Persuasion*; Rau-Ru (Sidney Poitier), a former black overseer, joins the Union army in *Band of Angels*; Gabriel (Eugene Jackson, Jr.), a worker rather than a slave, becomes a member of the Union forces in *Shenandoah*. But only with *Glory* (1989) did Hollywood—covering the story of the first major black combat unit—finally start to deal with the subject of the 178,000 African American soldiers who for the most part fought courageously and well in the Civil War.

Glory and after

Glory was the story of Colonel Robert Gould Shaw (Matthew Broderick), a white officer from Boston in the Union army, and his command, the 54th Massachusetts Volunteer regiment made up of black soldiers. Shaw himself was real—his letters are quoted at various moments in the film. The beginning of the film represented a real event: the battle of Antietam, in which Shaw was wounded. The ending of the movie was also "real": a recreation of the regiment's attack on Confederate-held Fort Wagner in Charleston Harbor, a suicidal assault in which half the regiment (and Shaw) died. The film used fiction, however, to recount the experience of black soldiers in the 54th. The principal African American characters were themselves composite inventions: Sergeant-Major John Rawlins (Morgan Freeman), a former gravedigger; Private Trip (Denzel Washington), an escaped slave; Corporal Jupiter Sharts (Jihmi Kennedy), a rural black; and Corporal Thomas Searles (Andre Braugher), a Boston-educated middle-class freeman. Most of the events in the film apart from the opening and closing battles were also fictional, being intended to demonstrate the racial prejudice against African Americans in the Union army: their inferior pay, being charged for their own uniforms, and not being issued with weapons or even boots (since, as Vincent Canby observed in the *New York Times*, "it is assumed they will never see battle").[50]

In interviews, Edward Zwick, the director of *Glory*, claimed that the story of the 54th had been excluded from the American history and literature he had studied in college. He had grown up believing in myths: that the Civil War "was fought by white people" and that freedom had been "paternalistically given" to black slaves. The history of the 54th challenged this perception, underlining the fact "that black men fought for their own freedom."[51] As Robert Burgoyne points out, however, *Glory* created a mythical history of its own: "of collective martyrdom . . . as the price of national affiliation." In the hands of Zwick and screenwriter Kevin Jarre, "the story of the 54th is . . . constructed as the genesis . . . of black historical consciousness."[52] In the process, much of black history itself was effectively sidelined. Whereas Shaw was a dominant figure in the film, particularly through his voice-over at key points, there was no reference to the real blacks who served in 54th.[53] The omission is particularly striking since two sons of black abolitionist Frederick Douglass, Lewis and Charles, were members of the regiment, with Lewis becoming a sergeant-major. Instead of characters based on real African Americans, *Glory* ultimately offered little more than "an ensemble of [racial] stereotypes, in which the 'Wild Tom' and the 'Uncle Tom,' the 'Buppie' and the rural hick are plainly represented."[54]

While *Glory* offered a different take on the Civil War to most of its predecessors (historian James M. McPherson hoped that it would "throw a cold dash of realism over the moonlight-and-magnolia portrayal of the Confederacy"), its main focus in the build-up to the doomed charge on Fort Wagner—as Thomas Cripps points out—was not so much on how African Americans experienced army life as the struggle between "white politicians and soldiers over the place to be taken by black soldiers in the Army."[55] It is only in the last, Fort Wagner sequences that the film becomes a tribute to African American heroism and sacrifice. "The dreadful toll is less awful," comments Thomas Doherty, "than the obvious certainty of it—nobody ducks for cover or hits the ground, they just march onward."[56]

Glory, with its very title, evoked an era before Vietnam when Americans could, without irony, see military courage and fortitude as desirable virtues in themselves. At the end of the assault, Doherty notes, the Confederate flag is unfurled from Fort Wagner "but it signals no failure. The mission was never really to take the garrison. It was, as Rawlins tells Trip in a riveting eye-to-eye encounter, to 'ante up and kick in like men'—to pay in blood for the price of freedom."[57] "Freedom" in this sense meant more than an end to slavery, something seemingly attained six and a half months earlier with the Emancipation Proclamation. It had to do with demonstrating that black soldiers, looked down upon by many in the Union army, could fight at least as well as whites, underpinning their wider claims to social equality. Yet the scenes of men dying and being maimed at Fort Wagner also have great poignancy, since most audiences will be aware that the Union victory in the Civil War did not secure racial equality. The sacrifice was in vain.

Glory was a financial gamble for Tri-Star, part of the Columbia Studio, to make. It cost an estimated $18,000,000 to produce and eventually made back nearly $27,000,000 in the United States. Over the years, it would become a staple of American history teaching in schools.[58] It did not, however, encourage a more informed treatment of African Americans in later Hollywood films about the Civil War. Two of these, *Gettysburg* (1993) and *Gods and Generals* (2003), were produced with the support of media mogul—and Civil War buff—Ted Turner.[59] *Gettysburg* was based on the 1974 novel by Michael Shaara, a former parachutist in the 82nd Airborne division. As Jim Cullen observes, the film "retains his [Shaara's] celebration of military valor and detail, at the expense of almost everything else."[60] There was no attempt to sketch out the social and political context of the battle. *Gettysburg*'s focus, noted the *Variety* critic, was "almost entirely on the officers" of both sides.[61] There were no African Americans in speaking roles and race, as a subject, was dealt with only superficially. While both Colonel Joshua Chamberlain (Jeff Daniels) and his younger brother Tom (C. Thomas Howell) declare that the North is fighting to free the slaves, Confederates deny that slavery has anything to do with the war. A captured Confederate soldier from Tennessee insists he "ain't fighting for no darkies" but "for my rights." Lieutenant-General James Longstreet (Tom Berenger) bizarrely asserts at one point that the South "should have freed the slaves, then fired on Fort Sumter."[62] *Gettysburg* failed to find a significant audience, making back less than 11 million dollars on estimated production costs of 25 million.[63]

Gods and Generals, released ten years later and based on a novel by Michael Shaara's son, Jeff, was intended as a prequel to *Gettysburg*, following the career of Lieutenant-General Thomas "Stonewall" Jackson (Stephen Lang) from the beginning of the Civil War until his death (accidentally shot by his own side) at Chancellorsville. The film was much-criticized for its length (nearly four hours) and slowness, its Southern bias (Robert Koehler pointed out that it was only at "nearly the one-hour mark" that the first serious Northern character, Joshua Chamberlain, appeared[64]), and its racial politics.[65] The major black characters are Martha (Donzaleigh Abernathy), a youthful but loyal slave who worries about her white family and stays behind to protect their property while also dreaming of freedom, and Jim Lewis (Frankie Faison), Jackson's cook. When Lewis asks Jackson how "a good Christian man" can tolerate slavery, Jackson predicts that African Americans will soon be free and wonders if "the southern government will have the sense to do it first." There is no historical evidence to suggest that Jackson favored ending slavery in this way.[66] *Gods and Generals* earned back an even smaller proportion (less than a quarter) of its total production costs, estimated at $56 million, than its predecessor.[67]

Two other Civil War movies of the 1990s, both set in borderlands away from the main areas of military conflict, were similarly commercial failures. *Pharoah's Army*, a movie made for TV that had a limited theatrical release, was based on interviews by a folklorist in 1941. It dealt with an isolated rural area, in Kentucky's Cumberland Mountains, where locals were divided more or less equally between supporters of the Union and the Confederacy. But the great political issues of the war are largely absent from the story, which revolves around Union Captain John H. Abston (Chris Cooper)'s arrival with a small detail of cavalry at the farm of Sarah Anders (Patricia Clarkson), whose husband is away fighting for the Confederacy. But what *Variety* called "the evolving relationship" between the two in the end has no chance against the bitter hatreds stirred up by a war in which neighbor at times fought neighbor.[68] *Ride With the Devil* again showed neighbors at war, this time on the western frontier of Missouri. Its main protagonists are a group of

Confederate Bushwackers: Jacob "Jake" Roedel (Tobey Maguire), Jack Bull Chiles (Skeet Ulrich), George Clyde (Simon Baker), and Daniel Holt (Jeffrey Wright), a former slave—a combination that, as Gary Gallagher remarks, transcends "nineteenth-century racial boundaries in ways that seem highly unlikely."[69] While there are occasional references to broader issues—the families of Chiles and Clyde both own slaves—the brutal and savage war between Bushwackers and Jayhawkers had more to do with local and family grievances. The Bushwackers themselves, as *Premiere* commented, are "more *Birth of a Nation*-esque wackos" than "*Gone With the Wind*-style, gray-uniformed gentlemen soldiers."[70] There are "bad" Bushwackers who participate in the massacre of civilians at Lawrence and "good" Bushwackers (Jake and Daniel) who do not. Some critics liked the movie, but even they had reservations. Stephen Hunter in the *Washington Post* admired the courage of director Ang Lee in making a film "about the wrong men on the wrong side of the wrong campaign in the wrong war," but pointed out that it was "anti-epic," "anti-romantic," and featured no stars. Stephen Holden in the *New York Times* saw it as "visually arresting but dramatically flat."[71] The film failed comprehensively at the box office, producing very little return on its estimated budget of $35 million.[72]

Cold Mountain

When *Cold Mountain* was released in December 2003, Todd McCarthy of *Variety* accurately predicted that this "handsomely made and vividly acted" film was likely "to connect with the intended discerning mass audience, resulting in solid domestic B[ox] O[ffice] . . . and perhaps better in many foreign territories." With an estimated budget of $83 million, the film grossed $95.6 million in the United States by June 25, 2004 but $173 million worldwide by January 2008, making it the most profitable Civil War movie for decades.[73] The film opens with Confederate infantryman Inman (Jude Law) wounded after the Battle of the Crater at Petersburg on July 30, 1864. As he recovers in hospital, flashbacks show his romance with Ada Monroe (Nicole Kidman), daughter of the preacher (Donald Sutherland) in the town of Cold Mountain, North Carolina. Ada has written asking him to return home and Inman is tired of fighting. He leaves the hospital, deserting the army and setting off back to Cold Mountain. His adventures on this journey—which becomes a kind of a Homeric Odyssey—make up one of two parallel stories in the movie. The other covers Ada's struggle to survive after the death of her father, her fruitful relationship with the highly practical Ruby Thewes (Renee Zellwegger) and the wartime harassment of the local community by Teague (Ray Winstone), the leader of the Home Guard.

Cold Mountain was very different from *Gods and Generals*, also released in 2003, for other reasons besides its commercial success. The only battle shown in *Cold Mountain* is the opening sequence at Petersburg. While *Gods and Generals* dealt principally with the wartime career of Stonewall Jackson and other senior officers on both sides in the war, *Cold Mountain* focused on the Southern home front and the struggles of ordinary people to survive. As John C. Inscoe noted, it offered an "unflinching . . . portrayal of the bleak and unsettling realities of a far-less-familiar version of the Civil War . . . that would have been all too recognizable to thousands of hardscrabble Southern men and women who lived through it."[74] This was a wartime world in which women, deprived of the company and labor of men, had to work for their own salvation—and a world in which a small herd of goats or even a solitary pig could make all the difference between survival or starvation. Until Ruby comes along to show her what can be done to turn Black Cove once again into a working farm, the cultured but dreamily impractical Ada survives mainly on the charity of other women: her neighbor Sally Swanger (Kathy Baker) and the woman in the local post office/store who gives her salt pork while turning down the offer of her father's watch.

If the film shows women supporting each other—and sometimes men, as when Inman is rescued and nursed back to health by the goat-farmer (Eileen Atkins)—at a time of violence and civil disorder, it also shows them as victims of male power in two major ways. First, *Cold Mountain* presents the war as a male idea. It is difficult to find a single woman in the movie who supports it. Ada is skeptical from the beginning and her letter helps persuade Inman to desert. The woman in the town store loudly states (within Teague's hearing): "The sooner we lose this war the better. They say not one boy in ten is coming home to these mountains." "Every piece of this is man's bullshit," Ruby furiously declares with respect to the war.[75] Secondly, the movie shows women as victims of men's violence both personally and sexually. As Anna Creadick perceptively points out, this "gratuitous sex and violence" is an example of Hollywood's interest in presenting (for profit) "violence threatened or committed against women's bodies." In Charles Frazier's novel, which provided the basis of the film's story, Sally Swanger "is not tortured by Teague's Guard, nor is her family massacred in front of her." Equally, the young widow Sara (Natalie Portman) is not threatened with rape while the river girl "does not offer herself up sexually to Inman and the lecherous Reverend [Philip Seymour Hoffman], and does not get shot."[76] In the film's telling, violence begets violence: Sara shoots one of the men who has threatened her and her baby in the back and, in the Western-style shoot-out at the end, even Ada, the gentle minister's daughter, shoots at Teague's men and knocks Teague himself off his horse with a shotgun butt.[77]

If *Cold Mountain* foregrounded sex and violence, it also—like most movies about the Civil War with the exception of *Glory*—paid virtually no attention to the issue of race. Historical and military adviser Brian Pohanka emphasized the level of detailed accuracy in the very first sequence of the film: the caps of the Union troops digging the mine underneath the Confederate fortifications at Petersburg had a "48" on to show they belonged to a regiment from a coal-mining area of Pennsylvania.[78] The mine blows up to form a crater in which attacking Union troops are trapped and killed: what the film does not show is that many of these soldiers were black.[79] African Americans are rarely shown in the film and never speak. We see only in passing the two slaves riding in the wagon to help carry Ada's piano, the pregnant black woman Inman prevents the white minister from drowning, and the slaves picking cotton outside the Confederate Army hospital. Pushing the idea of the "benevolent slave mistress" to the limit, Ada is shown carrying a tray of root beers to the slave cabins during the party, but it appears this is only a tactic to talk privately with Inman. We later learn from Sally that Ada (who is happy to have escaped from Charleston and what she terms "a world of slaves and corsets and cotton") has freed her slaves. Race remains the great "absent presence" in *Cold Mountain*. At one point in Inman's long journey, a group of runaway slaves appears like silent ghosts from the corn stalks. Inman tries to talk to them, but they walk off down the road (he is, after all, a white man) (Figure 4.1). Once they disappear, we hear shots as the local Home Guard discover them. This is a key sequence in the racial politics of the film: black people are shown as little more than palimpsests of their own history.

In relation to the politics of the war itself, there were differing views. Silas House thought that the "Yee-Haw, We Got Us a War, Boys!" sequence was overdrawn, like a Western North Carolina version of the scene at Twelve Oaks in *Gone With the Wind*. House considered such unanimous

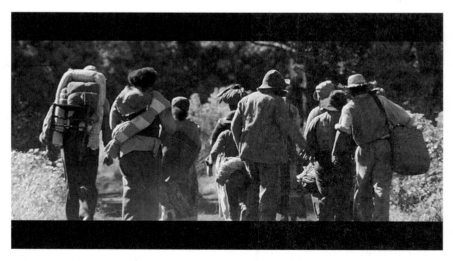

FIGURE 4.1 *Escaping slaves ignore Inman (Jude Law) in* Cold Mountain.

enthusiasm for war unlikely in the Appalachian mountains, where few people owned slaves and Union sentiment remained strong. John C. Inscoe disagreed, pointing out that the enthusiastic beginning of the war was historically accurate and that North Carolina's mountain counties sent proportionately more troops to the Confederate Army than the eastern part of the state.[80] Inman later becomes convinced that he has been duped ("like every fool sent off to fight with a flag and a lie") but never explains what he thinks the lie has been. The main spokesman for the view that the war is being fought to protect the interest of slave-owners is the sardonic doctor in the military hospital, who invites his nurses to look at the slaves picking cotton outside: "See what these poor fools are dyin' for. How many would still lose a leg for the rich man's slave?" Teague is based on an historical character, referred to by Martin Crawford as "the notorious Haywood County Home Guard leader."[81] The film suggests that Teague's motivation in pursuing (and killing) deserters so fiercely is to regain the wealth his family has lost on Cold Mountain. On the other hand, deserters, people avoiding conscription, and other social renegades—often organized into bands of bushwackers—were a serious problem for the local communities in many highland areas.[82] Teague explains the role of the Home Guard as chasing deserters and Union raiders, but the only representatives of the latter we see are the three who arrive to steal food from (and in two cases to attempt to rape) Sara, the lonely widow.[83]

In *Cold Mountain*, Inman and Ada meet up again despite all the odds and enjoy one night of intimacy. The next day Inman is killed in a shoot-out with the Home Guard, making the movie in part about doomed romance. The film itself, like *Gone With the Wind*, *Tap Roots*, and *Shenandoah*, deals primarily with the home front in the South. The two main female characters, Ada and Ruby, not only survive the war but emerge strengthened. The final sequence of the film, set several years later, shows Ada and Inman's daughter, Grace, who is growing up as part of an extended family in which women are the dominant influence. Beautifully shot in the Carpathian mountains of Romania, standing in for North Carolina,[84] and featuring three major stars, *Cold Mountain* suggested—after a long run of failures—that the Civil War could still be the setting for a commercially successful movie. To achieve this, however, it ignored almost completely—in common with most of its predecessors— the overriding issue of race in the Civil War era.

Filmography

The Birth of a Nation (dir. David W. Griffith; Epoch, 1915).
Hands Up! (dir. Clarence G. Badger; Famous Players-Lasky, 1926).
The General (dir. Clyde Bruckman/Buster Keaton; Buster Keaton/Joseph M. Schenck, 1926).

The Heart of Maryland (dir. Lloyd Bacon; Warner Bros., 1927).
Morgan's Last Raid (dir. Nick Grinde; MGM, 1929).
Only the Brave (dir. Frank Tuttle; Paramount, 1930).
Secret Service (dir. J. Walter Ruben; RKO, 1931).
Operator 13 (dir. Richard Boleslawski; MGM, 1934).
So Red the Rose (dir. King Vidor; Paramount, 1935).
The Littlest Rebel (dir. David Butler; Twentieth-Century Fox, 1935).
Hearts in Bondage (dir. Lew Ayres; Republic, 1936).
Gone With the Wind (dir. Victor Fleming; Selznick International/MGM, 1939).
The Man from Dakota (dir. Leslie Fenton; MGM, 1940).
Tap Roots (dir. George Marshall; Walter Wanger/Universal, 1948).
The Red Badge of Courage (dir. John Huston; MGM, 1951).
Drums in the Deep South (dir. William Cameron Menzies; King Brothers/RKO, 1951).
The Raid (dir. Hugo Fregonese; Panoramic, 1954).
Friendly Persuasion (dir. William Wyler; Allied Artists/B-M Productions, 1956).
The Great Locomotive Chase (dir. Francis D. Lyon; Walt Disney, 1956).
Raintree County (dir. Edward Dmytryk; MGM, 1957).
Band of Angels (dir. Raoul Walsh; Warner Bros., 1957).
The Horse Soldiers (dir. John Ford; Mirisch Corporation/Mahin-Rackin, 1959).
Advance to the Rear (dir. George Marshall; MGM, 1964).
Shenandoah (dir. Andrew V. McLagen; Universal, 1965).
Alvarez Kelly (dir. Edward Dmytryk; Columbia, 1966).
Journey to Shiloh (dir. William Hale; Universal, 1968).
The Beguiled (dir. Don Siegel; Malpaso, 1971).
Glory (dir. Edward Zwick; TriStar/Freddie Fields, 1989).
Gettysburg (Ronald F. Maxwell; TriStarTV/Esparza-Katz/Turner, 1993).
Pharaoh's Army (dir. Robby Henson; Cicada/Independent Television Service/ Kentucky Educational Television, 1995).
Ride with the Devil (dir. Ang Lee; Good Machine/Hollywood International MultiMedia Group/Maplewood, 1999).
Gangs of New York (dir. Martin Scorsese; Miramax, 2002).
God and Generals (dir. Ronald F. Maxwell; Turner Pictures, 2003).
Cold Mountain (dir. Anthony Minghella; Miramax/Mirage/Bona Fide, 2003).

CHAPTER FIVE

The War's Legacy: The Lost Cause and the Ku Klux Klan

The Civil War ended slavery. It did not reconcile the North and South; nor did it end racial problems in the South. In the years after the war was over, much of the white South resisted the attempt of Northerners—as it saw it—to impose their own social and cultural values on the South. Among the most potent weapons developed by Southerners were a complex of ideas that would come to be known as the "Lost Cause" and an organization called the Ku Klux Klan. The Lost Cause involved the redefinition, initially by pro-Southern writers, of the causes and course of the war from the Southern perspective. It would gain its widest currency through two films: *The Birth of a Nation* (1915) and *Gone With the Wind* (1939). The first part of this chapter looks at the origins and development of the Lost Cause up to and including *Gone With the Wind*. Although indicating the ways in which both *The Birth of a Nation* and *Gone With the Wind* articulated Lost Cause ideas, it also suggests that there were passages in both movies that can be read as criticism of some elements of the Lost Cause. The second part of the chapter explores how the Ku Klux Klan of the post-Civil War period—together with its twentieth-century successors—have been represented on film.

The Lost Cause

The American Civil War ended on April 9, 1865, when the principal Southern commander, General Robert E. Lee, surrendered the main surviving Confederate army to the Union army led by Ulysses S. Grant at Appomattox court house in Virginia. After four years of war, in which 620,000–750,000 Americans died—more than the figure killed in *all* other American wars from the War of Independence to Iraq and Afghanistan today—the North had achieved total victory over the South on the battlefield. Yet the end of military conflict between the sections was followed by a political and cultural struggle that lasted for many decades. This latter conflict still continues today in a number of respects but, for much of the time since 1865, it has been "won" by the South every bit as clearly and decisively as the North won the war itself.[1]

The main focus of this second "war" has been the fight to control the public memory of the Civil War. The South's main weapon in its enduring and mainly successful attempt to project a view of the war favorable to itself has been the myth of the so-called Lost Cause. That myth, as Thomas Connelly and Barbara Bellows have pointed out, emerged in two distinct phases. The first, the "inner" Lost Cause, was created by the Confederate generation that had fought and lost the Civil War. Led by men such as former President of the Confederacy Jefferson Davis and Southern military leaders, including General Jubal Early, it set out to justify why they fought and to explain away their defeat. Later came the "outer" Lost Cause that first emerged in the 1880s and 1890s, encouraged by mass-circulation magazines with their mainly Northern readership. It was largely the creation of a group of Southern writers who romanticized the "Old South": William Alexander Carruthers, John Esten Cooke, Mary Johnston, John Pendleton Kennedy, Sara Pryor and—perhaps above all— Thomas Nelson Page. Together, they created a myth of the Old South and the way in which it had fought the Civil War.[2]

As Alan T. Nolan has pointed out, the Lost Cause legend incorporated a range of different elements. According to the Lost Cause, slavery was not the primary reason for the Civil War. It was troublemaking abolitionists who had driven the tragic wedge between the sections that had finally led to war. If it had not been for outside interference, indeed, the South itself would ultimately have got rid of slavery on its own initiative. In the meantime, the slaves themselves had been happy and thoroughly content with their status. Southern plantation society (which, of course, meant *white* society) had been marked by superior grace and gentility. It had descended from the Norman cavaliers who had once conquered the Anglo-Saxon tribes (predictably, perhaps, Northerners were seen as having "Anglo-Saxon" origins). In the end, Southerners had been compelled to exercise their lawful right to secede from the Union, to protect their liberty, way of life, independence, and states' rights. Led by impressive, saintly figures such as Lee, Confederate soldiers had proven themselves gallant and heroic on the battlefield, fighting equally gallant Union troops. Yet, confronted with a North vastly superior in both manpower and industrial capacity, it was inevitable that they would lose in the end, and after four years of courageous resistance the South was finally overwhelmed.[3]

By the time of the emergence of cinema in the last decade of the nineteenth century, therefore, there was already a culturally dominant view of the Civil War based on a rereading of the era that was deeply sympathetic to the South. Initially, it appeared that cinema itself might challenge that view. One of the earliest and most important of American film genres was the "civil war" picture. Since these were at first made by Northern production companies such as Biograph and designed mainly for Northern and Western audiences, it was only natural in the beginning that they would look back on the war predominantly from a Northern perspective. The tide began to turn, however, in 1909 when *The Old Soldier's Story*, made by the Kalem Company in its new Florida studio, was hailed by the *Moving Picture World* as the "first [film] ever made that represents the Southern side." Also in 1909, Kalem launched its series dealing with the exploits of Nan, the Southern "girl spy," and Biograph released D. W. Griffith's *In Old Kentucky*. Filmmakers quickly discovered that what Eileen Bowser referred to as "the more romantic, noble, and heroic ideals to be found in the defeated South" appealed to cinema-goers in the North as well as the South. Consequently, from 1911 onwards, films reflecting the Southern point of view in relation to the war and its causes became twice as numerous as films with a Northern bias.[4]

If, by early 1915, the South was decisively winning the cultural war over how the Civil War was to be remembered, it remained for two films—with almost a quarter century in between—to give the Lost Cause view its most widespread popular diffusion. The two were D. W. Griffith's *The Birth of a Nation*, first released in 1915, and the David O. Selznick-produced *Gone With the Wind*, first released in 1939.[5] Both were the principal "blockbusters" of their time, reaching mass audiences and continuing to circulate widely for many years after their initial screenings. One estimate suggested that *The Birth of a Nation* was seen by 50 million people in the first 15 years of its career.[6] *Gone With the Wind* became—and perhaps still is, if box-office figures are adjusted for inflation—the biggest-earning movie of all time. When first shown on television in 1976, it attracted a record audience.[7] It has since been shown many times on television and rereleased on video, DVD, and Blu-Ray. Both *The Birth of a Nation* and *Gone With the Wind*, by encapsulating major elements of the Lost Cause, worked together to help perpetuate the hegemony of that myth for many decades. Yet, as will be suggested here, the dedication of both films to the Lost Cause myth itself was neither complete nor entirely unproblematic.

If *The Birth of a Nation* had no character like Ashley Wilkes in *Gone With the Wind* to claim that the South itself would eventually have freed the slaves even without interference from the North, in other respects it followed—and helped disseminate—central tenets of the Lost Cause point of view. It suggested, as did exponents of the Lost Cause, that the war had been brought about primarily by fanatical abolitionists. The intertitle introducing the first real scene of the film—a minister praying over manacled slaves about to be auctioned—observed that "The bringing of the African to America planted the first seed of disunion." The second scene, also introduced by an intertitle, was of a meeting of abolitionists demanding an end to the institution of slavery.

The Birth of a Nation also followed Lost Cause notions with regard to the superiority of Southern white society and the benign nature of slavery. It is clear from their first appearance in the film that the Southern Cameron family belongs to the planter class. Clearly, they typify the "Old" South. An intertitle describes their home as a place "where life runs in a quaintly way that is to be no more." The Camerons seem very genteel: their daughter, Margaret, is introduced as "a daughter of the South, trained in the manners of the old school." Above all, perhaps, they are benevolent: Dr. Cameron, referred to in an intertitle as "the kindly master of Cameron Hall," sits reading a newspaper surrounded by pets. Clearly, such a man can be assumed to have treated his slaves with considerable compassion and thoughtfulness. This is confirmed (see Chapter Two) in the sequence of whites and blacks together outside the slave quarters.

When it came to explaining why the South fought, *The Birth of a Nation* adopted the same approach as exponents of the Lost Cause. The film begins to sketch out the states' rights argument for war with an intertitle insisting that "The power of the sovereign states, established when Lord Cornwallis surrendered to the individual colonies in 1781, is threatened by the new administration." No attempt is made to sketch in the political context by explaining why Abraham Lincoln's election as President in 1860 was such a threat to the South. When Lincoln calls for troops to suppress the rebellion, he is said to be "using the Presidential office for the first time in history to call for volunteers to enforce the rule of the coming nation over the individual states." Once the war ends, Lee's surrender to Grant is represented as "the end of state sovereignty."

Much of the first part of the film is intended to ensure that the South is seen as a victim and to suggest that the North was bound eventually to win the Civil War. After the shots of the Confederate regiment, led by now-Colonel Ben Cameron, marching off to war, there is a curious hiatus (suggested by an intertitle) of "two and a half years." Clearly, many things have gone wrong for the South during this period. The Southern economy has more or less collapsed and standards of living have greatly declined: young Flora Cameron "wears her last good dress" to give a touch of ceremony to the reading of one of Ben's letters from the front. Northerners appear to be having no difficulty in invading the South: the film shows a group of mainly black guerrillas attacking the Camerons' hometown of Piedmont itself. General Sherman has begun to march and burn his way to the sea, bombarding and taking Atlanta in the process. In the meantime, the Camerons sell the "last of their dearest possessions . . . for the failing cause." Finally, in the "last grey days of the Confederacy," Southern soldiers in besieged Petersburg, Virginia, are reduced to eating nothing but "parched corn."

Thus far, *The Birth of a Nation* can be seen to have encapsulated Lost Cause ideas and themes. But as the editors of *Cahiers du cinéma* argued more than 40 years ago, even films that seem to articulate the most hegemonic myths and ideas at times contain contradictions that undermine the myths they ostensibly express.[8] Whatever David Wark Griffith's broader intentions, *The Birth of a Nation* has sequences that draw attention to the inaccuracies and contradictions that made up the myth of the Lost Cause. One of the most obvious is that while Griffith emphasizes in intertitles how poor and ill-equipped Southern soldiers are by the end of the war, as a cinematic showman he is unable to resist depicting the Confederate artillery endlessly bombarding Union lines at Petersburg. The idea that the Civil War was mainly a conflict between heroic and gallant white men on both sides is undercut by the scenes of brutal hand-to-hand combat in the trenches at Petersburg and the sequence in which Tod Stoneman and Duke Cameron, the two pre-war "chums," meet again on the battlefield. Tod is about to bayonet Duke, who is already lying wounded on the ground, when he recognizes him and lowers his gun. He is then shot in the back by a Confederate soldier hiding in the bushes behind him.

Even more crucially, perhaps, the myth of the benevolent master and loyal slaves is dramatically exploded in the second part of the film when Dr. Cameron is arrested by Northern soldiers, brought before his former slaves and taunted by an African American woman who spits at his feet and leads the others in abusing him. The reversal of status is particularly emphasized by the fact that Dr. Cameron is shown wearing chains—something that foregrounds the real, coercive nature of slavery (slaves had, for example, often been chained together in the holds of the ships that carried them from Africa—or while they were subsequently being sold, transported, or disciplined). The role of the woman (played by black actress Madame Sul-Te-Wan) is also important. The second part of *The Birth of a Nation* revolves around miscegenation, which the film portrays as the pursuit of innocent white women by aggressive, sexually rapacious black men. Under slavery, however, the true reality behind such relationships—as this sequence, with its depiction of a bitter, vengeful former slave woman perhaps suggests—had been the sexual exploitation of black female slaves by white slave owners, together with their sons and overseers.

Twenty-four years after *The Birth of a Nation* appeared, the myth of the Lost Cause received its ultimately most influential expression with the release of *Gone With the Wind*. In several respects, the Lost Cause was faithfully represented in Selznick's film. Southern plantation society was depicted as far more wealthy—and in many respects far more civilized— than in *The Birth of a Nation*. The comparatively modest Cameron Hall of

The Birth of a Nation had now given way to the elegant grandeur of Tara and Twelve Oaks. The film itself made great play with the idea of Southern "ladies" and "gentlemen." It also presented the planter class as descendants of the cavaliers. The opening intertitle, famously written by Ben Hecht, declared that:

> There was a land of Cavaliers and Cotton fields called the Old South. Here in this pretty world, Gallantry took its last bow. Here was the last ever to be seen of Knights and their Ladies Fair, of Master and of Slave. Look for it only in books, for it is no more than a dream remembered, a Civilization gone with the wind. . . .

A later intertitle revisited the same idea:

> Home from their lost adventure came the tattered Cavaliers . . . Grimly they came hobbling back to the desolation that had once been a land of grace and plenty . . .

Slavery in *Gone With the Wind* was also presented as a benign and necessary institution. Mammy, though a slave, is clearly a major part of the O'Hara household. She has a considerable degree of autonomy in plantation society—as does Big Sam, the black foreman who (improbably) gets to call "quittin' time" in the cotton fields of Tara. Pork is close enough to Gerald O'Hara to inherit his master's watch when Gerald dies. Ashley later declares that slaves had been better treated than the white convicts Scarlett intends to hire for the Kennedy lumber mill in Atlanta, and speaks warmly and nostalgically about the "high soft negro laughter from the [slave] quarters" wafting up to the plantation house at Twelve Oaks in "the warm still country twilight." Scarlett herself, when she meets "Big Sam" and the field hands going off to dig trenches for the Confederacy (thereby perpetuating their own apparently contented status as slaves),[9] greets each of the slaves individually by name, suggesting the (supposed) great intimacy of master-slave relationships on the plantation. And Gerald O'Hara, just before his death, explains to Scarlett the mixture of benevolence and strictness that—at least according to exponents of the Lost Cause—had been used to treat slaves: "You must be firm with inferiors, but you must be gentle with them, especially darkies."

When it came to outlining the causes of the Civil War, there was no specific reference in *Gone With the Wind*—unlike *The Birth of a Nation*—to the actions of abolitionists, although Gerald O'Hara suggests at the men's brandy and cigars session after the Twelve Oaks barbecue that the South has had "enough insults from the meddling Yankees." Gerald also, in his remarks, endorses the Southern view of the Civil War as a struggle over state sovereignty. According to the "states rights" view, the Federal Constitution of 1787 had been the result of an agreement or "compact" between the original states. But the states themselves, according to this perspective, reserved for themselves the ultimate right to leave the Union if they believed it to be threatening their own institutions and rights. Gerald O'Hara articulates this viewpoint very clearly at Twelve Oaks, claiming "'Tis the right of the sovereign state of Georgia to secede from the Union."

Gone With the Wind also, at a number of points, followed the Lost Cause perception of the inevitability of Southern defeat in the war itself. This is initially suggested by Rhett Butler in his attempt to dampen the war-fever of the men at the Twelve Oaks barbecue: "The Yankees are better equipped than we. They've got factories, shipyards, coal mines and a fleet to bottle up our harbors and starve us to death. All we've got is cotton, and slaves, and—arrogance." Once the war starts, the South clearly experiences many casualties—something emphasized by the casualty lists distributed after the battle of Gettysburg in July 1863 and the large numbers of wounded and dying men in the railroad yards in Atlanta. By the Christmas after Gettysburg, when Ashley is given leave to spend the holidays with his family, things are obviously going very badly for the Confederacy. Union soldiers are increasingly numerous and better-equipped. As Ashley confesses, while predicting the "end of the war and the end of our world": "Oh, Scarlett, my men are barefooted now. And the snow in Virginia is deep. When I see them, I see the Yankees coming and coming, always more and more." In reality, Ashley's defeatism was highly premature. It was by no means clear in December 1863 that the South had lost the war. According to some modern scholars, indeed, it could actually have won it at several points until the late summer of 1864.[10]

Although Gone With the Wind, therefore, helped implant deep in American culture and popular consciousness the ideas of a gracious white planter society, the essential benevolence and necessity of slavery as an institution, the war as a struggle over state sovereignty, and the inevitability of a Confederate defeat, just as in The Birth of a Nation there are key moments in the film that appear to question major aspects of the Lost Cause. Both Scarlett O'Hara and Rhett Butler are to a degree detached from traditional plantation society—the so-called Old South— and often regard it with a jaundiced eye. Looking at the long casualty lists after the battle of Gettysburg, Rhett remarks bitterly: "Look at them. All these poor tragic people. The South sinking to its knees. It will never rise again. . . . [All for] the cause. The cause of living in the past is dying right in front of us." Rhett and Scarlett are also both highly skeptical of the male codes of honor that have inspired Southern "gentlemen" to go to war in the first place. Sitting in a wagon amid the mass of defeated, often wounded, Confederate soldiers escaping from besieged Atlanta, Rhett observes ironically: "They were going to lick the Yankees in a month. Poor gallant fools." Scarlett is even more critical: "They make me sick. All of them. Getting us into this mess [with their] swaggering and boasting."

There are also moments in the film when the broadly favorable image of slavery is undercut. The shot of one little black girl tiredly stroking her hair (Figure 5.1), as she fans the sleeping white belles before the barbecue at Twelve Oaks, suggests the racial exploitation of slavery—as does Scarlett's treatment of Prissy.

Prissy herself is the only slave we see subjected to physical violence—Scarlett slaps her face. Scarlett also threatens to "whip the hide off" her if she upsets Melanie and, in one of the most revealing phrases in the whole film, threatens to sell Prissy "south." Slave-owners often did sell recalcitrant slaves to the frontier parts of states such as Mississippi, where conditions were much harder and death-rates higher than in the plantation areas of Georgia and the Carolinas. The slave concerned was also separated in the process from his or her family (we know Prissy has a family since she tells Rhett her mother would not approve of her entering the saloon where Belle Watling apparently—this is after all the era of the Hays Code—runs her brothel). The film contains one other reference to the slave trade. When Dolly Meriwether is worried by the nature of the fund-raising efforts at the charity ball—asking men to bid for their preferred dance partner—she bitingly describes it as a "slave auction."

When it came to discussing the causes of the Civil War, it was not simply that *Gone With the Wind* followed the Lost Cause only partially

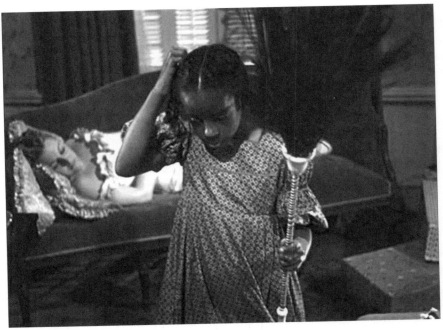

FIGURE 5.1 *Young female household slave in* Gone With the Wind.

(it foregrounded states' rights but not the role of radical abolitionists). In two comments in the men's "brandy and cigars" sequence at the Twelve Oaks barbecue, Gerald O'Hara undermines the Lost Cause mythology in two crucial ways. In the first place, he makes it plain that slavery—not the actions of abolitionists—was the principal cause of the war by insisting that "It's time we make . . . [the Yankees] understand we'll keep our slaves with or without their approval." Secondly, Gerald acknowledges—something *The Birth of a Nation* or its characters never did—that the war had actually been started by the South. As he excitedly insists at the barbecue, "After we fired on the Yankee rascals at Fort Sumter, we've *got* to fight. There's no other way."

Finally, while much of the film supports the Lost Cause view of the inevitability of Northern victory, one scene largely contradicts it. When Scarlett goes to the Atlanta railroad yards in her failed attempt to persuade Dr. Meade to help with Melanie Wilkes' labor, the camera—in a justly famous crane shot—pulls back to show thousands of wounded and dying men lying on the ground (Figure 5.2).

On seeing this sequence for the first time at the Atlanta première, Margaret Mitchell's husband apparently remarked that "if we'd had that many soldiers, we'd have won the war."[11]

FIGURE 5.2 *Confederate casualties at the railroad yards in* Gone With the Wind.

For much of the twentieth century, American movie—and later TV—audiences were consistently given a view of the Civil War era in which the South was presented very positively. Two films—each the most commercially successful of its time—perhaps did more than anything else to disseminate a romantic and biased view of the Lost Cause to a mass American audience. In so doing, they almost certainly helped perpetuate Southern racial injustices. In reality, however, both *The Birth of a Nation* and *Gone With the Wind* included some aspects of the Lost Cause while contradicting others. They were not simple expressions of the Lost Cause mythology. In a number of cases, indeed, they challenged the very foundations on which the legend itself was constructed.

The Ku Klux Klan in the movies

The Ku Klux Klan is a secret order with its own membership rituals. Born originally in the South, as a movement of protest against Northern domination after the Civil War, it had virtually disappeared by the mid-1870s. Reborn in 1915, also in the South, it spread over much of the United States in the decade that followed. Dwindling away again during the late 1920s and the 1930s, it revived as a protest against the civil rights movement of the 1950s and 1960s. Relatively few Hollywood films have ever dealt with the Klan. Those that have done so in recent years have usually presented it as sinister (*The Klansman* (1974), *Mississippi Burning* (1988)) or ludicrous (*Blazing Saddles* (1974), *O Brother, Where Art Thou?* (2000)). Associated with violence, racism, and xenophobia, it has been defined in negative terms by most American filmmakers since *The Northern Schoolteacher*, a 1909 movie showing the Klan persecuting a Yankee teacher in the South during the Reconstruction era. Yet, in the second decade of the twentieth century, David W. Griffith made a film that constructed the Klan as a positive good. Released in 1915, *The Birth of a Nation* was not only the first real masterpiece of American cinema, it also encouraged the rebirth and expansion of the Klan itself.

The Birth of a Nation and the original Klan

The Birth of a Nation derived its principal fictional characters and much of its essential narrative (particularly in relation to the Klan) from Thomas Dixon, Jr. Born in 1864 in North Carolina, Dixon would embrace a dizzying range of careers, being successively lawyer, politician, minister, lecturer, novelist, dramatist, actor, theatrical and motion picture producer, and real estate entrepreneur. Although Dixon himself would later claim that some of his earliest memories dealt with the Ku Klux Klan (including watching the hanging of a black convict convicted of raping a white women), it is impossible to establish the correctness or otherwise of his assertions. The process of Reconstruction in North Carolina after the Civil War effectively came to an end in 1871, with the whites back in control of both houses of the state legislature and the subsequent impeachment of the "radical" Republican governor, William H. Holden. Its objectives achieved, and increasingly targeted by a Federal government intent on the implementation of the Force Acts of 1870 and 1871 and the Ku Klux Klan Act of 1871, the Klan quickly disappeared. What is clear, however, is that Dixon's uncle, Colonel Le Roy McAfee, had been one of its local leaders and his father had also been a member of the hooded organization. Dixon, whatever the accuracy or otherwise of his childhood recollections, belonged to a family that looked favorably on the Klan.[12]

Once Dixon—called to churches in the North—was no longer living in the South, he discovered that others had a very different perspective on both the South itself and the issues of the Reconstruction period. Soon after he first arrived in Boston in 1887, he heard a speaker at Tremont Temple argue that the South was both still a "problem" and an enduring threat to the American nation. The vehemence of Dixon's protests against this viewpoint came close to causing a riot. Leaving the ministry in 1899, he carved out a lucrative career for himself as a lecturer. On one of his lecture tours, in 1901, he saw a performance of a stage version of Harriet Beecher Stowe's novel, *Uncle Tom's Cabin*. Furious at what he saw as the play's criticism of white Southerners and its misunderstanding of the real nature of African Americans, Dixon resolved to write a novel telling the "true story" of Southern postwar history.[13] His *The Leopard's Spots: A Romance of the White Man's Burden* (1902) was intended both as a refutation and a sequel to Stowe's work (it included some of the characters from *Uncle Tom's Cabin*). In 1905, Dixon published a second novel dealing with the Reconstruction era: *The Clansman: A Historical Romance of the Ku Klux Klan*. Both books dealt with the supposed chaos and anarchy of the Reconstruction period, the exclusion of whites from power by fraud and intimidation, the danger allegedly posed by lascivious black men to white women, and the role of the Klan in putting down such threats and restoring white rule.[14]

Dixon's second novel apotheosizing the Klan was subsequently turned with some success into a play.[15] In 1912, an unsuccessful attempt was made to film the play in color.[16] Two years later, David W. Griffith directed *The Clansman* (later retitled *The Birth of a Nation*), a 12-reel film based on Dixon's story. Although Griffith had grown up in Kentucky, he seems to have had no personal connection with the Klan. In fact, in 1911, he had made *The Rose of Kentucky*, a one-reel Biograph film dealing in a hostile way with a group of contemporary Klan-style nightriders supposedly operating in his home state. Kentucky itself had never undergone Radical Reconstruction, blacks had been unable to vote until after the Fifteenth

Amendment was adopted in 1870, and whites remained fully in control of the state all the way through the Reconstruction era.[17] But Griffith was very pro-Southern in outlook (his adored father had been a colonel in the Confederate Army) and rapidly realized that Dixon's story could provide an excellent basis for the first truly "spectacular" American motion picture. Reading Dixon's novel for the first time, Griffith—by his own admission—was excited by the cinematic possibilities of this story of the Klan of half a century ago: he "skipped quickly through the book until I got to the part about the Klansmen . . . I could just see those Klansmen in a movie with their white robes flying."[18]

The first part of *The Birth of a Nation* follows the fortunes of the Southern Cameron family and the Northern Stonemans during the Civil War. The second part begins with Lincoln assassinated and Republican congressman Austin Stoneman able to subject the defeated South to his policies of radical "Reconstruction." Blacks now jostle whites on the sidewalks of the Camerons' home town, Piedmont. On election day, with leading whites disfranchised and black voters cheating, the blacks win a majority in the state legislature and Silas Lynch (George Siegmann), Stoneman's mulatto protégé, is elected lieutenant-governor. Law and order collapse. Black magistrates and juries acquit fellow African Americans of crimes, white families are dispossessed, and blacks who refuse to take the side of the radicals are beaten or killed.

FIGURE 5.3 *The Klan ride in* The Birth of a Nation.

In the state legislature, politically dominant blacks adopt a resolution requiring all whites to salute black officers on the streets and pass a law allowing the intermarriage of blacks and whites. Ben Cameron (Henry Walthall), the only surviving Cameron son, feels helpless at the subjugation of the whites until, watching black children flee from two white children who have covered themselves with a sheet, he has the idea for the Ku Klux Klan. Flora Cameron (Mae Marsh), Ben's adored "Little Sister," sets off alone for the well but is pursued by a black captain, Gus (Walter Long), who says he wants to marry her. Panicked, Flora runs away and, to escape him, kills herself by jumping off a high cliff. When Gus is found, he is "tried" by the Klan, executed, and his body left on the front steps of Lynch's house in Piedmont. Lynch takes up the challenge by ordering black militiamen to fill the streets while the Klan begins to gather in order to disarm all blacks. Dr. Cameron (Spottiswoode Aitken), Ben's father, is arrested as a suspected member of the Klan. When Elsie Stoneman (Lillian Gish), the daughter of Austin Stoneman, goes to Lynch to ask for his help, he asks her to marry him. Horrified, Elsie refuses, and is then imprisoned by Lynch, who starts preparations for a "forced marriage." Meanwhile, helped by their black servants, Dr. Cameron escapes and—together with several other members of his family and Austin Stoneman's son, Phil (Elmer Clifton)—takes refuge in a cabin owned by two Union veterans. The Klan has now been fully mobilized. Led by Ben Cameron, it first confronts and vanquishes the black militia in Piedmont and frees Elsie, before moving on to rescue the group in the cabin. The blacks are disarmed by the Klan, which demonstrates its ascendancy by parading through the main square of Piedmont while blacks are shown slinking back to their quarters. At the next election, armed Klansmen prevent African Americans from voting. Symbolizing a reunited white nation, the northern and southern families are linked by two marriages: Ben Cameron weds Elsie Stoneman and Phil Stoneman marries Ben's sister, Margaret (Miriam Cooper).

The way in which the Klan was represented in *The Birth of a Nation* encouraged false impressions of the organization in many important respects. Far from having its origins in the imagination of the fictional Ben Cameron in South Carolina, the Klan was actually founded in Tennessee in December 1865 by ex-officers in the Confederate Army looking for high-spirited entertainment.[19] It did not spread to South Carolina until 1867, when R. J. Brunson, one of the original founders, organized dens in the state.[20] In South Carolina, the courts were never dominated by blacks in the way the film implied and ex-Confederates experienced only "partial and temporary disfranchisement."[21] While blacks were in a numerical majority in the state legislature, they never actually controlled the state. There was no real attempt by black leaders to make intermarriage between the races more acceptable. The rape of white women by black men, the nightmare of many white Southerners, was more fantasy than reality. While law and order *did* collapse in many areas of South Carolina, this had much more to do with the aggressiveness of whites toward blacks than the other way round. Most of the justifications advanced by the film for Klan activity, therefore, were fallacious. On a more minor factual note, the burning of crosses was not a part of the ritual of the Reconstruction-era Klan. It was imagined by Thomas Dixon, Jr.—who in turn may have plagiarized it from the work of British novelist Sir Walter Scott.[22]

On the other hand, some aspects of the portrayal of the Klan in the film were rooted in historical fact. The Klan *did* justify itself (however unreasonably) as a response to black criminality: the first shot of Klansmen is accompanied by an intertitle stating that they are terrorizing "a Negro disturber and barn burner."[23] The same scene emphasizes the belief of Klansmen in the superstition and credulity of blacks: a Klansman is shown drinking from a bucket, a direct reference to the legend—promoted by the Klan itself—that its members were the ghosts of former members of the Confederate Army who had not had a drink since they were killed at the battle of Shiloh.[24] The name given to the Camerons' home-town—Piedmont—accurately underlines the fact that the main strength of the Klan in South Carolina was in the "up country" or "piedmont" area of the state.[25]

Unlikely, moreover, as the pitched battles between the Klan and the black militia shown in the film appear, they came close to happening on at least two occasions in Reconstruction-era South Carolina. The state legislature in 1869 passed a law permitting the organization of a militia and Governor Robert K. Scott, to prevent his Republican regime being defeated by white force and intimidation during the elections of 1870, recruited and armed 14 regiments of black militiamen. Although most violence and intimidation continued to come from whites, including Klansmen, opposed to the radical Republican regime, armed black militiamen drilled, moved in groups around towns, and may—in some places—have pushed white people out of their way. There were a number of incidents, including the so-called Laurens riot on the day after the 1870 election. Armed blacks confronted around 2,500 whites, mainly Klansmen, in the town of Laurens. The blacks were finally disarmed by the sheriff and a white posse of around a hundred men, though only after several of the African American militiamen had been killed.[26] In Unionville, where black militia shot and killed a one-armed Confederate veteran, the Klan mounted two successive raids on the town jail to seize and execute the men thought responsible.[27] Finally, in an incident that could have provoked a violent confrontation, the Klan in Yorkville issued a proclamation that it would execute ten leading blacks if there were any further arson attacks. With black militia patrolling the town, there were more fires on the night of January 25, 1871. Many armed Klansmen arrived in the town and conflict was only averted when the black militia withdrew from the streets.[28] In each of these cases, as in *The Birth of a Nation*, Klansmen were summoned by courier from neighboring counties. Also, however, in each case the black militia—when confronted with the possibility of the kind of armed conflict shown in the film—preferred to back down instead of continuing organized resistance.

The Birth of a Nation not only idealized the Klan of the Reconstruction period, it inadvertently prepared the ground for the reemergence of the Klan in the early twentieth century. Not only did it romanticize the violent Klan of former times, but it helped refound an organization that—detached from the context of the Civil War era—even Thomas Dixon perceived as thoroughly evil.[29]

The role of *The Birth of a Nation* in the revived Klan

The new Klan came into existence as the result of a series of factors and events. On April 27, 1915, 14-year-old Mary Phagan was found raped and murdered in the basement of the building where she worked in Marietta, Georgia. Her employer, Leo M. Frank, was tried and convicted for the murder. Sentenced to death on the basis of evidence that was both slender and confused, the life of Frank, a Jew originally from New York, was temporarily spared when the governor commuted his sentence to one of life imprisonment. Tom Watson, a prominent Georgia politician, whose early dalliance during the Populist revolt of the 1890s with the notion of cooperating with African Americans had hardened over time into a virulent hatred of blacks, Catholics, and Jews, exhorted his fellow-Georgians to redress this injustice. On August 16, 1915, responding to Watson's call, a team of 25 men abducted Frank from the prison farm where he was incarcerated and hanged him. Precisely two months later, some of the members of this lynch party—who referred to themselves as the Knights of Mary Phagan—climbed Stone Mountain, 18 miles from Atlanta, and burned a huge cross that was "visible throughout the city." A few weeks earlier, Watson, applauding the lynching itself, had suggested in one of the periodicals he published that "another Ku Klux Klan" be organized "to restore HOME RULE."[30]

It was not Watson, however, but another Southerner—William J. Simmons—who effectively relaunched the Klan in 1915. Born in central Alabama in 1880, Simmons was too young to have personal memories of the original Klan. His father, however, had been a member in the 1860s and he himself grew up—as he would later confess—"fascinated by Klan stories." Seeking adventure on his own account, Simmons volunteered to fight as a private in the Spanish-American War. Once the war was over, he became a Methodist circuit-rider in the backwoods of Florida and Alabama. Simmons was not a very good minister, outraged many Methodists by his fondness for whiskey, and sank deeper and deeper into debt. In 1912, he was suspended for inefficiency by the annual conference of his church. For a time, he wandered from job to job, before finally finding his niche as an organizer for a fraternal order, the Woodmen of the World. In 1914, he moved to Atlanta as district manager. Early in 1915, he was injured by an automobile and spent three months in bed. During this time, he began to dream obsessively of founding a fraternal order of his own, based on the model of the Ku Klux Klan of Reconstruction days.[31]

The manner in which Georgians reacted to the Frank lynching convinced "Colonel" Simmons (his honorary rank in the Woodmen) that reestablishing the Klan was a timely idea. Gathering together 34 men, including some drawn from the Knights of Mary Phagan and two who had ridden as Klansmen during the Reconstruction era, he applied on October 26, 1915 to the State of Georgia for a charter for the Knights of the Ku Klux Klan as a fraternal order. A month later, on Thanksgiving Day, Simmons told his charter members that he planned to revive "the ancient glories" of the Klan by lighting another fiery cross on Stone Mountain. Since it was a cold night, only 15 of the original 34 agreed to go with him to the mountain in the sightseeing bus he had chartered. On arrival, Simmons filled his canteen from a spring of sparkling water (making "a few remarks on purity and honor" in the process). He and his colleagues then gathered together some boulders to make a rough altar, and covered it with an old American flag, laying a Bible on top of the flag. Simmons lighted the cross with a match and, while it burned, administered the oath of membership. "And thus," he would later assert, "on the mountain top that night at the midnight hour . . . bathed in the sacred glow of the fiery cross, the Invisible Empire was called from its slumber of half a century to take up a new task and fulfil a new mission for humanity's good."[32]

Simmons was well aware at the time of his improvized ceremony of the existence of *The Birth of a Nation*. Premièred on the west coast on February 8, 1915 at Clune's Auditorium in Los Angeles and on March 3 on the east coast at the Liberty Theater, New York, the film had prompted wonder (and a good deal of criticism) in most places where it had played. By the start of December 1915, it had already been shown very successfully in several Southern cities and its first showing in Atlanta was due. Simmons realized that here was an opportunity too great to be missed to publicize his new organization, which finally received its charter from the state of Georgia on December 4. Consequently, the same edition of the *Atlanta Constitution* that announced the opening of *The Birth of a Nation* in Atlanta on December 6, 1915 also carried an advertisement of the Klan's rebirth as a "HIGH CLASS ORDER FOR MEN OF INTELLIGENCE AND CHARACTER." The actual première itself was preceded by a parade in which Simmons and his first recruits rode down Peachtree Street wearing bedsheets and fired rifle salutes in front of the large queues of people waiting to enter the Atlanta Theater. It was, as Wyn Craig Wade has commented, "an enormously effective stunt."[33]

As both film and Klan subsequently spread across the South, they became locked in a marriage of publicity-oriented convenience. Ushers in some states alternated between wearing Confederate uniforms and the sheets of the Klan. In many towns, Klansmen rode through the streets in full regalia in advance of screenings of the film.[34] Moreover, by the early 1920s, as the Klan spread beyond its base in the South— where, as David Chalmers commented, "Georgia was its citadel and Atlanta its holy city"—it continued to exploit *The Birth of a Nation* as part of its recruitment drive. In February 1922, the film was screened at two New York theaters—helping, according to critics, the local Klan in its campaign to increase membership. Two years later, the Ulysses S. Grant Klan of Chicago, Illinois, showed the film successfully over two weeks at the Auditorium Theater.[35] By 1925, when 40,000 masked Klansmen paraded in Washington, DC, the Klan itself was strong in many states of the North and West, including Maine, Massachusetts, Rhode Island, New York, New Jersey, Pennsylvania, Ohio, Indiana, Illinois, Wisconsin, Kansas, Oklahoma, Colorado, California, and Oregon. The new Klan, at least outside the South, was no longer simply anti-black. Reflecting changing social circumstances, it was critical of Catholics, Jews, Orientals, and recent immigrants—in fact, all who were considered to challenge traditional American social hierarchies and values—as well. Besides giving the new Klan an idealized view of its predecessor and important propaganda symbols (the figure of a Klansman on a rearing horse holding a fiery cross, copied from the movie's publicity stills, became the principal insignia of the order), Griffith's film may also have appealed to Klan recruits for its clear endorsement of white supremacy and intense hostility to interracial relationships ("mongrelization").[36]

Despite the use by the Klan of *The Birth of a Nation* as a means of attracting and keeping its members—something that continued at least until the end of the 1970s—it is difficult to estimate the precise influence of the film on the expansion of the order in the early years after its reemergence in 1915.[37] Certainly, as a contributor to the *Confederate Veteran* observed in April 1916, the film had "done more in a few months' time to arouse interest" in the original Klan "than all the articles written on the subject during the last forty years." "No one who has seen the film," declared journalist Walter Lippmann in 1922, "will ever hear the [Klan's] name again without seeing those white horsemen." Asked in 1928 whether the Klan would have grown as quickly without the film, "Colonel" Simmons himself answered "no . . . *The Birth of a Nation* helped the Klan tremendously."[38] On the other hand, the really rapid growth of the Klan did *not* occur in its early years, when *The Birth of a Nation* was at the peak of its influence and availability. By 1919, the organization had no more than a few thousand members. It was only in the summer of 1920, with the hiring of publicity agents Edward Young Clarke and Mrs Elizabeth Tyler, that the real expansion of the Klan began. By the summer of 1921, it had around 100,000 members. By the middle years of the 1920s, it may—according to Nancy Maclean—have reached a peak of five million members spread across the nation in almost 4,000 local chapters.[39]

Thereafter, the Klan started to decline in numbers. There was a popular revulsion against the violence with which it had become associated. In order to advance its agenda, in many states the Klan had become involved in politics and began to be torn apart by factionalism and disputes over patronage. There were also a number of scandals, perhaps the worst being the 1925 conviction of the leader of the Indiana Klan, David C. Stephenson, for the murder of a secretary.[40] *The Mating Call*, a Paramount film of 1928, reflected the Klan's declining reputation. "A mechanical sub-plot," observed *Variety*, "deals with a klan leader who drives a girl to suicide and then turns suspicion upon the hero." It was not simply the narrative of the film that was at fault: the same reviewer noted that the "subject of the K. K. K. is pretty blah for dramatic purposes at this late date, anyhow."[41] As David M. Chalmers remarks, "by the beginning of the great Depression, the Klan's power and glory were almost gone."[42] The Depression itself further undermined its efforts at recruitment. As the Memphis *Commercial-Appeal* correctly observed, "Not many persons have $10 to throw away on an oversized nightshirt." There were signs, moreover, that the film with which the Klan was most closely associated was very definitely starting to look its age. In December 1930, *The Birth of a Nation* was reissued in a shorter version with a new soundtrack. Audiences, according to the *New York Times*, liked the action sequences but laughed openly at the film's archaic sentiments. "Today," claimed the *Outlook* magazine, "it carries but little of its old punch."[43]

1930s films critical of the Klan

Although *The Birth of a Nation* was not the last pro-Klan film to be made—Maxim Simcovitch cites the approval expressed for a movie called *While Brave Men Die* in a Klan magazine[44]—it was certainly the most profitable and influential. From the 1930s onward, films dealing with the Klan and Klan-like activities tended to criticize their underhand and repressive nature. Mob violence seemed a real threat in Depression-era America, and Hollywood responded with a cycle of anti-lynching films, including *Fury* (1936) and *They Won't Forget*

(1937). The same period also saw two films that adopted a hostile
attitude toward the violence of a xenophobic, Klan-like organization
in the Middle West in the 1930s: *Legion of Terror* (1936) and *Black
Legion* (1937). *Black Legion* drew its name from the black robes worn
by members. It was founded in Ohio in the mid-1920s by men trying to
revive the local Klan, but soon turned into an organization in its own
right. Many of its members were white workers drawn from the South
to work in the auto industry. Its main focus was Detroit, where it was
anti-union and anti-communist, as well as sharing the Klan's dislike
of blacks, Jews, and Catholics. The Black Legion was very violent,
bombing union headquarters and the homes of strikers. When members
of the organization murdered Charles Poole, an organizer for the New
Deal's Works Progress Administration in May 1936, the ensuing trial
(and the sentencing of 11 of those responsible to life imprisonment)
effectively broke the power of the Legion.[45]

Reviewers saw both *Legion of Terror* and *Black Legion* as thinly veiled
accounts of what had actually happened. "The grip of the organization
on the life of the mythical city of the film and the nocturnal antics of its
hooded votaries," declared one critic of *Legion of Terror*, "are accurately
copied from newspaper reports." "Beneath its fictional veneer," asserted
Walter S. Nugent in the *New York Times*, *Black Legion* "is the quasi-
documentary record of the growth and activities of the hooded organization
that terrorized the Midwest in 1935–36, cloaking its cowardice, bigotry,
selfishness, stupidity and brutality under the mantle of '100 per cent
Americanism.'" At the core of *Black Legion* was the story of how "homes
were burned and shops destroyed and men flogged and lynched" by
members of a Klan-like organization. It also dramatized the murder of
Charles Poole by a character named "Frank Taylor" (Humphrey Bogart),
a man corrupted and destroyed by the seductive rhetoric of the Legion.
Taylor, Nugent wrote, was

> A typical American workman, proud of his wife and son, planning to
> buy a new car, hoping to be promoted to the foreman's job–and then,
> losing the promotion to a "foreigner," ripe for stupid blatherings about
> "Americanism," joining the legion, sharing in its outrages, brutalized,
> finally a killer.[46]

While the events related in the two films were already in the past at the
time of their release, it can be argued that the production of both Columbia's
Legion of Terror and Warner Bros.' *Black Legion* marked a significant step
in the evolution of Hollywood's attitude toward secret orders such as the
Klan. The two films suggested that such orders achieved success only by
duping and misleading their members. As the *Variety* critic wrote of *Legion
of Terror*, the whole film was "a warning against being a sucker for schemes
of the K. K. K. ilk."[47]

Postwar films and the Klan

In the aftermath of the Second World War, as social tensions rose in American society and the Klan itself began to revive,[48] a number of films appeared that mounted a direct attack on the Klan itself. Jacques Tourneur's *Stars in My Crown* (1950) challenged the historical presentation of the Klan in *The Birth of a Nation* as an organization that had saved the South from the depredations of black rule. In Tourneur's film, Josiah Gray (Joel McCrea), a tough Tennessee parson, prevents the Klan from lynching an elderly black man (Juano Hernandez) whose land they want to steal soon after the end of the Civil War. As part of its cycle of late 1940s "problem" films, moreover, Hollywood also indicted the modern-day Klan. The exposé of the Klan in *The Burning Cross* (1947), noted a contemporary reviewer, was "probably inspired by recent reports that the Klan was on the move again in various sections of the country."[49] Other critics praised the fact that Screen Guild, the independent producers, had made the film after a number of major studios had considered and rejected the idea of a Klan picture.[50] "With the recent Klan outbreaks in the South still fresh in the minds of the public," noted *Variety*, "the film should do okay." At the same time, most critics thought the film poorly made. Following the story of a demoralized ex-GI who is convinced by Klan propaganda of the need to keep "America a place for Americans," and dealing with Klan efforts to keep blacks from voting and the murder of a black veteran, it relied very heavily on what the *New York Times* reviewer termed "manifestations of barbaric physical violence, tarring and feathering of victims, both white and Negro, and other acts of unconscionable sadism and vandalism" to put across its point. Yet while exposing the "bigotry and brutality" of the Klan, the same writer continued, it could not be seen as offering "a thoughtful and literate contemplation of the insidious anti-social and religious philosophy that is propagated in defiance of guaranteed constitutional liberties by the hooded, bullying Klansmen."[51]

The fact that *Storm Warning*, Hollywood's next anti-Klan film, was made at all—in 1950 at the height of the Cold War and the anti-communist witchhunt at home—observed a critic in the *Motion Picture Herald*, "must be considered a real tribute not only to the people who made it, but also to the country in which it could be made."[52] Such complacent self-congratulation from the movie industry's main trade paper was wide of the mark. The era of "social consciousness movies," as discussed in Chapter Eight, was about to come to an end. As Bosley Crowther pointed out in the *New York Times*, Warner Bros., the studio that produced the film, had in the past shown "a passion for social crusading," as demonstrated earlier in *Black Legion* and *They Won't Forget*. But Crowther thought that passion reemerged only "fitfully" in *Storm Warning*. The story revolved around the arrival of Marsha Mitchell (Ginger Rogers) in a Southern town. Mitchell inadvertently witnesses the murder of an "outside" reporter by the Klan. She is pressured into remaining silent until, changing her mind, she helps a fearless young prosecutor (Ronald Reagan) crack the case and defeat the Klan. "As a bulletin forecast of possible pressures by unprincipled groups in our widespread land," Crowther wrote, in a fairly unsubtle reference to McCarthyism, *Storm Warning* "may have some shocking impact, but it doesn't go into the more dramatic 'hows' and 'whys.'"[53] Although no critic pointed this out, *Storm Warning* had another major deficiency: it downplayed the racism of the Klan by having no major black characters at all.

The civil rights era and after

As the civil rights movement began to take off in the 1950s and early 1960s, the Ku Klux Klan—with its dedication to white supremacy and violent methods—found itself once more as popular among many Southern whites as it had been in the late 1860s and early 1920s.[54] Hollywood, which found it hard to deal with the civil rights movement, found it even harder to deal with Klan opposition to it. There were brief mentions in *The F.B.I. Story* (1959) and *The Cardinal* (1963)—the latter dealing anachronistically with Catholics defending racial integration from Klan hostility in 1930s Georgia. There was also *The Black Klansman* (1966), an independent production, which according to *Variety* was "patently aimed at cashing in on present Ku Klux Klan activities in the South and [the] civil rights agitation which is sweeping the country."[55] The film focused on a light-colored African American who, while he is in Los Angeles, learns that his daughter has been killed by a Klan bombing of a church in Alabama. In order to find the killer, he returns to Alabama and joins the Klan. The movie was not very successful. Such rare examples apart, the Klan was largely ignored by American filmmakers until the civil rights era was over.

Paramount's *The Klansman* (1974) returned retrospectively to the theme of racial violence by the Klan in a small Alabama town at the time of the civil rights agitation. Vincent Canby, writing in the *New York Times*, declared that "the events that bring about the final bloody shoot-out (an accumulation of rapes and murders and an invasion by Northern liberals who want to aid a voter registration drive) are not without a certain relation to recent history." Yet Canby also believed "the subject . . . should have been much better served." Alexander Stuart, in *Films and Filming*, agreed, arguing that the movie "shows no real concern for its subject. It sensationalises the violence of the Klan and the xenophobia it represents without examining the roots of the problem." The anonymous reviewer for *Variety* went much further, arguing that "there's not a shred of quality, dignity, relevance or impact in this yahoo-oriented bunk." "The only social impact of the film," the same critic insisted, "is likely to occur in those situations where audiences make known their displeasure to management." So bad was the film ("substandard in most all creative areas") that this writer even fantasized about "racially-integrated displays of unanimous disapproval."[56]

Since the 1970s, there have been sequences about the Klan in a number of films. In *Places in the Heart* (1984), Robert Benton showed the Klan active in the small-town of Waxahachie, Texas, in 1935. *Forrest Gump* (1994) simulated footage of some of the scenes originally shown in *The Birth of a Nation*. There has been a growing tendency to present the Klan as a floating signifier of racial prejudice, anachronistically present in periods when the real Klan was absent or inactive. Thus, *A Time to Kill* (1996) had a racially controversial murder case reviving a defunct local Klan and "making modern Canton [Mississippi] look like the South in pre-civil rights days."[57] *Posse* (1993) had black cowboys fighting Klansmen at the time of the Spanish-American War of 1898 and *Django Unchained* (2012) has a hilarious sequence in which, two years before the Civil War, proto-Klansmen complain about the size of the eye-holes in their white costumes. Klansmen were also parodied in *Blazing Saddles* (1974), a spoof Western by Mel Brooks, and the Coen brothers' *O Brother, Where Art Thou?* (2000). The phrase used by the black sheriff (Cleavon Little) to provoke the Klansmen in *Blazing Saddles* ("Where are the white women?") recalls the justification for the Klan's existence originally advanced in *The Birth of a Nation*. *O Brother, Where Art Thou?* treats the Klan of the 1930s as a joke by using one of their rallies as the basis for a musical number with Busby Berkeley-type features.

Throughout the twentieth century, we can trace the growing disapproval of the Klan on the part of movie producers and critics. Such disapproval, however, usually manifested itself *after* the periods in which the Klan itself was at its strongest: the first part of the 1920s and the two decades after the Second World War. There were exceptions to this: MGM and Warner Brothers both produced films attacking the contemporary Klan in 1949–50. But most films about the Klan were looking back on the Klan from a post-Klan era. They recognized that the Klan was, in a very literal sense, history.

Mississippi Burning (1988) was one such film. Based on a real case, the murder of three civil rights workers by the Klan in Mississippi during the "Freedom Summer" of 1964, it showed the FBI "breaking" the case—though not in the manner in which it really happened—and successfully prosecuting those involved. There were many historical inaccuracies in the film (see Chapter Ten). But its reception appeared to underline the fact that the Klan had once again, as in the 1870s and late 1920s, effectively been marginalized. John Slavin watched the film early in 1989 in a small Southern town. Most of the audience was made up of youngsters of both races who had been born since 1964. These young people, Slavin noted, were "products of the desegregated South" who "found the hatred and violence of the film not so much upsetting as unbelievable." As Slavin pointed out, 1989 was also the year in which David Duke—"avowed Klansman and white supremacist"—was elected to the state legislature in Louisiana. But the response of the young people to *Mississippi Burning* observed by Slavin emphasized the difference a quarter of a century had made: Klansmen such as Duke were no longer part of the mainstream of Southern politics.[58]

While there may continue to be films about the Klan, it is more probable that they will also deal with the past rather than the present. The Klan still exists, but its numbers are reduced to a few thousand, organized into chapters that seem more and more disconnected. It is also facing competition from many other right-wing organizations, including the sort of white supremacist groups depicted in *American History X* (1998). As Brian Palmer points out in a recent article in *Slate* magazine, many of the members of such organizations communicate with each other primarily via the internet. The refounded Klan of the 1910s and 1920s was effective at deploying new technology—the movie *The Birth of a Nation*—to help it recruit and retain members. Its modern successor has failed to do the same using the web and social media.[59]

Filmography

The Northern Schoolteacher (Kalem, 1909).
The Rose of Kentucky (dir. D. W. Griffith; Biograph, 1911).
The Birth of a Nation (dir. D. W. Griffith; Epoch, 1915).
Fury (dir. Fritz Lang; MGM, 1936).
Legion of Terror (dir. Charles C. Coleman; Columbia, 1936).
Black Legion (dir. Archie Mayo; Warner Bros., 1937).
They Won't Forget (dir. Mervyn LeRoy; Warner Bros., 1937).
Gone With the Wind (dir. Victor Fleming; Selznick International/MGM, 1939).
The Burning Cross (dir. Walter Colmes; Somerset-Screen Guild, 1947).
Stars in My Crown (dir. Jacques Tourneur; MGM, 1950).
Storm Warning (dir. Stuart Heisler; Warner Bros., 1950).
The F.B.I. Story (dir. Mervyn LeRoy; Warner Bros., 1959).
The Cardinal (dir. Otto Preminger; Otto Preminger/Columbia, 1963).
The Black Klansman (dir. Ted V. Mikels; SGS Productions, 1966).
The Klansman (dir. Terence Young; Atlanta/Paramount, 1974).
Blazing Saddles (dir. Mel Brooks; Warner Bros., 1974).
Places in the Heart (dir. Robert Benton; Delphi II/Tristar, 1984).
Mississippi Burning (dir. Alan Parker; Orion, 1988).
Posse (dir. Mario van Peebles; Polygram/Working Title, 1993).

Forrest Gump (dir. Robert Zemeckis; Paramount, 1994).
A Time to Kill (dir. Joel Schumacher; Regency/Warner Bros., 1996).
American History X (dir. Tony Kaye; NewLine Cinema/Savoy/Turman-
   Morrissey, 1998).
O Brother, Where Art Thou? (dir. Joel Coen; Touchstone/Universal/StudioCanal,
   2000).
Django Unchained (dir. Quentin Tarantino; Weinstein Company/Columbia,
   2012).

CHAPTER SIX

The Good Indian: *Dances With Wolves*

Dances With Wolves (1990), directed by and starring Kevin Costner, was released two years before the five-hundreth anniversary of Columbus' arrival in the Americas. It helped direct attention to the treatment of Native Americans by Americans of European descent. The film, based on Michael Blake's 1988 novel, told the story of John Dunbar (Costner), a lieutenant in the Union army during the Civil War, who is wounded in battle. Instead of having his leg amputated, he prefers to try to commit suicide by riding a horse close to the Confederate lines. Members of the Union army attack the distracted Confederates and Dunbar becomes an accidental hero, offered whichever post in the army he prefers. He chooses the West and ends up alone at Fort Sedgwick on the frontier. His only companion at first is his horse Cisco, although he later makes friends with a wolf he christens Two Socks. Soon, however, he encounters Indians in the form of Lakota Sioux and, over the course of time, begins to find ways of communicating with them and discovers they are nothing like his cultural preconceptions of what Native Americans are like.[1] Ultimately, he is so impressed by their values and way of life that he is reborn as "Dances With Wolves," a member of the Lakota tribe.

When Dunbar first meets Major Fambrough (Maury Chaykin), the mad officer who sends him to Fort Sedgwick, he explains why he has chosen to be posted to the West: "I've always wanted to see the frontier—before it's gone." For Dunbar, the frontier is a *place* or *location*—an area of unspoilt natural wilderness that would soon disappear beneath an advancing tide of white settlement. Yet when Dunbar arrived in the West in 1863, almost no one expected the frontier to disappear as fast as it did (in 1890, the US Census Bureau announced that there was no longer a continuous line of unsettled land in the West, and the frontier was now closed). As shrewd an observer as Abraham Lincoln thought it would take a century to settle the half-continent between the thin line of settlement existing west of the Mississippi and the Pacific Coast. One of the great population movements of history, aided by the growth of railroads (five transcontinental networks had been built by the early 1890s), proved him wrong. Dunbar seems instinctively to understand how vast this movement will be (he later explains to the Indians in a powerful piece of imagery for a people living close to nature that the influx will be "like the stars"). Yet at no stage of the film do we see a single white settler.

Richard White has suggested that popular understanding of the frontier since the 1890s has revolved around two very different interpretations. The first was that of historian Frederick Jackson Turner, who saw it as the settlement of free land that accounted for America's unique development as a nation. To Turner, the process was fairly peaceful, though he did note that "the United States Army fought a series of Indian wars in Minnesota, Dakota, and the Indian Territory."[2] The second interpretation was that associated with army scout, professional hunter, and later showman William F. (Buffalo Bill) Cody, which emphasized the endemic violence of frontier development.[3] *Dances With Wolves* is closer to Cody than Turner, but in focusing on the relationship between microcosms of the US Army (Dunbar) and the Plains Indians (a band of Lakota Sioux), it offers a glimpse of the road not taken: the development of friendship and understanding between whites and Native Americans.

At the heart of the film are two narratives of discovery. One is Dunbar's own voyage of self-discovery, the second the discovery of "real" Lakota as opposed to white assumptions about them. Both are deeply intertwined. We never learn anything of Dunbar's past: where he comes from, who his parents are, how he has been educated, why he finds himself on a battlefield at "St. David's Field, Tennessee" in 1863. All we can know is that he is literate and has some talent as an artist (both demonstrated in the journal he keeps) and that he has been brought up as a Christian ("Forgive me, father" he murmurs, starting his suicidal ride, at the climax of which he releases the reins and raises his arms in imitation of Christ on the cross). Dunbar has a strong sense of duty, or at least loyalty to the army, that keeps him going in the early, solitary days at Fort Sedgwick. But he has little understanding of his own psyche ("I'd never really known who John Dunbar was," he later confesses) and is in most respects a *tabula rasa* on his arrival in the West. Journeying with Timmons (Robert Pastorelli) and his mule-train to Fort Sedgwick, he seems most interested in natural phenomena—he sketches a shooting star across a clear night sky. But the presence of Indians somewhere in the background begins to emerge as a motif of the film. Major Fambrough has asked him if he is "an Indian-fighter" and told him the journey to Fort Sedgwick will cover "many miles of wild and hostile country." On the prairie, he sees the skeleton of a man killed by an arrow, and looks curiously at the arrow. He asks

Timmons why they have seen no Indians and is rewarded with a racist outburst ("You'd better not see them unless the bastards are dead. Nothing but thieves and beggars"). But Dunbar sees nothing foolish in remaining on his own in the abandoned fort. It is only after seeing his first Indian, Kicking Bird (Graham Greene), that he begins to make preparations for defending his post.

The first contacts between Dunbar and the Indians seem to live up to Timmons' description—they *are* "thieves," unsuccessfully attempting to steal his horse.[4] But both sides are curious about the other and, despite language difficulties, begin to try to communicate (Figure 6.1).

Gifts are exchanged and Dunbar is invited to the Lakota camp. He finds, in the Lakota community, a rich culture and shared lifestyle he has never known before. He particularly admires the intelligence of Kicking Bird, who works hard to promote understanding between them ("You were the first man I ever wanted to be like," he confesses near the end of the movie). His journal becomes increasingly anthropological, focusing on Indian habits and clothes. Two huge leaps forward in his relations with the Indians come when Dunbar rides to tell the Sioux that buffalo have arrived and Kicking Bird persuades his adopted daughter Stands With a Fist (Mary McDonnell), whose original white family have been massacred by Pawnee, to act as translator. After participating in the buffalo hunt, Dunbar becomes something of a celebrity. Yet he is still a friend to the Lakota rather than a member of the tribe. In the last hour of the film, two violent confrontations change this.

While the warriors of the tribe are away chasing the Pawnee, those remaining at the Lakota camp hear that a Pawnee raiding party is about

FIGURE 6.1 *John Dunbar (Kevin Costner) invites his Lakota neighbors for coffee in* Dances With Wolves.

to attack. Dunbar rushes to Fort Sedgwick and digs up the guns he has hidden there. He then leads a motley army of elders, women (including Stands With a Fist, who shoots a Pawnee brave), and children against the Pawnee and drives them away. At the start of his journey to Fort Sedgwick, Major Fambrough addressed him as "Sir Knight." Dunbar has now truly become a knight-errant, fighting to protect women and children, as well as the food stores to see the Lakota through the winter. "I felt a pride I'd never known before," his voice-over confesses, and "as I heard my Sioux name [Dances With Wolves] being called over and over I knew for the first time who I really was." Dunbar's new sense of identity is further confirmed by the second confrontation. Returning, in Indian dress, to Fort Sedgwick for a final time to retrieve his journal, he is captured and beaten up by members of the US Army. He refuses to lead them to "the hostiles" ("there are no hostiles") and, when the questioning continues, speaks only in Lakota ("I am Dances With Wolves. I have nothing to say to you. You are not worth talking to"). When Dunbar is sent back east to be tried for treason, he is rescued by a Sioux war party and his army escort killed. He is now completely culturally assimilated as a member of the tribe: Chief Ten Bears (Floyd Red Crow Westerman) tells him that "the man the soldiers are looking for no longer exists. Now there is only a Sioux named Dances With Wolves." But Dunbar knows that the army will not stop pursuing him and, to protect the tribe, decides to leave to carve out a new role for himself as someone "who will speak to anyone that listens" on the Indians' behalf.

Dances With Wolves: A revisionist Western?

In the 1970s and 1980s, there were many challenges to the Western as a genre and the flood of Hollywood Westerns, especially during the 1940s and 1950s, died away to a trickle. *Dances With Wolves* was a huge commercial success, taking in $184,208,848 at the US box office and $240,000,000 in the rest of the world.[5] It had 12 Academy Award nominations and won seven Oscars in all: for Costner's direction, Dean Semler's cinematography, John Barry's lush romantic music, film editing, sound, writing (Michael Blake), and best picture.[6] The first Western to win the "best picture" award since *Cimarron* in 1931, it helped breathe new life into the genre. Several critics praised it for its revisionist approach to the Western. Stephen Tatum saw it as "a revisionist critique of the conquest mentality and its destructive consequences."[7] The *Motion Picture Guide Annual* similarly hailed it as a "revisionist western" and added that "the Sioux gave the film their own rave review by admitting Costner as a full tribal member."[8] But Alexandra Keller was much less certain. "By 1990," she declared, "it was hardly a radical revision to the Western to suggest that Anglos did horrible things to Native American nations who did nothing to provoke them." To Keller, the film may have been "revisionist in content," but it was nostalgic in form because it offered a "traditionally historiographic" approach, allowing a white man renamed by the Sioux "to speak in place of them while seeming to speak for and even with them."[9]

To understand the degree to which *Dances With Wolves* was or was not revisionist means seeing it in the context of earlier Westerns. Seventeen years before its release, on March 27, 1973, Marlon Brando sent Sacheen Littlefeather, an Apache Indian and President of the National Native American Affirmative Image Committee, to the Academy Awards ceremony to turn down the "best actor" Oscar he had won for his role in *The Godfather* (1972).[10] Brando did so, Littlefeather explained, because of "the treatment of American Indians today by the film industry and on television in movie reruns and also with recent happenings at Wounded Knee" (where a group of Indian activists occupying the town in protest over a long list of grievances were involved in an at-times violent 71-day standoff with Federal marshals and the National Guard).[11] Brando's point about television reruns was a good one. A high proportion of the Westerns made up to the 1950s, whether by small specialist studios such as Republic and Monogram or the larger studios, showed Indians as hostile savages attacking the whites. "Probably the most indelible image in all Western cinema," writes Kim Newman,

> is the big action sequence in [John Ford's] *Stagecoach* (1939) . . . Geronimo's renegade Apaches pursue the stagecoach across Monument Valley, firing at everything but the horses. John Wayne proves his heroism . . . but just when it looks as if even the Duke's formidable presence will not be enough to avert a massacre, and gambler John Carradine is saving his last bullet for young mother Louise Platt, the 7th cavalry appear, bugles blaring, and charge to the rescue, routing the Apaches.[12]

In the many sequences of this kind, the Indians are represented as motiveless and insanely violent. They are merely the backcloth to the inevitable white settlement of the West. The fact that there were already Native Americans present in the West received short shrift historically from advocates of "Manifest Destiny," the right of white Americans to occupy the entire continent. They were an inconvenient reality, to be moved out of the way of the tide of white settlement and corralled on reservations. The background to *Stagecoach* was the escape of Geronimo from a New Mexico reservation in 1881 and the subsequent five years in which he led a band of Apache on raids. There is no suggestion in *Stagecoach* that Geronimo and his warriors might have had legitimate grievances against the US Government for breaking agreements and forcing them to live in restricted circumstances. As in many other films, they are presented only as hostile savages. They are also potential rapists: when Hatfield (John Carradine) attempts to kill Lucy Mallory (Louise Platt) to save her from the sexual depredations of the Apache, he is following the filmmaking tradition of saving the "last bullet" for the white woman that goes back at least as far as David W. Griffith's *The Battle at Elderbush Gulch* (1913). Since the Indians are a faceless mass, with no individuality or apparent culture of their own, there is no apparent explanation for the violence of their assaults on whites.

While Griffith also made a number of films that were, in Newman's phrase, "reasonably sympathetic" to Indians[13] and there were a number of noble, self-sacrificing Native Americans on screen, including Naturich in three versions of *The Squaw Man* (1914, 1918, 1931) and Nophaie in *The Vanishing American* (1925), there were very few films that could truly be characterized as pro-Indian before *Broken Arrow* (1950). Four decades before *Dances With Wolves*, *Broken Arrow* showed Tom Jeffords (James Stewart) discovering that Apaches were human in their emotions, with their own culture and values. The film, based on Elliott Arnold's novel *Blood Brothers* (1947), was set in Arizona in the early 1870s. The Apaches, who have complied with the treaties they signed with the Federal government, are fighting against white settlers encroaching on their land. Jeffords, a former officer in the Union Army, becomes a mediator between the army and the Indian chief, Cochise (Jeffrey Hunter). In the course of negotiations, he falls in love with and later marries an Indian girl, Sonseeahray (Debra Paget). But Jeffords and Cochise are ambushed by a group of whites who reject the idea of a ceasefire and, attempting to defend her husband, Sonseeahray is killed. Jeffords wants revenge but, in the cause of peace and racial understanding, is finally persuaded out of this by Cochise.

Broken Arrow introduced major changes in how Indians were represented on film. Most Native Americans in talking Westerns up to this point had been inarticulate or had said very little. Cochise is a persuasive speaker. He does not conform to the stereotype of the violent, aggressive Indian: he is a firm advocate of peace and racial reconciliation. The Apaches themselves are the injured party: they have obeyed the law but their rights have been infringed and their land invaded. It is unscrupulous whites, out to make profit and disregarding the treaties that have been agreed, who this time function as the aggressors. But, in common with the whites, the Indians are divided into "good" and "bad" elements: the "good" or pacific Cochise and the "bad" Geronimo, who tries to sabotage peace. The film shows Jeffords being educated out of his initial distrust and dislike of Indians. It demonstrates, above all, that the Apache are human. The men have a sense of fair play and the women worry about their children. They have family lives and courtship rituals (Sonseeahray explains that as an unmarried girl, she must not speak to any man, but that there can be "meetings by accident"). *Broken Arrow* still has limitations in its presentation of Indians. Cochise, the principal Native American character, is played by a white actor. The Indians only speak English. The treatment of the interracial marriage of Jeffords and Sonseeahray is very conservative: Sonseeahray's death means the film never has to address the issue of mixed-race children or how the family will be accepted by white society. But the film as a whole was a major departure in how Indians were depicted on screen.

In the aftermath of *Broken Arrow*, there was an important cycle of films presenting Indians in positive ways: *Devil's Doorway* (1950), *The Savage* (1952), *Hondo* (1953), *The Indian Fighter* (1955), *War Drums* (1957), and many more. Others (*Apache* (1954); *Run of the Arrow* (1957)) showed Native Americans as cynically realistic, even at times with a sense of humor. While this cycle had spent itself by the 1960s, most new Westerns now displayed at least some understanding of the life and motivations of Indians of the previous century. In 1964, John Ford released *Cheyenne Autumn*, an account of the desperate trek in 1878 of hundreds of Cheyenne from their reservation in the Indian territory (present-day Oklahoma) to their old hunting grounds in Wyoming Territory, a movie that was almost universally seen as Ford's apology for using Indians simply as the violent "other" in earlier films. In 1970, Dee Brown published *Bury My Heart at Wounded Knee*, a stunning and sustained analysis of how white men had mistreated the Indians.[14] The same year saw the release of several films with the same theme as the book. *Little Big Man* told the story of the conflict between whites and Indians by Jack Crabb (Dustin Hoffman), a white man raised by the Cheyenne, who had been present at the annihilation of Lieutenant-Colonel George A. Custer's 7th Cavalry by Indians at the Little Bighorn in 1876. *Soldier Blue* reproduced the Sand Creek Massacre of 1864, when 200 Cheyenne, mainly women and children, were killed by a force of Colorado militia. These and other Vietnam-era Westerns showed both life among the Indians and their victimization by whites in considerable detail. They and their predecessors made Brando's complaint about the way Indians were still being treated by American filmmakers in 1973 seem both out-of-date and out-of-touch.

Indians and their culture in *Dances With Wolves*

In the light of changes in the Western genre since the appearance of *Broken Arrow* in 1950, what did *Dances With Wolves* offer that was really new? All the major Indian parts in the film were played by Native American actors, a "first" for a mainstream Hollywood production. Around a third of the dialogue in the film was in Lakota Sioux, with English subtitles. The fact that Dunbar himself learns the language and speaks it added greatly to the film's sense of "authenticity." Lakota linguist Doris Leader Charge, comments Native American scholar Edward D. Castillo, "translated Michael Blake's screenplay into Lakota, coached the actors in the language, and played a small role in the film."[15] After the film's release, there was controversy when Indian activist and actor Russell Means suggested that Dunbar and some of the Indians had been speaking the female-gendered version of the language rather than the male. An expert on the Lakota Language Forum dismisses this idea and, despite some inaccuracies, defends the use of the Lakota tongue in the film as "an achievement which is nothing short of remarkable."[16] *Dances With Wolves* was not the first Western to use spoken Indian languages. *Little Big Man*, for example, began with Cheyenne, but quickly moved to English.[17] *Windwalker* (1981) used Cheyenne and Crow with English subtitles (Trevor Howard in the titular role as the old Cheyenne chief had his voice dubbed). However, *Dances With Wolves* used Lakota language in a dedicated and consistent way, introducing it for the first time to a mass audience.[18] The costumes worn by the Sioux—hailed by *Variety* as "striking combinations of paint, feathers and deerskin"—were based on drawings and paintings done in the 1830s by "Western" artists George Catlin and Karl Bodmer and, an overenthusiastic press release for the film claimed, had been made as accurately as possible "down to the last elk tooth decoration."[19]

In terms of the impact of the film on audiences, the attention to detail in terms of language and costume may have been less important than the general portrait of Lakota society and culture and the creation of characters who are likable and, above all, intensely human. "For the first time," declared Native American writer Marilou Awiakta, "a highly commercial film portrays Native Americans as individuals—intelligent, complex, humorous. *Civilized!*"[20] "They have a gentle humor I enjoy," Dunbar writes of the Sioux in his journal, "I've never seen a people so eager to laugh and so dedicated to family." Humor and family are tied together in the sequence in which Kicking Bird goes to bed, looks briefly uncomfortable, then tosses the child's doll he has been lying on across the tent. All families everywhere are the same, the scene suggests. Kicking Bird and his wife Black Shawl make love and talk together like any married couple, though Black Shawl notices changes in personal relationships much quicker than her husband. The camp is full of grandparents, parents, and children, some of who misbehave. It is an economic unit that works together: the men are warriors who hunt buffalo and defend the community; the women fetch water, prepare food, make clothes and tents, carry wood for fires, and do laundry. The film evokes very well the everyday life of the Sioux. Men meet together in the tent of Chief Ten Bears to smoke their pipes and discuss issues of importance to the tribe. In the oral culture of the Plains Indians, importance is given to storytelling (at the celebration after the buffalo hunt, Dunbar is made to recount his feats—including saving the life of Smiles a Lot (Nathan Lee Chasing His Horse)—over and over again). The camp is bound together by ceremonies (weddings, dances) and rituals (the rites attached to mourning). Yet audiences know, at the same time as they watch all these things, that they represent a form of society that will soon disappear forever, giving poignancy to the film's depiction of a doomed way of life.

The Indians and their community are made to seem even more attractive by virtue of the contrast between them and the film's whites. The judgment of the Union general (Donald Hotton) who interprets Dunbar's attempt at suicide as a heroic act is clearly flawed. Major Fambrough, the commander of Fort Hayes, who sends Dunbar to Fort Sedgwick before committing suicide, is deranged. Timmons, the wagon driver who takes Dunbar to his new post, is crude and vulgar (Dunbar describes him as "quite possibly the foulest man I've ever met").[21] In John Ford's *Stagecoach* and many other Westerns, the US cavalry are the heroes, rescuing vulnerable whites in the nick of time. In *Dances With Wolves*, what *Variety*'s critic called "this loutish and brutal mob" have changed places with the Indians: the army are now savages, the Indians civilized. The troops who have reoccupied Fort Sedgwick, argues Armando José Prats, "exist primarily to establish the pervasiveness of the racism that has so far been Timmons's alone."[22] Since Dunbar is wearing Indian costume, they try to shoot him on sight (but actually kill Cisco, his faithful horse). Dunbar is beaten up and imprisoned. The journal he has been keeping is stolen by Spivey (Tony Pierce), who is illiterate and uses it as toilet paper. When Spivey and his friends are detailed to escort Dunbar back to Fort Hays for trial as a traitor, they amuse themselves on the journey by shooting at and killing Two Socks, a wolf Dunbar has partly tamed. When Dunbar tries to stop them, he is beaten again. The only member of the army who tries to protect Dunbar from the brutality of the soldiers is Lieutenant Elgin (Charles Rocket). Ironically, when the Sioux massacre the escort detail and rescue Dunbar/ Dances With Wolves, Elgin is the first to die.

If whites are presented in *Dances With Wolves* in an even more disparaging way than in many earlier "pro-Indian" movies, some elements in Costner's film were by no means new. In the early twentieth century, artist Charles M. Russell published the story of a young boy who runs away from his family and is welcomed by Indians: his initiation rite, like Dunbar's, is a buffalo hunt after which, again like Dunbar, he is offered the raw liver of a dead buffalo to eat.[23] Thirty-three years before *Dances With Wolves* was released, *Run of the Arrow* (1957) had a Civil War veteran, former Confederate private O'Meara (Rod Steiger), travelling to the West to join the Sioux. The opposition between "good" and "bad" Indians had been a feature of *Broken Arrow* in 1950. *Dances With Wolves* changed it into an intertribal conflict between Lakota Sioux and Pawnees, with the Pawnees aggressively raiding the Lakota.[24] In reality, the history of the two tribes was often the opposite of this. In August 1873, ten years after the fictional events narrated in *Dances With* Wolves, a hunting party of Pawnees near the Republican River in Nebraska was attacked by a large war band of Lakotas and many of the Pawnees were killed. The Pawnees were worn down by contagious diseases and conflicts with the Sioux and Cheyenne: by the Census of 1910, there were less than 700 left.[25]

Dances With Wolves failed to delve very deeply into many aspects of Lakota life and culture. There is almost no reference to the tribe's religious beliefs and spiritual life. We only know that Kicking Bird is a holy man/shaman because Stands With a Fist tells us. We do not see him *do* anything apart from marry Dunbar/Dances With Wolves and Stands With a Fist. During the wedding, Dunbar's voice-over focuses on his love for Stands With a Fist, fading out completely the voice of Kicking Bird who is explaining the duties of a Sioux husband. There is a vague suggestion of belief in reincarnation (Wind in His Hair (Rodney A. Grant) confesses that he now thinks Dances With Wolves has come to replace Stands With a Fist's dead Sioux husband). There clearly are tribal rites for mourning the dead, but they are not really spelt out (although Stone Calf (Jimmy Herman) tells Dunbar it is "not polite to speak of the dead"). Stands With a Fist is very anxious that there is no gossip about her growing relationship with Dunbar until the mourning period for her Sioux husband is over. Apart from the seriousness with which it is conducted, we learn nothing about the pipe-smoking culture of the Sioux men. There are several dances in the Indian camp—one interrupted by Dunbar, another on the eve of the hunt, a third in celebration afterwards, a fourth after the victory over the Pawnee raiding party—but their social and cultural role is not defined. We see horses decorated for the hunt and men with painted faces but the significance of these things is never explained.[26]

There is also a suspicion in relation to *Dances With Wolves* that the Lakota it depicts are simply "generic" Indians, in the way John Ford, for example, used Native Americans from the Navajo reservation near Monument Valley to represent, as needed, Apache, Cheyenne, Comanche, Crow, Sioux, or Pawnee. Although the film used Indian actors for major roles, only Chief Ten Bears and Smiles a Lot were really Lakota. Kicking Bird was played by Graham Greene, an Oneida Indian born in Canada. His wife Black Shawl was also Canadian in origin: Cree/Chippewa actress Tantoo Cardinal. Rodney A. Grant, playing Sioux Warrior Wind in His Hair, was an Indian from the Omaha tribe.[27] Michael Blake's 1988 novel, on which the film was based, was set on the southern plains and the Indian tribe involved was Comanche. (Ten Bears was the name of a Comanche chief.[28]) The movie, however, was shot principally in South Dakota on the northern plains, to take advantage of the single surviving, 3,500-strong herd of buffalo.[29] Costner and Blake changed the identity of the Indians from Comanche to Sioux to fit better with the location. But the change introduced at least one major historical error. To explain why he is unconcerned about the impending arrival of white settlers, Ten Bears produces a Spanish conquistador's helmet and insists that "eventually we drove them out." The tribe had also seen off the Mexicans and the Texans. Yet the Lakota would not have encountered these three groups of invaders on the northern plains.[30]

The most sustained critique of what he saw as the movie's many inaccuracies was advanced by Wayne Michael Sarf, who would subsequently publish a book on the Little Bighorn campaign of 1876 that ended with the destruction of Lieutenant-Colonel George A. Custer's command by a combined force of Lakota Sioux and Cheyenne Indians.[31] According to Sarf, *Dances With Wolves* was "dishonest, cowardly, poorly written, historically ludicrous, and, worst of all, afflicted with a Southern Californian social conscience." The Plains Indians, he argued, were addicted to war, since war "provided the average male's only avenue to social status, and a warlike spirit was nurtured from early childhood." The Sioux had a long tradition of slaughtering other Indians and stealing their land. They had also been involved in the murder of many whites ("Dunbar seems too dumb to consider the possibility that an Indian might want to kill him"). In the light of what he saw as the Sioux's long record of violence against noncombatants (Sitting Bull "proudly recorded his killings of women in pictographs") and their use of rape (captured women "were routinely gang-raped before becoming the property of a single captor"), Sarf found Costner's presentation of them as peaceable, cultured, and family-oriented to be highly misleading. He also questioned the movie's attempts to present the Lakota as protective of the natural environment since, like other Plains Indians, they "overkilled game, slaughtered animals for furs (traded to whites for firearms and other goods), and killed a half-dozen eagles to make a war bonnet."[32]

The myth of the ecological Indian

Sarf's last point is particularly damaging since Indians have long been regarded in American culture as pioneers of ecology, a people living in a state of harmony with the natural environment. From the 1820s onwards, popular literature had emphasized the superior "skill in nature" of the Indians compared with whites, and their ability to survive while still respecting both land and resources. Toward the end of the nineteenth century, an Indian writer himself contributed greatly to this perception. Charles Eastman "contrasted Indians who kill animals because they need them with whites who kill them wantonly."[33] More recently, particularly with the growing concern for the environment in the 1960s and after,

Shepard Krech III argues, the "ecological Indian" became a much-used cultural symbol: someone living "in nature who understands the systemic consequences of his actions, feels deep sympathy with all living forms, and takes steps to conserve so that the earth's harmonies are never imbalanced and resources never in doubt."[34]

One image of this "ecological Indian" would become iconic to millions of Americans. To celebrate the first Earth Day on April 22, 1970, the organization Keep America Beautiful launched one of the most celebrated public interest campaigns in the history of advertising. Its star was Iron Eyes Cody, probably the most celebrated Native American in the United States at the time from his more than a hundred roles in Hollywood movies. The 60-second TV spot showed Cody paddling a canoe in an unspoilt wilderness. Then the bow of the canoe begins to push through floating garbage. The camera pulls back and the canoe is now travelling through a hellish industrial landscape, with endless factories belching smoke. Cody grounds the canoe. Where he lands, the soil is covered with litter. A voiceover tells viewers that "There are some people who have a deep, abiding respect for the natural beauty that used to be this country. Some people don't." There is a shot of someone tossing garbage out of a car window. It lands at Cody's feet. The camera zooms in on Cody's face. There is a close-up of his right eye that shows him crying.

The message of the spot was crystal clear. America had brutalized the Indian, whose heritage the land had really been, and now American capitalism was brutalizing the land itself. Native Americans are in touch with the land and the native environment. Many Americans who are not Indians are not. This Public Service Announcement (PSA) became the most widely seen in television history. It was followed by a whole publicity campaign in which magazine ads featured the crying Indian. Cody's tearful face shaped American public consciousness of the environment as no other ecological symbol (including pictures of oil disasters such as the *Exxon Valdez* (1989) and the Deepwater Horizon Oil Spill in the Gulf of Mexico (2010)) ever has.[35] In 1982, the US Postal Service used it on a stamp. Cody also became a major national and international celebrity, being invited to the White House by two successive presidents (Jimmy Carter and Ronald Reagan) and having an audience with the Pope.

Cody's role as a symbol of Indian concern for the natural environment was itself based on a personal fiction. Film scholar Angela Aleiss subsequently discovered that this archetypal "Indian" actor was born and raised in Louisiana and his parents were two Italian immigrants. When he moved to Hollywood to try to break into the movies, Cody simply reconstructed his identity from Italian to Indian to try to secure more regular work. As Patricia Nelson Limerick writes,

> While there are probably many descendants of European immigrants in the United States who care deeply about pollution and environmental

degradation, a public service advertisement showing an Italian American in tears, grieving over the state of the earth, would probably have left viewers more puzzled than moved. The grieving Indian, by contrast, met expectation and made perfect sense.[36]

Since viewers were already *conditioned* to see Indians as close to nature, focusing on an "Indian" actor like Cody—and demonstrating his sorrow over the injuries done to the natural environment—helped the ad make its point.

In *Dances With Wolves*, Dunbar begins his stay in the west as if he has just seen the "Crying Indian" commercial. One of the first things he does on arriving at Fort Sedgwick is to try to clean up what humans have done to the natural environment. He removes the carcass of the dead elk that has deliberately been used to foul the waterhole. He subsequently tidies away the litter and debris left by the fort's previous occupants next to the caves in which they seem to have lived. Dunbar also demonstrates his respect for nature by his empathy with animals. His horse, Cisco, kidnapped several times by Indians, always returns faithfully to his master at Fort Sedgwick. Dunbar makes friends with a wolf he calls Two Socks, domesticating him to the point where the wolf will accept food from his hand. He also plays with him on the prairie, astonishing the watching Indians who—themselves constructed as being close to the natural world—do not believe any white man capable of such close contact with nature. This scene is the genesis of Dunbar's later Sioux name: "Dances With Wolves."

The main environmental focus of the film—and its principal claim to be regarded as an "eco-western"—is the difference it spells out between Native Americans and whites over attitudes to the buffalo on the Great Plains. For the Sioux, the buffalo function as the primary source not only of food, but also of clothing, shelter, tools, and weapons. Dunbar's relationship with the Indians takes a huge step forward when a vast herd of buffalo charge past his fort and he races to tell Kicking Bird and the other Lakota of their arrival. He is invited to join the party as the Indians set off on their buffalo hunt. But things do not initially go well. The hunting party discover a group of dead buffalo, left rotting on the ground, with one tiny calf left alive, bleating forlornly on its own. There are wagon wheels leading away from the spot, suggesting that those responsible are white. To the Lakota, buffalo are a natural resource, vital to their survival as a community. The whole tribe is involved in the hunt: they strike camp to follow the herd. The film suggests that they propose to kill only the buffalo they need. As Dunbar comments, the three-day hunt provides them with all the meat they need to fill their food stores for the winter. The white hunters, in contrast, are dedicated only to profit. They have no compunction about leaving behind the carcasses of the buffalo they have shot—killed, as Dunbar contemptuously remarks, "only for their tongues and the price of their hides" (Figure 6.2).

FIGURE 6.2 *The legacy of white hunters in* Dances With Wolves.

The essential relationship between the Sioux and the buffalo they live off, *Dances With Wolves* suggests, is balance. Since the Lakota kill just for their own subsistence, it is unlikely that the animals they slaughter will seriously diminish the surviving numbers of wild buffalo. The Indians are consequently represented as practitioners of conservation or sustainable usage in relation to the buffalo as a natural resource. To white hunters, by contrast, the buffalo is merely a commodity, to be exploited for capitalist profit, and with no thought for its availability for future generations. In practice, the difference between Native American and white hunters was not as clear-cut in environmental terms as the film indicates. "Frequently," remarked Alice Kehoe of the Plains Indians, "more animals were slaughtered than could be processed." In 1882, a large herd of buffalo wandered onto the Great Sioux Reservation: 5,000 were quickly killed by 600 Indians.[37] Yet, as discussed below, it was almost certainly whites rather than Native Americans who were principally responsible for driving the buffalo swiftly to the point of near-extinction.

The vanishing Sioux way of life

Dances With Wolves finishes with a credit crawl explaining the disappearance of the traditional Sioux way of life: "Thirteen years later, their homes destroyed, their buffalo gone, the last band of free Sioux submitted to white authority at Fort Robinson, Nebraska. The great horse culture of the plains was gone and the American frontier was soon to pass into history." The reference to a crucial event in the credit was accurate:

after the massacre of Lieutenant-Colonel's George A. Custer's 7th Cavalry unit at the Little Bighorn in June 1876, General Philip H. Sheridan launched a successful winter campaign to wear down militarily first the Cheyenne and then the Sioux. By spring 1877 only one Sioux leader, Crazy Horse, was undefeated. When he and his band of several hundred supporters surrendered at Fort Robinson in May 1877, the Indian wars came to an end.[38] The credit is accurate also in its comment on what followed: 13 years after the last Sioux band submitted, the frontier—as already noted—was declared closed by the US Census Bureau and did indeed "pass into history." But the reference to the "great horse culture of the plains" gives a deceptive sense of timelessness to a way of life that, in fact, lasted little more than a century. Spanish ranchers in what is now New Mexico trained Indians in handling and looking after horses in the early seventeenth century. Indians were using them on the Southern Plains by the 1690s and, by 1770, the western Sioux had acquired them and were transforming themselves into nomadic buffalo-hunters.[39]

What is entirely missing from both the film and final credit is the political and military context to the Indian wars. By the mid-nineteenth century, the western Sioux, perhaps 15,000 strong, dominated the region between the Platte and Yellowstone rivers. The Lakota in particular, Alice Kehoe argues, constituted "the principal threat to Euro-American domination of the Plains."[40] In the late 1840s, the US government, influenced by "manifest destiny" ideas and a desire to prevent Indians harassing white settlers moving west, endorsed a policy of forcing Plains tribes onto reservations. In the Fort Laramie or Horse Creek Treaty of 1851, they created a "Great Sioux Reservation."[41] Yet conflict between Sioux and emigrants continued and, in 1854, a war that would flicker intermittently into life for the next 23 years broke out when the Sioux massacred an army unit of 30 men attempting to teach them a lesson.[42] In 1862, during the Civil War, what was also to all intents and purposes a war broke out on the Plains when eastern (Santee) Sioux, starving because of the breakdown of food supplies on reservations, began attacking Minnesota settlers. As US troops started to suppress the rising, some Santee Sioux fled west to find refuge with other Sioux, including Lakotas.[43] There were rumors of a wider war and, in spring 1863, General Pope sent two columns of troops into Dakota territory in a failed attempt to overawe the Lakota. Both in September 1863 and July 1864, Sioux villages were attacked.[44] The Lakota themselves hit back, stopping transport by river and road and raiding settlers. As news of the Sand Creek massacre (November 1864) spread, Sioux joined with Cheyenne and Arapahoes in February 1865 to burn the town of Julesburg, Colorado, in revenge.[45] None of this background is alluded to by the film, which is apparently set in 1863–4. It would have made the slow and relatively innocent development of friendly relations between Dunbar and the Indians seem far less credible.

The credit at the end of the film also eliminates the tangled history of the US/Lakota relationship between 1865 and 1877. The Lakota, together with Cheyenne and Arapahoes, forcibly resisted the increasing numbers of miners using the Bozeman trail, across the center of northern Lakota territory. When the government responded by building forts, outright hostilities commenced—hostilities that resulted in one major Sioux success, when they massacred a force of 80 under the command of Colonel William J. Fetterman in December 1866.[46] In the years after the ending of the Civil War, the Federal government, very much aware of the rising tide of white settlement flowing into the West, intensified its policy of "concentration"—relocating tribes to reservations. The war with the Lakota ended temporarily in 1868 with a second Fort Laramie Treaty: the government abandoned the fortifications along the Bozeman trail. In return, the Indians agreed that they would occupy areas outside the Great Sioux Reservation, with much the same boundaries as those set in 1851, only "so long as the buffalo may range thereon in such numbers as to justify" hunting them.[47] After the treaty was signed, most Sioux moved onto the reservation and there was relative peace for four years. It was briefly threatened by the plans of the Northern Pacific railroad to cross Yellowstone Valley, but the Northern Pacific was bankrupted in the "Crash" of 1873.[48] When the Lakota resisted white attempts to exploit the Black Hills, where gold was found in 1874, the administration of President Ulysses S. Grant decided once and for all to confine the Sioux (in defiance of the Treaty of 1868) to their reservation: the result was the conflict that led to Custer's defeat at the Little Bighorn and the war of attrition that followed, eventually leading to Sioux defeat and Crazy Horse's surrender.[49] Some of the last sequences of the movie—showing the army pursuing Dunbar and the Lakota—suggest the implacability of white politicians and generals' intention to defeat the Sioux and finally break their power.[50] That implacability, as the final credit suggested, included the destruction of Indian homes: "our tepees were burned with everything in them," recalled one unfortunate victim. "I had nothing left but the clothing I had on."[51]

The disappearance of the buffalo

The final credit was also correct in identifying the disappearance of the buffalo as a major—perhaps *the* major cause—of the Indians' abandonment of their former, highly nomadic way of life. Yet *Dances With Wolves* offers very little explanation for the demise of the buffalo, 60 million of which are estimated to have roamed the Great Plains earlier in the nineteenth century.[52] If the Indians only killed (as the film implies) the buffalo they actually needed and could use, then the responsibility for their near-extinction could only be blamed on those like the unseen band of white hunters who kill buffalo simply as a delicacy (their tongues) and for the commercial value of their hides. But this itself is anachronistic. The film is set in 1863–4; tanners in the east only began experimenting on turning buffalo hides into leather in 1870. When the process was perfected, a vast, if short-lived, trade in buffalo hides quickly emerged—a trade made possible by the railroads, which made it increasingly easy to ship staggering numbers of hides back to tanneries in Pennsylvania and New York.[53] Professional hunters killed vast numbers of buffalo. One hunter, W. S. Glenn later suggested that "a remarkably good hunter would kill seventy-five to a hundred in a day, an average hunter about fifty, and a common one twenty-five." Kansan Thomas Linton killed 3,000 in 1872. William "Doc" Carver shot 5,700 in 1875. Orlando Brown was responsible for killing 5,855 buffalo over a two-month period in 1876—with the consequence, writes Andrew C. Isenberg, that "the nearly constant report of his .50-caliber rifle during that time rendered him deaf in one ear." Josiah Wright Mooar, one of the pioneers of the whole buffalo hide industry, claimed to have shot 20,000 between 1870 and 1879.[54]

There were other reasons for the decline and disappearance of the buffalo in addition to hunting them for their hides, as foregrounded in *Dances With Wolves*. As railroads spread into the west—four transcontinental lines with an increasing network of branch-lines had been built by 1884—the railroads hired gangs of professional hunters to kill buffalo for their construction gangs to eat. One of the most famous of these men was "Buffalo Bill" Cody. There was also a strong element of wantonness to some of the killing. The railroads would subsequently advertise three-day excursions on which amateur hunters could, for ten dollars, ride on the train and shoot buffalo from the windows. Carcasses were left to rot, as in *Dance With Wolves*, in mid-prairie.[55]

Yet killing buffalo for their hides, as food for railroad workers and as sport even when added together still made up only part of the story. There is a sequence in John Ford's *The Searchers* (1956) that hints as something more sinister. After his niece Debbie (Nathalie Wood) has been kidnapped by Comanche Indians who have slaughtered her family, Ethan Edwards (John Wayne), accompanied by his sidekick Martin Pawley (Jeffrey Hunter), launches a seven-year search to find her. It is mid-winter and Ethan and Martin approach a herd of buffalo in search of meat. Martin shoots the buffalo they need but, as the rest of the herd flees, Ethan begins shooting at them indiscriminately. Martin is appalled: like the Indians in *Dances With Wolves*, he wants only to kill the animals they need. But Ethan, a psychotic Indian-hater, has a rational explanation for what he is doing. By destroying buffalo, he is also destroying the basis of the Indian way of life. As he shoots more and more buffalo, he defends what he is doing with the justification that "At least, they won't feed any Comanches this winter" (Figure 6.3).

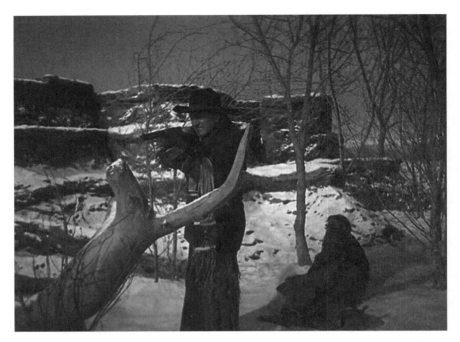

FIGURE 6.3 *Ethan Edwards (John Wayne) shooting indiscriminately at buffalo in* The Searchers.

Fanatical as Ethan appears, there is considerable evidence that what he was suggesting was—for a time in the 1870s—the formal policy of the Federal Government and of the US Army attempting to carry out its orders. In 1874, Columbus Delano, Secretary of the Interior in President Ulysses S. Grant's administration, testified before Congress that:

> The buffalo are disappearing rapidly, but not faster than I desire. I regard the destruction of such game as Indians subsist upon as facilitating the policy of the Government, of destroying their hunting habits, coercing them on reservations, and compelling them to begin to adopt the habits of civilization.[56]

Two years later, reporter John F. Finerty wrote that the government's allies among the Indians "killed the animals in sheer wantonness" saying "better kill buffalo than have him feed the Sioux."[57] Generals Phil Sheridan and William T. Sherman were enthusiastic supporters of a policy aimed at undercutting the Indians' capacity to continue armed struggle against the United States, with Sheridan insisting that "if I could learn that every buffalo in the northern herd were killed I would be glad."[58] (The so-called northern herd was a recognition of the effects of the building of the first transcontinental railroad line (1862–9), which had divided the surviving buffalo into two herds—one north of the railroad, the other south.)

Not every member of the army approved. Several officers protested at the policy of what they regarded as irresponsible destruction to Henry Bergh, president of the American Society for the Prevention of Cruelty to Animals. In 1873, Secretary of War William W. Belknap approved an attempt by one local officer, Colonel DeLancey Floyd Jones, "to put a stop to their wholesale destruction."[59] Nevertheless, there were enough remaining officers and men convinced that exterminating the buffalo would undermine the ability of Indians to continue resistance to the policy of forcing them onto reservations to make the army itself a major force in the culling of the wild buffalo.[60]

Miscegenation

While being very limited in explaining the decline of the traditional Lakota lifestyle, Dances With Wolves was also careful, even timorous, in approaching the subject of interracial relationships. Anxieties relating to such relationships across racial lines (which would later come to be known as "miscegenation," a term invented during the Civil War) had existed from the early years of European settlement in the United States. To Hollywood, the most controversial miscegenation involved black-white relationships, and after The Birth of a Nation (1915) these were largely avoided in movies until the 1970s. A number of Westerns, however, including Cecil B. De Mille's The Squaw Man (1914), explored the theme of Indian-white miscegenation. Most of them dealt with white men in relationships with Indian women and in nearly all, from The Squaw Man (which would be remade in 1918 and 1931) through Broken Arrow (1950) to Little Big Man (1970), the relationship ended with the death of the Indian woman.

The main romance in Dances With Wolves is between Dunbar/Dances With Wolves and Stands With a Fist. As Black Shawl, Kicking Bird's wife points out, it "makes sense" to the Lakota for them to marry since "they are both white." The film is conservative and safe in the sense that it does not directly confront the question of miscegenation, which it would necessarily have done if Dances With Wolves had married a Sioux woman. Yet there is another reference to miscegenation in the film: when we first see her, Stands With a Fist is in mourning for her first husband, a Sioux warrior.

There is a considerable literature on white women who spent time living with Indians. Starting with the publication of Mary Rowlandson's book in 1682,[61] most of them dealt with women who had been kidnapped or held captive. These "captivity narratives" were very popular in the late eighteenth and early nineteenth century; by the later nineteenth century they were being told in "dime" novels. The women concerned (sometimes real, more frequently fictional) had usually been abducted by force. They had often been obliged to watch the murder of family members. They faced (if only in their imaginations) threats of rape or forced marriage. The captivity narrative traditionally contrasted the Christian victim with pagan Indians and preached the need for faith in confronting adversity. Some, including Rowlandson, were at times strangely sympathetic in their portrait of Native Americans. Yet the general impression they created was that white women suffered from living, for however short a period, with Indians.[62] For a small minority of real women abducted by Indians, including Mary Jemison (1743–1833) and Cynthia Ann Parker (c. 1827–1870), the experience was very different. Both embraced Indian life and culture, married Indians, had children with them, and demonstrated no desire to return to living with whites. Parker, reabducted by Texas Rangers, appears to have starved herself to death on being separated from her beloved Comanches.[63]

In *Dances With Wolves*, Stands With a Fist's original name is Christine. She has not been abducted, but found and looked after by Kicking Bird after the Pawnees have slaughtered her original white family. She has grown up with the tribe, regarding Kicking Bird as her adopted father. She has thrived, learning to stand up for herself and resist bullying by an older women—hence the story of how she acquires her Indian name. She is fully acculturated with the Sioux, speaks their language, and has no desire to leave the tribe. As Stephen Tatum observes, "in a neat reversal of the white captivity narrative, [she] is afraid initially that Dunbar will capture her and return her to white society."[64] Over the years, she has reached sexual maturity and married a Sioux warrior, the best friend of Wind in His Hair. We learn almost nothing of her husband, who has recently died. When Dunbar first meets her, she is injured and bleeding, having slashed herself with a knife. Is this self-harm part of her mourning? It appears that Stands With a Fist has greatly loved her Sioux husband (Black Shawl tells her husband, Kicking Bird, that she has "found love again" with Dunbar). She may have responded to her sense of loss and desolation after his death with a suicide attempt. By never showing or even naming Stands With a Fist's first husband, the movie avoids confronting directly the issue of miscegenation, but it seems to be suggesting that this Indian/white marriage has been a success even if—like most examples of such marriages in Hollywood films—it ends with the death of one of the partners.

Conclusion

Dances with Wolves makes it clear that both whites and Indians see each other in terms of cultural stereotypes—stereotypes that promote fear and loathing. "Nothing I had been told about these people is correct," Dunbar confesses. "They're not beggars and thieves. They're not the bogeymen they have been made out to be." When the soldiers who have reoccupied Fort Sedgwick first see Dunbar, he is dressed as an Indian—a member of the group they have been conditioned to think of as "hostiles"—and they instantly open fire. The strength of ingrained racism encourages feelings of horror and disgust at the idea that a white soldier would want to become an Indian, underpinning Sergeant Bauer (Larry Joshua)'s baffled question: "[you] turned Injun, didn't you?" But Indians are equally prejudiced against whites: "They don't ride well," Wind in His Hair tells the council in Ten Bears' tent. "They don't shoot well. They are dirty." A key moment in the film is when Dunbar and Wind in His Hair confront each other for the first time. Dunbar could shoot Wind in His Hair with his gun; Wind in His Hair could skewer Dunbar with his spear. Both draw back from what they are culturally conditioned to do, making it possible for each to get to know the other. Out of knowledge comes understanding, respect, and eventually friendship. This particular aspect of the film seems to have struck home. Lynne Dozier incorporated *Dances With Wolves* into the work of a ninth-grade class in Texas. Discussing the film, she wrote, "promoted harmony, expanded thinking skills, and generated enthusiasm for storytelling in my classroom. Knowledge replaced prejudice, and students looked past skin color to find friendship and respect in the class, just as the Indians and Dunbar did in the movie." For all its omissions, mistakes, and misperceptions, *Dances With Wolves* embodied a powerful social and cultural message. As one perceptive member of the class wrote, summarizing the general response, the movie demonstrated "that to overcome problems, we must put color and stereotypes aside and look at real people for who they are."[65]

Filmography

The Battle at Elderbush Gulch (dir. David W. Griffith; Biograph, 1913).
The Squaw Man (dir. Cecil B. De Mille/Oscar Apfel; Jesse L. Lasky Feature Play, 1914) (later versions in 1918 and 1931).
The Vanishing American (dir. George B. Seitz; Famous Players-Lasky, 1925).
Stagecoach (dir. John Ford; Walter Wangar, 1939).
Broken Arrow (dir. Delmer Daves; Twentieth-Century Fox, 1950).
Devil's Doorway (dir. Anthony Mann; MGM, 1950).
The Savage (dir. George Marshall; Paramount, 1952).
Hondo (dir. John Farrow; Warner Bros./Wayne Fellows, 1953).
Apache (dir. Robert Aldrich; Hecht-Lancaster/Linden, 1954).
The Indian Fighter (dir. André de Toth; Bryna, 1955).
The Searchers (dir. John Ford; Warner Bros./C. V. Whitney, 1956).
Run of the Arrow (dir. Samuel Fuller; RKO/Globe, 1957).

War Drums (dir. Reginald Le Borg; Schenck-Koch/Bel-Air, 1957).
Cheyenne Autumn (dir. John Ford; Warner Bros./Ford-Smith, 1964).
Little Big Man (dir. Arthur Penn; Cinema Center/Stockbridge-Hiller, 1970).
Soldier Blue (dir. Ralph Nelson; AVCO-Embassy/Katzka-Loeb, 1970).
Windwalker (dir. Kieth Merrill; Santa Fe International/Windwalker, 1981).
Dances With Wolves (dir. Kevin Costner; Tig Productions/Majestic Films, 1990).

CHAPTER SEVEN

"The Golden Door":
Hester Street and
The Godfather Part II

In 1886, the Statue of Liberty—a gift from the people of France to the United States—opened on an island in New York harbor. Three years earlier, Emma Lazarus, who belonged to a family of Sephardic Jews that had immigrated to New York in colonial times, had written a sonnet she called "The New Colossus." Lazarus was a gifted writer who had been greatly influenced by Emerson. In the last years of her life (she died in 1887), she became increasingly preoccupied with the rise of anti-semitism in Europe. Her poem was written to help raise money to build a pedestal for the Statue of Liberty. It celebrated the statue itself, an image of Libertas, the Roman goddess of freedom, as the "Mother of Exiles." The poem was engraved on the pedestal when it finally opened in 1903. In the last five lines, it included the words:

> Give me your tired, your poor,
> Your huddled masses yearning to breathe free,
> The wretched refuse of your teeming shore.
> Send these, the homeless, tempest-tost to me,
> I lift my lamp beside the golden door!

1882, the year before the poem was written, was the peak year for immigration into the United States in the nineteenth century: over three-quarters of a million people arrived, of whom almost a third came from Germany. Much smaller numbers came from Italy (32,000), Austria-Hungary (28,000), and Russia and the Baltic (17,000).[1] Beginning around the time Lazarus wrote her poem, major changes, if not yet in the total size of European immigration but in its origins, began to emerge. Instead of coming from northern and western Europe, as their predecessors had done, immigrants increasingly came from southern and eastern Europe. This "new" immigration, as it became known in contrast to the "old," prompted growing concern on the part of many native-born Americans. The newcomers were drawn from a much wider range of ethnicities than "old" immigrants. They were suspected of being less skilled, less educated, and generally less assimilable into American society than their predecessors. The condescension—even hostility—toward them this would create was (unconsciously) hinted at in the words of Lazarus's poem: immigrants were "yearning to breath free"; they were also "tired," "poor," and "wretched refuse" of a "teeming shore."

Between the 1880s and the 1920s, the two largest groups of "new" immigrants were Italians and Jews from Russia and Poland. The two groups differed in language and religion. They differed in where they settled: although many Italians lived in cities, others spread out in smaller communities across the country; by the early 1890s, two-thirds of all American Jews lived in New York, Philadelphia, Boston, and Chicago, with most of the rest in other large cities.[2] Most Italian immigrants came from the south of the country and were unskilled and not very educated; most Jews were skilled and better educated. A high proportion of Italians (just under half in the period 1908–14) returned from the United States to Europe. The reemigration rate for Jews, facing political and religious repression in addition to discrimination in their European homelands, was little more than seven percent.[3] Both groups were similar in being looked down upon by native-born Americans and earlier immigrants. Both were regarded as clannish, having little interaction with broader American society. And both were suspected of involvement in criminal behavior: Theodore Bingham, the police commissioner of New York City, alleged in a magazine article of 1908 that "half the criminals" in New York were Jewish; sociologist Edward A. Ross insisted that crime rates had fallen in Italy "because all the criminals are here."[4] This chapter analyzes two films dealing with aspects of this "new" immigration: *Hester Street* examines the Jewish community of New York in the 1890s and *The Godfather Part II* recreates New York's "Little Italy" of the 1910s and 1920s.

Hester Street (1975)

By 1914, 1.4 million Jews would be residents of New York City. The Lower East Side of the city was effectively a Jewish ghetto—so overpopulated, indeed, that in 1893 the 10th Ward of the city, with 700 Jews per acre,[5] was probably the most crowded place in the entire world. At the heart of the Lower East Side was Hester Street. Horizontally located between

Grand Street in the north and Canal Street in the south, and vertically between Essex Street in the east and Center Street in the west, Hester Street was a principal focus of Jewish life and culture. In the 1890s, it had the busiest outdoor street market in New York. "There is hardly a square foot of ground on Hester Street that is not covered with people during the day," commented the *New York Times* in 1895. "The whole place seems to be in a state of perpetual motion, and the occasional visitor is apt to have a feeling of giddiness."[6] When director Joan Micklin Silver produced a film about the Jewish community in New York in the 1890s, therefore, it was only natural that she would title it *Hester Street*. Based on the short novel *Yekl: A Tale of the New York Ghetto* by Abraham Cahan, a Lithuanian-born Jewish writer and journalist, who had arrived in the United States in 1882, Silver's film dealt with the stresses of living and acculturation among a group of New York City Jews in 1896, the year Cahan's story was published.

In the first sequences of the film, we learn that Jake (Steven Keats), a Jewish immigrant from eastern Europe, has prospered since his arrival in the United States. He is very good at his job of sewing clothes on a machine and, in good times, earns as much as 12 dollars a week. He dresses in a sharp suit and cultivates an American-style appearance. He speaks fluent English, with only a little inflection. He acts like a single man, frequenting dancehalls in the evening, and acquires a sophisticated girlfriend, Mamie (Dorrie Kavanaugh), a 23-year-old Jewish girl from Poland who has lived in America for seven years and become thoroughly acculturated. But Jake is already married and has a son. He has followed the classic route of a married eastern European Jew—leaving on his own for the New World to establish himself before sending the money for his family to follow. Enjoying the pleasures of the single life in New York, however, Jake has been in no hurry to invite Gitl (Carole Kane), his wife, and Yossele (Paul Freedman), his son, to join him. He would almost certainly have waited still longer—or never done so at all (many men in a similar situation simply made new lives for themselves in America)—if it had not been for the death of his father.[7] With no other relations remaining in the Old World to look after his wife and son, Jake is finally obliged to ask them to join him.

The film shows him climbing the staircase at the immigrant reception depot on Ellis Island to meet them and help with the formalities. Jake looks far from confident. He has been in America since 1893, so would himself have arrived at Ellis Island, which on January 1, 1892 replaced Castle Garden on the Battery as the center for processing new immigrants arriving in New York. Jake almost certainly is reliving the humiliations of three years earlier, when he was inspected and interviewed to see if he was worthy of admittance to the United States. In the film, new prospective immigrants are waiting to be interviewed behind a wire cage, emphasizing their near-prisoner status. Jake does not immediately recognize Gitl and Yossele (maybe he does not really want to see them?). It is Gitl who first recognizes him and starts to become excited, pointing out to Yossele that the man waiting behind the wire is his father. Jake remains impassive, showing no similar interest or enthusiasm. He is clearly repulsed by Gitl's appearance: her dowdy clothes and *sheitel*, the ornamental wig worn by Orthodox Jewish women to cover their hair as a sign of modesty. He does not seem particularly interested either in his son, although Yossele looks as pretty as a girl with his long, curly blonde hair. Later in the film, over Gitl's screams of protest, Jake will cut Yossele's hair to make him look more American. From his initial reaction to his wife and son, it is clear that Jake—who has been getting along perfectly happily on his own—sees them as a threat to his new life as a "real Yankee fella."

The interview with the immigration official that follows brings all Jake's latent cultural insecurities to the fore. In the first place, the inspector is sitting behind a high desk denoting authority: he looks down on Jake and his family and has the power to decide whether Gitl and Yossele are allowed to enter the United States. Then, while Jake is smartly dressed in what he thinks of as "American" fashion, the inspector treats him patronizingly as a "foreigner" by speaking to him slowly and carefully in English. While the immigration official is clearly arrogant and unpleasant, reveling in his power, there is also a grain of practicality and common sense in his repeated question to Jake: "For what purpose are you bringing this woman in?" (Figure 7.1).

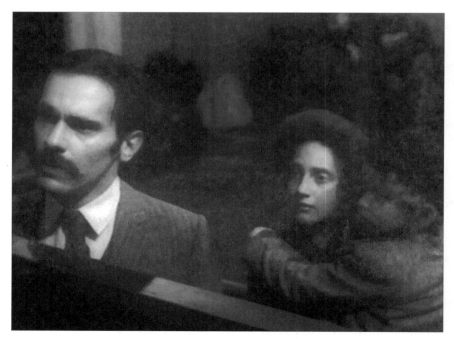

FIGURE 7.1 *"For what purpose are you bringing this woman in?"* (Hester Street).

There had been a suspicion for some time that many female immigrants entered the country for immoral purposes: the third section of the Page Act of 1875, the first Federal immigration law, had banned the importation of women for the purposes of prostitution. At the same time, Gitl and Jake do look so different that it is hard to see an obvious relationship between them. But the inspector's questioning quickly flusters Jake, undermining his self-image as a would-be Yankee. He snaps at Gitl (in Yiddish) to produce their marriage certificate and, when she hands him Yossele to hold, slaps his squirming son's face. Jake's humiliation is complete when the inspector is handed the marriage certificate. It is all in Hebrew and the official turns it round as if trying to work out the correct way of reading it. Disdainfully, he hands it back to Jake together with the ornamental ribbon of material used to tie it up. For this little family, there will be no pleasant memories of their reunion.

Hester Street is a story of the social and cultural relationships between new immigrants in the United States. It is also a movie produced by independent filmmakers—director Joan Micklin Silver and her husband Raphael—working on a small budget ($400,000). It consequently misses out completely the backstory of Gitl and Yossele's journey from Russia to New York, something of an epic in its own right. After the funeral of Jake's father, there would have been the complex process needed to acquire passports to cross both regional and national boundaries, followed by a long rail journey, probably in boxcars with uncomfortable benches, to a port for embarkation. Gitl would have carried all their possessions, mainly clothes, and some food wrapped up in a patterned blanket or quilt (she has this with her at Ellis Island). At the port, perhaps Hamburg or Bremen in Germany, they would have had to have their exit papers checked, prove they had sufficient resources to prevent them becoming a public charge (required by US legislation of 1882), and buy tickets. They would probably have had medical inspections, been bathed, and had their clothes and luggage fumigated. They would then have been allowed to board their ship where, in the cramped and crowded conditions of steerage, they would have to survive for up to two weeks in close proximity to other emigrants. Gitl regards herself as a respectable married woman, but maintaining modesty and respectability in such surroundings cannot have been easy. On arriving at the docks in New York, Gitl and Yossele must have been tagged with numbers and taken by barge or ferry to Ellis Island. Once they reached the bedlam of the main building, their numbers were called out in a variety of languages and they were shepherded in single file past a succession of doctors checking that they had no contagious diseases (prohibited under legislation of 1891) and were fit enough to enter the United States (approximately one in five failed and were deported). It was only after surviving this final ordeal that Gitl and Yossele were allowed to wait in the cage for Jake to arrive and for their final interview. The film, for understandable reasons, assumes rather than shows all this. It leaves

Gitl to reveal her strength of character only through her experiences once in New York. In reality, that strength had already been demonstrated in the journey, with her young son, from Russia.

Life in New York for Gitl is mainly about humiliation. Though they have obviously had a physical relationship in the past, and despite her readiness to resume one, Jake is simply not interested (preferring to visit a prostitute who recognizes him as a regular client). To him, Gitl represents a "greenhorn"—an unacculturated reminder of the Old World he is anxious to leave behind. Slowly, Gitl begins to give in to Jake's pressure to turn herself into a truly "American" woman. After much angst, she first stops wearing her wig and replaces it with a kerchief. Then she abandons the kerchief in favor of her own hair. Gitl also tries to wear a corset and dress in the way she thinks Jake wants. In the end, nothing works. When Jake rejects her violently as she tries to show him her new dress, she decides it is time for a Jewish divorce or *get*. Gitl, not having a job and confined to her role as an exemplary housewife, is much slower to speak English than Jake—or Yossele, who quickly begins to pick up the language, so much so that his mother is soon asking him the English meaning ("stove") of Yiddish words. But she is just as "American"—in Jake's sense of being materialistic—as Jake himself. When Jake sends a shyster lawyer to see her to bribe her with Mamie's money to agree to a divorce (which she wants anyway), Gitl manages by shrewdly remaining silent effectively to gain all the money ($300) Mamie has saved in her seven years in America.

Gitl brings with her to the New World the values of the Old. She is profoundly respectful of their lodger, Bernstein (Mel Howard), because he is a product of a *yeshiva* (a school devoted to the study of rabbinic literature and the Talmud) and was formerly a biblical scholar who had intended to become a rabbi. The film hints that Bernstein has been too passionate in his relations with women to become a true rabbi, and that he has fled to America to overcome his disappointment. But he still looks Orthodox in appearance (unlike Jake, he still has a beard) and spends most of his spare time studying religious literature. In the Old World, in Poland and especially Russia, it was commonplace for women to earn the money to support a family while their husbands studied.[8] Gitl, using the money she has acquired from Jake and Mamie, plans to follow this pattern. She will buy and run a grocery business, and Bernstein will be both her new husband and her formal partner. In practice, as we quickly realize from the dialogue between them, she will run the business and Bernstein will continue with his Talmudic studies.

On the face of it, Gitl still has strong echoes of her Old World upbringing. She is superstitious, for example, putting salt into the pockets of Yossele/Joey to ward off evil and asking a Jewish pedlar to sell her a love potion that will make Jake care for her again.[9] We can wonder how the family life she proposes with Bernstein will work out in practice: in America, social and cultural pressure would revolve more about men going out to work while their wives stayed at home to look after the children.[10] Equally, however, Gitl in what seems to be a relatively short period—the timescale of *Hester Street* is unclear— seems to have acquired a reasonable fluency in English and, through her negotiations over the divorce, enough money to start her own business. She is thus, without any very obvious skills apart from as a homemaker, poised to join in the restless search for social mobility that characterized many recently arrived members of the New York Jewish community in the 1890s.

And what of Jake and Mamie? The last sequence of the film shows Mamie wearing a wedding veil as the two walk towards City Hall to get married. Mamie will not allow them to take a cab—or even the subway— because, as she says, "two nickels is two nickels." Their dream of buying a dance academy has temporarily collapsed: Gitl has taken as the price for agreeing to divorce Jake all the money Mamie has saved in her time in America. They must both start working and saving again to pursue their dream of buying their own business. Like Gitl and Bernstein, the couple are ambitious to be socially mobile. They do not want to spend their lives living in the ghetto and working for other people. Although Jake and Mamie are in some ways a brasher, less appealing couple than the more diffident Gitl and Bernstein, we know—or at least suspect—at the end of the film that both couples are going to succeed, primarily because in each couple it is the wife who will provide the drive and ambition and discipline necessary to guarantee their success. If, as a common belief in the Jewish community expressed it, the journey uptown from Hester Street to Lexington Avenue was a ten-year trek, both families in a decade's time will be living on the upper East Side (or moving out to the suburbs of the Bronx or Brooklyn).[11]

The film ends making it reasonably clear what the future of the two couples is likely to be. But what will happen to Yossele? While the film does not tell us, it is possible to speculate. Jake has already rechristened him Joey and cut his hair to make him fit in with other American children. He is shown to be quick at picking up English—and Bernstein has begun to teach him to read Hebrew. In one of the final sequences of the film, when Gitl is chatting with the rabbi's wife after the divorce, she declares very firmly: "His name is Joey." Gitl by this stage has accepted the logic that to become American is to change, that the expectations of the Old World are not those of the New. As a result of the ambition of his mother and the education of his new father, Joey will go to public school in Manhattan, where he will be encouraged to succeed. At a time, in the first decade of the twentieth century, when only one American in five went to school after the age of 12, Joey will stay on at school and eventually go to college. His parents may want him to go to a local university, such as the free City College (where by 1915 85 percent of the student body were Jewish) or New York University (one-fifth Jewish).[12] But they may set their sights higher, perhaps on Harvard or Yale. He will be the first member of his family to graduate from an American university. Joey, in the film, seems about five in 1896. He would have been 18 in 1909. The next few years would see not only a number of important achievements for Jews in America—including the elevation of Louis D. Brandeis to the Supreme Court in 1916—but also the beginnings of a trend that would take off in the 1920s for American universities to adopt quota systems designed to limit the number of Jewish students they accepted.[13] But Joey would not need to have worried about any of that. He was fortunate in both his parents (at least from his mother's second marriage) and his birth-date. To Joey, the United States must truly have appeared a golden land [*goldene medina*].

Hester Street was shot in black-and-white cinematography to save money. The effect, however, is to give the film a restrained, at times almost documentary character. The exterior sequences were mainly filmed on Morton Street in Greenwich Village (Joyce Antler points out that the real Lower East Side by the 1970s "appeared too modern").[14] The film is made to seem more accurately "historical" by the use of Yiddish (subtitled into English) for part of the dialogue. But reviewers disagreed over whether *Hester Street* had succeeded as a historical reconstruction of ghetto life. Laurence Green, in *Films and Filming*, found

> the period atmosphere . . . so scrupulously accurate—from the bearded machinists wearing skull caps, sitting sewing at small tables in the garment factory [the sweatshop where Jake and Bernstein work], to the bustling market atmosphere of this tightly packed ghetto street flanked by tenements and lined with stalls . . . that it has the effect of an animated family album.[15]

Richard Eder, in the *New York Times*, praised the film's "fine balance between realism and fable" with the exception of the street market sequence, which he thought as crowded and unrealistic as "a stage set."[16] In sharp contrast, Robert F. Horowitz in *Film and History* believed there was almost nothing realistic about its presentation of immigrant life. "There is," he wrote,

> no real sense of economic deprivation or social pressure. The clothes which the characters wear are too fine to be the garments of penniless workers. . . . The streets, the alleys, Jake's tenement apartment, and the apartment halls are too neat, too garbage free. Silver fails to convey the noise, the filth, and the smells which assaulted the immigrants in their dilapidated and disease-ridden dumbbell tenements. One does not get a true feel for the congested and explosive conditions of the lower East Side at the turn of the century.[17]

Leaving aside the issue of how a movie can convey odors, Horowitz criticized the film on three counts: that the clothes worn by the characters were not of the kind immigrants would have worn; that the apartment occupied by Jake, his family, and Bernstein, as well as various apartment halls, are shown as too clean and well-maintained; and that the tense and crowded state (what Horowitz termed "the air of clamorous abrasiveness") of the lower East Side was not well represented. The question of what the major characters wear is an important one in *Hester Street*. Jake wants to "look American" not just by shaving off his beard and earlocks (*payess*) but also by dressing the part. This was a common attitude of newcomers. As Irving Howe commented, "to be an American, dress like an American, look like an American, and even, if only in fantasy, talk like an American became a collective goal."[18] The first time Gitl sees Jake after her arrival at Ellis Island, he seems to her "a nobleman," because in Russia only lords dressed so differently. Gitl, meeting Mamie for the first time, also thinks she must be "nobility" or "a real lady" because of her clothes. But "in America," Jake tells her, "anyone can dress like that." While this was not true for many immigrants in the 1890s who would have struggled to afford good clothes, none of the main characters in *Hester Street* who work is "penniless." Bernstein, the poorest, earns only six dollars a week, wears the same suit all the time and is obliged to lodge with Jake. But Jake and Mamie both work in the garment trade: Mamie has saved $300 dollars from her wages and Jake is described by his boss (Martin Garner) as "one of the locusts from Egypt" who earns 12 dollars a week, considerably higher than the average wage. While it is true that making clothes is a seasonal trade—at one point we see Jake during the "slack" season carrying his sewing-machine home in order to do piecework there—both Jake and, especially, Mamie are comparatively well-off. Working in the garment business, like around 60 percent of employed immigrant Jews,[19] they would also have been up-to-date with the latest fashions.

Horowitz's criticism of the accommodation shown in the film is far more convincing. Most of the real residents of Hester Street in the 1890s lived in "dumb-bell" apartments. These took their name from the fact that a New York law of 1879 required that all apartments have at least one window and access to air. Architects met the requirements of the law by building blocks of tenement apartments side by side, with an air shaft in the middle, thus giving the appearance of the kind of dumbbell used in weightlifting, with the air shaft as the narrow link between the weights. The air shaft itself was usually narrow, meaning that it admitted very little light through the windows looking down upon it. It was also often fouled with garbage thrown down it. In the average five-storey apartment, there would be four apartments on each of five floors grouped around the air shaft. There would be no running water in the apartments and toilets would be on the landing outside for communal use. These, as Oscar Handlin delicately remarked, "were open to the custom of all comers, charged to the care of none, and left to the neglect of all."[20] The apartments themselves were cramped, rarely wider than 11 feet at any point. In the summer, when all the windows onto the air shaft were open, the noise and smell would be indescribable.

The apartment where Gitl, Jake, Yossele, and Bernstein live in the film, by contrast, seems relatively light (it could be on the top floor) and spacious. None of the din from outside seems audible. The apartment halls shown in the film are unusually well-lit and empty—when Jake has his argument with Mamie outside her apartment, only one neighbor appears (in reality, there would probably have been an interested crowd). But the film is correct in its representation of a number of things. To pay the rent, Jake is compelled—like many of those in the ghetto—to share his accommodation with a boarder.[21] Mrs. Kovarsky (Doris Roberts), the landlady, praises the way Gitl keeps the apartment clean—and one feature of immigrant Jewish life was the lower than expected mortality rate in the ghetto, which some city health officials attributed to careful attention to cleanliness and hygiene (as well as orthodox rituals in food preparation).[22] Finally, there is one sequence that does suggest the crowded conditions in which many new immigrants lived. When Mamie wants to be alone with Jake, she cannot take him to the apartment she shares with her landlady to protect her reputation as a respectable young woman. Instead, she takes him up to the crowded roof where "hot-bedding" tenants are crammed together separated only by thin muslin curtains.

Horowitz's suggestion that the "air of clamorous abrasiveness" of the ghetto is also not well conveyed in the film has merit too. The crowdedness of the Hester Street market—and the outdoor shots in general—is muted. There are only a few children (and certainly not Joey) playing together in the street. In practice, much of the life of the ghetto took place at street level, to get away from cramped and fetid tenement apartments. In this sense, as Oscar Handlin observed, the street was both "artery and escape." It was also hardly ever cleaned.[23] Silver's Hester Street has been "sanitized," but so too has the sweatshop where Jake and Bernstein work. The workroom we see is light, airy, and not overcrowded. The sweatshop is on several floors: we see two women working in the room with Jake and Bernstein and Jake's ex-girlfriend Fanny (Lauren Frost) comes down from above, passing Jake and Bernstein on the stairs. The sweatshop itself therefore resembles the Triangle Shirtwaist Company near Washington Square Park where, 15 years later, a fire would take the lives of 146 garment workers, mainly immigrant women, who were locked in workrooms on the upper floors and unable to escape. There is no sign in the film of child labor, a common occurrence in New York sweatshops in the 1890s. The owner of the sweatshop is himself Jewish, a former pedlar who taunts Bernstein, the former *yeshiva* student, with the reversal of the social and cultural values of the Old World that their relationship represents. Although the boss is a stickler for continuous working, the fact he recognizes Jake's productivity by paying him so highly gives a misleading impression of sweatshop life. This consisted, for most garment workers, of "long hours, low wages and constant toil."[24] As muckraking journalist Lincoln Steffens, who was a reporter in New York during the 1890s, would later recall, there were at times bitter strikes.[25]

"I kept wishing," commented Deidre Mack in *Films in Review*, "for more about life on Hester Street than the problems of Jake and Gitl."[26] Most of the Jewish immigrants of the 1890s were Orthodox in religion, but Jake has abandoned any faith he may once have had in his dream of becoming a real "American." He goes to the rabbi to have the letter announcing his father's death read to him (he is illiterate). He then dons a mourning shawl but, since he is still wearing his American Derby (bowler) hat, he looks ridiculous as he peers at himself in the mirror. He and Gitl have a religious divorce, since civil divorce in New York at the time was both difficult and expensive, but he has to be taken slowly and carefully by the rabbi through the necessary ritual and responses. Bernstein is a more interesting case. He has clearly not abandoned religion completely. Indeed, Patricia Erens notes, he is "traditional in all respects, he has a beard, covers his head indoors, and prays before meals."[27] He also continues with his Talmudic studies. Yet, as he cynically informs Gitl, leaving for America—a country he regards as godforsaken ("Goodbye, O lord, I'm going to America")—ultimately means abandoning everything Jewish. While Bernstein is the first to begin to teach Joey his Hebrew letters, there is no sign during the film that the boy goes to—or is about to go to—school. For many Jewish children, attending public school "Americanized" them more effectively than anything else, in part because of education in English, in part because of peer-group pressure, and this frequently created a "generation gap" in cultural terms between them and Orthodox parents who had little or no command of English.[28] The film does not touch on this phenomenon.

Hester Street does, indeed, offer little insight into the vibrant Jewish culture of the lower East Side. It shows Joe Peltner's dance hall, which Jake and Mamie both attend and is clearly an agent of Americanization ("No Yiddish Spoken Here" it says on the wall). There were, as Joyce Antler points out, many dance halls like this in the ghetto.[29] It also shows two cafés, in both of which—unlike in New York saloons—respectable women are present.[30] Such meeting places fostered the new view of sexual relations to which both Jake and Mamie subscribe. Marriage in the Old World had been essentially a contract, sometimes arranged by matchmakers. Jake, at one point, displays his contempt for Bernstein by suggesting that he ask the *shadkhn* [matchmaker] to find him a deaf or hunchback woman with money, a wife who will support him financially by running a shop. (Ironically, although Gitl is no hunchback, this is what will happen to Bernstein at the end of the movie.) But Jake and Mamie have both accepted that the idea of romantic love prevails in America. When they are with a group of others at a café, somebody suggests she pay greater attention to an older, wealthy man who comes to the dance hall. "What is this?," she says contemptuously. "The old country? This is Poland, this is Russia?" Far from wishing to marry a wealthy man, Mamie wants to marry for love and on terms of equality. "I don't want no man to say," she insists, "I had to take her just as she was, without a penny." Jake himself declares that "in America, they marry for love," although it is Mamie's savings and later her earning power that he obviously sees as part of her attraction.

There is no reference in *Hester Street* to some significant aspects of Jewish life. Many Jews had been radicalized before they left eastern Europe. Arriving in New York, they became deeply involved in the socialist and anarchist movements. Abraham Cahan, the author of the novella on which the film was based, was active in socialist politics. A few months after the time depicted in the film, Cahan would join with others in founding the *Jewish Daily Forward*, a socialist paper in Yiddish that he would edit from 1903 to 1946. The film also ignores another feature of what Judith Thissen terms the "dynamic, Yiddish-speaking community" of the lower East Side: theater-going. "The popularity of the Yiddish stage and its famous actors, such as Jacob Adler, Boris Thomashevsky and Danid Kessler," she comments, "has been impressed upon us by Jewish-American memoir literature."[31] Moreover, the impression of the New York Jewish ghetto conveyed by *Hester Street*, as Patricia Erens comments, is "as insular as the *shtetls* [small Jewish towns] of [eastern] Europe."[32] At one point in the film, Gitl, Jake, Joey, and Bernstein all travel by train for an hour to spend time in the countryside outside the city. But Gitl, though she is physically removed from the ghetto, is still there in her imagination. "Where in America is the gentiles [non-Jews]?," she asks Bernstein. In practice, of course, there would have been non-Jews on the lower East Side, including teachers, some shopkeepers, firemen, and police. The absence of police in particular also emphasizes the lack of coverage of ghetto crime, though prostitution is referred to.[33] The concentration on Jewish characters alone conveys some of the self-absorbed character of the ghetto, but it also effectively excludes consideration of wider issues such as growing anti-semitism and demands for immigration restriction in the 1890s. The rhetoric of agrarian radicals of the time was often based on absurd fears of an international conspiracy by Jewish bankers. "One of the most striking things about the Populist [party's presidential nominating] convention [of 1896 in St. Louis]," wrote one reporter, "is the extraordinary hatred of the Jewish race."[34] Moreover, anti-semitism in the form of discrimination and even physical assault was common in many American cities.[35]

Hester Street, independently produced on a shoestring, was not immediately exhibited in the United States. But it was well-received at the Cannes Film Festival in France in May 1975. A critic for *Variety* remarked that it was a potential "sleeper" that dealt "with an intrinsically American subject that has been treated in Hollywood films before but rarely with any lasting renown."[36] The reviewer was correct: "ghetto films" had emerged as a subgenre of melodrama around 1910 and reached a peak during the 1920s with movies such as *The Jazz Singer* (1927).[37] In 1948, *My Girl Tisa*, an independent production dealing with a recent immigrant, a young female garment worker, who is saved from deportation by President Theodore Roosevelt in 1905, was distributed by Warner Brothers. But *Hester Street* was an expression of the new interest in ethnicity that had first shown itself in Daniel Patrick Moynihan and Nathan Glazer's book *Beyond the Melting Pot* (1963).[38] That interest and self-awareness had been greatly encouraged by the civil rights movement. By the early 1970s, growing academic and popular interest in ethnicity had begun to be reflected in Hollywood. Elia Kazan's *America, America* (1963), dealing with a Greek immigrant to America, had been followed by Arthur Hiller's *Popi* (1969) about a Puerto Rican, Martin Ritt's *The Molly Maguires* (1970) on a group of emigrant Irish miners, and Francis Ford Coppola's *The Godfather* (1972) and Martin Scorsese's *Mean Streets* (1973) on Italian-Americans.[39] *Hester Street* was Joan Micklin Silver's contribution to a growing field.

In choosing the subject for her first film, Silver was obviously influenced by the history of her own family in America. She chose a storyline based on Cahan's novel *Yekl*, described by John Higham as "the first full-fledged immigrant novel in English."[40] Some aspects of the film, however, reflected a modern consciousness. The relationship between Gitl and Mrs. Kovarsky—and that between Gitl, Mrs. Kovarsky, and the rabbi's wife (Eda Reiss Merin) at the end of the divorce sequence—echoed the second-wave feminism that had begun in the 1960s. As Sonya Michel notes, it "shows clearly that a strong network of both emotional and practical support existed among the women of the ghetto."[41] On the back of its successful showing at Cannes, *Hester Street* was exhibited in New York in October 1975 and subsequently attracted a popular audience in other major urban centers.[42] In 2011, it was chosen by the Library of Congress for preservation in the National Film Registry on the grounds that it offered "a portrait of Eastern European Jewish life in America that historians have praised for its accuracy of detail and sensitivity to the challenges immigrants faced during their acculturation process."[43]

The Godfather Part II (1974)

The Godfather Part II, released in 1974, was both a prequel and a sequel to *The Godfather* (1972), Francis Ford Coppola's highly profitable film about the fictional New York crime family, the Corleones. It showed both the origins of the family and the ways in which it starts to fall apart. As the movie opens, the young Vito Andolini (Oreste Baldini) is in Sicily, where his father, mother, and brother are killed by crime boss Don Ciccio (Giuseppe Sillato) in a vendetta. Vito himself is the only member of his family to escape, and to save his life he sets off for the United States. For the rest of the film, Vito's experiences during the 1910s and 1920s, as he establishes himself in New York, becomes involved in criminal activity, and starts a new family alternate with the problems facing his son and successor Michael (Al Pacino) in 1958. The story is very much that of Vito's rise and Michael's fall. The later chronological sequences, John Yates points out, emphasize "the devastating inadequacy of Vito's example as a model for action in Michael's generation."[44] Under Michael's leadership, the Corleone family have abandoned their New York Italian-American roots by moving to Nevada. The family business has deteriorated into a soulless business corporation and the family itself is torn apart by betrayal and the revolt of wives against male patriarchy. "Always out of step with his family," remarks Anthony Ambrogio, "when he thinks he is acting most like his father, he is actually most unlike him; he tries too hard, and destroys his family while trying to preserve it."[45]

The sections of the film dealing with Vito's early life and career shed considerable light—both for what they deal with and what they do not—on the Italian immigrant experience, and it is these sections that will be covered here. At the beginning of the film, the father of nine-year-old Vito Andolini has been killed for insulting local Mafia boss Don Ciccio. During the funeral procession, shots are heard. Vito's elder brother Paolo, who has sworn vengeance on Don Ciccio and gone off to hide in the hills, has been found and killed.[46] Vito's mother (Maria Carta) takes Vito to Don Ciccio to plead with him to spare her son's life. When he refuses (boys will grow up determined on revenge), she pulls a knife to threaten him, but is disarmed and shot. Vito runs away and, despite the warnings and blandishments of Don Ciccio, relatives or friends (it is not made clear) smuggle him out of Corleone in the pannier of a donkey. He is next seen sailing on a boat past the Statue of Liberty into New York harbor.

For all its beautiful cinematography, this opening sequence gives little information on the mass emigration that was taking place at this time from southern Italy, the region known as the *mezzogiorno*. The narrative is compressed within a framework of crime and the mafia. We learn almost nothing of the society of the town of Corleone. Don Ciccio lives in an elegant villa, guarded by armed retainers. He is clearly a man of great power in the community. But nothing is said about the class or status of others, including the Andolinis. It is implied that Sicily is a rural area (the landscape behind the funeral procession and the dependence for transport on donkeys). It is also a male-dominated society, tetchy and proud, in which the destruction of a family appears a normal and natural response to a personal insult. In reality, most emigrants from the mezzogiorno were peasants (*contadini*), escaping from the extreme poverty caused by antiquated farming methods, absentee landlords, the endless subdivison of land they owned themselves necessitated by inheritance law, and economic blows from abroad (competition from fruit-growers in Florida and California, high French tariffs on imported Italian wine).[47]

In common with *Hester Street, The Godfather Part II* ignores the hardships of the journey to America. Vito would have needed assistance to get to Naples, the main port for southern Italians leaving for the United States, perhaps by steamer from Palermo. He would have needed help with documentation, maybe with the assistance of the Emigrant Aid Society. On sailing day, he and his small bag of possessions would have been taken in a small boat to a ship in the bay of Naples, where he would have been inspected by police and health officials. For a nine-year-old boy on his own, with no family, the journey would have been difficult and dangerous. At Ellis Island, much more of the procedure for vetting potential new immigrants is shown than in *Hester Street* (Coppola viewed Elia Kazan's *America, America* (1963) and a documentary on the subject while shooting these scenes).[48] Vito, wearing a large card with his name and number (7) on it, is checked by a doctor for trachoma, an eye disease then very common in southern Europe. The queues for interview (filmed in the old fish market in Trieste, Italy) are much more chaotic than in *Hester Street*. Vito is asked his name and the interpreter explains that he is Vito Andolini from Corleone. The immigration official, either mishearing or deliberately careless, writes down Vito Corleone, renaming him like so many others in the same situation. Vito moves on to one final medical examination where a doctor, suspecting smallpox, orders him into quarantine for three months. At the end of this sequence, Vito enters a small bare cell, with an improbable view of the Statue of Liberty,[49] and starts to sing as he begins the weeks of solitary confinement that will finally be followed by his entry into the United States (Figure 7.2).

The next flashback sequence is set in New York in 1917. Vito Corleone (now Robert De Niro) is married with a baby son, Santino. He works for a grocer, Abbandando (Peter LaCorte), who, he acknowledges, "looked after me like a father." At an Italian-speaking music-hall, he and a friend see (for the first time in Vito's case) Fanucci (Gaston Moschin), who is running an extortion racket in the neighborhood. When Vito asks who he is, his friend replies "The Black Hand." Rather than being a criminal organization, like the mafia, the Black Hand was more of a method. Practiced by individuals, small groups, and sometimes larger gangs, it concentrated on extorting money from the wealthier members of the Italian community through threats of violence and bombings. Vito is not wealthy enough to attract Fanucci's interest, although "the whole neighborhood" is apparently paying him for protection. In reality, an Italian Vigilance

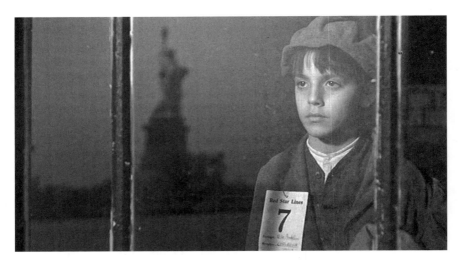

FIGURE 7.2 *Vito Andolini/Corleone (Oreste Baldini) in quarantine in*
The Godfather Part II.

Protective Association had been founded to resist black-handism in 1908
and by 1917 the phenomenon was in decline.[50] But Fanucci nonetheless
has an impact on Vito's life: he forces Abbandando to fire Vito from his
job in order to hire his own nephew.

The second and third flashback sequences are good at conveying the
lively market and street culture of Mulberry Street, the heart of "Little
Italy," located to the north and west of the Jewish ghetto on the lower
East Side. They are less impressive when it comes to representing living
conditions. Despite the fact that Vito is only a grocer's assistant, the
Corleones seem to live in an apartment that, while dark, is quite spacious.
By 1900 there were 145,000 Italians living in New York, and by 1920 this
had grown to 391,000.[51] A high proportion of these were very poor and
lived in the worst tenement accommodation. "Italian neighborhoods,"
according to one historian, "were uniformly decayed and congested;
more so than those inhabited by any other group of immigrants."[52] These
sequences are much better at conveying the importance of the family
unit in *contadini* society. "For me, there's only my wife and son," Vito
declares. He has huge personal pride: he will not accept a basket of fruit
and vegetables from Abbandando, his former employer. But when Peter
Clemenza (Bruno Kirby) offers him the gift of a carpet in exchange for
an earlier favor (Vito has concealed two guns for Clemenza), he accepts
because he thinks his wife will be pleased. But Clemenza has not told the
whole truth: the carpet is inside the apartment of a wealthy neighbor,
and Vito's help in stealing it marks the beginning of his criminal career.
By the start of the third flashback, Vito and his two friends are doing
well enough from theft to attract the attention of Fanucci, who demands

that they show him "respect" by paying him part of the proceeds of their latest robbery. Otherwise, he will tip off the cops, who "will come to your home. And your family will be ruined." By this stage, Vito has three sons in all (Santino, Fredo, and Michael). Threatening his family is a step too far. Vito takes one of the guns he has hidden and kills Fanucci. After the murder, he goes back to his apartment, picks up his youngest son, Michael, and tells him "your father loves you very much."

The fourth flashback begins some time later. Vito is now a much-respected figure in "Little Italy." Although nothing is said, it is probable that people realize he was behind the death of the unpopular Fanucci. Vito has also come to appreciate the importance of a culture involving reciprocal favors. In the opening scene, he accepts a gift from a greengrocer, offering to do something in return. His wife brings a widow, Signora Colombo, to see him. The dog she and her son own has been unpopular with the neighbors, and her landlord, Signor Roberto (Leopoldo Trieste), is about to evict her. Vito, acting according to Roger Ebert, "more like a precinct captain than a gangster," tries to persuade Roberto to change his mind.[53] He offers money in compensation. "Do me this favor," he tells Roberto, "Ask your friends in the neighborhood about me. They'll tell you I know how to return a favor." Roberto refuses, but shortly afterwards, terrified, since he now knows who he is dealing with, turns up at the office of the olive oil and cheese importing business Vito is building up as a front for his other activities. He agrees that Signora Colombo can keep her apartment at a lower rent and rushes away to get as far as possible from Vito Corleone.

In the fifth flashback, Vito and his family arrive back in Corleone by train. In common with two out of five Italian emigrants, they have returned home. They are wearing expensive, fashionable clothes (showing other members of the town the success that could be gained in America) and are greeted by the town band. The trip has three purposes. The first is to reconnect with old friends and the families of Vito's parents, which seem both large and prosperous (everyone has lunch in the sunshine outside a big house). Their comparative wealth suggests that, had it not been for the vendetta, Vito would never have gone to America. The second purpose is to make deals for the import of olive oil from local producers into the United States through Vito's new company, Genco. The third purpose, more nefarious, is finally to take revenge for the deaths of Vito's parents and brother. Vito, his old friend Tommasino (Mario Cotone) and two other men arrive at Don Ciccio's villa, which seems to have gone to seed—as has Don Ciccio, who is now very old and partly deaf. When Tommasino introduces Vito as an oil merchant, Don Ciccio asks the name of his father. Vito leans forward to say "Antonio Andolino" and, as Don Ciccio starts to realize who he is, kills him with a large knife. So potent is the power of the Sicilian vendetta that Vito is prepared to risk his life, the lives of his friends (Tommasino is shot and crippled by a guard as they escape), and the security of his new family to avenge what happened 20 years earlier in Corleone.[54]

Almost all the conversation in the "Vito" sections of the film is in Italian with a Sicilian accent (De Niro and other cast members were given special coaching).[55] This contributes to the "authenticity" of the flashback sequences, as do the lively reconstructions of the street life of "Little Italy" (dressed and filmed in the Ukrainian area of New York's East Village).[56] We see shops (such as the grocery where Vito works), street stalls, barber shops, and cafés. There is a religious *festa*, perhaps a foretaste of the celebration of Naples' patron saint, San Gennaro, which would be introduced in New York in 1926. There is also the Italian-speaking theater or music hall, where Vito sees Fanucci for the first time. But, as in *Hester Street*, concentration on some aspects of immigrant life meant the neglect of others. During the "Little Italy" sequences, Vito's children are too young to go to school so the issue of education is not touched upon (many Italians from a *contadini* background disliked American public schools as threatening the family by depriving them of children's labor and encouraging them to challenge their parents' values).[57] Religion is present in the film only as spectacle (the *festa*) or ritual (Fanucci crosses himself before the figure of Christ and is applauded for attaching a large denomination note to the base of the figure, Clemenza crosses himself before eating, and Vito has a picture of Madonna and child on the wall behind him in his Genco office). It has no discernible impact on people's actions. The movie has little to say about the work most Italians did. Coppola apparently planned or researched shots of Italians building the New York subway (three-quarters of all New York's construction workers in 1897 were Italian) and the garment industry (where New York Italians "were second only to the Jews") but these were missing from the final film.[58]

The focus on "Little Italy"—like that on the ghetto in *Hester Street*—directed attention away from the way such ethnic groups were regarded in the wider American society. There was considerable criticism of Italian immigrants in that society. They were seen as unskilled and ill-educated. They undercut wages paid to other groups, especially through the operation of the *padrone* system, in which an Italian who had come earlier to the United States supplied immigrants in gangs to employers.[59] Italians lived in overcrowded slums. They were perceived as parochial, people with different values who did not blend easily with Americans. They were also feared for their apparent association with violence and criminality. This association, argues George De Stefano, had its roots in American press coverage of attempts by the Italian government to suppress criminal bands and societies in southern Italy—the camorra in Naples and the region around, the "ndrangheta in Calabria and the mafia in Sicily." In 1890, when Police Superintendent David Hennessy was shot dead in New Orleans while "investigating extortion among the mostly Sicilian members of the city's Little Italy," 14 Italians were arrested. (A mob broke into the jail and killed

11 of the suspects.) Subsequently, popular newspapers often published sensational but untrue stories about Italian criminals and more upmarket magazines debated "whether Italians were predisposed to criminality by dint of genetics, culture, or both."[60] It was additionally unfortunate that during these years Italians were also acquiring a reputation for radicalism and political violence: Gaetano Bresci, an Italian-born anarchist who had lived for several years in the United States, returned to Italy in 1900 to assassinate King Umberto.[61]

Nineteen years after the killing of Hennessy occurred another landmark murder that, according to De Stefano, "quelled any doubts among Anglo-Saxon 'nativists' that the Southern Italian and Sicilian immigrants were a lawless bunch bent on establishing their old world crime syndicates on American soil." In 1909, Italian-born New York detective Joseph Petrosino was shot dead in Palermo. Petrosino was in Sicily investigating the background of Italian-born criminals in the United States and of others who had already returned to Italy. Yet newspapers reported that he was probing connections between Italian-American gangs in the United States and the mafia in Italy and, when an important Palermo mafia figure claimed credit for the killing, the linkage appeared beyond question. "Petrosino's murder," DeStefano asserted, "was a calamity for Italian-Americans . . . In the wake of the detective's death came massive police raids on Italian neighborhoods and vilification by public figures and the press."[62]

Hester Street and *The Godfather Part II* appeared at the same historical moment. They were very different types of film—a black and white independent production and a colorful, glossy Hollywood movie. *Hester Street* appealed mainly to an art-house audience while *The Godfather Part II* was a highly successful blockbuster. Both had their origin in a major movement of people from the Old World to the New. Both were based on novels by members of the ethnic group depicted: Abraham Cahan's *Yekl* and Mario Puzo's *The Godfather*. Each was directed by a member of that group: Joan Micklin Silver and Francis Ford Coppola. Each (*The Godfather Part II* only partially) dealt with the stresses of adapting to American life. Both ethnic groups represented were unpopular with many native-born Americans or earlier generations of immigrants. That unpopularity underpinned the preference expressed by the Dillingham Commission in 1911 for "old" immigrants over the "new," increasing demands that all immigrants be required to pass a literacy test and, finally, the Johnson-Reed Act of 1924. The latter imposed quotas on different nationalities allowed to enter the United States. Since the quotas were calculated on the basis of the Census of 1890, before the greatest waves of Jews and Italians arrived, it was clearly intended to discourage further immigration by members of those groups. Neither *Hester Street* nor *The Godfather Part II* dealt with this attempt to close what Emma Lazarus had 41 years earlier dubbed "the golden door." Yet in focusing so clearly *only* on the members of the groups concerned—and, in *The Godfather Part II*, on their associations with criminality[63]—the two films unconsciously reflected the fears of nativists of the 1920s that Jews and Italians were less desirable (because less easily assimilated) than the immigrants who had come before.

Filmography

The Jazz Singer (dir. Alan Crosland; Warner Bros., 1927).
My Girl Tisa (dir. Elliott Nugent; United States Pictures, 1948).
America, America (dir. Elia Kazan; Warner Bros./Athena Enterprises, 1963).
Popi (dir. Arthur Hiller; Herbert B. Leonard Productions, 1969).
The Molly Maguires (dir. Martin Ritt; Paramount, 1970).
Mean Streets (dir. Martin Scorsese; Warner Bros., 1973).
The Godfather Part II (dir. Francis Ford Coppola; Paramount, 1974).
Hester Street (dir. Joan Micklin Silver; Midwest Films, 1975).

CHAPTER EIGHT*

The Limits of Hollywood History: *The Grapes of Wrath* and the Great Depression

The release of the movie *The Grapes of Wrath* in January 1940 provoked a heated debate. William R. Weaver, writing in the trade journal *Motion Picture Herald*, remarked that—like the John Steinbeck novel on which it was based—the film was "daring, significant and controversial." Although Weaver praised the technical aspects of the film, he thought it dealt with "a melancholy subject" and concluded that, in its attempts to be faithful to the original, it included "much that does not fit into the accepted conception of family entertainment." Martin Quigley, in the same issue of *Motion Picture Weekly*, contributed a special editorial in which he condemned the film as "a new and emphatic item of evidence in support of the frequently repeated assertion in these columns that the entertainment motion picture is no place for social, political and economic argument."[1] Edwin Locke, writing for the liberal *New Republic*, emphatically disagreed, attacking Quigley's insistence that movies should offer only ill-defined "entertainment." To Locke, *The Grapes of Wrath* had "dramatized and memorialized one wretched section of the victims of American history," setting in the process a crucial precedent "for contemporary and historical honesty in movie-making."[2] Critical disagreements over *The Grapes of Wrath* went to the heart of the debate over what Hollywood films ought to be trying to do and the themes they could legitimately explore. At the same time,

*An earlier version of this chapter was published in Cornelis A. van Minnen and Sylvia L. Hilton, eds, *Frontiers and Boundaries in U. S. History* (Amsterdam: VU University Press, 2004). It has been extensively revised and appears here by permission.

critics themselves (including Quigley himself) often commented on the film's technical and cinematographic innovations. It was not simply that *The Grapes of Wrath* was on the boundary of what was permissible for a mainstream film in 1940, but it also extended the frontiers of moviemaking in aesthetic terms too.

Hollywood and the Depression

The man who decided to make a film of Steinbeck's novel in the first place was Darryl F. Zanuck, vice-president in charge of production at the Twentieth-Century Fox studio. Zanuck had begun his career at Warner Bros., where he had written films first for a dog (Rin Tin Tin), then for human stars, and finally—not yet 30—had been promoted to head of production. At Warner Bros., he was primarily responsible for the cycle of "social exposé" films produced in 1931–2: *The Match King* (critiquing business ethics), *The Cabin in the Cotton* (on the exploitation of Southern share-croppers), *Two Seconds* (attacking capital punishment), and *I Am A Fugitive From a Chain Gang* (dealing with the deficiencies of the penal system in the South).[3] Such films were by no means unusual for their time: other studios were producing movies that were—according to Terry Christensen—"questioning and pessimistic, torn between group solidarity and strong leadership as possible solutions to the crisis of the Depression."[4] By 1933–4, however, the cycle of critical and socially conscious movies produced by Hollywood had practically come to an end. There were a number of reasons for this. The inauguration of Franklin D. Roosevelt in March 1933 brought about a major change in the political climate. However successful or unsuccessful New Deal programs were, they at least created the impression that the Federal government was now actively involved both in fighting the Depression and attempting to alleviate its social consequences. Moreover, partly as a result of the Depression, the film industry had become extremely vulnerable to outside pressures.

Hollywood itself had been hard hit by the economic slump. Total box office income fell from a peak of $732,000,000 in 1930 to $482,000,000 in 1933.[5] Such a 34 percent fall in income seemed even more disastrous because, as a result of the costs of acquiring theater chains and innovating sound in the late 1920s, most of the major studios were under the financial control of their banks.[6] Conscious of its own weakness, the industry faced both public and private threats to its autonomy. During the 1920s, Protestant organizations such as the Reverend William H. Short's Motion Picture Research Council and Canon William S. Chase's Federal Motion Picture Council had pressed for Federal censorship of films to be introduced. In 1928, Short managed to secure funding from the Payne Fund for a series of sociological investigations into the impact of movies.

Most of the results of these surveys were published in 1933, together with *Our Movie-Made Children*, a book by popular journalist Henry James Forman summarizing the findings of the project. What the Payne Fund studies seemed to prove, through apparently impartial scientific research, was that the movies had a bad effect on young people, encouraging them to act and behave in antisocial ways. Their publication consequently gave an important boost to demands for federal regulation of the film industry as a whole.[7]

The Catholic approach to the problem of what to do about the movies was very different. Martin Quigley, publisher of the *Motion Picture Herald* (in which he would much later criticize *The Grapes of Wrath*), did not believe in government censorship (which was always vulnerable to pressure from corrupt politicians). He preferred to ensure that films were made without the inclusion of questionable material through a tighter system of movie industry self-regulation. In late 1929, he took the draft of a new "Production Code" written by fellow-Catholic Daniel Lord to Will H. Hays, chairman of the Motion Picture Producers and Distributors of America (MPPDA). Hays quickly realized its usefulness and secured its acceptance by the major film producers. After its formal adoption in 1930, however, the Production Code was more honored in the breach than the observance. It was supposed to ensure that Hollywood produced only entertainment that was "correct" and "moral." The Code itself was overwhelmingly concerned with the treatment of sex, but it also insisted that good always be preferred to evil, that crime must not be presented sympathetically, and that the judicial system must never be represented as unjust.[8] Yet the period after 1930 saw the release, among many other examples, of the sex comedies of Mae West, a series of "fallen women" films, and an early cycle of "gangster" films (*Little Caesar, Public Enemy,* and *Scarface*)—all of which, in one way or another, challenged aspects of the Production Code.[9]

This situation changed, however, in 1934. Catholics, disappointed with the operation of the Production Code, formed the Legion of Decency. This was a major force because the principal weapon it wielded—the threat of a boycott of some films by the US's 20 million Catholics—seemed particularly worrying to Hollywood at a time when audience figures were already depressed. (Because American Catholics were predominantly concentrated in urban areas, had their own national press, and the disciplined leadership of a church hierarchy, they could threaten Hollywood with the possibility of impressively united action.) Moreover, 1934 saw the establishment of the film industry's own "alphabet agency": the Production Code Administration (PCA) under Catholic Joseph I. Breen.[10]

After the introduction of the PCA, the Production Code itself was rigorously enforced for the first time. Some genres and film cycles were no longer made. Other subjects became taboo so far as the major studios were concerned. These included, for the most part, attempts at social exposures and anything to do with the history and consequences of the Depression. After 1934, as Robert Sklar has pointed out, most "of the important moneymaking pictures . . . had little to do with contemporary life."[11] Most Hollywood movies of the mid to late 1930s offered "entertainment" that allowed audiences to escape from the problems of the Depression years. "Nothing," Thomas H. Pauly has pointed out, "could have been further from the bread lines and the deprivation photographed by Dorothea Lange than the social comedies of Lubitsch, the slapstick of the Marx Brothers, and the polished dance routines of Fred Astaire and Ginger Rogers."[12]

Darryl Zanuck, who had left Warners in 1933 to found the new studio Twentieth Century (which merged with Fox in 1935), found himself doing the same as the rest of Hollywood. Turning his back on contemporary and historical realism, he concentrated on musicals, Shirley Temple vehicles, and genre pictures. One deeply unimpressed writer for the *New Masses* described Zanuck at this time as "a digger of some of the largest voids in the field of culture."[13] For all the complaints of left-wing critics, however, it is important to emphasize the fact that films produced during what David Bordwell, Kristin Thompson, and Janet Staiger have called "Classical" Hollywood were industrial products.[14] They were produced by vertically integrated corporations that existed solely for that purpose. The principal aims of these companies were to maximize the opportunity for profit and to minimize risks. Within this system, Zanuck was a highly skilled operator. Under him, Twentieth-Century Fox achieved the third best financial record (after MGM and Warner Bros.) for productions in 1938–9. This success, together with the growing demand for A-class movies in first-run houses created by the beginnings of economic recovery, would create the conditions for the making of *The Grapes of Wrath*.[15]

The Grapes of Wrath: From novel to screen

John Steinbeck's novel *The Grapes of Wrath* was published in March 1939. Two months later, Zanuck paid $70,000 for the movie rights, making it the most expensive cinematic property acquired that year.[16] His reasons for doing so may have included the desire to acquire a presold property (Steinbeck's novel had swiftly become a best seller) and awareness of a contemporary trend among the studios (as international tensions rose in Europe) to make films out of adaptations of novels and plays dealing with American subjects.[17] But, in signing a deal that bound Fox to preserve the theme of Steinbeck's book (the only book he would later recall ever reading all the way through), Zanuck must have been aware that he was embarking on a deeply controversial project.[18] The California Chamber of Commerce was bitterly opposed and the representatives of large farmers in the state called for a boycott of all Fox productions if the movie was made. Twentieth-Century Fox itself and its main banker, Chase National in New York, came under intense pressure to abandon the project. Zanuck, strengthened by evidence from private investigators that the plight of migrant workers in California was even worse than Steinbeck had suggested, refused to back down. Opening a war on another front, he also threatened to launch a public campaign against the Hays Office if the PCA attempted to intervene.[19]

Throughout his career, Zanuck displayed an interest in making "social consciousness" movies. By the late 1940s, indeed, for reasons that will be examined later, he was probably the *only* head of production for a major studio with such an interest. In 1943, on his return from Second World War duty as a colonel in the signal corps, Zanuck criticized the Hollywood obsession with films that "radiated sweetness and light" at a Writer's Congress meeting at the University of California, Los Angeles. It was time, he urged, for the industry

> to move onto new ground, break new trails . . . we must play our part in the solution of the problems that torture the world. We must begin to deal realistically in film with the *causes* [my italics] of wars and panics, with social upheavals and the depression, with starvation and want and injustice and barbarism under whatever guise.[20]

Zanuck himself, worried about the possibility that the United States would lapse back into isolationism, produced *Wilson*—a biopic of the twenty-eighth president who had fought for the League of Nations—in 1944 and considered filming a version of Wendell Wilkie's internationalist tract, *One World*.[21] Yet it would be wrong to perceive Zanuck as in any sense radical. A safe Republican in politics (he voted for Wilkie rather than Franklin D. Roosevelt in 1940), he championed historically realist and "social consciousness" pictures only in part for idealistic reasons. He was also convinced that they appealed to the interest of audiences and, therefore, helped the studio's balance sheet. *The Grapes of Wrath* itself justified this belief, being Fox's most profitable production of 1940.[22]

Critics hostile to *The Grapes of Wrath* tended to perceive the film as an accurate adaptation of the book. Martin Quigley, in his *Motion Picture Herald* editorial, saw the screenplay as "guided by the heavy and designing hand of John Steinbeck." William R. Weaver, in his review, described it as "an extremely literal and very nearly complete transcription of the Steinbeck novel."[23] Other critics—while writing positively of the film as a whole—emphasized that crucial aspects of the novel had disappeared or been toned down. Some of these changes were inevitable. The Hays Code, for example, did not permit swearing in movies. More seriously, the still-birth of Rosasharn's child and her subsequent attempt to save the life of a starving man by permitting him to suckle her breasts were completely unacceptable (for a whole variety of reasons) to the PCA. Apart from such omissions, there were also a number of additions or changes that helped make the story less depressing. Although the adaptation of the novel was credited to Nunnally Johnson, a Fox contract writer, it was almost certainly heavily influenced by Zanuck himself. Traditionally, Zanuck involved himself closely in story development at the studio; his two- to four-hour daily story conferences were legendary. Johnson himself would later concede that he "was a collaborator on anything I ever did."[24] Consequently, it may well have been Zanuck who suggested transforming the Weed Patch Camp of the novel into the Wheat Patch Camp, and placing the Joads' arrival at the camp toward the end of the movie, thus setting the scene for a much more optimistic ending than in Steinbeck's novel. The clear association of the camp with the New Deal—from the sign at the entrance announcing it as part of a program run by the Department of Agriculture to the depiction of its director as a prototype FDR[25]—may also have been due to Zanuck. Aware that his film would be attacked by right-wingers, Zanuck may have thought that identifying it with the popular Roosevelt (who was triumphantly reelected while it was in the middle of being shot) might make it less vulnerable to such criticism.

Once shooting actually started on September 28, 1939, John Ford and his cinematographer, Gregg Toland, had their own chance to put flesh on the bones of the script produced by Johnson and heavily influenced by Zanuck. Their movie differed from other contemporary American feature films not simply because of its social concern, but also through its visual appearance. "It has been photographed in the flat, newsreel technique," noted William R. Weaver on the film's release. "Similarly, the players wear no more makeup than flood sufferers." Philip T. Hartung, another contemporary critic, also applauded the absence of "Hollywood" production values: "No artificial make-up, no false sentiment, no glamour stars mar the authentic documentary form of this provocative film."[26] The film still appeared fresh and innovative several decades later. Terry Christensen writes that it "retains a documentary quality that is radically different from the style of other films but perfectly suited to *The Grapes of Wrath*."[27] One of Ford's biographers has suggested that the film's aesthetic style had its roots in several sources: contemporary photojournalism, British and American documentaries, expressionism in the cinema, and the paintings of Thomas Hart Benton.[28] Other students of film have underlined the efforts by the young and innovative Toland to expand the frontiers of filmmaking. Experimenting with wide-angle lens, high-speed film, new lighting techniques, "roofed-in" sets (as in the diner scene), and deep-focus cinematography, he was well on the way to developing the stylized form of realism that would soon impress the whole movie industry in *Citizen Kane*.[29] Certainly, in aesthetic terms, *The Grapes of Wrath* was very much on the frontiers of Hollywood filmmaking in 1939.

The fact that John Ford was the director of *The Grapes of Wrath* came about because Zanuck had formed a "Ford unit" at Twentieth-Century Fox. Ford himself had just finished three films back to back—*Stagecoach*, *Young Mr. Lincoln*, and *Drums Along the Mohawk*. With *Stagecoach* he had made his first Western since *The Iron Horse* in 1924 and, in the process, had reinvigorated a genre that seemed to have bumbled along on the lower half of the bill—the classic "B" movie—during the Depression years. *The Grapes of Wrath*, as some left-wing critics of the time perceptively noted, was itself in many respects a Western, albeit a revisionist one. Instead of the pioneers moving West in wagon trains and menaced by Indians, it was the Joad family—together with countless other Okies—heading for California in their old jalopy, threatened this time not by Indians but by poverty and starvation. Moreover, unlike earlier Westerns (including Ford's), *The Grapes of Wrath* dealt with the real social consequences of the western migration. Only with *The Grapes of Wrath*, argued Edward Locke in his contemporary review, had Hollywood—"by touching on some of the results of land speculation, submarginal farming, agricultural mechanization, and the California latifundia"—at last "given us a picture that totalled, in human values, some of the results of our drive to the frontier."[30]

Dust storms and tractors

The Grapes of Wrath is a film about "history" in the most literal sense: its action is set in the past, even if that past was a relatively recent one. "The story of the southern plains in the 1930s," comments Donald Worster, "is essentially about dust storms, when the earth ran amok."[31] When Muley Graves (John Qualen) explains to Tom Joad (Henry Fonda) and Casy (John Carradine) why everybody has to "get off" their Oklahoma farms, he blames "the dusters" for creating the situation: "Blowin' like this, year after year, blowin' the land away, blowin' the crops away." A drought beginning in 1931 had dried out the topsoil across large areas of the plains, making it friable and easily blown away as dust when winds came. The Soil Conservation Service charted the rising tempo of dust storms: 14 (1932); 38 (1933); 22 (1934); 40 (1935); 68 (1936); 72 (1937); 61 (1938). In 1937, the worst year, at one location in the panhandle of northwestern Oklahoma the dust storms lasted in all for 550 hours. After 1938, as the drought eased up, the number of such storms declined sharply.[32] There are no dates in Ford's *The Grapes of Wrath*, but the fictional Joads appear to have set off for California in the latter part of the 1930s, most probably around 1937. The Wheat Patch Camp (Figure 8.1) where they rest up for a time after their long journey was based on the Weedpatch Camp in Kern County, California,

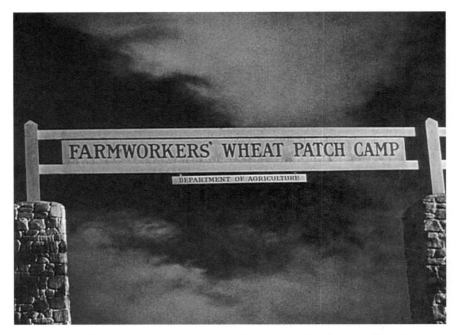

FIGURE 8.1 *The entrance to the Wheat Patch Camp in* The Grapes of Wrath.

founded in 1935 with residents living in tents. By 1937, it offered 23 homes in all.[33]

The film version of Steinbeck's novel offers two main explanations for the plight of the Joad family and the other Okies who live on the land. Listening to the dust storm howling around the Joads' abandoned farm, Muley describes such storms as "some of what done it . . . Started it, anyway." The drive to exploit the land for profit and the availability of technology have completed the process. The city man in the car who is shown in a flashback giving Muley his notice to quit explains to him that

> after what them dusters done to the land, the tenant system don't work no more. It don't even break even, much less show a profit. One man on a tractor can handle twelve or fourteen of these places. You just pay him a wage and take all the crop.

The film presents sharecroppers such as Muley and the Joads simultaneously as victims of the environment (the dusters), capitalism (the drive for profit), and technological progress (the development of mechanized tractors). It does not suggest, what was also true, that overproduction of agricultural staples played a significant role and that the dust storms, to a significant degree, had been produced by man.

Sharecropping had its roots in the impoverished South after the Civil War. Landowners negotiated for the labor they needed to produce crops on the basis, not of wages, but a share of the crop once it had been harvested and sold. The system usually developed in association with local stores, who would extend credit (often at very high rates of interest) until each crop was sold. Once caught up in the toils of the sharecropping system, it was difficult to escape. Sharecropping families sometimes lived for many years on the same land in a condition that was close to economic peonage: Muley talks of his grandfather settling on "his" land 70 years earlier and Tom claims "we been here fifty years." Both families—improbably—can trace their roots in Oklahoma before it became either a territory (1890) or a state (1907). The Joads come from Sallisaw, in Sequoyah county (Connie (Eddie Quillan) is from neighboring Cherokee county), in the southeast of Oklahoma. This placed them squarely in the cotton belt (as Pa (Russell Simpson) says in the final sequence "Be glad to get my hand on some cotton. That's the kind of pickin' I understand").[34] This dependence on one crop, grown for export, placed the sharecroppers at the mercy of prices on the world market, which were kept low by overproduction. At the same time, sharecropping—a conservative form of agriculture—tended to deplete the soil by growing the same crop year after year.

Donald Worster sees the problems of this area of the southern plains beginning well before the 1930s and continuing long after. They had their roots in the initial attempt of man to exploit the plains for profit. The area had originally been grassed over and the sod protected the soil, even to a degree on the southern plains "where the grass had always struggled to hold the land against powerful winds and recurrent drought." But farmers ploughed up the plains to plant wheat in the north and cotton in the south, exploiting the land for a cash return.[35] Undermined by the loss of grass, weakened by subsequent monoculture, large quantities of topsoil—when hit by drought—simply blew away. The push to mechanize farming came from the same profit imperative that had mandated the exploitation of the plains for commercial agriculture in the first place. The use of tractors, expanded greatly in the 1920s and 1930s, offered no solution to the problem of soil erosion, though as *The Grapes of Wrath* accurately showed, it did contribute to driving sharecroppers and tenant farmers off the land.[36] Yet, Worster maintains, "even without tractors Oklahoma could not have provided a permanent home for people like the Joads: too much of its soil had been destroyed." According to an estimate by the state agricultural college at Stillwater, 13 million out of Oklahoma's 16 million acres of cultivated land suffered from erosion.[37] Only the three northwestern counties of the Oklahoma panhandle (Cimmaron, Texas, and Beaver) were part of the "dust bowl," but most of the rest of the state was affected by soil erosion. It was these areas—including the Joads' Sequoyah county—that accounted for the bulk of migrants leaving Oklahoma. They did so, Worster explains, primarily because they were "victims . . . of an exploitative agricultural system: of tractors, one-crop specialization, tenant insecurity, disease, and soil abuse."[38] In blaming

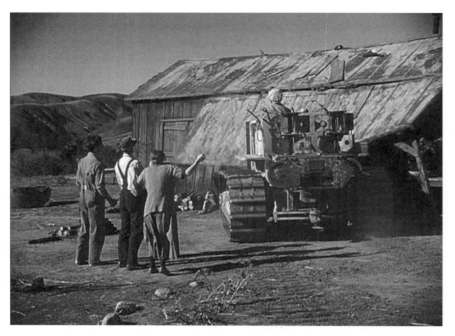

FIGURE 8.2 *The tractor destroys the house of Muley Graves (John Qualen) in* The Grapes of Wrath.

weather ("the dusters") Ford's *The Grapes of Wrath* diverted attention from reckless farming methods and their consequences.

A glaring absence in *The Grapes of Wrath*, until the Joads reach the Wheat Patch Camp in California, is any suggestion of assistance from the Federal government. When New Deal agricultural policy was formulated in 1933, its first priority was dealing with the surplus production of commodities. The Agricultural Adjustment Administration (AAA) established in May 1933 set out to pay farmers to cut acreage under cultivation in order to reduce the production of staple crops and raise commodity prices. Since the scheme was administered by local committees whose membership was drawn from the larger farmers, it offered little or no help to sharecroppers and tenant farmers.[39] The effect, indeed, was the opposite: reducing acreage, while allocating money that could be used for increasing mechanization, meant that more and more sharecroppers and tenants were evicted.[40] A few destitute farmers profited from early New Deal relief programs, just as some were later aided by the Resettlement Administration of 1935–6 and the Bankhead-Jones Tenancy Act of 1937.[41] But there was no attempt, for example, to pay people like the Joads directly to reduce acreage and the policies of the AAA in the end had the indirect effect of forcing many off their farms.[42]

California bound

When the Joads leave their homes and set off for California, they embark on an illuminating Depression-era tour of rural America. This makes clear the link between agriculture, which still employed 30 percent of the national workforce in 1933, and those who depended on it.[43] A former storekeeper from Arkansas, also on the road, ruefully remarks that "when the farms went the stores went too." Several scenes bring home the reality of starvation or near-starvation and the failure of efforts at relief: the man at the first wayside camp talking of his dying children "layin' in the tent with their bellies puffed out an' just skin on their bones" and the feverish rush of children in the later "Hooverville" camp to find receptacles for food when Ma Joad (Jane Darwell) offers to feed them. At the same time, it becomes clear that not everyone is suffering. The truck drivers at the hamburger stand not only eat well, they leave generous tips—a tribute, perhaps, to the power of early unionization by the Teamsters. There are policemen and security guards everywhere—including the cop (Ward Bond) in the first Californian town the Joads arrive in, who had migrated from neighboring Cherokee county, Oklahoma, two years earlier.

In the film, the Joads are persuaded to set out on their epic journey by a handbill advertising 800 jobs for picking peaches in California. The film is correct in suggesting that Californian growers encouraged immigration into the state. With the exception of the 1937–8 recession, James N. Gregory points out, "the Californian economy grew steadily" in the late 1930s. Agricultural production expanded during this period but, during the Depression, much of the established Mexican labor force had been repatriated.[44] Growers did indeed advertise for labor.[45] In the first camp in which the Joads spend the night, a crowd of men are all carrying handbills advertising jobs. One disillusioned Okie, on his way back from California, explains the tactic to them:

> this man wants 800 men. So he prints up 5,000 of them handbills and maybe 20,000 people sees them. And maybe two-three thousand starts moving, [on] account of this handbill. Two-three thousand folks that's crazy with worry heading out for 800 jobs.

Later, in the Hooverville, an unlicensed labor contractor arrives with a police escort, making airy promises of "about thirty cents" an hour for fruitpicking. In the original filmscript (cut from the film) Floyd (Paul Guilfoyle) pulls out a handbill and asks suspiciously "how do we know you ain't one of the guys that sent these things out?"[46] To Floyd, and many real-life labor organizers, the handbills represented a conscious strategy of exploitation by the growers, designed to bring in Okies as strikebreakers and reduce still further the already low level of wages on offer.[47]

The Joads' journey to California shows the disdain many locals had for people who have little money to spend. To the guard on the Arizona border, it only matters that they are not carrying any plants that might infect local crops with disease—and that they are not planning to remain in the state. Once they cross into California, however, it is obvious to everyone they meet that they have come as a family to stay. The film advances only one reason for the hostility of many Californians to Dust Bowl migrants: that they will take the jobs of native Californians. When the Joads find the road to one town blocked off, the leader of the locals tell them that "we don't want any more Okies in this town. We ain't got work enough for them that are here already." The point is further emphasized by handmade signs along roads saying "NO WORK" and "NO HELP WANTED." In practice, there were a complex of reasons for widespread anti-Okie sentiment. Okies tended to concentrate in the state's agricultural counties.[48] The camps in which many lived were associated by health authorities and newspapers with diseases and health problems.[49] Okies were blamed for the increased cost of schools, health, and sanitation.[50] They were deemed principally responsible for the sharply rising costs of relief payments (there was a leap of 344 percent in relief caseloads in the San Joaquin Valley between 1937 and 1939).[51] They were also suspected of being left-wing ("reds") in politics and wrongly blamed for the election of a Democrat, Culbert Olsen, as governor in 1938, breaking the Republican hegemony in the state.[52]

According to Charles J. Shindo, the main difference between John Steinbeck's novel *The Grapes of Wrath* and John Ford's film based upon it was that the novel "championed progressive ideas about reform and relief" while the movie "reinforced more traditional beliefs in moral values and the family."[53] In the film, the Joads have only two jobs in California. They first find work on the Keene ranch, where they pick peaches and are used as strikebreakers. They live in a dirty shack and can only buy food from the overpriced company store. When the strike is defeated, their reward is to have their wages cut, since there will always be needy people willing to take their place. The second job, much more briefly shown, is working for a local farmer laying pipes. The lessons the family take from the experience of life in California are mainly those derived from the Keene ranch. But those lessons point in very different directions: Shindo's view of the film's message focuses mainly on the impression left by Ma's final speech. But that was itself a product of last-minute studio anxieties.

The film that Ford shot seems to have stayed close to the shooting script written by Nunnally Johnson and approved both by Zanuck and Steinbeck himself. It ended with Tom Joad going on the run from the law, leaving his family in the Wheat Patch Camp. In the scene in which he says goodbye to Ma Joad, Tom's speech is heavy with references to startling social inequalities and injustice. It also demonstrates his new commitment to activism and collective action. At the end of this scene, Tom strides off

THE LIMITS OF HOLLYWOOD HISTORY

into the dawn in order to become a radical agitator or follow in Casy's footsteps as a labor organizer. At this point, Ford turned over the cans of film he had shot to Zanuck for final editing and left to go on vacation. For Ford himself, this was standard practice. He hated cutting rooms and was happy that Zanuck (whom he regarded as "a great film editor") should take over responsibility for this.[54] But Zanuck was by this stage clearly worried about possible difficulties with the PCA, and his gut feeling was that a more upbeat ending was needed to expand the film's popular appeal. In Ford's absence (through probably with his verbal agreement), Zanuck himself shot a new ending in which the Joads abandon the Wheat Patch Camp in search of work elsewhere. Ma Joad is now clearly the head of the family ("I ain't no good any more," Pa confesses),[55] and she delivers a long speech (written by Zanuck himself according to his biographer) in which she praises the qualities and staying power of "the people," suggesting that they—like the Joads—will triumph in the end.[56]

There can be little doubt that the new ending undermined the radical character of the film Ford had shot. It moved *The Grapes of Wrath* closer to the type of populist cinema produced by Frank Capra in the late 1930s and early 1940s. Capra's populism showed how "the people" could be saved when one heroic individual took on the political and economic system and won.[57] There is no real suggestion, other than in Ma's speech, that this is likely to happen in *The Grapes of Wrath*. If anything, it is implied—in his goodbye scene with Ma—that Tom is most likely to suffer the same fate as Casy, who has been murdered for being a strike leader. Left-wing critics at the time of the film's release were unenthusiastic about Zanuck's new ending (Edwin Locke regretted "that the woolly lines about how the people go on and on are handed to Ma to end the picture").[58] Later scholars have been equally hostile. Tag Gallagher, in his study of Ford's films, declared that Ma's speech "virtually destroys the film's trajectory toward inevitable *disintegration*/revolution, in favour of *perseverance*/abidance."[59] Until Ma's homily to "the people" and their capacity for survival, the film had concerned itself primarily with what Thomas Pauly sees as "[t]he futility of individualism and the breakdown of the family."[60] Even the Wheat Patch Camp is shown as offering only temporary respite, since Tom leaves it as a fugitive from justice and, soon after, the surviving Joads abandon it in a new search for temporary work.

By focusing so narrowly on the Joads, Ford's movie avoids dealing with the California context of the time. It suggests that accusing those challenging the status quo of being "reds" is a common tactic on the part of local conservatives ("Every time you turn around," Tom complains, "[there's] somebody calling somebody else a red.") Communists had indeed formed part of the Cannery and Agricultural Workers Industrial Union (CAWIU)'s successful cotton strike of 1933, but the growers had subsequently combined into the Associated Farmers' organization (1934) and quickly destroyed the union through "a campaign of violent harassment and criminal syndicalism prosecutions."[61] A new union, the United Cannery, Agricultural, Packing and Allied Workers of America (UCAPAWA) appeared on the scene in 1937. Its defeat in a cotton strike two years later, remarks James N. Gregory, "ended serious efforts to organize field workers."[62] It was always difficult, of course, to unionize migrant workers who were usually highly mobile. But the film draws attention to two other main reasons for the failure of unionization in agriculture. The first was the anti-communist propaganda ("reds") referred to by Tom. Many Okies were patriotic and politically conservative: their antipathy to communism made them susceptible to such campaigns.[63] They were also instinctively drawn to ideas of "individualism and family self-sufficiency" rather than those involving collective action.[64] Tom emphasizes this in telling Casy why the Joads will not join the strike against the Keene ranch: "You think Pa's going to give up his meat on account of some other fellows? Rosasharn needs milk. You think Ma's going to starve that baby just on account of fellows yelling outside a gate?"

While the movie version of *The Grapes of Wrath* is less bleak than the novel, it still offers no obvious justification for the optimism expressed both in Ma's final speech or Tom's parting regret that he will not be there "when you and Pa get settled in a nice little place." The extended Joad family has largely collapsed: the grandparents have died, Connie has abandoned the pregnant Rosasharn (Dorris Bowdon), Tom is on the run from the law. The "about" two hundred dollars they have saved for the journey must be nearly exhausted: the truck to carry them cost 75, petrol probably around ten dollars more. The remaining family members are now migrant labor with no permanent home, dependent on exploitative agribusiness for their wages. Yet, while the story told by Steinbeck and Ford ends at this point, it is likely that the downward spiral in the family's fortunes will shortly come to an end. The impact of the Second World War will make itself felt in California a year before Pearl Harbor when, notes Walter J. Stein, "the defense boom pulled the Okies into the urban areas where they took jobs in the shipyards and the munitions plants and began their slow process of assimilation into the state." Even the radical press noticed "a decline of interest in the Joads" as the Okie migration was subsumed into what was seen as a wider "defense migration." Some Okies, of course, did not abandon agriculture: as wartime labor scarcity made itself felt, they "became accustomed to high earnings and a new sense of pride."[65] Ma and Pa probably had their "nice little place" after all.

Aftermath of *The Grapes of Wrath*

If the final version of *The Grapes of Wrath* was less radical than Ford's film—itself considerably less bitter than Steinbeck's original novel—it was still unusual in being a Hollywood film that confronted some of the historical realities of the Depression. As Gallagher notes, it is "difficult to recall any other movie from a major studio whose tone was anywhere near so 'aware.'"[66] To the surprise and dismay of critics such as Quigley, the film proved popular with audiences (albeit more so in cities than in the countryside, where recollections of the sufferings of farmers were still raw). Premièred at the Rivoli in New York, it broke all of the theater's opening day records. In its eight-week run there, it made $273,000 (or one-seventh of the total cost of producing it.)[67] In his favorable review in *The New Republic*, Edwin Locke observed that "audiences . . . are crowding the box offices and breaking into spontaneous applause after each screening of the picture." The manager of the Criterion Theater in Oklahoma City (possibly reflecting the special interest of "Okies" in the film) greeted it as "[o]ne of the greatest pictures of our time. Honesty fearlessly on screen." What *The Grapes of Wrath* seemed to prove was that socially aware movies could succeed at the box office. Its success, observed *Variety*, "may lead other producers to explore the rich field of contemporary life which films have neglected and ignored."[68]

A year later, Zanuck, pleased with *The Grapes of Wrath*'s career, returned to the theme of dispossessed farmers and—again with a script by Nunnally Johnson and with Ford as director—set out to make a movie adaptation of another sensational novel, Erskine Caldwell's *Tobacco Road*. Shortly after the film's release, however, the United States became involved in the Second World War. Not only did the war itself distract attention from domestic problems, the mobilization of millions of men into the armed forces and the conversion of the economy to full wartime production practically eliminated unemployment and most of the remaining effects of the Depression. In his speech to the Writers' Congress at UCLA in 1943, however, Zanuck looked forward to a postwar world in which Hollywood would no longer be afraid to deal with the darker and more problematic side of the American experience in historical and social terms. Once the war ended in 1945, it looked for a time as if his hopes might be justified. A number of films were released that looked at social problems: alcoholism (*The Lost Weekend* (1945); *Smash-Up* (1947)); rehabilitating war veterans (*The Best Years of Our Lives* and *Till the End of Time* (both 1946)), and anti-semitism (*Crossfire* and *Gentleman's Agreement* (both 1947)). After 1947, however, the number of "social problem" films dropped, with Zanuck's Twentieth-Century Fox and independent producer Stanley Kramer responsible for most of the ones that were produced.[69]

There were two main reasons for this decline. The first was the state of the American movie industry itself. Movie attendance started to decline after 1946, its peak year. The postwar baby boom and the emergence of new leisure pursuits (there were one million television sets in the United States in 1948 and 11 million by 1950) undercut the profitability of Hollywood. By 1948, industry profits had halved since 1946. Overseas markets were also down, as countries such as Britain and France adopted policies designed to protect their domestic film industries from American competition.[70] In 1948, moreover, the Supreme Court issued its Paramount decree, undercutting the long-term stability and profitability of the major studios by forcing them to sell off their chains of movie theaters. The increasing economic vulnerability of Hollywood discouraged attempts at making movies that might alienate significant sections of the national audience by presenting controversial historical or social views.

The second reason for the fall in the number of social problem films was the advent of the Cold War. With the Soviet Union as the United States' principal international threat, right-wing Americans were eager to avoid anything that—by criticizing the workings of American capitalism—would give aid to the communist opponent. "Don't Smear the Free Enterprise System"/"Don't Deify the Common Man"/"Don't Show That Poverty is a Virtue . . . and Failure is Noble," warned a guide published by Ayn Rand in 1947.[71] In terms of The Grapes of Wrath (which was shown in the Soviet Union to underline the extent of poverty in the United States), right-wingers adopted a dual approach. They tried to restrict its circulation (as well as other "critical" movies) abroad.[72] They also set out to make it impossible to make similar, unflattering films in future. "We'll have no more Grapes of Wrath, we'll have no more Tobacco Roads," declared Eric Johnston, head of Hollywood's Motion Picture Association of America (MPAA), in March 1947. "We'll have no more films that show the seamy side of American life."[73]

Perhaps the most effective of all right-wing organizations of the time, the House Committee on Un-American Activities (HUAC), began its investigation into possible communist subversion in the movie industry with secret sessions in Los Angeles in May 1947. In October of that year, it held public hearings in Washington with a number of "unfriendly" (communist or once-communist) witnesses. When they refused to cooperate, these witnesses—who quickly became known as the "Hollywood Ten"—were cited for contempt of Congress. In November 1947, in the "Waldorf Statement," movie producers introduced a formal blacklist of those with communist associations. The next step was inescapable. In December 1947, the same edition of the Motion Picture Herald that announced the rerelease of The Grapes of Wrath also included news of the firing of the Hollywood Ten.[74]

In the climate of the time, it was now much harder to produce a film that dared to be critical of any aspect of American society or history. Journalist Lillian Ross, interviewing William Wyler, the director of The Best Years of Our Lives, reported that "he is convinced that he could not make [it] today and that Hollywood will provide no more films like The Grapes of Wrath and Crossfire."[75] Only Zanuck's Twentieth-Century Fox, among the major studios, continued to produce a small

number of "social problem" films.[76] Two of these—*Pinky* (1949) and
No Way Out (1950)—dealt with race, the one area in which the MPAA
(supported by the National Association for the Advancement of Colored
People (NAACP)), resisted the attempt by right-wing forces to prevent
the making of critical or controversial movies.[77] Otherwise, with the
Cold War intensifying (in 1949, the Soviet Union exploded its first
atomic bomb and China was "lost" to communism; in 1950, the Korean
War began), the production of "social problem" pictures—indeed of all
pictures that retold the history of the United States in a different and
critical way—came virtually to an end. The rise of "McCarthyism" and
the rumors surrounding the possibility of another HUAC investigation
into the movie industry (which finally began early in 1951) made them
too dangerous to handle.

From the introduction of the PCA in 1934 until 1939, Hollywood
largely ignored the social and economic history and effects of the
Depression, producing films that were primarily intended to distract
Americans from their problems by offering pure entertainment. Two
things changed this situation: the publication of John Steinbeck's best-
selling novel of 1939 and the growing demand for A-quality pictures
created by the start of economic recovery. In combination, these things
gave Darryl Zanuck the chance to return to the "social consciousness"
style of filmmaking he had once preferred. With the Depression at last
starting to come to an end it finally became practicable for a major
studio to make a movie about it.[78] If *The Grapes of Wrath* could not
have been made earlier, moreover, it also could probably not have been
made later, in the highly charged atmosphere of the Cold War. It was—
and would long remain—very much on the frontier of what was possible
for a mainstream Hollywood film dealing with the history of current
problems.

Filmography

The Match King (dir. Howard Bretherton/William Keighley; First National, 1932).
The Cabin in the Cotton (dir. Michael Curtiz; First National/Warner Bros., 1932).
Two Seconds (dir. Mervyn LeRoy; First National/Vitaphone, 1932).
I Am A Fugitive from a Chain Gang (dir. Mervyn Leroy; Warner Bros., 1932).
Our Daily Bread (dir. King Vidor; King W. Vidor Productions, 1934).
The Grapes of Wrath (dir. John Ford; Twentieth-Century Fox, 1940).
Tobacco Road (dir. John Ford; Twentieth-Century Fox, 1941).
The Lost Weekend (dir. Billy Wilder; Paramount, 1945).
The Best Years of Our Lives (dir. William Wyler; Samuel Goldwyn, 1946).
Till the End of Time (dir. Edward Dmytryk; Dore Schary Productions/Vanguard/
   RKO, 1946).

Smash-Up: The Story of a Woman (dir. Stuart Heisler; Universal, 1947).
Crossfire (dir. Edward Dmytryk; RKO, 1947).
Gentleman's Agreement (dir. Elia Kazan; Twentieth-Century Fox, 1947).
Pinky (dir. Elia Kazan; Twentieth-Century Fox, 1949).
No Way Out (dir. Joseph L. Mankiewicz; Twentieth-Century Fox, 1950).

CHAPTER NINE*

HUAC and Hollywood:
The Way We Were and *Guilty*
by Suspicion

One type of film that Hollywood has shown continuous—and often highly profitable—interest in is movies about Hollywood itself. Films of this type have covered a whole spectrum from sentimental idealization, as in *Ella Cinders* (1926) and *Going Hollywood* (1933), through nostalgic reminiscences of the studio era, such as *Singin' in the Rain* (1952) and *The Eddie Cantor Story* (1953), to the sardonic and satirical, including *Sunset Boulevard* (1950) and *The Player* (1992).[1] But this enthusiastic self-reflexivity comes to a virtual full stop when the relations between Hollywood and the anti-communist "inquisition" of the late 1940s and early 1950s are foregrounded. There are, indeed, only two modern mainstream Hollywood films—*The Way We Were* (1973) and *Guilty by Suspicion* (1991)—that deal with the direct effects on Hollywood itself as a community of the investigations into the movie industry launched by the House Committee on Un-American Activities (popularly if inaccurately known as HUAC) during that time.[2]

Of course, there have been other feature films discussing the *impact* of HUAC and Senator Joseph R. McCarthy on filmmaking in more general terms. In 1976, *The Front* dealt with the story of a man who allowed his name to be used by a blacklisted writer so that he could carry on working in television in New York. In 1989, *Fellow Traveller*, an Anglo-American

---

*An earlier version of this chapter was published in Cornelis A. van Minnen and Sylvia L. Hilton, eds, *Political Repression in U. S. History* (Amsterdam: VU University Press, 2009).

production, also dealt with the travails of a blacklisted writer, in this case living in exile in London. *The Majestic*, released in 2001, was (again) about a blacklisted writer who overcomes depression, drunkenness, and memory loss to challenge HUAC successfully on First Amendment grounds—a position, as Ernest Giglio notes, "that was never accepted either by Congress or the courts."[3] And *Good Night and Good Luck* (2005) did a good job of looking at the circumstances, personal and institutional, that led broadcaster Edward R. Murrow to speak out against McCarthy and his methods on CBS television (though the film appeared to have *two* targets: not just McCarthy himself but the banality of much of 1950s American commercial television). But *The Way We Were* and *Guilty by Suspicion*, even after more than 60 years, still remain the only mainstream Hollywood films to look at the impact of the anti-communist inquisition on the film community itself.[4]

In chronological terms, the two films book-ended the serious involvement of HUAC with Hollywood. Several sequences of *The Way We Were* had Katie Morosky (Barbra Streisand), once famed on campus as a communist activist ("Communist K-K-K-Katie"), joining in the initial attempt to fight HUAC at the start of its first serious investigation into Hollywood in 1947. Katie, married to glamorous but superficial movie screenwriter Hubbell Gardiner (Robert Redford), leaves him behind in Hollywood to go to Washington to join the protest of the Committee for the First Amendment (CFA) at HUAC's treatment of those who were about to become the "Hollywood Ten."[5] *Guilty by Suspicion* opens with HUAC taking secret testimony from friendly witnesses in Los Angeles in September 1951 and ends with the climactic scene of the December 1951 hearings in Washington.

There are, of course, reasons why the American film industry would shy away from making many films about HUAC and Hollywood. Many studio heads, including Jack Warner and Walt Disney, supported the Committee's efforts.[6] Hollywood's institutional collaboration with the anti-communist crusade led it to produce a major cycle of anti-red films, including *The Red Menace* (1949), *I Married a Communist* (1949), *I Was a Communist for the F.B.I.* (1951), *Big Jim McClain* (1952), *My Son John* (1952), and *Pickup on South Street* (1953).[7] Members of the Motion Picture Alliance for the Preservation of American Ideals, led by its president John Wayne (the star of *Big Jim McClain*), egged the committee on.[8] Major stars, including Gary Cooper and Adolphe Menjou, had acted as "friendly witnesses" and named names before the Committee. Unions, including the Screen Actors Guild, introduced a loyalty oath.[9] Hollywood would have many reasons, in later years, to feel embarrassed by its relationship with HUAC. One symptom of that embarrassment was the refusal, until very recently, to acknowledge the wrong done to blacklisted directors and writers by restoring screen credits for their work done under pseudonyms or "fronts."[10]

The Way We Were covers the period between 1937 and 1947. The first sequence after the credits shows Katie Morosky addressing a student rally at what seems to be Harvard (the Charles River, Wentworth Field in Boston).[11] She is president of the Young Communist League and most of the audience, including Hubbell Gardiner, seem bored or hostile. But Katie builds a narrative around the victims of the Civil War in Spain, the fact that in 1937 the Soviet Union is the only country sending aid to the Republican cause, and the ambitions of Hitler and Mussolini ("using the Spanish earth as testing ground for what they want. Another world war!") She urges the crowd not to be scared of the "red bogeyman" since the Russians want "total disarmament now," and wins over the audience to her side (before being undermined by a crude practical joke) (Figure 9.1).

It is hard to believe that a speech of this kind could have made it into a mainstream Hollywood production (*The Way We Were* won two Oscars and was nominated for four more) of the 1940s, 1950s, or 1960s. It would have simply been too controversial during most of the Cold War. But *The Way We Were* was released in October 1973, 17 months after the first Strategic Arms Limitation Treaty was signed by the United States and Soviet Union. The second of three conferences that would lead to the Helsinki Accords of 1975 had begun work the previous month in Geneva. The process of *détente* (or relaxing tensions) between the United States and the Soviet Union was in full swing. For a comparatively brief moment (the movie would have provoked much more controversy after the Soviet invasion of Afghanistan in 1979), it seemed possible to include a scene of this type without stirring right-wing censure.[12]

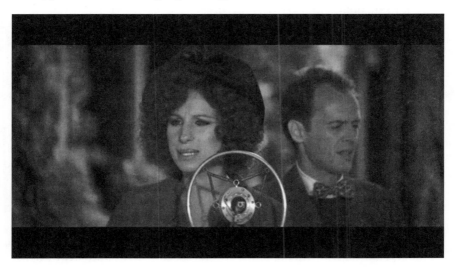

FIGURE 9.1 *Katie Morosky (Barbra Streisand) defends Soviet policy over the Spanish Civil War in* The Way We Were.

In the decade before the 1947 investigation by HUAC into Hollywood, Katie appears to have abandoned her membership in the Communist Party, although she can still criticize the delay in launching a Second Front "while the Russians were taking a beating" in the Second World War and has strong (but unexplained) views on the Yalta Conference (1945) at which Stalin, Roosevelt, and Churchill discussed plans for the postwar world. Her new hero is war leader President Franklin D. Roosevelt and she is desolate when Roosevelt dies two months after Yalta.[13] She and Hubbell subsequently move to California, where Hubbell has been offered a job as a screenwriter. Katie is one of the first in the Hollywood community to hear that HUAC has been taking testimony from witnesses in secret. In spite of Hubbell's objections (he does not want to lose the first real job he has ever had), Katie goes to Washington with a plane-load of other Hollywood protestors to defend the rights of the first hostile witnesses called by HUAC (the "Hollywood Ten"). When Katie and the rest of the group return to Los Angeles, they are met by a large group of right-wing demonstrators waving signs (all in red and black) with phrases such as "Go back to Moscow" and "Down With Commies."

Some of the film's coverage of the relations between HUAC and Hollywood is sketched out quite well. HUAC was a fairly marginal committee by congressional standards, and had chosen to investigate Hollywood principally to attract greater publicity.[14] As director George Bissinger (Patrick O'Neal) bluntly observes in the film, "they're just out to get election yardage by coupling their names to the great jerks of the silver screen." The movie producers, represented by Eric Johnston of the Motion Picture Association of America (MPAA), had initially given the impression both of being opposed to HUAC and supporting the 19 witnesses (later ten) summoned to testify.[15] But, as Paula Reisner (Viveca Lindfors) suggests, broadly summarizing the Waldorf Statement issued by Johnston on behalf of the MPAA on December 3, 1947, they had later "reversed their positions . . . and any employee who is an unfriendly witness before the committee is . . . fired . . . so now we have an official blacklist."[16]

In the film, the people who go to Washington to defend the first amendment are fairly peripheral figures: Vicki (Diana Ewing), the wife of George Bissinger, Paula Reisner, a member of Bissinger's production team, and Katie herself, who is a writer of movie synopses. The probable leader of the group (it is never made completely clear) is scriptwriter Brooks Carpenter (Murray Hamilton). In reality, the CFA assembled a major group of Hollywood A-listers. Formed on the initiative of screenwriter Philip Dunne, directors John Huston and William Wyler, and actor Alexander Knox, it brought together some well-known names.[17] Those on the plane to Washington on October 26, 1947 included Danny Kaye, Paul Henreid, Gene Kelly, Marsha Hunt, Lauren Bacall, and Humphrey Bogart (so high was Bogart's prestige at this time that journalists began talking of "Bogart's plane" and "Bogart's group").[18]

The film not only fictionalizes all the names of members of the committee who went to Washington: it fails to come to grips with what actually happened when they did arrive to attend the HUAC hearings. While Katie is away, we see Hubbell eating dinner morosely on his own and listening to the radio, which is broadcasting the allegations of one of the "friendly witnesses" naming names (and subversive organizations) to the committee. This was essentially what happened during the first week of the hearings, beginning on March 20. The representatives of the CFA arrived in time for the second week's hearings, with the "unfriendly witnesses" about to testify. Their arrival was timed specifically to support Eric Johnston, the president of the MPAA, who was scheduled to testify on Monday.[19] On Sunday evening, March 26, HUAC's position was not particularly strong (its work had been criticized by many newspapers)[20] and the studio establishment, represented by the MPAA, seemed on side. That night, the eve of the resumed hearings, there was a national radio broadcast ("Hollywood Fights Back"), sponsored by the CFA, to "denounce HUAC, uphold the First Amendment, and defend Hollywood."[21]

On Monday morning, March 27, Hollywood unity began to crumble. HUAC changed the order of witnesses to be called and, from the testimony of the first "unfriendly" witness, screenwriter John Howard Lawson, things began to go wrong. Lawson, annoyed by the fact that he was not permitted to read a prepared statement (as the "friendly" witnesses had been allowed to do) began by refusing to answer the question as to whether he was or had been a member of the communist party. His confrontation with committee chair J. Parnell Thomas degenerated into a shouting match that ended when Thomas terminated the testimony, cited Lawson for contempt of Congress, and had him forcibly removed.[22] This pattern of confrontation, citation, and physical removal would be followed with the rest of the "Hollywood Ten." Public opinion began to change very quickly. It seemed to many that the shouting and confrontation were undignified. It also increasingly appeared that the "unfriendly witnesses" had something to hide: that they had been communists and some still were. The members of the CFA who had gone to Washington to fight for a constitutional principle now found themselves standing on very shaky ground.

One effect of the hearings was increased public criticism of "unfriendly witnesses." Some of those who appeared at a rally in Philadelphia were greeted with shouts of "Shut up, you Communists" and "Go Back to Russia, you bums."[23] As a consequence of their appearance at HUAC in the same week as the "Hollywood Ten," some may have wrongly suspected members of the CFA as also having communist members (in reality, both to protect themselves and give greater clout to their protest, the CFA had been careful to discourage communist involvement in the group).[24] The fictional sequence in *The Way We Were* in which the returning members of the committee are met at the station in Los Angeles by anti-communist demonstrators suggests that public opinion had changed and that they were now seen by many as left-wing subversives. What the film does not do, however, is to chart the swift decline of the CFA which, Larry Ceplair and Steven Englund argue, "disappeared from the fray within two weeks of the end of the hearings."[25] The demise of the CFA as an organization was followed (again something not covered in the film) by pressure from the studios to persuade those who had flown to Washington to quit the political arena. Humphrey Bogart was one of the first to do so, confessing in *Photoplay* in March 1948 that he and the other protestors had been "American dopes" and assuring his readers that "I'm about as much in favor of Communism as J. Edgar Hoover."[26]

While *The Way We Were* was unusual in its favorable presentation of Katie Morosky as a communist in the early part of the film, its coverage of Hollywood's resistance to HUAC in 1947 (and especially that of the CFA) was sketchy and misleading. In its failure to recognize (and name) those members of the CFA who went to Washington to confront HUAC, the film almost certainly reflected the continuing embarrassment of the Hollywood community over its role in the events of 1947. Some of the members of that community had supported HUAC. Hollywood had also adopted and operated for many years a blacklist of left-wing political activists. To save their careers, directors, actors, and screenwriters had been obliged to turn their backs on friends and renounce political beliefs. It was probably too early in 1973 for a mainstream studio production to attempt to face up to what had happened in Hollywood during the anti-communist inquisition.

The first film to try to do so was *Guilty by Suspicion* (1991). Since the inquisition was still a difficult subject for Hollywood to deal with,[27] it was not surprising that the original idea for this film came from someone outside the American film industry: French film director Bertrand Tavernier. Tavernier's first idea was to make a movie about blacklistees such as Joseph Losey, Jules Dassin, and Jack Berry, who had chosen the path of exile in Europe. Tavernier brought together writer-director Abraham Polonsky, himself once on the blacklist, with veteran producer Irwin Winkler.[28] Polonsky produced the first draft of a screenplay that opened with a scene at the HUAC hearings. Both Winkler and Tavernier felt this scene ought to be the climax of the film instead of the beginning. Polonsky decided that in that case, as he expressed it, "it's no longer a survival-in-Europe story. It should be a picture about Hollywood. And if it's a picture about Hollywood, it will have to be a picture about the political controversy."[29] Subsequently, Tavernier dropped out of the project and Winkler signed on to direct the movie. He also began to rewrite the screenplay. The most crucial change involved changing the story's protagonist, David Merrill, from the communist he had been in Polonsky's original screenplay into a nonpolitical innocent who had attended a few part meetings in the 1930s and finally been thrown out of the party for "arguing too much."

The film in its final form begins with the grilling of screenwriter Larry Nolan (Chris Cooper) by HUAC in secret session in Los Angeles. Nolan says to HUAC what actor Larry Parks really said, in almost exactly the same words: "I beg of you, please don't make me do this. Don't make me crawl through the mud. You *know* who they are. They're my friends."[30] That same evening, David Merrill (Robert De Niro), a film director, returns from France where he has been doing the groundwork for a film. In his absence, Merrill has been named as someone who had formerly attended Communist Party meetings. Darryl F. Zanuck (Ben Piazza), head of Twentieth-Century Fox, insists that he has to appear before the committee and clear himself before he can resume work on his film. When it is explained to Merrill by Felix Graff, the lawyer Zanuck sends him to—ironically played by sometime blacklistee Sam Wanamaker—that he will have to "name names," he refuses.[31] The rest of the film is dominated by the choice between living up to his conscience or working at the job he adores. Merrill is barred from the studio lot and finds it hard to hold down the most menial job even after moving to New York. But—when he does finally agree to testify—changes his mind and defies the committee in words very similar to those used by Army Counsel Joseph Welch in his denunciation of McCarthy during the Army-McCarthy hearings of 1954.[32]

In historical terms, *Guilty by Suspicion* got a lot right. As Larry Nolan says, the committee already knew who most of the communists in Hollywood were. Witnesses were asked to "purge" themselves by undergoing a ritual humiliation and providing the names of friends and colleagues. As Jeanne Hall notes, this transformed HUAC's supposed "investigations" into what Edward Herman and Noam Chomsky have termed "'flak'—actions meant to be punitive and threatening rather than fact-finding or truth-seeking."[33] The film also worked hard to show the reality of life on the "graylist"—made up of men and women who had supported the Hollywood Ten or worked for liberal causes and were consequently victims of "guilt by association" (or, as the title of the film has it, "guilty by suspicion"). The FBI surveillance of many graylistees is shown in the film (though not the extensive phone-tapping that took place). FBI men note down the registration numbers of the cars at the party given to welcome Merrill back from France and carry on harassing him in New York. He becomes so paranoid he thinks he is being followed by a stranger on Christmas Eve. Of course, as someone once said, just because you are paranoid does not mean they are not out to get you. Merrill's final, unsuccessful strategy before the committee is realistic: like Lillian Hellman, he tries to talk about his own actions but not those of others (the so-called diminished Fifth [Amendment]). Finally, the fact that HUAC pursues Merrill even though he is not and has never been a communist underlined the fact that the accusers and clearance committees *did* get things wrong: John Henry Faulk of CBS successfully sued the anti-communist organization *Aware* for wrongly suggesting he had been a communist.[34]

At the same time, the fact that Merrill is not nor has he ever been a communist is a major weakness of the film.[35] This plot change caused Polonsky to remove his own name from the movie's credits. It makes little sense in historical terms: Merrill had almost nothing to "purge." Someone like him would never have been subpoenaed by HUAC: he would have submitted a studio-drafted letter of apology to the committee, and that would have been that. Yet Winkler was convinced, as he declared in an interview, that if the movie was "about a communist, the end result would be perceived as a defense of Communism."[36] Winkler had a point: the immediate context of his film's production was the collapse of the communist regimes in Eastern Europe and the massacring of pro-democracy protestors in Tiananmen Square by an arthritic communist leadership intent on clinging to power in China. In 1991, the year of the film's release, the Soviet Union finally collapsed. At the beginning of the 1990s, seeing communism either as a threat or as a faith that had once appealed to many thousands of Americans had become quite literally incredible. On the other hand, as Victor Navasky observed, Winkler's decision not to focus on a communist also emphasized the result of 70 years of cultural and political repression: a deeply engrained hostility to communism that demonstrated just "how far . . . [Hollywood] and the political culture at large still have to go."[37]

Winkler's decision transformed *Guilty by Suspicion* into what was in effect a melodrama: the fall and (at least in terms of character) rise of David Merrill. In the entire film, there is only one avowed communist: director Joe Lesser, played in a cameo role by Martin Scorsese. In his only scene, Lesser arrives with a suitcase to see Merrill and two other directors at a secret four a.m. meeting. Lesser explains that he is one jump ahead of a subpoena and is leaving that night for London. Although based on the actual flight to Europe of Joseph Losey—the "film" Lesser is directing that he asks Merrill to finish for him is Losey's *The Boy With Green Hair* (1948)—this brief sequence gives little understanding of the difficulty and trauma that often accompanied expatriation. In actual fact, Losey's last memory of his homeland was hiding in a darkened house to avoid being served with his subpoena.[38]

Having Merrill as a noncommunist and Lesser run away, the film consciously forecloses any possibility of covering the communist fight-back against HUAC. There can be no reference, for example, to the efforts of Herbert Biberman and the Blacklist Company to produce their own films— even if that initiative ended with the failure of *Salt of the Earth* (1954).[39] So far as Merrill is concerned, rather than the personal becoming the political, the political becomes the personal. "In the end," remarks Jeanne Hall, "David defies the Committee for a number of very personal reasons: it has kept him from working, injured his friends, frightened his son, implicated his wife, and generally pissed him off"[40] (Figure 9.2).

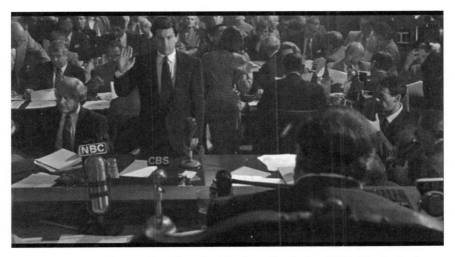

FIGURE 9.2 *David Merrill (Robert De Niro) testifies before HUAC in* Guilty by Suspicion.

The triviality (in historical terms) of Merrill's reasons for decisively opposing the committee—in the full knowledge that this will mean blacklisting and possible imprisonment—points up other weaknesses in the film's approach. The fact that Merrill is unaware of the activities and threat of HUAC when he returns from a two-month trip to France in 1951 is frankly unbelievable. As Dalton Trumbo later pointed out, the only innocents—in the sense of knowledge—were the original Hollywood Ten, including Trumbo himself. After 1947, everyone in Hollywood knew what the consequences of the Committee's actions would be. "All the people who took the First and Fifth Amendments after us," Trumbo declared, "knew something we had not known, namely, that they would not work for years . . . We didn't know how hot the water was."[41]

Another curious impression left by the film came from the fact that, when it begins, David Merrill and his wife are divorced and living apart. When the film ends, the couple are together, having been reunited in opposition to HUAC. The notion of HUAC as a catalyst for marital reconciliation is, to put it mildly, eccentric. As Jeanne Hall comments, "the blacklist was known for breaking up families, not bringing them back together."[42] The representation of the role of informers in the film is also rather limited and unconvincing. Larry Nolan is shown as caving in completely to the committee, not only giving them the names of his friends (including Merrill) but also his wife's name. (Nolan seems to be a composite character, partly based on actor Larry Parks, and partly on screenwriter Richard J. Collins, the husband of Dorothy Comingore. Nolan's naming of his wife, Dorothy, as a communist and his accusations that she is an alcoholic and an unfit mother are probably based on the experience of Comingore.) "Bunny"

Baxter (George Wendt) is a nice guy driven, in desperation, to ask his best friend Merrill if he can name him to the committee (on the grounds that Merrill is "already dead").[43] In the end, both Baxter and Merrill defy the committee, but it seems apparent that in both cases this means reneging on earlier commitments to name names. The film creates the impression that informing was something done only by the weaker members of the film community in response to great pressure from HUAC. It ignores the actions of "friendly witnesses" who were ready, even eager, to name names within their own social circles.

What *Guilty by Suspicion* does not do, moreover, is to present the confrontation between HUAC and Hollywood in anything other than the simplest black and white terms. It offers what is in essence a broadly liberal perspective on the "inquisition" of the early 1950s. Yet the view of Hollywood and HUAC it puts across is doubly inadequate in terms of history. Not only is much of the context of the early 1950s missing, but also the longer historical backcloth to the events of 1951–2. Audiences are not really informed of the fact that, in 1951 and 1952, anti-communism was a mainstream American phenomenon with much institutional support.[44] In fact, it is possible to regard the repression of the period as supported by a democratic consensus. Moreover, most scholars have interpreted the Hollywood inquisition as a stage in the repressive history of HUAC. But there may also be a case for perceiving HUAC itself as only a stage in the repressive history of Hollywood.

Political repression in the United States, argues Robert Goldstein, "consists of government action which grossly discriminates against persons or organizations viewed as presenting a fundamental challenge to existing power relationships or key government policies, because of their perceived political beliefs."[45] Only rarely has the ruling American elite decided its interest was being seriously threatened and embraced repression, often together with a manufactured political hysteria, as a means of protecting its power and status. By contrast with European history, in consequence, American repression has on the whole been considerably more episodic.[46]

Popular hysteria and repression have traditionally gone hand in hand in American history. According to Murray Levin, several elements have contributed to this pairing. Quite consciously, elites have from time to time deliberately fostered the idea that a conspiracy exists to undermine the American way of life. While they *may* sincerely believe this, it is also the case that alleging the existence of a conspiracy also has very tangible benefits. Among these, Levin observes, have been:

> strike-breaking, stereotyping opposition leaders as alien and radical, the justification of military expenditures and additional personnel for law enforcement agencies, expanding newspaper circulation, profits and fees for superpatriotic societies and speakers, and . . . the creation

of scapegoats so that failure of the economy and policy will be neither traced to the party in power nor to dominant American values.[47]

Levin identifies three situations that have encouraged American elites to abandon the normal techniques for exercising power and to engage in repression: first, the sudden, dramatic decline of a formerly dominant party (such as the Federalists facing the rising strength of Jeffersonianism in the late 1790s); secondly, in more modern times, the rising strength of organized labor (causing US Steel and other business corporations to throw their support behind the "Red Scare" of 1919–20); thirdly, the temptation facing political leaders (including A. Mitchell Palmer and Joseph McCarthy) to build a future power base by helping to create an anti-radical hysteria.[48]

Contrived leadership by an elite is only part of the explanation for the Federalist pursuit of sedition in the 1790s or the "Red Scares" of 1919–20 and 1947–54. Historians such as Richard Hofstadter and David Brion Davis long ago drew attention to the tendency of groups of ordinary Americans from time to time to become obsessed with the idea of a conspiratorial threat to the whole American way of life.[49] Political hysteria as a mode of repression is something manufactured by elites, but it could not succeed without mass popular acquiescence and approval. The roots of this popular acceptance may be found deep in the soil of American culture and, to an extent, also in the American psyche (Levin suggests that "the evil conspirator on the march" in reality reflected "the hated and feared secret self, finally out of control.")[50]

The difficulty with the linkage established between political repression, conspiracy, and popular hysteria by scholars such as Levin is that it relies on an interpretation of history in which politicians in their own interest manufacture national panics without any real cause and some Americans, for reasons of their own, support crusades against spectral enemies. Yet there have also been organized groups in American society who—sometimes long in advance of politicians—have led campaigns to repress what they perceived as subversion and sedition. Some of these have been organizations in the public domain. Frank Donner, for example, has documented the history of police repression in American cities, from the "red squads" established to fight subversives in the Gilded Age to their more modern equivalents.[51] Others have been private groups and organizations. Prominent among such groups were the bosses of the Hollywood studio system.

The conventional view of the events of 1947 and 1951–2 in Hollywood suggests that, in Terry Christensen's words, "the HUAC investigations provided an opportunity for pipsqueak politicians to bring mighty Hollywood to its knees." The movie industry "caved in, turned itself inside out, surrendered its workers to the committee's witch-hunters, and denied employment to talented people because of alleged past associations with communism."[52] Seen in this way, HUAC's interventions in Hollywood were straightforward examples of political repression by forces external to Hollywood itself. Research by Dorothy B. Jones seemed to confirm the success of HUAC's actions in terms of film content. Jones, a social scientist who had served for two years during the war as head of the Film Reviewing and Analysis section of the Office of War Information, found that what she termed "social theme movies" (defined as films with "social and psychological themes") declined from 28 percent of Hollywood's output in the second half of 1947 to 9.2 percent in 1954, a fall of two-thirds.[53] Yet this is to ignore Hollywood's troubled history of labor relations long before HUAC came on the scene.

The early days of the film industry on the West Coast had often witnessed bitter struggles between the film companies and their employees. Attempts by the American Federation of Labor to unionize the studio construction crafts had led to three strikes in the period 1916–21. Indeed, as Murray Ross argued, the formation in 1922 of the Motion Picture Producers' and Distributors' of America ("an open-shop organization of seventeen studios") was very largely an attempt to create "a unified labor policy among Hollywood's major film producers." In 1926, nine major film studios and five unions reached the Studio Basic Agreement—the first example of union recognition in Hollywood. Yet a combination of technical changes and, after 1929, economic depression worsened labor relations within the film industry. Technical changes created new occupations that were fought over by competing unions: a 1933 struggle over who should represent soundmen between the International Brotherhood of Electrical Workers and the International Alliance of Theatrical Stage Employees (IATSE) led to the comprehensive defeat of the latter. The depression led screenwriters, actors, and directors to fight for the recognition of unions of their own, organized in imitation of medieval guilds.[54]

Against a background of endemically poor industrial relations, studio bosses sought—sometimes with the help of organized crime—to control their unruly workforce.[55] It was during this period that they adopted the strategy of labeling those who opposed them as "un-American" or "communists." Another tactic that first appeared in this period was the blacklist: labor organizer Irv Hentschel, who helped found the IA Progressives within IATSE in 1937, lost his job as a consequence of his union activities. He soon discovered that no one else would hire him: his name had been placed on an invisible blacklist.[56] Both blacklist and anti-communism, therefore, were long-established tactics used to discipline the studio workforce and keep it tractable even before HUAC appeared on the scene.[57]

The years during the Second World War were essentially peaceful ones on the labor front. Labor unions remained committed to their "no strike" pledge (which was also supported by the American Communist Party). Yet immediately after the end of the war in Europe, a major dispute over who had jurisdiction over set decorators broke out between the revived IATSE and a new combination of craft unions, the Conference of Studio Unions (CSU). After an initial eight-month strike, the dispute rumbled on into 1946. Eventually, the CSU became victim of the studios' determination to break the influence of militant labor unions in Hollywood. In September 1946, studios locked out the carpenters, bought off the mob-dominated IATSE with a lucrative wage offer, and set out to break down the CSU through a combination of violence on the picket lines and mass arrests. By early 1947, the union was effectively destroyed.[58]

This conflict (which helped shape the Labor Management Act of 1947, better known as the Taft-Hartley Act, with its anti-union—and anti-communist—provisions),[59] also formed the immediate context for HUAC's investigation of Hollywood. It was no accident that those primarily targeted by HUAC were deeply involved in union and other off-screen activities. The studio bosses found an ally in HUAC, which helped destroy union militants through the same tactic as Hollywood: identifying them as communists. In November 1947, at their meeting at the Waldorf Hotel in New York, they also used the excuse of HUAC to give their preexisting blacklist policy far wider application. Far from the usual image of HUAC repressing the Hollywood community, it was in many ways acting as an instrument of one section of that community—the studio elite—in its own campaign to repress union militancy.

Filmography

The Boy With Green Hair (dir. Joseph Losey; RKO, 1948).
The Red Menace (dir. R. G. Springsteen; Republic, 1949).
I Married a Communist (dir. Robert Stevenson; RKO, 1949).
I Was a Communist for the FBI (dir. Gordon Douglas; Warner Bros., 1951).
Big Jim McClain (dir. Edward Ludwig; Warner Bros., 1952).
My Son John (dir. Leo McCarey; Paramount/Rainbow, 1952).
Pickup on South Street (dir. Samuel Fuller; Twentieth-Century Fox, 1953).
The Salt of the Earth (dir. Herbert J. Biberman; Independent Production Company, 1954).
The Way We Were (dir. Sydney Pollack; Columbia, 1973).
The Front (dir. Martin Ritt; Columbia, 1976).
Fellow Traveller (dir. Philip Saville; HBO/BFI/BBC, 1989).
Guilty by Suspicion (dir. Irwin Winkler; Warner Bros., 1991).
The Majestic (dir. Frank Darabont; Castle Rock, 2001).
Good Night and Good Luck (dir. George Clooney; Warner, 2005).

CHAPTER TEN

Remembering the 1960s:
Mississippi Burning and *JFK*

In the United States, as in much of the world, the 1960s was a period of great social and political upheaval. Many challenged the status quo. The baby-boomer generation reached adulthood. The modern women's and gay liberation movements were born. Violence became more prevalent and there were a series of grisly assassinations of major public figures: President John F. Kennedy, Martin Luther King, Senator Robert F. Kennedy, Malcolm X. At the heart of much of the turmoil of the times were two crucial influences: the movement for black civil rights and American involvement in the war in Vietnam. This chapter examines two films, one (*Mississippi Burning* (1988)) dealing with a grave incident in the civil rights movement, the other (*JFK* (1991)) which suggested that President Kennedy was killed as a result of a conspiracy to prevent him ending American military involvement in Vietnam. Each was made by a director, Alan Parker and Oliver Stone respectively, who brought his own background and convictions to the film. Each was much criticized for introducing his personal views into the movie concerned and, in essence, fictionalizing the narrative. Yet both, by working out their own ideas in dealing with the events concerned, made it possible to view them to some extent in a new light.

Mississippi Burning (1988)

On the afternoon of June 21, 1964, three young men drove 50 miles from Meridian, Mississippi, to Longdale in Neshoba County. In Longdale, they looked over what was left of the Mount Zion United Methodist Church, a mainly black church that had been burned to the ground five days earlier. The young men were civil rights activists. James Chaney, a black Mississippian, worked for the Congress of Racial Equality (CORE) in Meridian. His companions, Michael Schwerner and Andrew Goodman, had come from New York to help register blacks to vote during the "Freedom Summer" of 1964. Late in the afternoon, Neshoba County police deputy sheriff Cecil Ray Price—a member of the Ku Klux Klan—stopped their blue Ford station wagon and arrested Chaney for breaking the speed limit. The trio spent several hours in jail in Philadelphia, the county seat of Neshoba County, until Chaney was fined $20 and all three were ordered to quit the county. Price followed them and stopped their car once again, using his police siren, before they reached the Neshoba County line. He took them to an isolated spot to meet a group of Ku Klux Klansmen, who shot dead all three. Their bodies were taken away to be interred in the packed earth foundations of a dam under construction and their car was burned.[1] The publicity generated by the disappearance of the three activists prompted President Lyndon B. Johnson to order the FBI to investigate. The subsequent discovery of their bodies led to a series of trials of those involved that would continue into the twenty-first century.[2] The case also inspired the making of Alan Parker's film *Mississippi Burning* (1988).

Mississippi Burning begins, during the opening credits, with two sequences to an accompaniment of Gospel music: a white man and a black boy drink at water faucets marked respectively "White" and "Colored," followed by a shot of a wooden building burning. As the music turns ominous, we see three young men (who are never named) driving along a country road at night. They are followed by several other cars, harassed by a truck and then stopped by a police car. They are shot dead inside their car. Although the circumstances are *slightly* different from what happened in the case of Chaney, Goodman, and Schwerner, the intertitle accompanying the sound of gunshots (Mississippi 1964) makes it clear that the movie is based on their case. Two FBI men—Rupert Anderson (Gene Hackman) and Alan Ward (Willem Dafoe)—are shown driving to investigate the disappearances. From the beginning, they meet a wall of silence from hostile local whites (particularly the sheriff's office) and blacks too intimidated to talk. The Klan harasses the two FBI men and continues victimizing African Americans. Ward, the younger but more senior of the two, drafts in many more agents to help in the search. Anderson, a former sheriff in another Mississippi town, adopts a more subtle approach, establishing a relationship with Mrs. Pell (Frances McDormand), the wife of deputy-sheriff Clinton Pell (Brad Dourif), whom the FBI men suspect of involvement. Eventually, Mrs. Pell contradicts her husband's alibi and tells Anderson where the murder victims are buried. Pell beats up his wife in response and Anderson has a furious confrontation with Ward, who forces him not to take immediate revenge on Pell. In return, Ward gives Anderson *carte blanche* to crack the case open. The mayor of the town

(R. Lee Ermey) is kidnapped and taken to a remote shack where a black FBI man (Badja Djola) threatens him with castration until he reveals the names of those involved in the murders. The FBI picks the weakest of the team of murderers, Lester Cowens (Pruitt Taylor Vince), who is persuaded that the Klan is out to kill him for giving evidence against them and, to save himself, does exactly that. Seven men are seen coming out of court and intertitles tell us what has happened: Sheriff Ray Stuckey (Gailard Sartain) has been acquitted but six men, included Clinton Pell, have been sentenced to terms of between three and ten years in jail. The film ends with a mixture of optimism and pessimism. Mrs. Pell tells Anderson she plans to stay in the town because "there's enough good people round here know what I did was right" and Anderson and Ward attend a biracial church service, held in the open air because the church itself has been burned. In the final shot of the film, the camera pans across the graveyard to focus on a vandalized and broken tombstone with the date "1964" and the legend "Not Forgotten." This—though the film never says so—is the grave of James Chaney (Figure 10.1).

Director Alan Parker had been much criticized for his earlier film *Midnight Express* (1978), dealing with the experiences of a young American imprisoned for drug smuggling in Turkey, which claimed to be "based on a true story."[3] Determined not to repeat the experience, he made sure that the credits for *Mississippi Burning* finished with the statement that "This film was inspired by actual events which took place in the South during the 1960's. The characters, however, are fictitious and do not depict real people either living or dead." This curiously ambiguous claim was accepted neither by former Philadelphia Sheriff Lawrence Rainey, who launched a

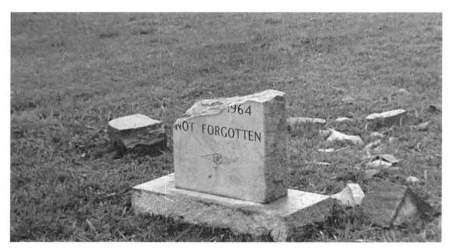

FIGURE 10.1 *The tombstone of murdered black civil rights worker James Chaney* (Mississippi Burning).

lawsuit against Parker claiming $7 million for defamation,[4] nor by the movie's army of critics.

Mississippi Burning was better than many reviewers thought in conveying the reality of race relations in Mississippi in 1964. The very first sequence, involving the water faucets, undercut the legal basis of racial segregation—the Supreme Court's 1896 *Plessy v. Ferguson* decision accepting the constitutionality of state laws requiring persons of different race to use different facilities provided they were "equal." The fictional nature of this equality was underlined in the movie: the white faucet is an electric water-cooler, the colored a small washbasin with a dripping fountain. Filmed entirely on location in the South, mainly in the towns of Lafayette, Alabama, and Jackson, Mississippi,[5] *Mississippi Burning*—as one commentator who had lived in the South in the early 1960s confirmed—effectively recreated the atmosphere of the time, getting "the climate of fear and hatred exactly right."[6] The local state courts, as the film makes plain, were racially prejudiced and unlikely to deliver justice to blacks.[7] The movie correctly identified black churches and their congregations as crucial targets of racist attack. Churches were a major focus of black life and frequently used for political meetings, including those connected with voter registration. The burning of black churches in Mississippi provided Parker's film with its title: 31 such burnings took place in the summer of 1964, the first being the one at Longdale visited by Chaney, Goodman, and Schwerner before their deaths.[8] The suggestion in the film that some white Mississippians regarded the disappearance of the students as a hoax was true[9]—as was the shot of a news cameraman from the North being attacked by local racists.[10]

For many critics, however, *Mississippi Burning* was a betrayal of the civil rights movement to which Chaney, Goodman, and Schwerner belonged and for which they died. After setting the scene for an investigation of the circumstances surrounding the 1964 murders, the film metamorphosed into a more traditional "Hollywood" product: a combination of buddy movie and police story. Sean French pointed out that the "struggle between a fervent young officer who believes in playing it by the book and an experienced middle-aged cop who realises that you must . . . bend the rules when necessary" was a familiar staple, as seen, for example, in Dennis Hopper's *Colors*, released a few months before Parker's film.[11] Given the nature of the genre, the ongoing conflict between Anderson and Ward becomes the principal theme of the movie, eclipsing in the process, as Gavin Smith remarked, "the conflict going on in society at large (over civil rights)—without even remotely mirroring it."[12] Although Anderson and Ward are entirely fictional characters, the film makes clear that they are by no means strangers to Mississippi: before working for the FBI, Anderson has been the sheriff in a small Mississippi town just across the state border from Memphis, Tennessee, and Ward—while working for the Department of Justice—has been shot in the shoulder in the riots following African American James Meredith's admission to the University of Mississippi in October 1962. Their experiences could have been used to offer greater background to the fight for equal rights. Instead, *Cineaste* commented in an editorial, "a film which rightfully should have dealt with the character and ideology of the civil rights movement has been turned into *Dirty Harry Meets the KKK*."[13]

The favorable way in which the FBI was portrayed in the film attracted considerable criticism. The *Cineaste* editorial condemned Parker for turning the civil rights movement "into a historical footnote" while transforming J. Edgar Hoover's FBI "into a heroic force." In his review, Thomas Doherty quoted Jimmy Breslin's comment that, under Hoover, the FBI was "always more concerned . . . with pinkos handing out leaflets than with civil rights violations or organized crime."[14] Before the deaths of Chaney, Goodman, and Schwerner, the FBI had been fairly hostile to civil rights activists, spying on or harassing them. Mississippi civil rights worker Michael Yarrow would later recall that Student Non-violent Coordinating Committee members distrusted the FBI, who at times turned statements they had made over to the local police.[15] The disappearance of the civil rights workers, however, changed the position: there was huge media publicity (in part because two of the victims were white) and, under political pressure from Lyndon Johnson, the Bureau was obliged to act. After six weeks, the FBI—on the basis of information apparently supplied by a paid informer—had located and recovered the bodies.[16] *Mississippi Burning*, by contrast, shows Ward and Anderson constantly at odds, FBI agents in regulation blue suits and narrow neckties blundering around in a swamp, Ward spending money

FIGURE 10.2 *FBI agents Rupert Anderson (Gene Hackman) and Alan Ward (Willem Dafoe) first come into contact with the Klan in* Mississippi Burning.

like water—and the bodies of the lost activists finally located by means of threatened castration (by a black agent although the FBI was all-white in 1964) and simulated Klan violence. To defeat the Klan, the film suggests, requires behaving like them. It is no accident that at one point FBI men dress as Klansmen. The two, to all intents and purposes, have become indistinguishable. The resort to violence by the FBI is not only fictional; it diverts attention from the achievements of the real civil rights movement, which adopted a courageous, resolute, and ultimately successful policy of nonviolence.[17]

Mississippi Burning, as many critics pointed out, told a story of the struggle for black rights essentially from a white perspective. With the exception of two courageous African American boys, a minister who declares he is "sick and tired of going to the funerals of black men who have been murdered by white men," and the anachronistic black FBI agent, blacks appear in the film according to one reviewer "only as passive victims, silent observers or gospel singers."[18] This is not entirely correct: many blacks—and some whites—are shown walking together in a protest march through the streets of the town and, later, following the body of the slain black activist to the cemetery. But it is true that the film has no major black characters, despite being set in a state that produced, among many other civil rights leaders, Medgar Evers, James Meredith, Fannie Lou Hamer, and Anne Moody. Alan Parker explained the absence of major black characters in his film as the product of commercial necessity: the movie was aimed at a predominantly white audience, in the United States and elsewhere, and the film probably could not have been made without white heroes. The director insisted he was "not making movies for 14 intellectuals at the Cinematheque in Paris" but was trying "to find a wide audience."[19] An unimpressed *Cineaste* dismissed Parker's version of "conventional box office wisdom" as a "cop-out" ignoring the recent success of movies with mainly black casts such as *A Soldier's Story* (1984) and *The Color Purple* (1985), as well as the box-office drawing power of black actors like Eddie Murphy and Richard Pryor.[20]

Ultimately, *Mississippi Burning* has more to say about the roots of Southern racism than the fight against it. The film offers two main explanations of bigotry and racism. Mrs. Pell sees it as a cultural phenomenon. "Hatred isn't something you're born with," she tells Anderson, "it gets taught. At school they said segregation is what's said in the bible . . . Genesis 9, verse 27.[21] At seven years o[f] age, [if] you['re] told it enough times you believe it." At both the televised Klan rally and the "political meeting" addressed by Klan leader Clayton Townley (Stephen Tobolowsky), there are small children—some young enough to be held in their mother's arms—who are listening avidly to (and sometimes applauding) the speeches about protecting "Anglo-Saxon, Christian" civilization.[22] A slightly older boy is shown jeering the civil rights march through the town. Children follow the lead of their parents. "It's ugly, this whole thing, it's so ugly," declares Mrs. Pell, and Alan Parker famously made sure—by careful selection of local extras—that the ugliness of spirit of adult racists was reflected in the ugliness (and contemptuousness) of their faces.[23] Mrs. Pell herself has been brought up within this system, but is capable of standing outside it. Victimized by male patriarchy—her father has lost the family home in a poker game and her husband requires her to give him an alibi for racist murder—she is on good terms with local blacks. When a black boy is beaten up and dumped on main street, she pauses on the way back into her hairdressing salon to pat an elderly black man sympathetically on the arm.[24] She talks happily in the garden with her black laundress Mary, and plays with the baby of Mary's sister, but as soon as Clinton Pell appears, the atmosphere becomes strained and Mary quickly picks up the baby and leaves.

Parker's second explanation of the origins of racism was grounded in his London working-class origins and socialist convictions. He suggested that racism is closely tied up with class exploitation. There is a conflict between Parker and screenwriter Chris Gerolmo over the degree to which Parker rewrote the script (Parker claimed it was "totally overhauled"). But there is one scene in which Parker's claims to authorship seem undeniable. It comes when Anderson and Ward are sharing a motel room together, and have their one and only conversation about the roots of racism. In answer to Ward's question, "Where does it all come from, all this hatred?" Parker claimed, "I wanted to point out that it is economic, that what was invented was an underclass which happens to be black."[25] Anderson answers the question with a story from his boyhood:

Anderson: You know, when I was a little boy . . . there was an old negro farmer lived down the road from us, name of Monroe. And he was . . . Well, I guess he was just a little luckier than my daddy was. He bought himself a mule. That was a big deal around that town. My daddy hated that mule. 'Cos his friends were always kidding him about that they saw Monroe ploughin' with his new mule . . . and Monroe was gonna rent another field now that he had a mule. One morning that mule just showed up dead. They poisoned the water. After that there was never any mention about that mule around my daddy. Just never came up. One time we were drivin' down the road and we passed Monroe's place and we saw it was empty. He'd just packed up and left, I guess. Gone up North or somethin'. I looked over at my daddy's face . . . and I knew he'd done it. And he saw that I knew. He was ashamed. I guess he *was* ashamed. He looked at me and he said. "If you ain't better than a nigger, son, who *are* you better than?"

Ward: Do you think that's an excuse?

Anderson: No, it's not an excuse. It's just a story about my daddy.

Ward: Where does that leave you?

Anderson: With an old man who was so full of hate that he didn't know that bein' poor was what was killin' him.

Ward knows that Anderson has lived in Mississippi before leaving to join the FBI. He is curious—and concerned—to know what Anderson's take on Mississippi racism is, but he does not understand the point of the story. Yet to Anderson, as a Southerner, the story illuminates because it has its roots in a discourse about racism that goes back to the 1890s.

The Reconstruction period after the Civil War had seen a comparatively brief attempt on the part of northern Republicans, sustained by Union troops, to bring African Americans into the political life of the Southern states. It failed, in part because of white opposition, in part because blacks were not economically independent enough, and in part because the Republican leadership either disappeared from the scene or became distracted with other issues. One by one, the "radical" Republican governments of the South, heavily dependent on black votes, were defeated and replaced with Democratic administrations.[26] Yet, for a few years, there were not huge changes in how blacks were treated in the South. Many continued to vote and race lines were fairly fluid.[27] But agriculture, the economic mainstay of the still mainly agrarian South, was in deep trouble by the mid-1880s. Farmers faced falling prices for their produce, higher transportation and borrowing costs, exploitation by middlemen, and the fact that most did not own farms, but were working either as tenants or sharecroppers. This resulted in the birth of the cooperative Farmers' Alliance movement in Texas in 1885. Increasingly, white Southern farmers found that the Democratic party—led by so-called Bourbons who often had close ties with financial interests and railroads—had no interest in helping them. In the elections of 1890, farmers ran insurgent campaigns within the Democratic party to elect their own men. The old Democratic guard was humiliated in South Carolina, Georgia, and Tennessee. But in the months after the election, as southern farmers discovered that their local successes cut little ice with Democratic politicians in Washington, many began to move toward the idea of founding their own party.[28]

Thomas E. Watson, elected a congressman from Georgia in the revolt of 1890, became one of the leaders in the new movement. At a convention in Omaha, Nebraska, in July 1892, representatives of Southern farmers joined with westerners to launch a new third party: the People's or Populist Party. In the South, Populists became the first American political party to argue that the main problem facing the South was one of poverty, not race. Tom Watson and others defended the right of African Americans to vote and attempted to form a political coalition between the poor and disadvantaged of both races.[29] Although the Populists did not do as well as they had hoped (Watson lost his seat in the US House of Representatives in the fall elections of that year) and effectively committed political suicide by joining with the Democrats to run the same presidential candidate (William Jennings Bryan) in 1896,[30] the Democratic Party establishment in the South had suffered a mighty scare. It responded with moves to bring an end to African American voting. Mississippi had led the way in 1890. A new constitution tightened residency requirements, required all voters to pass a literacy test and pay all their taxes (including the poll tax) by a certain date in election year, and banned those who had committed crimes from voting. Other Southern states followed, for example, Louisiana in 1898 and North Carolina in 1900.[31] The impact was devastating: the number of registered black voters in Louisiana fell from 130,344 in 1896 to 5,320 in 1900. Sadly, Tom Watson reversed himself and helped lead the successful campaign for disfranchisement in Georgia in 1908.[32] Thereafter, until the 1960s, the Democratic party maintained its power in the South by racist appeals to white unity. It was this culture that the three real civil rights workers (Chaney, Goodman, and Schwerner), whose story inspired *Mississippi Burning*, were committed to change. Much of what they were doing in Mississippi had to do with challenging the white political elite by persuading African Americans to register to vote.

In his story of his father, Anderson returned to the political lesson briefly offered by the Populists of the 1890s: that the main problem of the South was not race but poverty, and that the latter would continue as long as the white political and social elite used racist tactics to keep poor whites and blacks apart. While Alan Parker's analysis of the class origins of racism was not popular with modern American critics—who, he thought, believed in the American Dream and its promise of self-advancement—it had strong roots in radical late nineteenth-century American thought.[33]

Afterword

The shooting (in part) and reception of *Mississippi Burning* in Mississippi raised the question of just how much had changed in race relations there. Alan Parker, Gene Hackman, and Willem Dafoe, Thulani Davis noted, "each suggested that attitudes have not completely changed in the towns in which they've shot."[34] Perhaps the most revealing story came from Philadelphia, Mississippi, the real-life focus of the 1964 investigation. Lullu Ellis, the owner of the town's only theater, announced that its manager, her son Shelly Steiger, had first decided not to show *Mississippi Burning* "because church groups had threatened to boycott the theater if it screened the film." Steiger had later changed his mind arguing that the film "would bring negative publicity no matter what he did." *The Hollywood Reporter* commented that "during most movies" at the Ellis Theater, "blacks customarily sit in the balcony while whites, a few blacks and Choctaw Indians sit down in the orchestra seats." Steiger quickly explained that "this was by custom and was not required by the theater management," attempting to side-step criticism that—25 years after the Civil Rights Act became law on July 2, 1964, itself 11 days after the murder of civil rights workers James Chaney, Andrew Goodman, and James Schwerner—he was breaking the law by continuing to run a segregated movie-theater.[35]

JFK (1991)

Rarely has a movie excited the same controversy as Oliver Stone's *JFK* (1991). Six months before the film's release, George Lardner, Jr. published an article in the *Washington Post* attacking it. Basing his critique on an early draft of the screenplay, Lardner insisted that Stone was "chasing fiction" in his account of John F. Kennedy's assassination and flirting with "the edge of paranoia."[36] When the film finally arrived in theaters, Vincent Canby of the *New York Times*—who thought it "simultaneously arrogant and timorous"—predicted that "the ferocity of . . . outrage should now subside."[37] Canby was wrong. A few days later, George Will argued that "Stone's celluloid diatribe . . . falsifies so much he may be an intellectual sociopath, indifferent to truth." *JFK*, Will concluded, was "an act of execrable history and contemptible citizenship by a man of technical skill, scant education and negligible conscience."[38] Two well-known political figures added their names to the list of those attacking the film. Governor John Connally of Texas, who according to the report of the Warren Commission set up by President Lyndon B. Johnson to investigate the circumstances of the assassination had been hit by a bullet that already passed through John Kennedy's body, thought the movie was "insulting" in the manner in which it implicated the Warren Commission in the whole assassination conspiracy. Connally also criticized Stone for making the investigation into the assassination launched by District Attorney Jim Garrison in New Orleans the centerpiece of the story, since that investigation had proved a "fiasco." Jack Valenti, a former Lyndon Johnson aide who had become long-serving president of the Motion Picture Association of America, issued a statement describing the film as a "hoax," a "smear," and "a monstrous charade."[39]

Oliver Stone, the director of *JFK* and target of many of the criticisms leveled against it, was born in New York City on September 15, 1946, the only child in an upper middle-class family. His father was a stockbroker, married to a French-Canadian woman. Stone attended expensive schools: Trinity School on the upper West Side and, later, the Hill School, a preparatory boarding school in Pottstown, Pennsylvania. In 1961, when he was 15, his parents divorced. Feeling betrayed, Stone learned soon afterwards that his father was deeply in debt. There was just enough money to pay for a college education, and Stone began studying for a degree at Yale. As an act of youthful rebellion, he dropped out after one year to spend two terms teaching Chinese students in Saigon. He arrived in South Vietnam in June 1965, four months after the first US combat troops were deployed. At this stage, Stone (who had supported conservative Republican Barry Goldwater for the presidency a year earlier) had no doubts about American involvement in the war. "We were going to win," he later wrote, "It was the war of my generation." When his teaching job finished, Stone worked his way back as a merchant seaman to the Americas, first to Oregon and later Mexico, where he finished a long novel about his Asian experiences. After it was rejected by Simon and Schuster, he returned to Yale. Frustrated and still restless, he quit again after one semester to join the army, turning down the chance of officer training to go as an infantryman to Vietnam. Experiencing the Vietnam war as a combat soldier would in many ways be the defining experience of Stone's life.[40]

Stone's motives for joining up were mixed: it was obviously in part to do with his inner demons but he also believed in the war. Arriving in Vietnam in September 1967, however, he realized that much had changed: the South Vietnamese who had welcomed Americans two years earlier were now much more critical. Corruption was widespread: some were making fortunes out of the war, while others were killed or injured. Stone himself was wounded several times in action and awarded a Purple Heart and a Bronze Star. Yet he would carry away with him a strong awareness of the fact that most American GIs were poor and uneducated. He also helped burn villages, saw the random killing of civilians, and learned of the frequency with which "gung-ho" officers and sergeants in the US army were killed by their own desperate-to-survive men. Stone lost his faith in the war yet, returning to New York after 15 months in Vietnam, was angry and embittered that few Americans seemed to care about the conflict.[41] His salvation appeared to come when he was accepted by New York University's film school, where one of his teachers was Martin Scorsese. Stone's first short film, *Last Year in Vietnam*, was about the difficulties of a returned Vietnam veteran. Yet his film studies did not immediately lead to anything: he would spend the next few years working at a succession of jobs while writing screenplays and directing one cheaply produced horror film, *Seizure*. In 1976, he wrote the screenplay for what would become *Platoon*. Although no studio showed any interest in the film, the writing was impressive enough for Columbia to invite him to produce the screenplay for Alan Parker's *Midnight Express*, for which he won an Academy Award.[42] This paved the way for more screenwriting assignments. In 1981, he wrote and directed *The Hand*, another low-budget horror film. He also directed and cowrote *Talk Radio* (1988) and *The Doors* (1991), a biopic about Jim Morrison. But, increasingly, he was drawn to films with a political slant: *Salvador* (1986) condemned US interventionism in the Central American republic and *Wall Street* (1987) the failings of American capitalism in the boom years of the 1980s. Stone's growing success also made it possible for him to return to the most haunting experiences of his youth and depict the Vietnam war on film. In 1986, ten years after writing the draft script, he directed *Platoon*, dealing with the experiences of a naive volunteer grunt. This was followed by *Born on the Fourth of July* (1989), based on the life of disabled veteran Ron Kovic (Tom Cruise), and *JFK* (1991), which covered the political origins of the war.

From his own experiences in Vietnam, Stone carried away a distrust of what the American government told its people. Events of the early 1970s, especially the Watergate scandal, increased his growing sense "that the US government is out of control or in the hands of secret agencies . . . [and] that our democratic heritage and institutions serve as a kind of ideology to cover the activities of greedy men."[43] Central to his analysis was the perception that something had been lost with Kennedy's assassination. "As he watched his country's troubles grow in subsequent years," commented Robert Brent Toplin, "Stone came to believe that 1963 constituted an important watershed. During the thousand days of Kennedy's presidency, much seemed right about America; in the following years, much seemed wrong." By the end of the 1970s, according to Randy Roberts and David Welky, "he had decided that the assassination of John F. Kennedy had drastically altered the course of the war [in Vietnam] and America's future."[44] In the years that followed, as Stone became an increasingly successful filmmaker, it is likely that his thoughts turned at times to the idea of a movie about Kennedy. What he lacked was an angle of approach, a way into the subject.

In 1988, in a scene that could have come straight out of *JFK*, publisher Ellen Ray handed him a copy of Jim Garrison's book *On the Trail of the Assassins: My Investigation and Prosecution of the Murder of President Kennedy* (1988) in an elevator in Havana, Cuba.[45] Garrison had been the only prosecutor ever to bring charges in connection with the assassination, accusing New Orleans businessman Clay Shaw of being involved in a conspiracy to murder Kennedy. Garrison's prosecution had been unsuccessful: a jury found Shaw not guilty. But reading and rereading the book convinced Stone not only that the Warren Commission had been wrong in its conclusion that Lee Harvey Oswald had been the "lone gunman" in the killing of the president—that there had, in fact, been a conspiracy—but also that the story of Garrison's prosecution could serve as the focus for a film.

Stone optioned Garrison's book (reportedly with $250,000 of his own money) and arranged to meet the author. He hired Zachary Sklar, who had helped write and edit *On the Trail of the Assassins*, as a cowriter on the film project. He optioned another book on the assassination controversies that had developed since 1963: Jim Marrs' *Crossfire: The*

Plot That Killed Kennedy (1989). Stone also recruited a recent Yale graduate, Jane Rusconi, as a researcher.[46] Over the course of time he also hired L. Fletcher Prouty, a retired colonel in the US Air Force who had been an aide to the Joint Chiefs of Staff during the Kennedy presidency, and John Newman, who had worked in US Army military intelligence and was currently finishing a PhD on Kennedy's policy in Vietnam. Although Prouty (who would provide the basis for "X" (Donald Sutherland) in the film) and Newman both agreed that Kennedy, if he had lived, would not have expanded the Vietnam war by committing American combat troops, they found it difficult to work together on the film.[47]

Stone, when starting to work with Sklar on the screenplay, cited two films as models.[48] The first, Constantin Costa Gavras' *Z* (1969), was based on the real-life assassination of Greek leftwinger Grigoris Lambrakis in May 1963—six months before Kennedy went to Dallas—and the investigation of the case by Christos Sartzetakis. It dealt, in part, with the efforts by right-wing elements to eliminate Lambrakis and conceal the conspiracy.[49] The second film, Akira Kurosawa's *Rashomon* (1950), examined the murder of a samurai warrior through a series of conflicting testimonies, underlining the difficulty of establishing what is really "true." As Adam Barker pointed out, there are at least two other films with strong resemblances to *JFK*: Alan J. Pakula's conspiracy thriller *The Parallax View* (1974) and the same director's *All the President's Men* (1976), an account of the investigation by two journalists, Carl Bernstein and Bob Woodward, into the Watergate scandal. *All the President's Men* introduced the idea of a "Deep Throat" character who provides background information but refuses to be identified, much the same role as "X" in *JFK*.[50]

JFK, like *Rashomon*, is a film that invites its spectators to consider and choose between the different views and perspectives that are on offer. What gives the film its underlying structure is that it focuses on two heroes (John F. Kennedy, Jim Garrison) and two conspiracies (the initial one to carry out Kennedy's assassination, the second to conceal what had occurred). Kennedy appears in the film mainly as victim, but there are two principal sequences that establish his claims to heroic status. The first is at the start of the film, following a shot of President Dwight D. Eisenhower speaking. This is succeeded by two and a half minutes of montage in which a bewildering array of brief shots, some from newsreels, television newscasts, and still photos, and others from what appear to be Kennedy family home movies, are used to convey—often subliminally—six essential points. First, in contrast to Eisenhower, Kennedy was youthful and somehow "a symbol of the new freedom of the 1960s." He had considerable style, being shown at times with his elegant wife Jacqueline in full evening dress. Second, he was a family man, with frequent shots of his children, parents, and siblings. Third, that he favored the civil rights struggle: footage of black sit-down strikers being hauled away, Martin Luther King speaking, southern cops beating up African Americans, and the 1963 civil rights march on Washington precedes Kennedy declaring his commitment "to the cause of freedom round the world."[51] Fourth, that he "inherited" a "war against the Communist Castro dictatorship" in Cuba—a war fought by the CIA and Cuban exiles that led to the futile "Bay of Pigs" invasion of Cuba in April 1961. Kennedy assumed public responsibility for the failure, but privately thought that the CIA headed by Allen Dulles (whose hand he pointedly avoids shaking) had tried to force him into an all-out invasion. In the following year, by imposing a naval blockade on Cuba, he compelled the Soviet Union to remove the missiles it had installed there, although there were rumors he had reached a secret "deal" with the Russians and was thus "soft" on communism. Fifth, Kennedy was skeptical over the legitimacy and prospects for survival of the US-supported noncommunist government in South Vietnam and insisted that "in the final analysis, it's their war. They're the ones who have to win it or lose it." Sixth, in his American University speech of June 1963, Kennedy was attempting to move beyond the Cold War and establish a new basis for peaceful coexistence with the Soviets on the grounds that "we all inhabit this small planet . . . we all cherish our children's futures."

The second sequence occurs later in the film when Garrison's informer, X, meets him at the Lincoln Memorial in Washington. X has been involved in Cold War "black ops" since the 1940s and much of his summary of these often-illegal operations takes place with the Washington Monument ironically in the background. X claims that Kennedy had been planning to end American participation in the war in Vietnam. He himself had "spent much of September 63 working on the Kennedy plan for getting all U. S. personnel out of Vietnam by the end of 1965." X later puts Kennedy's decision to begin to withdraw from Vietnam, as announced to his administration in National Security Action Memorandum (NSAM) 263, in a broader perspective. Kennedy had begun to make major changes in US foreign policy. He had refused to invade Cuba in 1962 and signed a nuclear test-ban treaty with the Soviets in October 1963. During his second term, X claimed, he planned to end the Cold War and abandon the race to the moon in favor of collaboration with the USSR in space. What Kennedy might or might not have done in a second term, of course, was pure speculation. Of far more importance was the suggestion that Kennedy had already begun a policy of disengagement from South Vietnam and, if he had lived, the long national nightmare of American involvement in the war could have been avoided.

Much of Stone's interpretation of Kennedy in *JFK* has been questioned by writers and scholars. In portraying the president as a husband and family man, it ignored his compulsive promiscuity. His record on race was patchy to say the least: he did not support the Freedom Rides or, initially, the March on Washington. He had appeared ready to negotiate with segregationalists before ultimately sending in US troops and federalized National Guardsmen to restore order during the riots after James Meredith enrolled at the University of Mississippi in 1962.[52] It is uncertain how much Kennedy (or his brother Robert, the Attorney-General) knew about plans to assassinate Cuban president Fidel Castro or disrupt the Cuban economy. Presenting Kennedy as an advocate of peace flies in the face of the fact that he had presided over what Alexander Cockburn describes as "the largest and most rapid military build-up in the peacetime history of the US." In two and a half years the American defense budget had risen from 39.5 billion dollars to around 52 billion.[53]

On the other hand, as Oliver Stone argued, Kennedy had clearly "changed enormously" during 1963.[54] Did that change mean that he truly wanted the United States out of Vietnam? *JFK* insisted that he did (though as Robert Rosenstone points out, "within the world of the film, the idea . . . rests on the mention of a single memorandum and the testimony of a fictional character [X]").[55] Yet the single memorandum, as Stone pointed out in an answer to his critics, was crucial. In NSAM 263, Kennedy specifically accepted the recommendations made in a report by General Maxwell Taylor and Defense Secretary Robert McNamara. The second of these was that "A program be established to train Vietnamese so that the essential functions now performed by U. S. military personnel can be carried out by Vietnamese by the end of 1965. It should be possible to withdraw the bulk of U. S. personnel by that time." (Stone paraphrased the final sentence.) The third recommendation was for the withdrawal of "1,000 U.S. military personnel by the end of 1963" with the aim of replacing them by "trained Vietnamese." The only recommendation of the report Kennedy rejected was the suggestion that the withdrawal of the 1,000 men be formally announced. As Stone explained, "Kennedy didn't want to be attacked [during the 1964 presidential campaign] for 'losing' Vietnam in the same way that the Republican Right had, in the 1952 election of Eisenhower, successfully accused the Democrats under Truman of 'losing' China."[56]

Both Stone and Sklar, the cowriters of the screenplay for *JFK*, insisted that Lyndon Johnson's NSAM 273, signed on November 26, 1963, differed from NSAM 263 in significant ways and prepared the ground for deeper US involvement in Vietnam.[57] *JFK* suggests that one of the reasons Kennedy was killed was to put Lyndon Johnson, a man more enthusiastic about fighting the war, in his place ("Just let me get elected, and then you can have your war"). Almost certainly, this is a misreading of Johnson's character. Stone, as he acknowledged, borrowed the quotation from Stanley Karnow's book on the Vietnam war. But Karnow had used it not to illustrate Johnson's aggressive intent but his "practice of making different promises to different factions."[58]

"It is difficult to believe," writes Robert Brent Toplin,

that Kennedy would have turned as quickly and extensively to placing U.S. combat troops in the country as did his successor . . . It is striking that in less than a year after Kennedy's assassination Lyndon

Johnson was promoting misleading interpretations of reports from the Gulf of Tonkin to win congressional justification for future military actions . . . In less than five years after the assassination Johnson had committed over a half-million American troops and billions of dollars in equipment to the U. S. effort in Vietnam.[59]

Johnson, however, was not instinctively a warlike leader. He wanted, above all, to be a great president in domestic affairs.[60] He had little knowledge or experience of foreign policy. Yet he could be assertive over what he saw as essential American interests and was more disposed to accept military advice than his predecessor. Largely as a result of their experiences over the Bay of Pigs and the Cuban missile crisis, both John Kennedy and his brother, Attorney-General Robert Kennedy, had become distrustful of the military. "I thought, as I listened," Robert Kennedy would later write of discussions in the National Security Council during the missile crisis, "of the many times that I had heard the military take positions which, if wrong, had the advantage that no one would be around at the end to know."[61]

Making District Attorney Jim Garrison the second hero of *JFK* was a controversial decision on Stone's part. Many commentators were critical of the real Garrison, whom they saw as extremely flawed. He was accused of manipulating the media, being forced out of the National Guard for a "severe and disabling psychoneurosis," taking bribes, Mafia connections, bullying witnesses, and lying in court.[62] Stone defended him against such charges,[63] yet, as he also made clear, had never intended his screen Garrison to be anything other than a "metaphoric protagonist."[64] He used Garrison, Roger Ebert declared, "as the symbolic center of his film because Garrison . . . is the only man who has attempted to bring anyone into court in connection with the fishiest political murder of our time."[65] "Garrison" in the film is a traditional Hollywood narrative device: the heroic individual who takes on the system in the cause of justice. As Vincent Canby observed in the *New York Times*, he is "a Frank Capra character," the man of decency and integrity played in Capra films by James Stewart or Gary Cooper (both of whom Stone had in mind as he wrote the script).[66]

The casting of Kevin Costner in the role of Garrison underlined this: to spectators of the film when it was released in 1991, Costner brought with him the integrity of Eliot Ness in *The Untouchables* (1987), the drive to restore lost American values of Ray Kinsella in *Field of Dreams* (1989) and something of the bewildered openmindedness of John Dunbar in *Dances With Wolves* (1990). Costner's casting gave credence to the storyline developed by Stone and Sklar and his performance, as the family man slowly and painfully coming to grips with the truth, provided the essential core of unity in a long, complex film. Yet Garrison in *JFK* is really a composite character rather than a historical individual. He is in possession of considerably more knowledge than the real Garrison had during his 1966–9 investigation. "I took the dramatic liberty," Stone explained, "of having Garrison and his staff uncover much of the evidence that was really uncovered by other . . . researchers such as Sylvia Meagher, Josiah Thompson, Mark Lane, Robert Groden, Peter Dale Scott, Paul Hoch, and Mary Ferrell."[67] Stone's Garrison, either while talking to his staff or in the Shaw trial itself, raises questions over the Warren Commission's report that had emerged in more than two decades of subsequent debate surrounding the assassination.

Stone established the foundation for his thesis that Kennedy's death was the result of a conspiracy in the very first sequence of the film. President Dwight D. Eisenhower, delivering his farewell address in January 1961, warns—in words written by Adam Yarmolinsky—against the growing power of the "military-industrial complex" in American life. In his review of *JFK*, Vincent Canby perceptively noted that "it never becomes much more specific than Ike [Eisenhower]."[68] The main figure claiming a link between the growing power of the military-industrial complex and the Kennedy assassination is the fictional "X," who explains to Garrison how profitable the Vietnam war is: $75 to $100 billion so far, maybe $200 billion before it ends. A failing company such as Bell Helicopters has been saved by the need to replace the 3,000 helicopters lost so far. General Dynamics also profits by building F-111 fighters. If Kennedy ends American involvement in the war, companies like this will suffer.

"I think it started like that," X believes, referring to grumbles among the corporate elite at the potential economic loss. "Defense contractors, oil bankers. Just conversation." Then "a call was made" to someone in the armed forces, the various branches of which have their own grievances. The military are frustrated by Kennedy's failure to invade Cuba in 1962, worried over the budget cuts he has announced in March 1963, deeply concerned by the possibility that he is (supposedly) planning to wind down the Cold War and withdraw American troops from Vietnam. The CIA is angry at Kennedy's attempt to rein it in after the fiasco of the Bay of Pigs (by handing responsibility for "covert paramilitary operations in peacetime" to the Joint Chiefs of Staff and by the dismissal of agency head Allen Dulles and two senior officers). "General Y," X's former superior in "Black Ops," possibly takes the call and arranges to fly in the team of assassins. "Maybe from the special camp we keep near Athens, Greece . . .," suggests X. "They'd be locals, Cubans, Mafia hire . . . Does it matter who shot . . . from what rooftop?"

The vagueness of the conspiratorial forces Stone suggested were behind the Kennedy assassination (the "military-industrial complex") was a weakness of the film. It evoked, in some respects, Senator Joseph R. McCarthy's description of the internal Communist threat as "a conspiracy so immense." It also tied *JFK* into the longer tradition of conspiracy theories in American history that marked out what Richard Hofstadter, in a famous essay, referred to as "The Paranoid Style in American Politics."[69] Stone responded that he found

> it so condescending that Hofstadter . . . is trotted out each time by the self-righteous media to attack those who investigate conspiracy in our culture. It's condescending simply because we've had so many *provable* conspiracies in our history—from the first gathering of conspirators against the Stamp Act, kicking off the Revolutionary War, to the conspiracy that murdered President Lincoln, and recently to the Watergate and the Iran-contra conspiracies.[70]

Arguing that there *had* been conspiracies in American history was not, of course, the same as justifying the claim that the military-industrial complex had acted to eliminate Kennedy. As Vincent Canby again observed, with its references to the army, Army Intelligence, the CIA, and politics (Lyndon Johnson), "the conspiracy includes just about everyone up to what are called the Government's highest levels, but nobody in particular can be identified except some members of the scroungy New Orleans-Dallas-Galveston demimonde."[71]

Stone made clear his belief there were *two* conspiracies: one to kill Kennedy, the other to cover up the killing. By focusing on Garrison's investigation and the trial of New Orleans businessman Clay Shaw for involvement in the conspiracy to murder the president, his film mainly dealt with the second conspiracy, which—he argued—had "another agenda" and involved "a larger series of players," although those players may not have been aware "who killed Kennedy and why." Stone claimed, for example, that Kennedy's successor, Lyndon Johnson, had an important role in the cover-up because he appointed the Warren Commission ("the worst single piece of investigation I've ever seen").[72] Given the nature of Garrison's investigation into Shaw, most of the many problems and setbacks the Garrison team experienced could be blamed on the cover-up. These included the death of witness Dave Ferrie (Joe Pesci), presented in *JFK* as murder, the refusal of the US Attorney in Washington to serve subpoenas on Allen Dulles, existing CIA director Richard Helms, and named FBI agents, the rejection of extradition requests by state governors, the disappearance or reluctance of witnesses called to testify, and the bugging of the District Attorney's offices, allegedly by the FBI. At the end of the trial, it took the jury less than an hour to find Clay Shaw not guilty on all charges. Yet the failure of Garrison's prosecution masked his courtroom success in undermining the main conclusion of the Warren Commission, that Lee Harvey Oswald had acted alone. The jury, while finding there was insufficient evidence to convict Shaw, was now convinced that "there had been a conspiracy to kill JFK."[73]

One prop of the Warren Commission's report was undercut by Garrison's trial and, later, even more widely by Stone's movie. This was the "single" or "magic bullet" theory formulated by Arlen Specter and adopted by the Commission. The arguments over this bullet are arcane and some have suggested that it did not operate precisely in the way Garrison describes in court in the film. There continue to be disagreements over whether Oswald was capable of firing three bullets in 5.6 seconds with the necessary degree of accuracy—or whether there were, in fact, more bullets fired, either by Oswald or other assassins. Many of these arguments start from the home movie shot by Abraham Zapruder, while standing on a concrete block in Dealey Plaza. For five years after the assassination, the film was locked in the files at *Time-Life* corporation in New York. Garrison's subpoena of it as evidence in the trial made it possible to see the film in court. Stone's use of the Zapruder film in *JFK* gave it, for the first time, a mass audience.[74] According to Robert Burgoyne, it provided a "clock" for the assassination, "giving the lie to the 'magic bullet' theory, which would have us believe that a bullet could suspend itself in midflight for one and a half seconds."[75] Yet the Zapruder footage did something else going well beyond arguments over the magic bullet and number of shots. It showed audiences for Stone's film the fatal shot, in which Kennedy's head jerks *backwards* (the Book Depository from which Oswald allegedly fired his shots was behind him) and there is a flash of blood at the back of his head. Doctors have argued that a neurological reaction to shock made Kennedy's body jerk backwards when hit by a bullet from behind.[76] But this flies in the face of many people's common sense reaction, which is that Kennedy jerked backwards because he was shot from the *front* (Stone himself remarked that "you don't have to be a combat veteran to know that generally the target goes with the impact and velocity of the bullet"[77]). The Zapruder footage, wrote film critic Roger Ebert, has "made it forever clear that the Oswald theory [of the lone assassin] is impossible—and that at least one of the shots must have come from in front of Kennedy, not from the Texas Schoolbook Depository behind him."[78]

JFK was a film of great complexity, crowding an enormous amount of information of various kinds—visual and auditory—into its three-hour running-time. Stone used various strategies to bind parts of the film together, including the narration by Martin Sheen in the course of the opening montage and the use of what Kenneth Turan in the *Los Angeles Times* called "reassuringly familiar faces" in minor roles (Jack Lemmon as Jack Martin, Ed Asner as Guy Bannister, Donald Sutherland as X, and Walter Matthau as Senator Russell Long).[79] Much of the film is what Robert Burgoyne terms "a form of radical pastiche," tying together by rapid editing reminiscent of MTV various forms of media output: newsreels and documentaries, simulated newsreels and documentaries, reenactments shot in original locations, and still photographs, all incorporated at times into flashbacks and flashforwards, with the result that chronology at times becomes hard to determine and fact is often indistinguishable from fiction.[80]

The film was much-criticized for this blurring of the line between truth and fiction. Commentators attacked the film's various inventions. These included scenes (the bullet left by a coconspirator on a hospital gurney, described by one reviewer as "just an overheated act of conjecture"[81]) and dialogue (e.g. the debates within the military introduced by X). They also included a number of fictional characters, the most crucial of these being Willie O'Keefe (Kevin Bacon) and X. O'Keefe, a male prostitute, is apparently a composite of several gay witnesses.[82] X is the *deus ex machina* who explains the background of the conspiracy to Garrison. The film also made many factual mistakes.[83] Finally, it was also attacked for its apparent bias against gays (the scenes of Shaw and Ferrie partying together) and women (especially what Desson Howe of the *Washington Post* referred to as the "second-rate domestic subplot" revolving around Garrison's relationship with his wife Liz (Sissy Spacek).[84]

Oliver Stone denied that his film was homophobic, insisting that the issue had only been raised because Shaw denied knowing Ferrie, whereas there was a photograph of them (used in the film) in drag together. "No one with a brain is going to walk away from *JFK*," he asserted, "thinking that all gays are president killers or that their homosexuality was the reason these particular men may have been involved."[85] Stone also refused to accept that he had distorted history by mingling together truth and fiction. He was not a historian, he argued, but a "dramatist" making use of artistic license.[86] His aim, he declared, was not to rewrite history but to shape a new "counter-myth to the conventional myth presented by the Warren Commission."[87] In making *JFK*, he conceded, it had been necessary to take some liberties with the facts, but he and his cowriter Zachary Sklar had "explained in depth what we combined, condensed, and collapsed" by publishing an annotated version of the screenplay.[88] Stone also insisted that he had emphasized with considerable frankness the fictional or unproven nature of much of the film's content. "In numerous interviews at the time and in press materials attached to the film when it was first shown at media screenings," he wrote, "I made it clear that the film was a blend of speculative fiction and facts, many of which were unagreed upon."[89]

The release of *JFK* stimulated debate over whether Kennedy, if he had lived, would have ended the American commitment in Vietnam.[90] More practically, it provoked growing political pressure for the release of papers collected by the Warren Commission and the House Select Committee on Assassinations (1976–8). The result was the passage of the President John F. Kennedy Assassination Records Collection Act of 1992 and the release of thousands of pages of documents over the next few years. When the Assassination Records Review Board set up by the Act came to an end in 1998, it specifically drew attention to the role of *JFK* in passing the 1992 law.[91] "Very few Hollywood filmmakers," wrote Robert Brent Toplin, "can claim that their productions helped to nudge Congress into legislative action."[92] The release of the documents chipped away further at the battered reputation of the Warren Commission. It was revealed that Warren Commission member (and future president) Gerald R. Ford had raised the place where a bullet entered Kennedy's back by two to three inches. According to Stone, Ford's "clarification" made the "magic bullet" theory a "minute physical possibility" instead of an outright absurdity.[93] Many American filmmakers have made movies representing events and people in American history. Few movies (only Griffith's *The Birth of a Nation* comes to mind) have stirred up as much controversy and had such practical consequences as Oliver Stone's *JFK*.

Filmography

Mississippi Burning (dir. Alan Parker; Orion Pictures, 1988).
JFK (dir. Oliver Stone; Warner Bros./Canal+/Regency, 1991).

NOTES

Introduction

1 See, for example, Robert Burgoyne, *Film Nation: Hollywood Looks at American History* (Minneapolis: University of Minnesota Press, 2010; rev. edn); idem, *The Hollywood Historical Film* (Malden, MA: Blackwell, 2008); J. E. Smyth, *Reconstructing American Historical Cinema from "Cimarron" to "Citizen Kane"* (Lexington: University of Kentucky Press, 2006); Robert Brent Toplin, *History by Hollywood: The Use and Abuse of the American Past* (Urbana and Chicago: University of Illinois Press, 1996). Robert A. Rosenstone's *Visions of the Past: The Challenge of Film to Our Ideas of History* (Cambridge, MA: Harvard University Press, 1995) discusses how film can be used to think historically, but discusses only three American historical films.

2 See, for example, John E. O'Connor and Martin Jackson, eds, *American History/American Film: Interpreting the Hollywood Image* (New York: Ungar, reissued in 1985); Peter C. Rollins, ed., *Hollywood As Historian: American Film in a Cultural Context* (Lexington: University of Kentucky Press, 1997; rev. edn); J. E. Smyth, ed., *Hollywood and the American Historical Film* (Basingstoke: Palgrave Macmillan, 2012).

3 Jeremy D. Stoddard and Alan S. Marcus, "The Burden of Hollywood Representation: Race, Freedom, and 'Educational' Hollywood Film," *Film and History*, vol. 36, no. 1 (2006), 28.

4 This point relates *solely* to subject-matter, since movies about slavery and Native Americans have almost invariably been made by whites with racial assumptions of their own. By contrast, the films used in this book to discuss Jewish and Italian immigration were written and directed by people who shared the same ethnic background as the characters in their films.

5 Janet Staiger, "'The Handmaiden of Villainy': Methods and Problems in Studying the Historical Reception of a Film," *Wide Angle*, vol. 8, no. 1 (1986), 20.

6 Toplin, *History by Hollywood*, 1–2.

7 David Thomson, *Showman: The Life of David O. Selznick* (London: André Deutsch, 1993), 676; Jim Cullen, *The Civil War in Popular Culture: A Reusable Past* (Washington, DC: Smithsonian Institution, 1995), 68; Robert Brent Toplin, ed., *Ken Burns's The Civil War: Historians Respond* (New York: Oxford University Press, 1996), xv.

8 Griffith, as quoted in Melvyn Stokes, *D. W. Griffith's "The Birth of a Nation": A History of "The Most Controversial Motion Picture of All Time"* (New York: Oxford University Press, 2007), 172.

9 Stanley Karnow, "*JFK*," in Mark C. Carnes, Ted Mico, John Miller-Monzon, and David Rubel, eds, *Past Imperfect: History According to the Movies* (London: Cassell, 1996), 273.

10 Exceptions to this may include David W. Griffith, Oliver Stone, and Steven Spielberg.

11 Elizabeth Grottle Strebel, "Renoir and the Popular Front," *Sight and Sound*, vol. 49, no. 1 (Winter 1979–80), 40.

12 Robert A. Rosenstone, "Oliver Stone as Historian," in Robert Brent Toplin, ed., *Oliver Stone's USA: Film, History, and Controversy* (Lawrence: University of Kansas Press, 2000), 32.

13 www.gettysburg.edu/news_Events/press_release_detail.dot?id=3376573, accessed April 17, 2013.

14 Ibid.

15 Rosenstone, "Oliver Stone as Historian," 34.

Chapter 1

1 *Midnight Ride of Paul Revere* (dir. Edwin S. Porter: Edison, 1907); *The Boston Tea Party* (dir. Edwin S. Porter; Edison, 1908); *The Spirit of 76* (dir. Francis Boggs; Selig Polyscope, 1908); *Washington at Valley Forge* (writer Gene Gauntier; Kalem, 1908); *Washington under the American Flag* (dir. J. Stuart Blackton; Vitagraph, 1909); *1776, or the Hessian Renegades* (dir. D. W. Griffith; Biograph, 1909); *The Battle of Bunker Hill* (dir. Oscar Apfel/J. Searle Dawley; Edison, 1911); *How Washington Crossed the Delaware* (dir. Oscar Apfel; Edison, 1912); *The Flag of Freedom* (Kalem, 1913); *The Midnight Ride of Paul Revere* (dir. Charles Brabin; Edison, 1914); *The Spy* (dir. Otis Turner; Universal Film Manufacturing, 1914); *Washington at Valley Forge* (dir. Francis Ford; Universal Film Manufacturing, 1914); *A Continental Girl* (dir. Joseph Adelman; Continental Photo-Play, 1915); *The Boston Tea Party* (Edison, 1915); *The Heart of a Hero* (dir. Émile Chautard; Peerless/World Film, 1916); *Betsy Ross* (dir. George Cowl/Travers Vale; World Film, 1917); *The Spirit of 76* (dir. George Siegmann; Continental Producing, 1917). See Clémentine Tholas-Disset, "Cinéma Muet et représentations des États-Unis: la mythification et l'universalisation de l'espace américain," PhD diss., University Sorbonne Nouvelle—Paris III, 2010, 272; www.imdb.com, accessed March 3, 2013.

2 Dir. John W. Noble; Messmore Kendall/Cosmopolitan Pictures, 1922.

3 Barry Schwartz, "Social Change and Collective Memory: The Democratization of George Washington," *American Sociological Review*, vol. 56, no. 2 (April 1991), 222–7, 230–2.

4 *"Betsy Ross," Variety*, September 7, 1917.

5 Alfred F. Young, *The Shoemaker and the Tea Party: Memory and the American Revolution* (Boston: Beacon Press, 1999), 7–9, 42–5, 87–8, 155–64. On the misuse of the "Tea Party" symbolism and other myths of the Revolution in contemporary America, see Jill Lepore, *The Whites of Their Eyes: The Tea Party's Revolution and the Battle Over American History* (Princeton: Princeton University Press, 2010).

6 One source lists Longfellow as the "writer" of the 1914 film. www.imdb.com, accessed February 26, 2013.

7 Lauren Thatcher Ulrich, "How Betsy Ross Became Famous: Oral tradition, nationalism, and the invention of history," *Common-Place*, vol. 8, no. 1 (October 2007), 14. Also see Marla R. Miller, *Betsy Ross and the Making of America* (New York: Henry Holt, 2010) and Lonn Taylor, Kathleen M. Kendrick, and Jeffrey L. Brodie, *The Star-Spangled Banner: The Making of an American Icon* (Washington, DC: Smithsonian/Collins, 2008).

8 Stokes, *D. W. Griffith's "The Birth of a Nation"*, 97–8.

9 Anthony Slide, ed., *Robert Goldstein and the "Spirit of '76"* (Metuchen, NJ: Scarecrow Press, 1993), xiii.

10 Anthony Slide, *"The Spirit of '76 and The Strange Case of Robert Goldstein," Films in Review*, vol. 27, no. 1 (January 1976), 2.

11 "Costly War Picture Banned; Courts Appeal Too [sic]," *The Motion Picture News*, vol. 15, no. 21 (26 May 1917), reprinted in Slide, *Robert Goldstein*, 203.

12 Slide, *Robert Goldstein*, xvi, 54–5; Michael Selig, "United States v. Motion Picture Film *The Spirit of '76*: The Espionage Case of Producer Robert Goldstein (1917)," *Journal of Popular Film and Television*, vol. 10, no. 4 (Winter 1983), 170.

13 Selig, "United States v. Motion Picture Film *The Spirit of '76*," 170.

14 Selig, "United States v. Motion Picture Film *The Spirit of '76*," 170. For the comments by reviewers, see Genevieve Harris, "*Motography* Commentary," *Motography*, vol. 17, no. 25 (June 23, 1917) and "*Exhibitor's Trade Review* Commentary," *Exhibitor's Trade Review*, vol. 2, no. 1 (June 9, 1917); both reprinted in Slide, *Robert Goldstein*, 204–5.

15 Slide, *Robert Goldstein*, 84; Selig, "United States v. Motion Picture Film *The Spirit of '76*," 170.

16 Slide, *Robert Goldstein*, xvii, 85.

17 G. P. Harleman, "'Spirit of '76' Confiscated by Government," *The Moving Picture World*, December 22, 1917, reprinted in Slide, *Robert Goldstein*, 212; Selig, "United States v. Motion Picture Film *The Spirit of '76*," 170–1.

18 G. P. Harleman, "*Spirit of '76* Film Called Part of Plot: Picture Incites to Mutiny is Allegation–Producer May be Given Penitentiary Sentence," *The Moving Picture World*, December 29, 1917, reprinted in Slide, *Robert Goldstein*, 214–15.

19 Selig, "United States v. Motion Picture Film *The Spirit of '76*," 171; Slide, *Robert Goldstein*, xviii.

20 Slide, *Robert Goldstein*, xviii.

21 Selig, "United States v. Motion Picture Film *The Spirit of '76*," 172; Slide, "*The Spirit of '76* and The Strange Case of Robert Goldstein," 4.

22 Selig, "United States v. Motion Picture Film *The Spirit of '76*," 172.

23 Ibid., 171–2.

24 G. P. Harleman, "Goldstein Is Sentenced to Ten Years: Producer of *The Spirit of '76* Is Sent to the Federal Penitentiary and Fined $5,000," *The Moving Picture World*, May 25, 1918, reprinted in Slide, *Robert Goldstein*, 219; ibid., xxi–xxii.

25 Ibid., 89.

26 Selig, "United States v. Motion Picture Film *The Spirit of '76*," 169.

27 Edward Weitzel, ""The Spirit of '76": Crude Concoction of Fact and Fiction, Written and Directed by Robert Goldstein, Is Released by All-American Company," *The Moving Picture World*, August 6, 1921; "*Photoplay* Commentary," *Photoplay*, vol. 20, no. 5 (October 1921); both here as reprinted in Slide, *Robert Goldstein*, 232–33.

28 George Mitchell, "*America*: 1924's Forgotten Classic," *American Cinematographer*, vol. 71, no. 10 (October 1990), 34.

29 Ibid., 34–5.

30 Richard Schickel, "The Sacrifice," *Film Comment*, vol. 21, no. 4 (July–August 1985), 71.

31 Mitchell, "*America*," 38. One of the soldiers, asked by Griffith where he had learned to die so realistically, brusquely answered: "In the Argonne." Ibid., 39.

32 Ibid., 35.

33 Ibid., 39.

34 Tim Pulleine, "Retrospective-*America*," *Monthly Film Bulletin*, vol. 46, no. 544 (May 1979), 104.

35 For other parallels between Lynch and Butler, see Cotton Seiler's comments on Butler in Seiler, "The American Revolution," in Peter C. Rollins, ed., *The Columbia Companion to American History on Film* (New York: Columbia University Press, 2003), 53.

36 *Photoplay* (May 1924); *Variety*, 28 February 1924; *Harrison's Reports*, March 1, 1924; all quoted in John DeBartolo, "*America*," *The Silent Film Monthly*, vol. 6, no. 4 (April 1998), 3

37 Slide, *Robert Goldstein*, 186.

38 Mitchell, "*America*," 40; Roy E. Aitken (with Al P. Nelson), *The Birth of a Nation Story* (Middelburg, VA: Denlinger, 1965), 24.

39 Mitchell, "*America*," 40; DeBartolo, "*America*," 3.

40 Mark Glancy, "The War of Independence in Feature Films: *The Patriot* (2000) and the 'Special Relationship' Between Hollywood and Britain," *Historical Journal of Film, Radio and Television*, vol. 25, no. 4 (October 2005), 528–9.

41 "*Love and Sacrifice*," *Bioscope*, vol. 61, no. 938 (October 2, 1924), 70–1.

42 Glancy, "The War of Independence in Feature Films," 526.

43 Don H. Poston, "*Janice Meredith*," *Films in Review*, vol. 28, no. 2 (February 1977), 123–4.

44 Ibid., 124.

45 Jim Beckerman, "Tales from the Crypt," *Film Comment*, vol. 27, no. 1 (January–February 1991), 79.

46 Seiler, "The American Revolution," 50.

47 J. Allen Smith, *The Spirit of American Government; A Study of the Constitution: Its Origin, Influence and Relation to Democracy* (New York: Macmillan, 1907); Algie M. Simons, *Social Forces in American History* (New York: Macmillan, 1911); Charles A. Beard, *An Economic Interpretation of the Constitution of the United States* (New York: Macmillan, 1913).

48 "Historical" films of this kind, of course, would look even more old-fashioned as time passed. When the long-lost *Janice Meredith* was revived at a film festival in Minneapolis in 1978, one disenchanted spectator commented that "It wasn't a lost film, it was in hiding." Beckerman, "Tales from the Crypt," 79.

49 Anthony F. C. Wallace, "*Drums Along the Mohawk*," in Carnes, *Past Imperfect*, 96–7.

50 Ibid., 94, 96.

51 John E. O'Connor, "A Reaffirmation of American Ideals: *Drums Along the Mohawk* (1939)," in John E. O'Connor and Martin A. Jackson, eds, *American History/American Film: Interpreting the Hollywood Image* (New York: Continuum, 1988; rev. edn), 98–100, 113, 115.

52 O'Connor, "A Reaffirmation," 110.

53 The film's screenplay was by Sidney Buchman who was both politically active and left-wing. In 1951, he would confess to the House Committee on Un-American Activities (HUAC) that he had been a member of the Communist party (1938–45). Blacklisted by Hollywood, he spent much of his subsequent life in France. www.imdb.com/name/nm0118227/bio, accessed February 27, 2013.

54 See Daniel Boorstin, *The Lost World of Thomas Jefferson* (New York: Henry Holt, 1948) and *The Americans: The Colonial Experience* (New York: Random House, 1958); Clinton Rossiter, *Seedtime of the Republic: The Origins of the American Tradition of Political Liberty* (New York: Harcourt, Brace and Co., 1953).

55 This was not a new theme. *The Spy* (1914) was based on an 1821 novel by James Fenimore Cooper but with an ending inspired by Charles Dickens' *A Tale of Two Cities* (1859). American spy Harvey Birch (Herbert Rawlinson) exchanges places in prison with Henry Wharton (J. W. Pike), a condemned British officer who is the brother of Frances Wharton (Ella Hall), whom Birch loves. Birch goes to the gallows, sacrificing himself to save the life of Frances' brother.

56 "*The Scarlett Coat* with Cornel Wilde, Michael Wilding and Anne Francis," *Harrison's Reports and Film Reviews, 1953–55, vol. 12* (Hollywood: Hollywood Film Archive, 1992), 103; "*The Scarlet Coat*," *Monthly Film Bulletin*, vol. 23, no. 267 (April 1956), 49.

57 Anonymous viewer from Maine, review dated March 22, 2001, found under *Johnny Tremain* on www.amazon.com website, February 6, 2004.

58 Elspeth Hart, "*Johnny Tremain*," *Films in Review*, vol. 8, no. 6 (June–July 1957), 282.

59 "Solemn and conscientious," commented one reviewer, it fell "victim to its own sincerity and laboriousness." "*Johnny Tremain*," *Monthly Film Bulletin*, vol. 24, no. 287 (December 1957), 151.

60 Abner Morison, "*John Paul Jones*," *Film Comment*, vol. 10, no. 6 (June–July 1959), 360: "*John Paul Jones*," *Monthly Film Bulletin*, vol. 26, no. 306 (July 1959), 89.

61 Morison, "*John Paul Jones*," 359.

62 Henry Goodman, "*The Devil's Disciple* and *The Doctor's Dilemma*," *Film Quarterly*, vol. 13, no. 2 (Winter 1959), 57.

63 Robert C. Roman, "*The Devil's Disciple*," *Films in Review*, vol. 10, no. 8 (October 1959), 494–5.

64 Goodman, "*The Devil's Disciple* and *The Doctor's Dilemma*," 57; Brenda Davies, "*The Devil's Disciple*," *Sight and Sound*, vol. 28, nos. 3 and 4 (Summer–Autumn 1959), 172.

65 Transcript of Meetings of the Planning Committee of the American Film Institute's American Revolution Film Project, July 27, 1970, 23, Reuben Library, British Film Institute (henceforth Transcript, Part I).

66 "There something about this mass of material," Taradash commented, "I don't know what it is, it seems to baffle." Ibid., 24.

67 Ibid., 17–18, 28, 84, 89.

68 Ibid., 27.

69 Ibid., 19; Transcript of Meetings of the Planning Committee of the American Film Institute's American Revolution Film Project, July 28, 1970, 10, Reuben Library, British Film Institute (henceforth Transcript, Part II).

70 Transcript, Part I, 29, 50–3; Part II, 11. Other parallels included so-called British efforts to win the "hearts and minds" of the colonists, their attempts at what one discussant termed "Angloization," and the emigration of many loyalists to Canada. Transcript, Part 1, 28, 33, 49.

71 Transcript, Part I, 39–41, 99, 107–8.

72 Transcript, Part I, 79–80, 82, 89.

73 Transcript, Part I, 10.

74 Transcript, Part I, 16, 18, 24, 45, 69, 71–2.

75 Transcript, Part I, 22–3, 26–7, 34–6.

76 Transcript, Part I, 25, 31, 53–4; Part II, p. 55.

77 Transcript, Part I, 18,19, 25, 59–60.

78 Transcript, Part I, 59–60; Part II, 18–19.

79 Transcript, Part II, 57–9.

80 Transcript, Part I, 27.

81 Thomas Fleming, "*1776*," in Carnes, *Past Imperfect*, 91.

82 Fleming, "*1776*," 90; Alexander Stuart, "*1776*," *Films and Filming*, vol. 19, no. 8 (May 1973), 52; Jan Dawson, "*1776*," *Monthly Film Bulletin*, vol. 40, no. 471 (April 1973), 83.

83 "Q & A," *Premiere* (US), no. 42 (December 1992), 42.

84 John Pym, "The Promissory Note: *Revolution*," *Sight and Sound*, vol. 55, no. 2 (Spring 1986), 132; Alain Garsault, "*Révolution*: Bas-de-Cuir et la révolution," *Positif*, no. 302 (April 1986), 66; Derek Elley, "*Revolution*," *Films and Filming*, no. 377 (February 1986), 38.

85 Elley, "*Revolution*," 38.

86 Elley, "*Revolution*," 38; Brent Lewis, "Revolution: The Making of Hugh Hudson's *Revolution*," *Films and Filming*, no. 374 (November 1985), 10; Garsault, "*Révolution*," 67.

87 Elley, "*Revolution*," 38.

88 *City Limits* (January 31–February 6, 1986), cited in Richard Combs, "Landscape After Battle or *Revolution*'s History Lessons," *Monthly Film Bulletin*, vol. 53, no. 626 (March 1986), 68. Combs also mentioned the criticism aimed at Pacino's "slipping and sliding Scots-Bronx accent." Ibid., 69.

89 Michael Brooke, "*Revolution*," booklet to accompany *Revolution-The Director's Cut* (London: BFI, 2012), 1–2; "Revisiting *Revolution* (2008)," a discussion between Hugh Hudson and Al Pacino, on DVD *Revolution-The Director's Cut*. Hudson's comment was in the documentary "Re-cutting *Revolution*: The Deleted Scenes" (2012), on DVD *Revolution-The Director's Cut*.

90 Brooke, "*Revolution*," 4; "Hugh Hudson on *Revolution*," on DVD *Revolution-The Director's Cut*"; "Revisiting *Revolution*."

91 "Re-cutting *Revolution*."

92 See Trevor McCrisken and Andrew Pepper, "Lessons from Hollywood's American Revolution," chap. 1 in McCrisken and Pepper, *American History and Contemporary Hollywood Film* (Edinburgh: Edinburgh University Press, 2005), 24.

93 Seiler, "The American Revolution," 55. See, for example, Gordon Wood, *The Creation of the American Republic, 1776–1787* (Chapel Hill: University of North Carolina Press, 1969); Eric Foner, *Tom Paine and Revolutionary America* (New York: Oxford University Press, 1976); Joan Hoff Wilson, "The Illusion of Change: Women and the American Revolution," in Alfred F. Young, ed., *The American Revolution: Explorations in the History of American Radicalism* (DeKalb: North Illinois University Press, 1976), 383–446; Gary B. Nash, *Urban Crucible: Social Change, Political Consciousness, and the Origins of the American Revolution* (Cambridge, MA: Harvard University Press, 1979); Ira Berlin and Ronald Hoffman, *Slavery and Freedom in the Age of the American Revolution* (Charlottesville: University Press of Virginia, 1983).

94 See Seiler, "The American Revolution," 56.

95 Mark Olsen, "*The Patriot*," *Film Comment*, vol. 36, no. 4 (July–August 2000), 74; "*The Patriot*," *Screen International*, no. 1265 (June 30, 2000), 20.

96 In a review in the *Journal of American History*, William Ross St. George, Jr. noted that Martin's character was "a composite of several partisan leaders, most notably Francis Marion, Thomas Sumter, and Andrew Pickens." St. George, Jr., "*The Patriot*," *Journal of American History*, vol. 87, no. 3 (December 2000), 1147.

97 Bob Fisher, "Images for the Ages," *American Cinematographer*, vol. 82, no. 6 (June 2001), 91; Olsen, "*The Patriot*," 75; Ian Nathan, "Patriot Games," *Empire*, no. 134 (August 2000), 90; "*The Patriot*," *Screen International*, 20.

98 *Premiere* (USA), vol. 13, no. 10 (June 2000), 54; Fisher, "Images for the Ages," 92; Nathan, "Patriot Games," 91–2.

99 Ian Nathan, "*The Patriot*," *Empire*, no. 140 (February 2001), 111; Colin Kennedy, "*The Patriot*," *Empire*, no. 134 (August 2000), 56; Philip Strick, "*The Patriot*," *Sight and Sound*, vol. 10, no. 9 (September 2000), 47.

100 "Gibson has another go at kicking British butt," observed one American critic with an inadequate understanding of the difference between British and English. "Future: *The Patriot*," *Empire*, no. 130 (April 2000), 40. Another reviewer dubbed *The Patriot* "Braveheart-versus-the-Redcoats." "Preview: *The Patriot*," *Interview* (July 2000), 30. Also see John Millar, "Independence Days," *Film Review*, no. 596 (August 2000), 76; James Mottram, "*The Patriot*," *Film Review*, c. Spec., no. 34, Year Book, 2001, 97.

101 "Future: *The Patriot*," 40.

102 Fisher, "Images for the Ages," 90.

103 Nathan, "Patriot Games," 92; "*The Patriot*," *Premiere* (USA), 54; Olsen, "*The Patriot*," 75.

104 Glancy, "The War of Independence," 535.

105 McCrisken and Pepper, "Lessons from Hollywood's American Revolution," 25.

106 St. George, Jr., "*The Patriot*," 1147.

107 Colin Kennedy observes that "racial divisions between militia and slaves are glossed over, smoothed out and generally ignored." Kennedy, "*The Patriot*," 56.

108 "Spike Lee Slams *Patriot*," *The Guardian* [London], July 6, 2000, www. guardian.co.uk/film/2000/jul/06/news.spikelee, accessed February 24, 2013.

109 "In reality," comments one reviewer, the slaves in the Gullah village " . . . were hiding from the Patriots. Thomas Sumter [one of the partisan leaders the character of Benjamin Martin was based upon] often used slaves seized from Tory owners to pay his militiamen." St. George, Jr., "*The Patriot*," 1147.

110 There was a lack of adult female characters generally in *The Patriot*, with Benjamin Martin's first wife dead and his relationship with his sister-in-law (Joely Richardson) largely undeveloped.

111 St. George, Jr., "*The Patriot*," 1148.

112 Ibid., 1147.

113 Estimated budget from www.imdb.com/title/tt0187393/business?ref_=tt_dt_bus, accessed March 2, 2013; McCrisken and Pepper, "Lessons from Hollywood's American Revolution," 37, n. 31.

114 Ibid., 28–9.

Chapter 2

1 *The Slave Hunt, Variety*, June 22, 1907; *The Slave's Vengeance, Variety*, February 1, 1908.

2 Thomas F. Gossett, *Uncle Tom's Cabin and American Culture* (Dallas: Southern Methodist University Press, 1985), 164–5, 183–4, 344, 339, 341.

3 Gossett, *Uncle Tom's Cabin*, 367–68, 370–1.

4 Janet Staiger has argued that this film only appears fragmentary and disconnected to modern viewers. The 14 discrete tableaux, to contemporary spectators familiar with the novel and play, "must have called up a whole causal chain of events, fully motivated in psychologies of characters, and complexly ordered into a story that involved a simultaneity of events as well as sequentiality." Staiger, *Interpreting Films: Studies in the Historical Reception of American Cinema* (Princeton: Princeton University Press, 1992), 105–18, quotation from 118.

5 Charles Musser, *The Emergence of Cinema: The American Screen to 1907* (Berkeley: University of California Press, 1990), 349, 361; Eileen Bowser, *The Transformation of Cinema, 1907–1915* (New York: Charles Scribner's Sons, 1990), 198, 203; Linda Williams, *Playing the Race Card: Melodramas of Black and White from Uncle Tom to O. J. Simpson* (Princeton: Princeton University Press, 2001), 87–95; Bruce Chadwick, *The Reel Civil War: Mythmaking in American Film* (New York: Vintage, 2002), 89–90.

6 Donald Bogle, *Toms, Coons, Mulattoes, Mammies and Bucks: An Interpretive History of Blacks in American Films* (New York: Continuum Press, 2003), 3–9.

7 Bogle, *Toms, Coons, Mulattoes, Mammies and Bucks*, 10–17.

8 There were occasional films showing the brutality of the slave trade. *The Slaver* (Crescent Picture, 1927) had a black African chief trying to buy a white girl from "a dissolute white sea captain." *Slave Ship* (Twentieth-Century Fox, 1937) had Warner Baxter and Wallace Beery as a pair of tough adventurers trafficking slaves from Africa to America. See *Variety*, December 14, 1927 and June 23, 1937.

9 See John D. Smith and John C. Inscoe, eds, *Ulrich Bonnell Phillips: A Southern Historian and His Critics* (Athens: University of Georgia Press, 1993).

10 David W. Blight, *Beyond the Battlefield: Race, Memory, and the American Civil War* (Amherst: University of Massachusetts Press, 2002), 103. Also see Thomas L. Connelly and Barbara L. Bellows, *God and General Longstreet: The Lost Cause and the Southern Mind* (Baton Rouge: Louisiana State University Press, 1982), 1–38.

11 Chadwick, *The Reel Civil War*, 8. Slavery in these stories, writes David W. Blight, was usually associated with "laughter, music, and contentment." Blight, *Beyond the Battlefield*, 103.

12 Jack Temple Kirby, *Media-Made Dixie: The South in the American Imagination* (Baton Rouge: Louisiana State University Press, 1978), 67.

13 Edward D. C. Campbell, Jr., *The Celluloid South: Hollywood and the Southern Myth* (Knoxville: University of Kentucky Press, 1981), 76.

14 Kirby, *Media-Made Dixie*, 70.

15 Campbell, *The Celluloid South*, 188; Helen Taylor, *Scarlett's Women: "Gone With the Wind" and Its Female Fans* (London: Virago, 1989), 2.

16 Wear, "*The Foxes of Harrow*," *Variety*, September 24, 1947.

17 Campbell, *The Celluloid South*, 20, 141, 166–8; Kirby, *Media-Made Dixie*, 115–16. As the reviewer for *Variety* noted, the main subject of the film was miscegenation, in part because of Amantha's mixed-race parentage, in part because of her growing relationship with Bond. See Whit, "*Band of Angels*," *Variety*, July 10, 1957.

18 Bosley Crowther, "*Band of Angels*," *The New York Times*, July 11, 1957, 21:1.

19 Rela, "*Slaves*," *Variety*, May 7, 1969.

20 The independently-produced *Slaves*, according to Jack T. Kirby, "was a poor film which apparently sold well only in predominantly black theaters." Kirby, *Media-Made Dixie*, 123.

21 *Slaves* also to some extent exploited this theme, depicting a master with a slave mistress.

22 On the subject of miscegenation in film generally, see Arlene Hui, "Miscegenation in Mainstream American Cinema: Representing Interracial Relationships, 1913–1956," PhD diss., University of London, 2006.

23 Although the Supreme Court of California had declared the state's miscegenation law unconstitutional in 1948, and seven other states repealed their laws against interracial marriage between 1951 and 1958, there were still 22 American states that forbade interracial marriage when Barack Obama was born of a white mother and black father in 1961. The Obama family was fortunate to be living in Hawaii, which had never enacted such legislation.

24 The film itself pulls its punches. The actual kiss was not photographed directly. Spectators see it taking place, in deep shadow, seen only through the mirror of a white taxi-driver who clearly disapproves.

25 Kirby, *Media-Made Dixie*, 116.

26 Edward Campbell notes the breakdown of the American cinema audience after 1965 into white suburban moviegoers and black inner-city spectators. Blaxploitation films were aimed at the latter. Other examples of the genre set in the era of slavery included *The Quadroon* (1971) and *Passion Plantation* (1978). Campbell, *The Celluloid South*, 174–5.

27 Vincent Canby, "*Mandingo*," *The New York Times*, May 8, 1975, 49:1; Murf, "*Mandingo*," *Variety*, May 7, 1975. On *Mandingo*, also see Catherine Clinton, *The Plantation Mistress: Woman's World in the Old South* (New York: Pantheon, 1982), 223–31.

28 *Mandingo* ranked eighteenth of the 104 most profitable films of 1975. Campbell, *The Celluloid South*, 175, n. 59.

29 Robin Wood, *Sexual Politics and Narrative Film: Hollywood and Beyond* (New York: Columbia University Press, 1998), 267.

30 Murf, "*Drum*," *Variety*, August 4, 1976. *Drum* did less well commercially than its predecessor, coming only seventy-first out of the top 116 films of 1976. Campbell, *The Celluloid South*, 175, n. 59.

31 Vincent Canby, "*Drum*," *The New York Times*, July 31, 1976, 11:1.

32 Allison Graham, *Framing the South: Hollywood, Television, and Race during the Civil Rights Struggle* (Baltimore: Johns Hopkins University Press, 2001), 184.

33 Campbell, *The Celluloid* South, 21.

34 Chadwick, *The Reel Civil War*, 270.

35 Ibid., 267–8.

36 Anne Crémieux, "La représentation de l'esclavage dans *Planet of the Apes* et *The Brother from Another Planet*," in Melvyn Stokes and Gilles Menegaldo, eds, *Cinéma et histoire/Cinema and History* (Paris: Michel Houdiard, 2008), 232–41.

37 Sally Hadden, "*Amistad* (1997): An Internet Review of Merit," *Film and History*, vol. 29, nos. 1–2 (1998), 66.

38 Todd Williams, "Troubled Waters," *Premiere* (January 1998), 56; Julie Roy Jeffrey, "*Amistad*: Steven Spielberg's 'true story,'" *Historical Journal of Film, Radio and Television*, vol. 21, no. 1 (2001), 77.

39 Jeffrey, "*Amistad*," 79.

40 Don Webster, "Slavery in American Cinema," *Ecrans d'Afrique*, no. 23 (first semester 1998), 101.

41 Wyatts, as quoted in Jeffrey, "*Amistad*," 79.

42 Jeffrey, "*Amistad*," 79–80; Thomas Osha Pinnock, "Checking Out Amistad," *Black Filmmaker*, vol. 1, no. 1 (February/March 1998), 10.

43 Jeffrey, "*Amistad*," 80.

44 See Ira Berlin, *Many Thousands Gone: The First Two Centuries of Slavery in North America* (Cambridge: Harvard University Press, 1998); Ira Berlin, *Generations of Captivity: A History of African-American Slaves* (Cambridge: Harvard University Press, 2003).

45 Jeffrey, "*Amistad*," 80.

46 Williams, "Troubled Waters," 56; Jeffrey, "*Amistad*," 80.

47 Jeffrey, "*Amistad*," 77.

48 Ibid., 79.

49 Armond White, "Against the Hollywood Grain," *Film Comment*, vol. 34, no. 2 (March–April 1998), 37; Jeffrey, "*Amistad*," 81.

50 Jeffrey, "*Amistad*," 83; Christopher Hemblade, "Chain Reaction," *Empire*, no. 105 (March 1998), 77–8.

51 Jeffrey, "*Amistad*," 83; Williams, "Troubled Waters," 54.

52 Jeffrey, "*Amistad*," 82. Former slave Frederick Douglass, for example, played an important role in the abolitionist crusade.

53 Rosenstone, *Visions of the Past*, 36, 57, 67–72, 74–5, 125–6.

54 Jeffrey, "*Amistad*," 91, 78.

55 This idea seems to have come straight from Debbie Allen. See Hemblade, "Chain Reaction," 78.

56 Jeffrey, "*Amistad*," 88.

57 Ibid.

58 Horrific as this sequence was, it was based on fact. Either because they were about to run out of provisions or to remove evidence that the ship was carrying slaves before inspection by British warships, it did sometimes happen that large numbers of slaves were simply thrown overboard.

59 Since the film focused so much on Cinque's influence on Baldwin and Adams, there was little opportunity—other than through the fictional character of Theodore Joadson—to represent abolitionists who campaigned for the Africans' release. The white abolitionists shown are either ridiculed or, in the case of Lewis Tappan, presented as cynically callous (Tappan suggests that the captives might be more use to the abolitionist cause dead than alive).

60 Philip Strick, "*Amistad*," *Sight and Sound*, vol. 8, no. 3 (March 1998), 38.

61 *Amistad* cost $40 million to produce but grossed only $44 million at the US box office. *Schindler's List*, by contrast, was produced for $25 million and earned $96 million domestically. Steve Lipkin, "When Victims Speak (Or, What Happened When Spielberg Added *Amistad* To His List)," *Journal of Film and Video*, vol. 52, no. 4 (Winter 2001), 27.

62 Jeffrey, "*Amistad*," 84.

63 Julie Roy Jeffrey makes the point that the manner in which the Africans are represented in the first scenes—especially the violence and the shouting, together with the absence of subtitles to explain what they are saying— makes them appear "savage, violent, murderous, incomprehensible." Jeffrey, "*Amistad*," 87.

64 Christopher Hemblade, "*Amistad*," *Empire*, no. 105 (March 1998), 34.

65 White, "Against the Hollywood Grain," 34.

66 McCrisken and Pepper, *American History and Contemporary Hollywood Film*, 40.

67 Ibid., 45.

68 *Amistad* cost approximately $40,000,000 in production costs. Released on December 10, 1997, its US gross by April 3, 1998 was only $44,175,394. www.imdb.com/title/tt0118607/business?ref_=tt_dt_bus, accessed on February 2, 2013.

69 *Boss Nigger*, also known as *The Black Bounty Hunter*, directed by Jack Arnold, Dimension Pictures, 1975.

70 Gerald Peary, *Quentin Tarantino: Interviews* (Jackson, MI: University Press of Mississippi, 1998), 172–3. The other movie was *Showgirls* (United Artists, 1995).

71 Steven Stowe, "Slaveholders, Large" and Russell R. Menard, "Plantation System," both in Randall M. Miller and John D. Smith, eds, *Dictionary of Afro-American Slavery* (Westport, CT: Praeger, 1997; updated edn), 668, 579.

72 Menard, "Plantation System," 580; Laurence Glasco, "Miscegenation," in Randall M. Miller and John D. Smith, eds, *Dictionary of Afro-American Slavery* (Westport, CT: Praeger, 1997; updated edn), 477.

73 Menard, "Plantation System," 580.

74 www.vibe.com/article/spike-lee-slams-django-unchained-im-not-gonna-see-it, accessed February 5, 2013.

75 Cosmo Landesman, "Here to blow you away," *The Sunday Times* [London], Culture section, January 20, 2013, 15.

76 What the fictional Candie defines as passivity, Marxist scholar Eugene D. Genovese saw as the product of acceptance by slaves of the "paternalist" vision of planters. This explained, he believed, why there were comparatively few slave revolts in the United States, compared to other slave societies. At the heart of Genovese's argument was the argument that slave-owners maintained their power and position by cultural means instead of physical coercion. Slaves accepted the idea of the plantation as a kind of family but, in return, had forced paternalist masters to accept that they also enjoyed a number of rights and privileges. See Genovese, *Roll, Jordon, Roll: The World The Slaves Made* (New York: Vintage Books, 1976).

Chapter 3

1 Merrill D. Peterson, *Lincoln in American Memory* (New York: Oxford University Press, 1994).

2 Barry Schwartz, *Abraham Lincoln and the Forge of National Memory* (Chicago and London: University of Chicago Press, 2000); Barry Schwartz, *Abraham Lincoln in the Post-Heroic Age* (Chicago and London: Chicago University Press, 2008).

3 Peterson devotes one paragraph to the depiction of Lincoln in D. W. Griffith's *The Birth of a Nation* (1915). He wrongly describes (344) the biopic of Lincoln made by the Rockett brothers and directed by Phil Rosen in 1924 "as the first attempt to film an American life." He briefly recounts aspects of the treatment of Lincoln in five other films. Peterson, *Lincoln in American Memory*, 169–70, 344–6. In Schwartz's first volume, the only film dealing with Lincoln to be discussed is *The Birth of a Nation*. The second volume refers briefly to the references to Lincoln in Frank Capra's *Mr. Smith Goes to Washington* (1939) and to the "biographical" films by Phil Rosen (*The Dramatic Life of Abraham Lincoln*, 1924); D. W. Griffith (*Abraham Lincoln*, 1930); John Ford (*Young Mr. Lincoln*, 1939), and John Cromwell (*Abe Lincoln in Illinois*, 1940). This comparative neglect of movies is surprising,

since Schwartz himself comments that "millions of people bought tickets for *Young Mr. Lincoln*." Schwartz, *Abraham Lincoln and the Forge of National Memory*, 220–1; Schwartz, *Abraham Lincoln and the Post-Heroic Age*, 156–7, 270–2, quotation from 271. Neither Peterson nor Schwartz analyze the filmic representations of Lincoln in any detail.

4 Frank Thompson, *Abraham Lincoln: Twentieth-Century Popular Portraits* (Dallas, TX: Taylor Publishing, 1999), 190–240. Mark S. Reinhart's annotated guide to Lincoln films over much the same period is less thorough than Thompson's and the comments on individual films address a limited range of issues, including how well the role of Lincoln is played and whether the film is "correct" in its representation of history. Mark S. Reinhart, *Abraham Lincoln on Screen: A Filmography of Dramas and Documentaries Including Television, 1903–1998* (Jefferson, NC: McFarland and Co., 1999). Both Thompson and Reinhart cover television films and documentaries as well as motion pictures. The present chapter concentrates only on movies for practical reasons (the subject is already a large one; the modes of production and conditions of reception of television programs are different from those of movies) and personal ones (the writer is a cinema historian).

5 Robert C. Roman, "Lincoln on the Screen," *Films in Review*, vol. 12, no. 2 (February 1961), 87–101; Martin A. Jackson, "Abraham Lincoln," in Peter C. Rollins, ed., *The Columbia Companion to American History on Film: How the Movies Have Portrayed the American Past* (New York: Columbia University Press, 2004), 175–9.

6 David Turley, "A Usable Life: Popular Representations of Abraham Lincoln," in David Ellis, ed., *Imitating Art: Essays in Biography* (London and Boulder, CO: Pluto Press, 1993), 53–80; Mark E. Neely, Jr., "The Young Lincoln," in Carnes, *Past Imperfect*, 124–7; Tony Pipolo, "Hero or Demagogue?: Images of Abraham Lincoln in American Film," *Cineaste*, vol. 35, no. 1 (Winter 2009), 14–21.

7 Bryan Rommel-Ruiz, "Redeeming Lincoln, Redeeming the South: Representations of Abraham Lincoln in D. W. Griffith's *The Birth of a Nation* (1915) and Historical Scholarship," in Peter C. Rollins and John E. O'Connor, eds, *Hollywood's White House: The American Presidency in Film and History* (Lexington, KY: University Press of Kentucky, 2003), 76–95; Andrew Piasecki, "Abraham Lincoln in John Ford's *The Iron Horse*: Both Trumpets and Silences," in Peter C. Rollins and John E. O'Connor, eds, *Hollywood's White House: The American Presidency in Film and History* (Lexington, KY: University Press of Kentucky, 2003), 62–75.

8 Eric F. Goldman, *The Tragedy of Lyndon Johnson* (London: Macdonald, 1969), 13.

9 Schwartz, *Abraham Lincoln and the Forge of National Memory*, 70; David H. Donald, *Lincoln Reconsidered* (New York: Vintage, 1989), 149.

10 John Nicolay and John Hay, *Abraham Lincoln: A History*, 10 vols (New York: The Century Company, 1890); Peterson, *Lincoln in American Memory*, 119, 126.

11 For a list of these films, see Thompson, *Abraham Lincoln*, 190–5.

12 Harold S. Wilson, *"McClure's Magazine" and the Muckrakers* (Princeton: Princeton University Press, 1970), 74.

13 William H. Herndon and Jesse W. Weik, *Herndon's Lincoln: The True Story of a Great Life*, 3 vols. (Springfield, IL: Herndon's Lincoln Publishing Co., 1889); also see Schwartz, *Abraham Lincoln and the Forge of National Memory*, 157–8.

14 Ida M. Tarbell, *The Life of Abraham Lincoln*, 2 vols. (New York: Doubleday and McClure, 1895); Mary E. Tomkins, *Ida M. Tarbell* (New York: Twayne, 1974), 43–51; Schwartz, *Abraham Lincoln and the Forge of National Memory*, 159–60.

15 See Russell Merritt, "Rescued from a Perilous Nest: D. W. Griffith's Escape from Theatre into Film," *Cinema Journal*, vol. 21, no. 1 (Fall 1981), 21; Richard Schickel, *D. W. Griffith and the Birth of Film* (London: Pavilion, 1984), 51.

16 Mark, "*Abraham Lincoln's Clemency*," *Variety*, November 12, 1910, 16.

17 Reinhart, *Abraham Lincoln on Screen*, 54–5.

18 William E. Gienapp, *Abraham Lincoln and Civil War America: A Biography* (New York: Oxford University Press, 2002), 185; David H. Donald, *Lincoln* (New York: Simon and Schuster, 1995), 567.

19 "*Lieutenant Grey of the Confederacy*," *The Moving Picture World*, vol. 10, no. 8 (November 25, 1911), 637.

20 Jack Spears, *The Civil War on the Screen and Other Essays* (South Brunswick, NJ: A. S. Barnes, 1977), 67; Thompson, *Abraham Lincoln*, 16.

21 "Ford's," *Star* [Baltimore], April 11, 1916, D. W. Griffith Papers, Library of Congress; "American Theater Notes," *Christian Science Monitor* [Boston], August 18, 1915, Griffith Papers; "'Birth of a Nation' at Grand Another Week," *Kansas City Post*, November 19, 1915, Griffith Papers; "Picture in Fourth Week," *Times-Picayune* [New Orleans], April 2, 1916, Griffith Papers; Carl E. Milliken to Will W. Alexander, August 9, 1930, National Association for the Advancement of Colored People Papers, Library of Congress.

22 Schickel, *D. W. Griffith*, 551.

23 The "conquered provinces" phrase was associated with Thaddeus Stevens, the Radical congressional leader from Pennsylvania on whom Stoneman's fictional character was based.

24 Eric Foner, *Forever Free: The Story of Emancipation and Reconstruction* (New York: Alfred A. Knopf, 2005), 79; Eric Foner, *The Fiery Trial: Abraham Lincoln and American Slavery* (New York: W. W. Norton, 2010), 331, 333.

25 Claude G. Bowers in *The Tragic Era* (1929)—a book that like Griffith's film saw Radical Reconstruction as a disaster—quoted a Georgian as saying something very similar: "Then God help us! If [Lincoln's death] is true, it is the worst blow that has yet been struck the South." Rommel-Ruiz, "Redeeming Lincoln," 86.

26 See Michael Rogin, "'The Sword Became a Flashing Vision': D. W. Griffith's *The Birth of a Nation*," in Robert Lang, ed., *The Birth of a Nation: D. W. Griffith, Director* (New Brunswick, NJ: Rutgers University Press, 1994), 281.

27 Blight, *Race and Reunion*, 87, 201–5, 216.

28 Joseph Smith, *The Spanish-American War: Conflict in the Caribbean and the Pacific 1895–1902* (London: Longman, 1994), 102; Frank Freidel, *The Splendid Little War* (Boston: Little, Brown, 1958), 33.

29 Schwartz, *Abraham Lincoln and the Forge of National Memory*, 221–2.

30 The first Africans to arrive in the British colonies in America seemingly were the 20 who landed at Jamestown, Virginia, from a Dutch frigate in 1619—12 years after the founding of Jamestown itself and a year before the Pilgrim Fathers sailed on the *Mayflower*. The idea of the existence of a white "Eden" before the arrival of Africans is unsustainable. See John Hope Franklin and Alfred A. Moss, Jr., *From Slavery to Freedom: A History of African Americans* (New York: Alfred A. Knopf 1994; 7th edn), 56.

31 See Stokes, *D. W. Griffith's "The Birth of a Nation"*, chap. 5.

32 Maldwyn A. Jones, *The Limits of Liberty: American History, 1607–1980* (New York: Oxford University Press, 1983), 412.

33 Kitty Kelly, "Flickerings from Filmland—Why Don't Chicago Managers Do This," *Chicago Tribune*, March 24, 1915; "Birth of a Nation Justifies Praise," *Kansas City Journal*, October 25, 1915; "Hosts of People Seeing 'The Birth of a Nation,'" *Marrett Weekly*, January 27, 1916; G. B. D., "The Birth of a Nation," *Battle Creek Morning Journal* [Michigan], February 4, 1916; all in Griffith Papers.

34 Schwartz, *Lincoln and the Forge of National Memory*, 2; Eric Foner, *Reconstruction: America's Unfinished Revolution, 1863–1877* (New York: Perennial Classics, 2002), 6. For a revisionist view of Lincoln's ideas on colonization, see Michael Vorenberg, "Abraham Lincoln and the Politics of Black Colonization," *Journal of the Abraham Lincoln Association*, vol. 14, no. 2 (1993), 23–46.

35 While this sequence was later removed, a number of film critics attested to its existence. See W. Stephen Bush in *the Moving Picture World*, 23 (March 13, 1915) and Francis Hackett in *The New Republic*, 7 (March 20, 1915), both reprinted in Lang, *The Birth of a Nation*, 178, 162.

36 Schwartz, *Abraham Lincoln and the Forge of National Memory*, 264.

37 Ibid., 286.

38 The first biopic featuring Lincoln had been released by Essanay in 1908. Although only a one-reeler, a reviewer praised it as covering "nearly every period" of Lincoln's life. Frank Wiesberg, "*Life of Abraham Lincoln*," *Variety*, October 17, 1908, 11. In 1915, Edison produced *The Life of Abraham Lincoln*, a two-reel picture.

39 "The Screen—Lincoln's Life," *The New York Times*, January 22, 1924, 17; Fred, "*Abraham Lincoln*," *Variety*, January 24, 1924, 26; Foner, *The Fiery Trial*, 297.

40 "The Screen—Lincoln's Life"; Fred, "*Abraham Lincoln*"; Marion, as quoted in Kevin Brownlow, "First Film on Lincoln," *Cineaste*, vol. 35, no. 2 (Spring 2010), 10.

41 Reviewers commented that it had "all the elements that make for a box-office success" and drew attention to the innovative methods used in publicizing it.

Fred, "*The Iron Horse*," *Variety*, September 3, 1924, 23; "*The Iron Horse*," *Harrison's Reports and Film Reviews, Vol. 2* (Hollywood, CA: Hollywood Film Archive, 1992), September 6, 1924, 143.

42 Piasecki, "Abraham Lincoln," 64.

43 Ibid., 65.

44 Ibid., 67–71.

45 Janey Place, "A Family in a Ford," *Film Comment*, vol. 12, no. 5 (September–October 1976), 46.

46 John F. Stover, *American Railroads* (Chicago: University of Chicago Press, 1961), 69, 74–6, 105–6.

47 Piasecki, "Abraham Lincoln," 73.

48 "The Screen—*The Iron Horse*," *New York Times*, August 29, 1924, 6.

49 Carl Sandburg, *Abraham Lincoln: The Prairie Years*, 2 vols (New York: Harcourt, Brace, 1926).

50 Turley, "A Usable Life," 59–60.

51 Arthur Lennig, "'There is a tragedy going on here which I will tell you later': D. W. Griffith and *Abraham Lincoln*," *Film History*, vol. 22, no. 1 (2010), 45.

52 Arthur Lennig comments that the dullness of the "debates" was worsened by "the series of slow dissolves linking them." Lennig, "There is a tragedy," 63.

53 Singing blacks, of course, emerged as one of the earliest tropes of sound-era cinema. King Vidor had directed an all-black musical, *Hallelujah!*, for MGM in 1929.

54 "*Abraham Lincoln*," *Variety*, August 27, 1930, 21; Mordaunt Hall, "The Screen—Mr. Griffith's First Talker," *The New York Times*, August 26, 1930, 24; "*Abraham Lincoln*," *Harrison's Reports and Film Reviews*, Vol. 4 (Hollywood, CA: Hollywood Film Archive, 1992), September 6, 1930, 142; Schickel, *D. W. Griffith*, 557.

55 Griffith quoted by Edmund Rucker, cited in Lennig, "There is a tragedy," 67.

56 Schickel, *D. W. Griffith*, 554–6. Arthur Lennig offers an alternative explanation for the inferiority of the assassination sequence: all the shots had to be completed on the final day of production. Lennig, "There is a tragedy," 56.

57 Vlada Petric, "Two Lincoln Assassinations by D. W. Griffith," *Quarterly Review of Film Studies*, vol. 3, no. 3 (Summer 1978), 347.

58 Schickel, *D. W. Griffith*, 558–9.

59 Andre Sennwald, "The Screen—Charles Laughton as a Famed Gentleman's Gentleman in 'Ruggles of Red Gap,' at the Paramount," *New York Times*, March 7, 1935, 26 (quotation); Kauf, "Ruggles of Red Gap," *Variety*, March 13, 1935, 15; "'Ruggles of Red Gap' with Charles Laughton, Charles Ruggles and Mary Boland," *Harrison's Reports and Film Reviews*, Vol. 6 (Hollywood, CA: Hollywood Film Archive, 1992), February 16, 1935, 27.

60 "*Mr. Smith Goes to Washington*," *Motion Picture Herald*, October 7, 1939, 35.

61 Andre Sennwald, "*The Littlest Rebel*," *The New York Times*, December 20, 1935, 30.

62 "'Of Human Hearts' with James Stewart, Walter Huston and Beulah Bondi," *Harrison's Reports and Film Reviews*, Vol. 7 (Hollywood, CA: Hollywood Film Archive, 1992), February 26, 1938, 35.

63 So far as American filmmakers were concerned, the last volumes in Sandburg's biography (*The War Years*, 4 vols, 1939) had considerably less influence.

64 Turley, "A Usable Life," 61.

65 Donald, *Lincoln*, 150–1; Neely, "The Young Lincoln," 124; Edward Eggleston, *The Graysons: A Story of Illinois* (New York: Harcourt Brace, 1970; originally published in 1887).

66 Neely, "The Young Lincoln," 124.

67 So deftly did Alice Brady play the role of Abigail Clay that the *Variety* critic observed that "it's almost her picture." *Variety*, June 7, 1939, 12.

68 Richard Abel, "Paradigmatic Structures in *Young Mr. Lincoln*," *Wide Angle*, vol. 2, no. 4 (1978), 25.

69 The mob sequence in the film was consistent with Lincoln's own views. In 1838, worried by violent attacks on abolitionists, he had delivered a speech criticizing mob violence to the Young Men's Lyceum in Springfield. Pipolo, "Hero or Demagogue?", 21.

70 Virginia Wright Wexman, "'Right and Wrong; That's [Not] All There Is To It!': *Young Mr. Lincoln* and American Law," *Cinema Journal*, vol. 44, no. 3 (Spring 2005), 27.

71 Eric Foner, *Free Soil, Free Labor, Free Men: The Ideology of the Republican Party before the Civil War* (New York: Oxford University Press, 1995).

72 Frank S. Nugent, "*Young Mr. Lincoln*," *New York Times*, June 3, 1939, 11; "*Young Mr. Lincoln* with Henry Fonda," *Harrison's Reports and Film Reviews*, Vol. 7, June 17, 1939, 94; Abel, "*Young Mr. Lincoln*," *Variety*, June 7, 1939, 12.

73 Abel, "*Young Mr. Lincoln*,".

74 Edelstein Amusement Co., Homer Theater, Hibbing, Minnesota, "What the Picture Did for Me," *Motion Picture Herald*, March 9, 1940, 71; Jim Haney, Milan Theater, Milan, Indiana, "What the Picture Did for Me," *Motion Picture Herald*, October 7, 1939, 57; C. H. Collier, Globe Theater, Drew, Mississippi, "What the Picture Did for Me," *Motion Picture Herald*, October 28, 1939, 66; J. E. Stocker, Myrtle Theater, Detroit, Michigan, "What the Picture Did for Me," *Motion Picture Herald*, January 13, 1940, 46.

75 "*Abe Lincoln in Illinois*—Showmen's Reviews," *Motion Picture Herald*, January 23, 1950, 50; Flin, "*Abe Lincoln in Illinois*," *Variety*, January 24, 1940, 14; Frank S. Nugent, "*Abe Lincoln in Illinois*," *New York Times*, February 23, 1940, 19; "*Abe Lincoln in Illinois* with Raymond Massey, Ruth Gordon and Gene Lockhart," *Harrison Reports and Film Reviews*, Vol. 7, January 20, 1940, 11.

76 Herndon, as quoted in Benjamin P. Thomas, "*Lincoln's Humor*" and Other *Essays*, ed. Michael Burlingame (Urbana: University of Illinois Press, 2002), xlii, n. 34.

77 Nugent, "*Abe Lincoln in Illinois*".

78 Raymond Massey, *A Hundred Different Lives: An Autobiography* (London: Robson, 1979), 253–4.

79 The one exception to this is in Lincoln's critique of the Dred Scott decision by the Supreme Court in his filmic campaign "debate" with Stephen A. Douglas. He attacks the fact that the Dred Scott decision defines blacks *only* as property.

80 Turley, "A Usable Life," 63–4; Nugent, *"Abe Lincoln in Illinois,"*; "*Abe Lincoln in Illinois," Harrison's Reports.*

81 *"Abe Lincoln in Illinois," Variety.*

82 *"Abe Lincoln in Illinois*—Showmen's Reviews," *Motion Picture Herald.*

83 In April 1939, Sherwood had launched a legal challenge against Twentieth-Century Fox alleging that *Young Mr. Lincoln* had plagiarized his own play and was an attempt "to reap undeserved financial gain" from its success. Reinhart, *Abraham Lincoln on Screen*, 25.

84 C. W. Mills, Arcade Theater, Sodus, New York, "What the Picture Did for Me," *Motion Picture Herald*, September 7, 1940, 51; Joe Schindele, Granite Theater, Granite Falls, Minnesota, "What the Picture Did for Me," *Motion Picture Herald*, August 3, 1940, 52; M. R. Harrington, Avalon Theater, Clatskanie, Oregon, "What the Picture Did for Me," *Motion Picture Herald*, June 22, 1940, 68; Alex Slendak, St. Clair Theater, St. Clair, Michigan, "What the Picture Did for Me," *Motion Picture Herald*, May 25, 1940, 58.

85 Peterson, *Lincoln in American Memory*, 312.

86 Thompson lists *Rock Island Trail* and *Transcontinent Express* as different 1950 pictures. The film was the same, but it was retitled as *Transcontinent Express.*

87 See, for example, *Lincoln in Illinois* (State of Illinois, 1950); *Abraham Lincoln* (Emerson Film Corporation/Encyclopaedia Brittanica, 1951); *The Face of Lincoln* (University of Southern California/Cavalcade Pictures, 1955).

88 *Lincoln Speaks at Gettysburg* (A.F. Films, 1950); *Lincoln's Gettysburg Address* (Sterling Films, 1951); *Lincoln at Gettysburg* (Pathé News, 1960); *Lincoln's Gettysburg Address* (Charlton Heston, 1973). *Nor Long Remember* (Jam Handy Organization, 1940) combined a scene of Lincoln (Sam Slade) delivering the Gettysburg Address with a group of people the next day discussing the impact of the speech.

89 Lincoln provided much of the inspiration for the King in *Anna and the King of Siam* (Twentieth-Century Fox, 1946); compare *The King and I* (Twentieth-Century Fox, 1956), the animated film with the same title (Morgan Creek Productions, 1999), and *Anna and the King* (Fox 2000 Productions, 1999).

90 See, for example, *The Battle of Gettysburg* (MGM, 1955). This category could also include *Bébé's Kids* (Hyperion Pictures, 1992), an animated film in which Pete Renaday played the voice of Abraham Lincoln.

91 Peter Coates, *In Nature's Defence: Conservation and Americans*, British Association for American Studies Pamphlets in American History, no. 26 (1993), 26.

92 Richard Corliss, "*The Conspirator*: Abraham Lincoln's 9/11," *Time Magazine*, September 17, 2010, www.time.com/time/arts/article/0,8599,2019832,00.html, accessed March 8, 2011.

93   In these three films, Lincoln was respectively played by Richard Craycroft, Richard Blake, and Charles L. Brame.

94   Eric Foner, *Our Lincoln: New Perspectives on Lincoln and His World* (New York: W. W. Norton, 2008), 270.

95   Schwartz, *Abraham Lincoln and the Forge of National Memory*, 2.

96   John Harlow, "Spielberg shows darker side of saintly Lincoln," *The Sunday Times* [London], March 18, 2001.

97   Doris Kearns Goodwin, *Team of Rivals: The Political Genius of Abraham Lincoln* (New York: Simon and Schuster, 2005).

98   Stax, "Logan Scripting Spielberg's Lincoln," December 7, 2001 (http://uk.ign.com/articles/2001/12/07/logan-scripting-spielbergs-lincoln); Stax, "Lincoln Update," January 23, 2003 (http://uk.ign.com/articles/2003/01/23/lincoln-update); Michael Fleming, "Lincoln Logs in at DreamWorks," January 11, 2005 (www.variety.com/article/VR1117916168/?refCatId=1238); Rodrigo Perez, "Spielberg Chased Daniel Day-Lewis for 9 Years, Wanted Him Before Liam Neeson to Play 'Lincoln' & More About the Film," IndieWire, November 7, 2012 (http://blogs.indiewire.com/theplaylist/spielberg-chased-after-daniel-day-lewis-for-9-years-went-after-him-before-liam-neeson-7-things-learned-about-lincoln-20121107); all accessed January 8, 2013.

99   Eric Foner, "Lincoln's Use of Politics for Noble Ends," *New York Times*, November 26, 2012.

100 Kate Masur, "In Spielberg's 'Lincoln,' Passive Black Characters," *New York Times*, November 12, 2012.

101 This may have been what Foner was referring to in his letter. On Sherman's Field Order, see Foner, *Reconstruction*; Michael Fellman, *Citizen Sherman: A Life of William Tecumseh Sherman* (New York: Random House, 1995); Joseph T. Glatthaar, *The March to the Sea and Beyond: Sherman's Troops in the Savannah and Carolinas Campaigns* (New York: New York University Press, 1985).

102 Donald R. Shaffer, "Race and Spielberg's Lincoln," November 25, 2012, http://cwemancipation.wordpress.com/2012/11/25/race-and-spielbergs-lincoln/, accessed February 8, 2013.

103 Harold Holzer, "Reel Lincoln: The Case for the Spielberg Film," *The Chronicle of Higher Education*, November 30, 2012, http://chronicle.com/blogs/conversation/2012/11/30/reel-lincoln-the-case-for-the-spielberg-film/, accessed February 13, 2013.

104 Foner argues that "the film grossly exaggerates the possibility that . . . the war might have ended with slavery still intact." Apart from the consequences of the Emancipation Proclamation, "Louisiana, Maryland, Missouri, Tennessee and West Virginia, exempted in whole or part from the proclamation, had decreed abolition on their own." Foner, "Lincoln's Use of Politics for Noble Ends."

105 Goodwin, *Team of Rivals*, 728. Goodwin points out that Lincoln's assassin, John Wilkes Booth, was in the audience for this speech. Its suggestion of black suffrage appears to have been the final straw persuading him to act.

106 Phillip W. Magness and Sebastian N. Page, *Colonization After Emancipation: Lincoln and the Movement for Black Resettlement* (Columbia, MO: University of Missouri Press, 2011).

107 Goodwin, *Time of Rivals*, 694–6. Secretary of State William H. Seward, who might have supported it, could not attend the cabinet meeting.

Chapter 4

1 Lillian Ross, *Picture* (London: Faber and Faber, 1998; first published in 1952), 172.

2 Ibid., 11, 58, 145–6, 158, 203, quotations from 11 and 203.

3 Ibid., 99, 193–4, 196, 251–64, 278, 299–303, 305–8, 310–11, 314–17, 333–8, 354, 356, 362–3, 375.

4 Brog, "*The Red Badge of Courage*," *Variety*, August 15, 1951; Bosley Crowther, "*The Red Badge of Courage*," *The New York Times*, October 19, 1951, 22:2.

5 Ross, *Picture*, 367.

6 Eileen Bowser, *The Transformation of Cinema, 1907–1915* (New York: Charles Scribner's Sons, 1990), 177.

7 Jack Spears, *The Civil War on the Screen and Other Essays* (New York: A. S. Barnes, 1977), 11, 12, 21–2, 24–6, 29–30; Thalberg quoted in Leslie Halliwell, *Halliwell's Screen Greats* (London: Grafton, 1988), 155. Selznick was well aware that *So Red the Rose*, made in 1935 starring Margaret Sullavan, had been commercially unsuccessful. David Thomson, *Showman: The Life of David O. Selznick* (London: André Deutsch, 1993), 212.

8 Cullen, *The Civil War in Popular Culture*, 2.

9 Guy Gugliotta, "New Estimate Raises Civil War Death Toll," *New York Times*, April 3, 2012, D1.

10 C. Vann Woodward, "The Inner Civil War," *New York Review of Books* 151:7 (April 7, 1994), 36. Compare Daniel Aaron, *The Unwritten War: American Writers and the Civil War* (Madison: University of Wisconson Press, 1987), esp. xix–xxii. The one exception to Woodward's general thesis was Stephen Crane's *The Red Badge of Courage*, published in 1895, which became a best seller. Modern fiction on Civil War themes has included Michael Shaara's Pulitzer Prize-winning *Killer Angels* (New York: McKay, 1974), whose graphic account of the battle of Gettysburg seems to have been the original inspiration for Ken Burns' documentary television series on the war, and Charles Frazier's *Cold Mountain* (New York: Atlantic Monthly Press, 1997).

11 Arthur Mayer, *Merely Colossal* (New York: Simon and Schuster, 1953), 178; Charles Eckert, "The Carole Lombard in Macy's Window," *Quarterly Review of Film Studies*, vol. 3, no. 1 (1978), 1–21.

12 Kathryn H. Fuller, *At the Picture Show: Small-town Audiences and the Creation of Movie Fan Culture* (Washington, DC: Smithsonian Institution Press, 1996), esp. chap. 8.

13 Alice Miller Mitchell, *Children and Movies* (Chicago: University of Chicago Press, 1929), 104–7; Richard Koszarski, *An Evening's Entertainment: The Age of the Silent Feature Picture, 1915–1928* (Berkeley: University of California Press, 1990), 28–9. The advent of audience research, beginning in 1937, confirmed the female lack of enthusiasm for war pictures. See, for example, Leo Handel, *Hollywood Looks at Its Audience* (Urbana: University of Illinois Press, 1950), 121–4.

14 For a discussion of what women like about *Gone With the Wind* and the meanings they continued to create from it, see Helen Taylor, *Scarlett's Women: "Gone With the Wind" and Its Female Fans* (London: Virago, 1989).

15 Thomas R. Cripps, "The Myth of the Southern Box Office: A Factor in Racial Stereotyping in American Movies, 1920–1940," in J. C. Curtis and Lewis Gould, eds, *The Black Experience in America: Selected Essays* (Austin: University of Texas Press, 1970), 121; "*Man from Dakota,*" *Variety*, February 21, 1940.

16 Cripps, "The Myth of the Southern Box Office," 121.

17 Abel, "*So Red the Rose,*" *Variety*, December 4, 1935; Land, "*The Littlest Rebel,*" *Variety*, December 25, 1935.

18 Thomas R. Cripps, "The Absent Presence in American Civil War Films," *Historical Journal of Film, Radio and Television*, vol. 14, no. 4 (1994): 367–9.

19 Kim Newman, *Wild West Movies: How the West Was Found, Won, Lost, Lied about, Filmed and Forgotten* (London: Bloomsbury, 1990), 28. Cripps himself remarks that "the first reel of many westerns seemed to be about the Civil War until the action moved westward." "The Absent Presence in American Civil War Films," 371–2.

20 For estimates of profits, see Richard Schickel, *D. W. Griffith and the Birth of Film* (London: Pavilion, 1984), 280–1, 324; and Roland Flamini, *Scarlett, Rhett, and a Cast of Thousands: The Filming of "Gone With the Wind"* (London: André Deutsch, 1976), 332–3, 336–7. On the music written by Joseph Carl Breil to be performed with *The Birth of a Nation* and Max Steiner's score for *Gone With the Wind*, see Schickel, *D. W. Griffith*, 243–4, 247; and Flamini, *Scarlett, Rhett, and a Cast of Thousands*, 300–1.

21 P. McDonald, "*Birth of a Nation* Award 'Is Racist,'" *Evening Standard* [London], December 9, 1992.

22 Bogle, *Toms, Coons, Mulattoes, Mammies, and Bucks*, 12.

23 Francis Hackett, "*The Birth of a Nation,*" in Stanley Kauffman with Bruce Henstell, eds, *American Film Criticism: From the Beginnings to "Citizen Kane"* (New York: Liveright, 1972), 89.

24 David M. Chalmers, *Hooded Americanism: The History of the Ku Klux Klan* (New York: Franklin Watts, 1981), 23–5; Scott Simmon, *The Films of D. W. Griffith* (Cambridge: Cambridge University Press, 1993), 125–6.

25 J. Morgan Kousser, *The Shaping of Southern Politics: Suffrage Restriction and the Establishment of the One-Party South, 1880–1910* (New Haven: Yale University Press, 1974); Joel Williamson, *The Crucible of Race: Black-White Relations in the American South since Emancipation* (New York: Oxford University Press, 1984), 117–18, 253; George C. Wright, *Racial Violence in Kentucky, 1865–1940: Lynchings, Mob Rule, and "Legal Lynchings"* (Baton Rouge: Louisiana State University Press, 1990), 108; Pierre Sorlin, *The Film in History: Restaging the Past* (Totowa, NJ: Barnes and Noble, 1980), 108.

26 Scott Simmon, for example, cites Walter Lippmann's later recollection of this period as "a happy time" when it was still possible to believe in "the inevitability of progress" and "the perfectability of man." *Films of D. W. Griffith*, 24.

27 Edward L. Ayers, *The Promise of the New South: Life after Reconstruction* (New York: Oxford University Press, 1992), 155; Ray Stannard Baker, *Following the Color Line: An Account of Negro Citizenship in the American Democracy* (New York: Doubleday, Page, 1908), 30–1; C. Vann Woodward, *Origins of the New South, 1877–1913* (Baton Rouge: Louisiana State University Press, 1951), 354–5; Williamson, *Crucible of Race*, 253–5.

28 Jack S. Blocker, *Retreat from Reform: The Prohibition Movement in the United States 1890–1913* (Westport, CT: Greenwood, 1976), 214, 216, 239; McKelway quoted in Hugh C. Bailey, *Liberalism in the New South: Southern Social Reform and the Progressive Movement* (Coral Gables, FL: University of Miami Press, 1969), 65.

29 Schickel, *D. W. Griffith*, 300. On the NAACP's background and its campaign against the film, see Stokes, *D. W. Griffith's "The Birth of a Nation,"* 1, 129–70.

30 Sara Evans, *Born for Liberty: A History of Women in America* (New York: Free Press, 1989), 167–8. On the image of the flapper, see Molly Haskell, *From Reverence to Rape: The Treatment of Women in the Movies* (Chicago: University of Chicago Press, 1987), 44, 74–82.

31 Evans, *Born for Liberty*, 204–16, 198; Susan Ware, *Holding the Line: American Women in the 1930s* (Boston: Twayne, 1982), 414–9, 90–4, 97–103, 111.

32 Marjorie Rosen, *Popcorn Venus: Women, Movies, and the American Dream* (London: Peter Owen, 1975), 169; Lester V. Chandler, *America's Greatest Depression, 1929–1941* (New York: Harper and Row, 1970), 5–6; Ray Wax quoted in Studs Terkel, *Hard Times: An Oral History of the Great Depression* (London: Allen Lane, 1970), 456.

33 *Harrison's Reports*, July 16, 1927. There had been two earlier screen versions of the play in 1915 and 1921.

34 A. D. S., "*Secret Service*," *New York Times*, December 14, 1931, 16:3.

35 Char, "*Secret Service*," *Variety*, December 15, 1931.

36 Bosley Crowther, "*Raintree County*," *New York Times*, December 21, 1957, 22:1.

37 Verr, "*The Beguiled*," *Variety*, March 10, 1971.

38 "*The Great Locomotive Chase* with Fess Parker and Jeffrey Hunter," *Harrison's Reports*, May 26, 1956.

39 Bosley Crowther, "*The Horse Soldiers*," *New York Times*, June 27, 1959, 13:1.

40 Mordaunt Hall, "A Civil War Farce," *New York Times*, February 8, 1927, 21:1; Fred, "*The General*," *Variety*, February 9, 1927; Howard Thompson, "*Mail Order Bride/Advance to the Rear*," *New York Times*, June 11, 1964, 27:3.

41 Bosley Crowther, "*The Horse Soldiers*," *New York Times*, June 27, 1959, 13:1.

42 John C. Tibbetts points out that there are several other movies dealing with the Border Wars and the Lawrence massacre. These include: *Dark Command* (1940), *Kansas Raiders* (1950), *Quantrill's Raiders* (1958), and *The Jayhawkers* (1959). *The Outlaw Josey Wales* (1976) and *The Long Riders* (1980) deal "more tangentially" with the subject. Yet as Michael Fellman has argued, the Border Wars had more to do with petty hatreds and personal revenges than they did with the politics and ideology of the Civil War era. John C. Tibbetts, "The Hard Ride: Jayhawkers and Bushwackers in the Kansas-Missouri Border Wars–Ride With the Devil," *Film/Literature Quarterly*, vol. 27, no. 3 (1999), 193; Michael Fellman, *Inside War: The Guerrilla Conflict in Missouri During the American Civil War* (New York: Oxford University Press, 1989).

43 Spears, *Civil War on the Screen*, 34, 55, 57.

44 Rollin G. Osterweis, *The Myth of the Lost Cause, 1865–1900* (Hamden, CT: Archon, 1973), 113. See Chapter Five of this book for a discussion of the "Lost Cause" on film.

45 For a good outline of the story, see James R. Kelly, Jr., "Newton Knight and the Legend of the Free State of Jones," *Mississippi History Now*, http://mshistory. k12.ms.us/index.php?s=extra&id=309, accessed March 25, 2013. Also see Victoria E. Byrnum, *The Free State of Jones: Mississippi's Longest Civil War* (Chapel Hill: University of North Carolina Press, 2009); Sally Jenkins and John Stauffer, *The State of Jones* (New York: Doubleday, 2009).

46 Whit, "*Shenandoah*," *Variety*, April 14, 1965.

47 See David Williams, *Bitterly Divided: The South's Inner Civil War* (New York: The New Press, 2008). Other scholars who have written books suggesting dissent and internal conflict within the Confederacy include Charles H. Wesley (1937), Charles W. Ramsdell (1944), Paul D. Escott (1978), Wayne K. Durrill (1990), Victoria E. Byrnum (1992), Drew Gilpin Faust (1996), John C. Inscoe and Gordon B. McKinney (2000), Martin Crawford (2001), and Jonathan Dean Sarris (2006).

48 See James A. Ramage, *Rebel Raider: The Life of General John Hunt Morgan* (Lexington: University Press of Kentucky, 1986); Edison H. Thomas, *John Hunt Morgan and His Raiders* (Lexington: University Press of Kentucky, 1975).

49 On the draft riots, see Iver Bernstein, *The New York City Draft Riots: Their Significance for American Society and Politics in the Age of the Civil War* (New York: Oxford University Press, 1990).

50 Vincent Canby, "The Brutality and the Chaos," *New York Times*, December 14, 1989; C15: 1. Another critic, however, commented that—by making Shaw alone responsible for the decision to have the 54th lead the attack on Fort Wagner—*Glory* avoided the issue of whether senior white officers had been using blacks troops only "as cannon fodder." Mac, "*Glory*," *Variety*,

December 13, 1989. On this point, see Cullen, *The Civil War in Popular Culture*, 156–7.

51 "Fighting Black–Ed Zwick interviewed by Armond White, " *Film Comment*, vol. 26, no. 1 (January/February 1990), 22; Robert Seibenberg, "*Glory*— Thirtysomething's Edward Zwick goes to war—the Civil War," *American Film*, vol. 15, no 4 (January 1990), 58.

52 Robert Burgoyne, "Race and Nation in *Glory*," *Quarterly Review of Film and Video*, vol. 16, no. 2 (1997), 136, 143.

53 Jim Cullen points out that the role of Shaw, in particular, inserts a patronizing subtext into *Glory* that suggests "it is whites who make the most dramatic contributions to the black cause." Cullen, *The Civil War in Popular Culture*, 164.

54 Ibid., 141, 143.

55 James M. McPherson, "The *Glory* Story," *The New Republic*, vol. 202, January 8, 1990, 22; Cripps, "Absent Presence," 375.

56 Thomas Doherty, "*Glory*," *Cineaste*, vol. 17, no. 4 (1990), 40.

57 Ibid., 41.

58 http://uk.imdb.com/title/tt0097441/business?ref_=tt_dt_bus, accessed March 26, 2013; Jeremy D. Stoddard and Alan S. Marcus, "The Burden of Historical Representation: Race, Freedom, and "Educational" Hollywood Film," *Film and History*, vol. 36, no. 1 (2006), 26–7, 31–3.

59 Turner himself played a cameo role as Colonel Waller T. Patton in both films.

60 Cullen, *The Civil War in Popular Culture*, 154.

61 Daniel M. Kimmel, "*Gettysburg*," *Variety*, October 4, 1993.

62 Gary W. Gallagher, *Causes Won, Lost, and Forgotten: How Hollywood and Popular Art Shape What We Know About the Civil War* (Chapel Hill: University of North Carolina Press, 2008), 57, 100.

63 www.imdb.com/title/tt0107007/business?ref_=tt_dt_bus, accessed March 27, 2013.

64 Robert Koehler, "*Gods and Generals*," *Variety*, February 17–23, 2003.

65 For a good summary of the case against the film, see Christopher Sharrett, "*Gods and Generals*,' *Cineaste*, vol. 28, no. 3 (Summer 2003), 36–9.

66 Gallagher, *Causes Won, Lost, and Forgotten*, 76–7, 80.

67 www.imdb.com/title/tt0279111/business?ref_=tt_dt_bus, accessed March 27, 2013.

68 Emanual Levy, "Pharoah's Army," *Variety*, April 24, 1995; Gallagher, *Causes Won, Lost, and Forgotten*, 64–5.

69 Gallagher, *Causes Won, Lost, and Forgotten*, 69.

70 "*Ride With the Devil*," *Premiere* (US), vol. 13, no. 3 (November 1999), 34.

71 Stephen Hunter, "When Johnny Doesn't Come Marching Home," *Washington Post*, December 17, 1999; Stephen Holden, "*Ride With the Devil*: Far from Gettysburg, a Heartland Torn Apart," *New York Times*, November 24, 1999.

72 www.imdb.com/title/tt0134154/business?ref_=tt_dt_bus, accessed March 27, 2013.

73　Todd McCarthy, "Love Story Warms Soldier's Odyssey," *Variety*, December 8–14, 2003, 50; www.imdb.com/title/tt0159365/business?ref_=tt_dt_bus, accessed March 30, 2013.

74　John C. Inscoe, "*Cold Mountain*," *Journal of American History*, vol. 91, no. 3 (December 2004), 1129.

75　The movie representation of Southern women as opposed to the war fits with the analysis of Drew Gilpin Faust, who has seen women—particularly elite women—as increasingly unsupportive of the Confederacy. See Faust, "Altars of Sacrifice: Confederate Women and the Narratives of War," *Journal of American History*, 76 (March 1990), 1220–8; Faust, *Mothers of Invention: Women of the Slaveholding South in the American Civil War* (Chapel Hill: University of North Carolina Press, 1996). Gary Gallagher, in contrast, argues that "the large majority of white southern women—especially slaveholding women like Ada Monroe—resolutely supported the Confederate nation until very late in the conflict." Gallagher, *Causes Won, Lost and Forgotten*, 86.

76　Anna Creadick, "When you are in Romania, you are in Cold Mountain," "APPALJ Roundtable Discussion: *Cold Mountain*, the Film," *Appalachian Journal*, vol. 31, no. 3/4 (Spring/Summer 2004), 330–1.

77　For a reflection on how guerrilla warfare releases women—including those of *Cold Mountain*—from "conventional gender roles," see John C. Inscoe, "Mountain Women, Mountain War," ibid., 343–7.

78　Linda Sunshine, ed., *Cold Mountain: The Journey from Book to Film* (New York: Newmarket Press, 2003), 86.

79　Gallagher, *Causes Won, Lost, and Forgotten*, 84; Inscoe, "*Cold Mountain*," 1128.

80　Silas House, "The Appalachian Factor in *Cold Mountain*," "APPALJ Roundtable Discussion: *Cold Mountain*, the Film," 340; "Inscoe's Response to House," ibid., 342.

81　Martin Crawford, "*Cold Mountain* Fiction: Appalachian Half-Truths," *Appalachian Journal*, vol. 30, no. 2/3 (Winter/Spring 2003), 183.

82　Inscoe, "*Cold Mountain*," 1128.

83　This sequence echoes a similar scene in *Pharoah's Army* and, in a more limited way, the arrival of the Yankee deserter at Tara in *Gone With the Wind*.

84　The film was much-criticized by some in the United States for this. See "In focus: Minghella feels cold shoulder," *Screen International*, no. 1440 (February 13, 2004), 4.

Chapter 5

1　On the "continuing" Civil War, see David Goldfield, *Still Fighting the Civil War: The American South and Southern History* (Baton Rouge: Louisiana State University Press, 2002), 1–2, 9, 299, 302–4.

2 Thomas L. Connelly and Barbara L. Bellows, *God and General Longstreet: The Lost Cause and the Southern Mind* (Baton Rouge: Louisiana State University Press, 1982), 1–38; David W. Blight, *Beyond the Battlefield: Race, Memory, and the American Civil War* (Amherst and Boston: University of Massachusetts Press, 2002), 103; David W. Blight, *Race and Reunion: The Civil War in American Memory* (Cambridge, MA: Harvard University Press, 2001), 211, 216–17, 221–7.

3 Alan T. Nolan, "The Anatomy of the Myth," in Gary W. Gallagher and Alan T. Nolan, eds, *The Myth of the Lost Cause and Civil War History* (Bloomington: Indiana University Press, 2000), 15–19.

4 Eileen Bowser, *The Transformation of Cinema 1907–1915* (New York: Charles Scribner's Sons, 1990), 178; Evelyn Ehrlich, "The Civil War in Early Film: Origins and Development of a Genre," *Southern Quarterly*, vol. 19, nos. 3–4 (Spring–Summer 1981), 77–8.

5 For further reflections on the interpretation of "history" in the two films, see Stokes, *D. W. Griffith's "The Birth of a Nation"*, chap. 7 and James Chapman, Mark Glancy, and Sue Harper, eds, *The New Film History: Sources, Methods, Approaches* (Basingstoke: Palgrave Macmillan, 2007), chap. 1.

6 Carl E. Milliken to Will W. Alexander, August 9, 1930, National Association for the Advancement of Colored People Papers, Library of Congress.

7 Helen Taylor, *Scarlett's Women: "Gone With the Wind" and Its Female Fans* (London: Virago, 1989), 2.

8 Jean-Louis Comolli and Jean Narboni, "Cinema/ideology/criticism" (1), originally published in *Cahiers du cinéma*, no. 216 (October 1969), 11–15, trans. Susan Bennett, in Nick Browne, ed., *Cahiers du cinéma, Vol. 3, 1969–72: The Politics of Representation* (London: Routledge/BFI, 1990), 58–67; "John Ford's *Young Mr. Lincoln*, a Collective Text by the Editors of *Cahiers du cinéma*," originally published in *Cahiers du cinéma*, no. 223 (August 1970), 29–47, trans. Helen Lackner and Diana Matias, *Screen*, vol. 13, no. 3 (Autumn 1972), 5–44.

9 The notion that field hands were content with their lot is contradicted later in the film: Scarlett arrives back at Tara to discover that only the black "house servants"/slaves remain. All the field hands have gone. This was in fact a fairly accurate portrayal of what happened in the South in 1864–5.

10 Nolan, "The Anatomy of the Myth," 22–4.

11 Quoted in "The Making of a Legend: *Gone With the Wind*," documentary produced by L. Jeffrey Selznick, written by David Thomson and directed by David Hinton, 1988.

12 Ray Allen Cook, *Fire from the Flint: The Amazing Careers of Thomas Dixon* (Winston-Salem, NC: John F. Blair, 1968), 7, 13–14; Ray Allen Cook, *Thomas Dixon* (New York, Twayne Publishers, 1974), 23–4.

13 Joel Williamson, *The Crucible of Race: Black-White Relations in the American South Since Emancipation* (New York: Oxford University Press, 1984), 155, 157–8.

14 Thomas Dixon, Jr., *The Leopard's Spots: A Romance of the White Man's Burden* (New York, Doubleday, Page and Co., 1902); Thomas Dixon, Jr., *The Clansman: A Historical Romance of the Ku Klux Klan* (New York: Doubleday, Page and Co., 1905).

15 Cook, *Fire from the Flint*, 136, 139–44, 148–9.

16 Jack Spears, *The Civil War on the Screen and Other Essays* (South Brunswick and New York: A. S. Barnes, 1977), 32–3.

17 Allen W. Trelease, *White Terror: The Ku Klux Klan Conspiracy and Southern Reconstruction* (Baton Rouge: Louisiana State University Press, 1995), 89.

18 James Hart, ed., *The Man Who Invented Hollywood: The Autobiography of D. W. Griffith* (Louisville: Touchstone Publishing Company, 1972), 89.

19 David M. Chalmers, *Hooded Americanism: The History of the Ku Klux Klan* (Durham, NC: Duke University Press, 1987; 3rd. edn), 8–9.

20 William P. Randel, *The Ku Klux Klan: A Century of Infamy* (Philadelphia: Chiltern Books, 1965), 53.

21 Trelease, *White Terror*, xxviii.

22 Wyn Craig Wade, *The Fiery Cross: The Ku Klux Klan in America* (New York: Simon and Schuster, 1987), 146.

23 In reality, the burning of white barns, stables, and saloons by African Americans seems to have been a protest against the far more numerous aggressions committed by whites against blacks. Chalmers, *Hooded Americanism*, 20; Trelease, *White Terror*, 364, 366.

24 Other battles were sometimes cited but Shiloh (Pittsburgh Landing, April 6–7, 1862) reflected the southwestern origins of the Klan, since the battle had taken place only 80 miles to the west of the Klan's birthplace in Pulaski, Tennessee.

25 The Klan had its main strength in the nine counties of the South Carolina piedmont in which President Ulysses S. Grant later (October 17, 1871) suspended habeas corpus: Spartanburg, Laurens, Union, Newberry, York, Chester, Fairfield, Lancaster, and Chesterfield. Stanley F. Horn, *Invisible Empire: The Story of the Ku Klux Klan, 1866–1871* (Boston: Houghton Mifflin, 1939), 217, 238; Chalmers, *Hooded Americanism*, 10, 16.

26 Horn, *Invisible Empire*, 218–20; Trelease, *White Terror*, 351–2. A similar incident took place in Yorkville. See Horn, *Invisible Empire*, 222.

27 Horn, *Invisible Empire*, 225–7; Randel, *The Ku Klux Klan*, 54–5; Trelease, *White Terror*, 356–8.

28 Trelease, *White Terror*, 364–5.

29 On Dixon's view of the revived Klan, see Cook, *Fire from the Flint*, 196–97; Anthony Slide, *American Racist: The Life and Films of Thomas Dixon* (Lexington: University Press of Kentucky, 2004), 16. After the publication of *The Clansman*, Dixon had rejected suggestions that he lead some kind of Klan revival. Chalmers, *Hooded Americanism*, 27.

30 Wade, *The Fiery Cross*, 143–4.

31 Ibid., 140–3; Chalmers, *Hooded Americanism*, 28–30.

32 Wade, *The Fiery Cross*, 144–5.

33 Ibid., 146–7.

34 Maxim Simcovitch, "The Impact of Griffith's *Birth of a Nation* on the Modern Ku Klux Klan," *Journal of Popular Film*, vol. 1, no. 1 (Winter, 1972), 48.

35 Chalmers, *Hooded Americanism*, 3; Simcovitch, "The Impact of Griffith's *Birth of a Nation* on the Modern Ku Klux Klan," 49, 51.

36 Chalmers, *Hooded Americanism*, 3–4, 31–3; Simcovitch, "The Impact of Griffith's *Birth of a Nation* on the Modern Ku Klux Klan," 49, 52.

37 The Klan of Oxnard, California exhibited it as a fundraiser and membership promotion device in August 1978, when Mexican-American and black associations protested, and violence broke out. In 1979, the Communist Workers Party disrupted a showing of *The Birth of a Nation* to Klansmen at a rally in China Grove, North Carolina. Janet Staiger, *Interpreting Films: Studies in the Historical Reception of American Cinema* (Princeton: Princeton University Press, 1992), 139; Wade, *The Fiery Cross*, 379.

38 Mrs. S. E. F. Rose, "The Ku Klux Klan and *The Birth of a Nation*," *Confederate Veteran*, vol. 24, no. 4 (April, 1916), 157; Nancy Maclean, *Behind the Mask of Chivalry: The Making of the Second Ku Klux Klan* (New York: Oxford University Press, 1994), 13; William G. Shepherd, "How I Put Over the Klan," *Collier's Magazine*, July 14, 1928, quoted in Simcovitch, "The Impact of Griffith's *Birth of a Nation* on the Modern Ku Klux Klan," 46.

39 Chalmers, *Hooded Americanism*, 31–3; Maclean, *Behind the Mask of Chivalry*, 5, 10.

40 Leonard J. Moore, *Citizen Klansmen: The Ku Klux Klan in Indiana, 1921–1928* (Chapel Hill: University of North Carolina Press, 1991), 46, 181–3, 185–6.

41 Rush, "*[The] Mating Call*," *Variety*, October 10, 1928.

42 Chalmers, *Hooded Americanism*, 4–5.

43 Wade, *The Fiery Cross*, 257.

44 Simcovich, "The Impact of Griffith's *The Birth of a Nation* on the Modern Ku Klux Klan," 52. I have not so far been able to uncover production details for this film.

45 See Stephen Harlan Norwood, *Strikebreaking and Intimidation: Mercenaries and Masculinity in Twentieth-Century America* (Durham: University of North Carolina Press, 2001), 196–200; Peter H. Amann, "Vigilante Fascism: The Black Legion as an American Hybrid," *Comparative Studies in Society and History*, vol. 25, no. 3 (July 1983), 490–524; http://apps.detnews.com/apps/history/index.php?id=151, accessed January 29, 2013.

46 J. T. M., "*Legion of Terror*," *The New York Times*, November 2, 1936, 24:2; Frank S. Nugent, "*Black Legion*," *The New York Times*, January 18, 1937, 21:1.

47 Edga, "*Legion of Terror*," *Variety*, November 4, 1936.

48 Chalmers, *Hooded Americanism*, 325–34.

49 "*The Burning Cross*," *Motion Picture Herald*, vol. 168, no. 4 (July 26, 1947), 3746.

50 Peter Noble commented that every national bank in the United States had refused finance for *The Burning Cross*. Noble, "The Cinema and the Negro 1905–1948," *Special Supplement to Sight and Sound*, index series no. 14 (March 1948), 19.

51 "*The Burning Cross*," *Variety*, August 13, 1947; T. M. P., "*The Burning Cross*," *The New York Times*, February 20, 1948, 19:1.

52 "*Storm Warning*," *Motion Picture Herald*, vol. 181, no. 10 (December 9, 1950), 605.

53 Bosley Crowther, "*Storm Warning*," *The New York Times*, March 3, 1951, 8:2.

54 Chalmers, *Hooded Americanism*, 343–85.

55 "*The Black Klansman*," *Variety*, June 15, 1966.

56 Vincent Canby, "Clumsy Adaptation of the Novel by Huie," *The New York Times*, November 21, 1974, 54:1; Alexander Stuart, "*The Klansman*," *Films and Filming*, vol. 21, no. 10 (July 1975), 43; Murf, "*The Klansman*," *Variety*, November 6, 1974.

57 Todd McCarthy, "*A Time to Kill*," *Variety*, July 15, 1996.

58 John Slavin, "Alan Parker's *Mississippi Burning*," *Cinema Papers*, no. 73 (May 1989), 56.

59 Brian Palmer, "Ku Klux Kontraction: How did the KKK lose nearly one-third of its chapters in one year?" www.slate.com/articles/news_and_politics/politics/2012/03/ku_klux_klan_in_decline_why_did_the_kkk_lose_so_many_chapters_in_2010_.html, accessed February 3, 2013.

Chapter 6

1 According to Jeffrey Ostler, the name Sioux originated in a word the French wrote as "Nadouessioux," eventually shortened to Sioux. The Lakota belonged to the Western, Teton, branch of the seven principal divisions of Sioux. Their dialect uses "l" in place of "d," hence their name. Jeffrey Ostler, *The Plains Sioux and U. S. Colonialism from Lewis and Clark to Wounded Knee* (Cambridge: Cambridge University Press, 2004), 21; Alice Beck Kehoe, *North American Indians: A Comprehensive Account* (Englewood Cliffs, NJ: Prentice Hall, 1992), 302–3.

2 Richard White, "Frederick Jackson Turner and Buffalo Bill," in James R. Grossman, ed., *The Frontier in American Culture* (Berkeley: University of California Press, 1994), 7–65; Frederick Jackson Turner, "The Significance of the Frontier in American History," paper originally delivered at the 1893 meeting of the American Historical Association in Chicago, here as reprinted in www.gutenberg.org/cache/epub/22994/pg22994.txt, accessed February 10, 2013.

3 White, "Frederick Jackson Turner and Buffalo Bill."

4 Alice B. Kehoe notes that stealing horses was approved of by Plains Indians as a means of gaining greater power for individual bands. Kehoe, *North American Indians*, 312.

5 www.imdb.com/title/tt0099348/business, accessed January 11, 2013.

6 http://awardsdatabase.oscars.org/ampas_awards/DisplayMain.
jsp?curTime=1360910966417, accessed February 15, 2013.

7 Stephen Tatum, "*Dances With Wolves*: A Review Essay," *Montana: The Magazine of Western History*, vol. 41, no. 2 (Spring 1991), 91.

8 *Motion Picture Guide Annual 1991* (Chicago: Cinebooks, 1991), 36.

9 Alexandra Keller, "Historical Discourse and American Identity in Westerns since the Reagan Administration," *Film and History: An Interdisciplinary Journal of Film and Television Studies*, vol. 33, no. 1 (2003), 48.

10 Littlefeather's speech is widely available on the internet. See, for example, www.youtube.com/watch?v=2QUacU0I4yU, accessed January 10, 2013.

11 Wounded Knee, in the Pine Ridge Indian Reservation, was the site of the 1890 massacre of between 150 and 300 Sioux men, women, and children by a detachment of the US Seventh Cavalry—the last massacre of the nineteenth-century Indian wars.

12 Kim Newman, *Wild West Movies: How the West was Found, Won, Lost, Lied About, Filmed and Forgotten* (London: Bloomsbury, 1990), 53.

13 Ibid., 67. According to Newman, these included *The Redman's View* (1909), *Ramona* (1910), *A Mohawk's Way* (1910), *The Squaw's Love* (1911), *The Chief's Daughter* (1911), *The Indian Brothers* (1911), and *The Chief's Blanket* (1912).

14 Dee Brown, *Bury My Heart at Wounded Knee: An Indian History of the American West* (New York: Sterling Innovation, 2009; originally pub. in 1970).

15 Edward D. Castillo, "*Dances With Wolves*," *Film Quarterly*, vol. 44, no. 4 (Summer 1991), 21.

16 www.russellmeansfreedom.com/2009/russell-means-interview-with-dan-skye-of-high-times/ and http://lakotadictionary.org/phpBB3/viewtopic.php?f=2&t=3610&p=44874&sid=d85e699ac74847b159aaec6745718f4c; both accessed January 12, 2013.

17 Castillo, "*Dances With Wolves*," 21.

18 Stephen Tatum points out that *A Man Called Horse* (1970), with Richard Harris in the title role, had Lakota as 80 percent of the dialogue, but did not provide English subtitles. Tatum, "*Dances With Wolves*," 91.

19 Daws, "*Dances With Wolves*," *Variety*, November 12, 1990.

20 Marilou Awiakta, "Red Alert! A Meditation on *Dances With Wolves*," *Ms. Magazine* (March–April 1991), 70.

21 "One can only suppose," Edward Castillo drily comments, "it was someone of Timmons's character that prompted Thomas Jefferson to observe that when the Indians encountered the typical frontiersman in the wilderness it was hardly an elevating experience for the Indians." Castillo, "*Dances With Wolves*," 16–17.

22 Daws, "*Dances With Wolves*," *Variety*, November 12, 1990; Armando José Prats, "The Image of the Other and the Other *Dances With Wolves*: The Refigured Indian and the Textual Supplement," *Journal of Film and Video*, vol. 50, no. 1 (Spring 1998), 8.

23 Robert Baird, "'Going Indian': *Dances With Wolves* (1990)," in Peter C. Rollins and John E. O'Connor, eds, *Hollywood's Indian: The Portrayal of the Native American in Film* (Lexington: University Press of Kentucky, 2003), 158. The story, first published in 1907, was reprinted in Russell's *Trails Plowed Under* (Garden City, New York: Doubleday, Page, 1927).

24 Shepard Krech III sees the construction of Indian stereotypes such as the "Ecological Indian" or the "Noble Indian" as masking "cultural diversity." There was a considerable range of character in every Indian tribe. Yet, in *Dances With Wolves*, the Sioux are without exception presented in a highly positive way. Any negative qualities or characteristics are displaced onto the Pawnees—who are uniformly evil—and the whites. Shepard Krech III, *The Ecological Indian: Myth and History* (New York: W. W. Norton, 1999), 26–7.

25 "The Sioux-Pawnee War," *Chicago Tribune*, August 30, 1873; Gene Weltfish, *The Lost Universe: Pawnee Life and Culture* (Lincoln: University of Nebraska Press, 1977), 3–4. One reason for the unpopularity of the Pawnee with other tribes was that, as suggested in *Dances With Wolves*, they acted as scouts for the US Army.

26 For reflections on earlier Sioux social life and customs by a physician who lived with them for almost two decades, see James R. Walker, *Lakota Society*, ed. Raymond J. DeMallie (Lincoln: University of Nebraska Press, 1982).

27 Castillo, "*Dances With Wolves*," 14–15. Kicking Bird was a chief, not shaman, of the Kiowas, a tribe also located on the southern plains.

28 Castillo, "*Dances With Wolves*," 17.

29 Ibid.

30 Ibid.

31 Wayne Michael Sarf, *The Little Bighorn Campaign: March-September 1876* (Conshohocken, PA: Combined Books, 1993).

32 Wayne Michael Sarf, "Oscar Eaten by Wolves," *Film Comment*, vol. 27, no. 6 (November–December 1991), 62–4, 67–8.

33 Krech, *The Ecological Indian*, 19.

34 Ibid., 21.

35 Since Cody was unable to cry on demand, the tears had been induced with glycerine eye-drops.

36 Angela Aleiss, *The Times Picayune* (New Orleans), May 26, 1996, 1, sec. D (also see Ron Russell, "Make-Believe Indian," *New Times* (Los Angeles), vol. 4, no. 14, 8–14 April 1999, 14–21); Patricia Nelson Limerick, "The American West: From Exceptionalism to Internationalism," in Melvyn Stokes, ed., *The State of U. S. History* (Oxford: Berg, 2002), 293.

37 Kehoe, *North American Indians*, 312; Ostler, *The Plains Sioux and U. S. Colonialism*, 128. Also see Krech, *The Ecological Indian*, 132, 134–5 on Indian wastefulness in relation to buffalo.

38 Philip Weeks, *Farewell, My Nation: The American Indian and the United States, 1820–1890* (Wheeling, IL: Harlan Davidson, 1990), 182–5, 188–9, 192; Ostler, *The Plains Sioux and U. S. Colonialism*, 81–3.

39 Kehoe, *North American Indians*, 297; Ostler, *The Plains Sioux and U. S. Colonialism*, 22.

40 Ostler, *The Plains Sioux and U. S. Colonialism*, 22; Kehoe, *North American Indians*, 303.

41 Ostler, *The Plains Sioux and U. S. Colonialism*, 19, 36–9.

42 Ibid., 40.

43 Weeks, *Farewell, My Nation*, 90–4; Ostler, *The Plains Sioux and U. S. Colonialism*, 44–45.

44 Weeks, *Farewell, My Nation*, 97; Ostler, *The Plains Sioux and U. S. Colonialism*, 44.

45 Weeks, *Farewell, My Nation*, 97; Ostler, *The Plains Sioux and U. S. Colonialism*, 45. The real Fort Sedgwick was located around a mile upriver from Julesburg. Built in the summer of 1864, it was originally named Fort Rankin. Its small garrison was unable to prevent the destruction of Julesburg. The base was subsequently enlarged and renamed Fort Sedgwick, after the late Union general John Sedgwick. In the late 1860s, it protected construction crews building the Union Pacific railroad from Indian attacks. www.over-land. com/fsedgwick.html, accessed February 13, 2013.

46 Ostler, *The Plains Sioux and U. S. Colonialism*, 45.

47 Weeks, *Farewell, My Nation*, 109–11, 123–7, 135–41; Ostler, *The Plains Indians and U. S. Colonialism*, 48–50, quotation from 50. On the boundaries of the Great Sioux Reservation, see Ostler, *The Plains Indians and U. S. Colonialism*, 19 and 37, fn. 62.

48 Weeks, *Farewell, My Nation*, 169, 172–3; Ostler, *The Plains Sioux and U. S. Colonialism*, 52–3.

49 Weeks, *Farewell, My Nation*, 174–89; Ostler, *The Plains Sioux and U. S. Colonialism*, 59–83.

50 This sequence is otherwise very curious. The pursuing army, with its Pawnee scouts, keeps coming across recently extinguished camp-fires—but these cannot belong to the Lakota band with whom Dunbar is staying, which is secure in its mountainous winter camp.

51 Weeks, *Farewell, My Nation*, 179.

52 Kehoe, *North American Indians*, 287.

53 Andrew C. Isenberg, *The Destruction of the Bison: An Environmental History, 1750–1920* (Cambridge: Cambridge University Press, 2000), 131–2.

54 Ibid., 136–7.

55 Isenberg, *The Destruction of the Buffalo*, 156; www.thbison.com/lordofplains. shtml, accessed January 24, 2013.

56 Robert Wooster, *The Military and United States Indian Policy, 1865–1903* (Lincoln: University of Nebraska Press, 1988), 171.

57 Ibid., 172.

58 Ibid., 171–2.

59 Ibid., 172.

60 Robert Wooster argues that "the slaughter of the buffalo" not only "severely reduced the Indians' capacity to continue an armed struggle against the United States," it also "helped to mask the military's poor performance in the Indian wars." Wooster, *The Military and United States Indian Policy*, 171.

61 Mary Rowlandson, *A True History of the Captivity and Restoration of Mrs. Mary Rowlandson* (New York: Garland, 1977; originally published in 1682).

62 On captivity narratives, see June Namias, *White Captives: Gender and Ethnicity on the American Frontier* (Chapel Hill: University of North Carolina Press, 1993); Richard VanDerBeets, *The Indian Captivity Narrative: An American Genre* (Lanham, MD: University Press of America, 1984).

63 James E. Seaver, *Narrative of the Life of Mary Jemison* (New York: Garland, 1977; first pub. 1826); Margaret S. Hacker, *Cynthia Ann Parker: The Life and the Legend* (El Paso: Texas Western Press, 1990).

64 Tatum, "*Dances With Wolves*," 91. When Dunbar first sees her, when she is "hurt," he has no suspicion that she might be a white captive who has escaped the Sioux. He takes her back to the tribe.

65 Lynne Dozier, "*Dances With Wolves*: Lessons from Loo Ten Tant's Journal," *The English Journal*, vol. 83, no. 1 (January 1994), 37.

Chapter 7

1 Leonard Dinnerstein and David Reimers, *Ethnic Americans: A History of Immigration* (New York: Columbia University Press, 2009; 5th edn), 56.

2 Dinnerstein and Reimers, *Ethnic Americans*, 65; Maldwyn A. Jones, *Destination America* (London: Fontana, 1977), 172.

3 Morton Rosenstock, "The Jews: From the Ghettos of Europe to the Suburbs of the United States," in Frank J. Coppa and Thomas J. Curran, eds, *The Immigrant Experience in America* (Boston: Twayne, 1976), 151.

4 Spencer Blakeslee, *The Death of American Anti-semitism* (Westport, CT: Praeger, 2000), 30; Dinnerstein and Reimers, *Ethnic Americans*, 62.

5 Rosenstock, "The Jews," 153.

6 *New York Times*, July 27, 1895.

7 Jewish husbands deserting their families was so common that, for many years, the Yiddish newspaper *Forward* ran a "Gallery of Missing Husbands." See Irving Howe, *The Immigrant Jews of New York: 1881 to the Present* (London and Boston: Routledge and Kegan Paul, 1976), 179–80.

8 Sonya Michel, "*Yekl* and *Hester Street*: Was Assimilation Really Good for the Jews?," *Literature/Film Quarterly*, vol. 5, no. 2 (Spring 1977), 142–3.

9 On peddling, see Howe, *The Immigrant Jews of New York*, 77–80.

10 Michel, "*Yekl* and *Hester Street*," 145.

11   Leonard Dinnerstein, *Uneasy at Home: Antisemitism and the American Jewish Experience* (New York: Columbia University Press, 1987), 20.

12   Dinnerstein and Reimers, *Ethnic Americans*, 77.

13   Dinnerstein, *Uneasy at Home*, 35, 50.

14   Joyce Antler, "Hester Street," in Carnes, *Past Imperfect*, 178.

15   Laurence Green, "Hester Street," *Films and Filming*, vol. 22, no. 4 (January 1976), 34.

16   Richard Eder, "Hester Street," *New York Times*, October 20, 1975, 44.

17   Robert F. Horowitz, "Between a Heartache and a Laugh: Two Recent Films on Immigration," *Film and History*, vol. 6, no. 2 (December, 1976), 75–6.

18   Howe, *The Immigrant Jews of New York*, 128.

19   Dinnerstein, *Uneasy at Home*, 22.

20   Oscar Handlin, *The Uprooted: The Epic Story of the Great Migrations that Made the American People* (Boston: Little, Brown, 1951), 153.

21   Dinnerstein, *Uneasy at Home*, 20; Howe, *The Immigrant Jews of New York*, 171, 178.

22   Jones, *Destination America*, 176.

23   Handlin, *The Uprooted*, 152–4.

24   Rosenstock, "The Jews," 154. Also see Howe, *The Immigrant Jews of New York*, 82–3; Dinnerstein, *Uneasy at Home*, 23.

25   Lincoln Steffens, *The Autobiography of Lincoln Steffens* (New York: Harcourt, Brace and Company, 1931), 210–14.

26   Deidre Mack, "*Hester Street*," *Films in Review*, vol. 26, no. 10 (December 1975), 635.

27   Patricia Erens, *The Jew in American Cinema* (Bloomington: Indiana University Press, 1984), 326.

28   See Steffens, *Autobiography*, 243.

29   Antler, "*Hester Street*," 180.

30   Dinnerstein and Reimers described the café or coffee-house as "the most popular cultural institution on the Lower East Side." Dinnerstein and Reimers, *Ethnic Americans*, 77.

31   Judith Thissen, "Jewish Immigrant Audiences in New York City, 1905–14," in Melvyn Stokes and Richard Maltby, eds, *American Movie Audiences: From the Turn of the Century to the Early Sound Era* (London: BFI Publishing, 1999), 15.

32   Erens, *The Jew in American Cinema*, 326.

33   On crime and prostitution in the New York Jewish community, see Howe, *The Immigrant Jews of New York*, 96–101.

34   Rosenstock, "The Jews," 160–1; Dinnerstein, *Antisemitism in America*, 50.

35   Dinnerstein, *Antisemitism in America*, 50–3.

36   Mosk, "*Hester Street*," *Variety*, May 14, 1975.

37   Erens, *The Jew in American Cinema*, 42.

38 Daniel Patrick Moynihan and Nathan Glazer, *Beyond the Melting Pot: The Negroes, Puerto Ricans, Jews, Italians, and Irish of New York City* (Cambridge, MA: MIT Press, 1963).

39 Horowitz, "Between a Heartache and a Laugh," 73.

40 John Higham, *Send These to Me: Jews and Other Immigrants in Urban America* (New York: Atheneum, 1975), 88.

41 Michel, "*Yekl* and *Hester Street*," 144. Michel points out that Mamie, however, with "few compunctions about taking Jake from Gitl," is the exception to this rule. Ibid.

42 Erens, *The Jew In American Cinema*, 326.

43 www.loc.gov/today/pr/2011/11–240.html, accessed on January 6, 2013.

44 John Yates, "Godfather Saga: The Death of the Family," *Journal of Popular Film*, vol. 4, no. 2 (1975), 162.

45 Anthony Ambrogio, "'The Godfather, I and II': Patterns of Corruption," *Film Criticism*, vol. 3, no. 1 (1978), 42.

46 In a careful piece of research by Coppola's team, the shot of the discovery of Paolo's body—even down to the position of his right arm—is based on a photograph of police leading the mother of 14-year-old Paolo Riccobono, killed in a Mafia vendetta, to his body. Frédéric Foubert, "Revoir Le Parrain: Une expérience cinématographique du temps (Watching the Godfather again: A cinematographic experience of Time)," *Vingième siècle: Revue d'histoire*, no. 92 (October–December 2006), 146.

47 Jones, *Destination America*, 193–5.

48 Peter Cowie, *The Godfather Book* (London: Faber and Faber, 1997), 95.

49 Would-be immigrants suspected of illness were quarantined on Hoffman Island, off Staten Island, about five miles south of the Statue of Liberty.

50 See www.gangrule.com.gangs/the-black-hand, accessed January 19, 2013.

51 Thomas Kessner, *The Golden Door: Italian and Jewish Immigrant Mobility in New York City 1880–1915* (New York: Oxford University Press, 1977), 17.

52 Jones, *Destination America*, 133.

53 See www.rogerebert.com/reviews, accessed January 19, 2013.

54 Vito's action did, however, fit the outlook of many Sicilians, according to which—Richard Alba notes—"justice was regarded as a private matter." Richard D. Alba, *Italian Americans: Into the Twilight of Ethnicity* (Englewood Cliffs, NJ: Prentice-Hall, 1985), 37.

55 Cowie, *The Godfather Book*, 87.

56 Ibid., 87–8.

57 Alba, *Italian Americans*, 59–61; Jones, *Destination America*, 209, 211.

58 Cowie, *The Godfather Book*, 79; Dinnerstein and Reimers, *Ethnic Americans*, 65.

59 Dinnerstein and Reimers, *Ethnic Americans*, 68–9; Jones, *Destination America*, 198.

60 George De Stefano, "Italian-Americans: Family Lies," *Film Comment*, vol. 23, no. 4 (July/August 1987), 23–4. On the Hennessy case, also see Luciano J. Iorizzo and Salvatore Mondello, *The Italian Americans* (Youngstown, NY: Cambria Press, 2006), 83–5; Alba, *Italian Americans*, 64–5.

61 Two decades later, anarchists Nicola Sacco and Bartolomeo Vanzetti were charged with the murder of two men during a robbery in 1920 in Massachusetts. Their trial took place during a peak of anti-foreign sentiment in the United States that followed the "Red Scare" of 1919–20. They were finally executed in 1927. Alba, *Italian Americans*, 65–6. Also see Michael M. Topp, *The Sacco and Vanzetti Case: A Brief History with Documents* (Boston: Bedford, 2004); Moshik Temkin, *The Sacco-Vanzetti Affair: America on Trial* (New Haven: Yale University Press, 2009).

62 De Stefano, "Italian-Americans: Family Lies," 24.

63 *Godfather I* and *II* revived the association on screen between Italians and organized crime that had existed in some films of the early 1930s. Rico (Edward G. Robinson) in *Little Caesar* (1931) and Tony (Paul Muni) in *Scarface* (1932), for example, had both been constructed as of "Italian" ethnicity, with *Scarface* loosely based on the career of crime boss Al Capone in Chicago.

Chapter 8

1 W.R.W. [William R. Weaver], "*Grapes of Wrath* . . . Movie of a Best Seller," *Motion Picture Herald*, vol. 138, no. 4 (January 27, 1940), 52; M. Q. [Martin Quigley], "*Grapes of Wrath*—An Editorial Viewpoint," ibid., 17.

2 Edwin Locke, "*The Grapes of Wrath*," in Stanley Kaufman with Bruce Hensell, eds, *American Film Criticism: From the Beginnings to Citizen Kane* (New York: Liveright, 1972), 385, 391.

3 Russell Campbell, "The Ideology of the Social Consciousness Movie: Three Films of Darryl F. Zanuck," *Quarterly Review of Film Studies*, vol. 3, no. 1 (Winter 1978), 49–50.

4 Terry Christensen, *Reel Politics: American Political Movies from "Birth of a Nation" to "Platoon"* (New York: Blackwell, 1987), 43.

5 Francis Bordat and Michel Etcheverry, *Cent ans d'aller au cinéma: Le spectacle cinématographique aux Etats-Unis, 1896–1895* (Rennes: Presses Universitaires de Rennes, 1995), 203.

6 Richard Maltby, "The Political Economy of Hollywood: the Studio System," in Philip Davies and Brian Neve, eds, *Cinema, Politics and Society in America* (Manchester: Manchester University Press, 1981), 46–7.

7 Gregory D. Black, *Hollywood Censored: Morality Codes, Catholics, and the Movies* (Cambridge: Cambridge University Press, 1994), 32–4; Robert Sklar, *Movie-Made America: A Cultural History of American Movies* (New York: Vintage, 1994), 134–40.

8   Black, *Hollywood Censored*, 34–46; "The Motion Picture Production Code of 1930," reprinted in Gerald Mast, ed., *The Movies in Our Midst: Documents in the Cultural History of Film in America* (Chicago: University of Chicago Press, 1982), 321–3.

9   Black, *Hollywood Censored*, 72–80; Lea Jacobs, *The Wages of Sin: Censorship and the Fallen Woman Film, 1928–1942* (Madison: University of Wisconsin Press, 1991); Melvyn Stokes, "The Gangster Cycle, the Impact of the Depression, and Cultural Struggles of the Early 1930s," in Trevor Harris and Dominique Daniel, *Le Crime Organisé à la Ville et à l'écran aux Etats-Unis, 1929–1951* (Tours: Publications de GRAAT, 2002), 17–27.

10 Black, *Hollywood Censored*, 149–92; James Skinner, *The Cross and the Cinema: The Legion of Decency and the National Catholic Office for Motion Pictures, 1933–1970* (Westport: Praeger, 1993), chap. 3.

11 Sklar, *Movie-Made America*, 189.

12 Thomas H. Pauly, "*Gone With the Wind* and *The Grapes of Wrath* as Hollywood Histories of the Depression," *Journal of Popular Film*, vol. 3, no. 3 (Summer 1974), 204.

13 Quoted in Campbell, "The Ideology of the Social Consciousness Movie," 50.

14 David Bordwell, Janet Staiger, and Kristin Thompson, *The Classical Hollywood Cinema: Film Style and Mode of Production to 1960* (London: Routledge and Kegan Paul, 1985).

15 Rebecca Pulliam, "*The Grapes of Wrath*," *Velvet Light Trap*, no. 2 (August 1971), 3; Thomas Schatz, *Boom and Bust: The American Cinema in the 1940s* (New York: Scribner's, 1997), 79.

16 Pulliam, "*The Grapes of Wrath*," 3.

17 Campbell, "The Ideology of the Social Consciousness Movie," 52; Schatz, *Boom and Bust*, 107.

18 Pulliam, "*The Grapes of Wrath*," 3; Campbell, "The Ideology of the Social Consciousness Movie," 51.

19 Campbell, "The Ideology of the Social Consciousness Movie," 52; Pulliam, "*The Grapes of Wrath*," 3.

20 Ian Hamilton, *Writers in Hollywood 1915–1951* (London: Heinemann, 1990), 275; Campbell, "The Ideology of the Social Consciousness Movie," 51.

21 Campbell, "The Ideology of the Social Consciousness Movie," 51.

22 Ibid., 52.

23 W. R. W., "*Grapes of Wrath*," 52; M. Q., "*Grapes of Wrath*," 17.

24 Johnson quoted in Campbell, "The Ideology of the Social Consciousness Movie," 50.

25 According to Jim Sanderson, the camp director (played by Grant Mitchell) "looks and acts like Roosevelt freed from his wheelchair, dressed for a summer evening in an upstate New York retreat, fearing only fear." Jim Sanderson, "American Romanticism in John Ford's *The Grapes of Wrath*: Horizontalness, Darkness, Christ, and F. D. R.," *Literature/Film Quarterly*, vol. 17, no. 4 (1989), 241.

26 W.R.W., "*Grapes of Wrath*," 52; Philip T. Hartung, "Trampling Out the Vintage," *Commonweal*, no. 31 (February 9, 1940), cited in Pauly, "*Gone With the Wind* and *The Grapes of Wrath* as Hollywood Histories of the Depression," 203.

27 Christensen, *Reel Politics*, 50.

28 Tag Gallagher, *John Ford: The Man and His Films* (Berkeley: University of California Press, 1986), 176–81.

29 Schatz, *Boom and Bust*, 93; Pulliam, "*The Grapes of Wrath*," 4; also see Locke, "*The Grapes of Wrath*," 388.

30 Locke, "*The Grapes of Wrath*," 389.

31 Donald Worster, *Dust Bowl: The Southern Plains in the 1930s* (New York: Oxford University Press, 1979), 13.

32 Ibid., 12, 15, 30.

33 Samuel Mason, "Hard Work: The Okie Migration to Kern County, California," MA diss., San Diego State University, Fall 2010, 48; Kevin Starr, *Endangered Dreams: The Great Depression in California* (New York: Oxford University Press, 1996), 236. Tom Collins, the manager of the Kern County Camp, "was [John] Steinbeck's most profitable source of information about migrant traditions." John H. Timmerman, "The Squatter's Circle in *The Grapes of Wrath*," in Barbara A. Heavilin, ed., *The Critical Response to John Steinbeck's "The Grapes of Wrath"* (Westport, CT: Greenwood Press 2000), 137. Steinbeck dedicated his book "To Tom, Who Lived It."

34 See the map in James N. Gregory, *American Exodus: The Dust Bowl Migration and Okie Culture in California* (New York: Oxford University Press, 1989), 5.

35 Worster, *Dust Bowl*, 13, 78–9, 97 (quotation).

36 Ibid., 57–8.

37 Ibid., 60.

38 Gregory, *American Exodus*, 5; Worster, *Dust Bowl*, 61.

39 Anthony J. Badger, *The New Deal: The Depression Years, 1933–40* (Chicago: Ivan R. Dee, 2002), 158–9, 187. *The Grapes of Wrath* was wrong to suggest that much land was controlled by companies, such as the Shawnee Land and Cattle Company, the owners of Muley's farm. "There were few farming corporations anywhere in Oklahoma," Donald Worster points out, ". . . independent operators were the rule, some of them large landowners, others not so large but caught up just as firmly in the web of commercialism." Worster, *Dust Bowl*, 58.

40 Norman Thomas, socialist candidate for president in the election of 1932, criticized Secretary of Agriculture Henry A. Wallace in 1934 for permitting Southern cotton-growers "to displace sharecroppers as part of the Triple-A's crop reduction program." Edward L. and Frederick H. Schapsmeier, "Henry A. Wallace: Agrarian Idealist or Agricultural Realist?", *Agricultural History*, vol. 41, no. 2 (April 1967), 133.

41 Worster, *Dust Bowl*, 39–40, 131; Badger, *The New Deal*, 171; Schapsmeier and Schapsmeier, "Henry A. Wallace," 134.

42 For what he saw as a missed opportunity, see David E. Conrad, *The Forgotten Farmers: The Story of Sharecroppers in the New Deal* (Urbana: University of Illinois Press, 1965), 206. Ironically, in view of the foregrounding of the Department of Agriculture in the shot of the sign for the "Farmworkers' Wheat Patch Camp," the Department of Agriculture on the whole looked down on sharecroppers and tenants, seeing them as unlikely to become prosperous, self-supporting farmers, and believing that it would be better both for them and agriculture itself if they moved to the cities. Theodore Saloutos, *The American Farmer and the New Deal* (Ames: Iowa State University Press, 1982), 261–2.

43 Badger, *The New Deal*, 147.

44 Gregory, *American Exodus*, 24.

45 Walter J. Stein, *California and the Dust Bowl Migration* (Westport, CT: Greenwood Press, 1973), 18–19.

46 www.dailyscript.com/scripts/grapes_of_wrath.html, accessed February 19, 2013.

47 Stein, *California and the Dust Bowl Migration*, 18–19.

48 Ibid., 45.

49 Gregory, *American Exodus*, 87; Stein, *California and the Dust Bowl Migration*, 49.

50 Gregory, *American Exodus*, 84–5; Stein, *California and the Dust Bowl Migration*, 54–7.

51 Gregory, *American Exodus*, 85.

52 Stein, *California and the Dust Bowl Migration*, 93–5.

53 Charles J. Shindo, *Dust Bowl Migrants in the American Imagination* (Lawrence: University of Kansas Press, 1997), 248.

54 Campbell, "The Ideology of the Social Consciousness Movie," 51.

55 This was not an unusual phenomenon in the Depression. Many men lost both their jobs and their role as "breadwinner," with women often becoming the principal source of income in families. The 1930s also saw women playing a more active role in politics and union organization. See Sara Evans, *Born to Liberty: A History of Women in America* (New York: The Free Press, 1989), 204–16 and Susan Ware, *Holding the Line: American Women in the 1930s* (Boston: Twayne, 1982), 41–9, 90–4, 97–103, 111.

56 Gallagher, *John Ford*, 179; Sanderson, "American Romanticism," 236; Pauly, "*Gone With the Wind* and *The Grapes of Wrath* as Hollywood Histories of the Depression," 208, 217 n. 13. As Leslie Gossage points out, Ma's final speech in the film is actually a combination of two of her speeches at different points in the novel. Gossage, "The Artful Propaganda of Ford's *The Grapes of Wrath*," in David Wyatt, ed., *New Essays on "The Grapes of Wrath"* (Cambridge: Cambridge University Press, 1990), 120–1.

57 Populism of the Hollywood variety revolved around the attempt to reassert traditional "American" values, including self-help and good neigborliness. Although it had some parallels with the Populist or People's Party of the 1890s, it lacked the ideology and detailed political program of the nineteenth-century Populists. See Wes D. Gehring, "Populist Comedy," in Wes D. Gehring,

ed., *Handbook of American Film Genres* (Westport: Greenwood Press, 1988), 124–43. On Capra, see Jeffrey Richards, "Frank Capra and the Cinema of Populism," *Cinema* [UK], no. 5 (February 1970), 22–8; Glenn A. Phelps, "The 'Populist' Films of Frank Capra," *Journal of American Studies*, vol. 13, no. 3 (1979), 377–92; Wes D. Gehring, *Populism and the Capra Legacy* (Westport: Greenwood Press, 1995), 1–27.

58 Locke, "*The Grapes of Wrath*," 387.

59 Gallagher, *John Ford*, 180.

60 Pauly, "*Gone With the Wind* and *The Grapes of Wrath* as Hollywood Histories of the Depression," 208.

61 Stein, *California and the Dust Bowl Migration*, 224–5; Gregory, *American Exodus*, 89.

62 Gregory, *American Exodus*, 155, 157.

63 Ibid., 160.

64 Ibid., 154.

65 Stein, *California and the Dust Bowl Migration*, 279–80. As the Okies became too expensive, California landowners began looking for cheaper migrant workers. In August 1942, the United States and Mexico signed a treaty for the importation of *braceros*. In the years to come, temporary Mexican laborers, both legal and illegal, would provide replacements for the Okies, most of whom were now living in cities. Ibid., 280–1.

66 Gallagher, *John Ford*, 176.

67 Pulliam, "*The Grapes of Wrath*," 4; "*Wrath*'s Start Breaks Records," *Motion Picture Herald*, vol. 138, no. 4 (January 27, 1940), 25.

68 Locke, "*The Grapes of Wrath*," 385; William Nable, Criterion Theater, Oklahoma City, Oklahoma, in "What the Picture Did for Me," *Motion Picture Herald*, vol. 138, no. 12 (March 23, 1940), 55; *Variety*, January 31, 1940, 14.

69 Twentieth-Century Fox released *The Snake Pit* (1948), dealing with mental illness, and two films on racism (both produced by Zanuck himself): *Pinky* (1949) and *No Way Out* (1950). Kramer's *Home of the Brave* (1949) dealt with racism in the army during the Second World War and *The Men* (1950) with the plight of paraplegics. Louis de Rochemont, who had pioneered "The March of Time" newsreels on the world situation, made two "problem" films: *Lost Boundaries* (1949), dealing with race, and *The Whistle at Eaton Falls* (1951), on the subject of labor relations.

70 Hamilton, *Writers in Hollywood*, 293, 301; Brian Neve, *Film and Politics in America: A Social Tradition* (London: Routledge, 1992), 84, 87–8.

71 Ayn Rand, *A Screen Guide for Americans*, quoted in Lary May, "Movie Star Politics: The Screen Actors' Guild, Cultural Convention, and the Hollywood Red Scare," in Lary May, ed., *Recasting America: Culture and Politics in the Age of the Cold War* (Chicago: University of Chicago Press, 1989), 145.

72 Christensen, *Reel Politics*, 52. In the Western-occupied zone of Austria, for example, the Information Services film section discouraged the distribution of critical movies such as *The Grapes of Wrath*. Reinhold Wagnleitner, "The Irony

of American Culture Abroad: Austria and the Cold War," in May, *Recasting America*, 294.

73 Schatz, *Boom and* Bust, 382.

74 *Motion Picture Herald*, vol. 169, no. 10 (December 6, 1947): 3966 [*sic*], 20.

75 Schatz, *Boom and Bust*, 393.

76 *Fortune* magazine commented that Zanuck "could risk a *Snake Pit* [on mental illness] because he had twenty-five or more other pictures a year and Betty Grable." Schatz, *Boom and Bust*, 384.

77 Richard Maltby, *Hollywood Cinema: An Introduction* (Oxford: Blackwell, 1995), 377.

78 *Our Daily Bread* (1934), directed by King Vidor, was an independent production dealing with city-dwellers who move to the countryside to set up a cooperative farming community that endures a drought and ultimately succeeds.

Chapter 9

1 On this type of self-reflexivity in general, see Rudy Behlmer and Tony Thomas, *Hollywood's Hollywood: The Movies About the Movies* (Secaucus, NJ: Citadel Press, 1975).

2 There are, by contrast, several books on the impact of the HUAC "Inquisition" on Hollywood. See for instance Larry Ceplair and Steven Englund, *The Inquisition in Hollywood: Politics in the Film Community, 1930–1960* (Berkeley: University of California Press, 1983); Bernard F. Dick, *Radical Innocence: A Critical Study of the Hollywood Ten* (Lexington: University Press of Kentucky, 1989); Michael Freedland with Barbara Paskin, *Witch-Hunt in Hollywood: McCarthy's War on Tinseltown* (London: JB Books, 2009); John J. Gladchuk, *Hollywood and Anti-Communism: HUAC and the Evolution of the Red Menace, 1935–1950* (New York: Routledge, 2007); Reynold Humphries, *Hollywood Blacklists: A Political and Cultural* History (Edinburgh: Edinburgh University Press, 2008); Robert Mayhew, *Ayn Rand and "Song of Russia": Communism and Anti-Communism in 1940s Hollywood* (Lanham, MD: Scarecrow Press, 2005); Victor S. Navasky, *Naming Names* (New York: Viking, 1980).

3 Ernest Giglio, *Here's Looking at You: Hollywood, Film and Politics* (New York: Peter Lang, 2005; 2nd. edn), 96.

4 There are, of course, a number of films (especially Westerns) that critics have suggested made indirect, metaphorical commentary on HUAC's investigations of Hollywood and the blacklist. These include *High Noon* (1952) and *Johnny Guitar* (1953).

5 The "Hollywood Ten" were the first ten "unfriendly witnesses," all communists or former communists, who were subpoenaed to appear before HUAC in October 1947. Most were screenwriters (Alvah Bessie, Lester Cole, Ring Lardner, Jr., John Howard Lawson, Albert Maltz, Samuel Ornitz, Adrian

Scott, and Dalton Trumbo), though Scott also worked as a producer. Herbert Biberman and Edward Dmytryk were both directors. All ten defied HUAC, were cited for "contempt of Congress," and eventually were jailed.

6 See Ceplair and Englund, *The Inquisition in Hollywood*, 157–8, 193, 210, 213, 258–9, 279–80, 281, 287, 299; Brian Neve, *Film and Politics in America: A Social Tradition* (London: Routledge, 1992), 108; Marc Eliot, *Walt Disney: Hollywood's Dark Prince* (London: André Deutsch, 1994), passim.

7 Nicole Potter, "Tales of the Red Menace," *Films in Review*, vol. 47, nos. 9–10 (September 1996), 33. Also see Dan Leab, "I was a Communist for the FBI," *History Today*, vol. 46, no. 12 (December 1996), 42–7. James Naremore terms these films "anticommunist noir" and notes that they were "neither artistically nor commercially successful," although *I Was a Communist for the F.B.I.* spun off into a syndicated television series called *I Led Three Lives*. Naremore, *More Than Night: Film Noir in Its Contexts* (Berkeley: University of California Press, 1998), 295, n. 29.

8 Potter, "Tales of the Red Menace," 30–1.

9 Giglio, *Here's Looking at You*, 104, 110; Ian Hamilton, *Writers in Hollywood, 1915–1951* (London: Heinemann, 1990), 285, 287; Potter, "Tales of the Red Menace," 31.

10 Giglio, *Here's Looking at You*, 100.

11 Most of this sequence was actually filmed at Union College, Schenectady, New York.

12 There might have been more controversy if it had been known that Dalton Trumbull, one of the Hollywood Ten, was one of the (uncredited) screenwriters on the film. www.imdb.com/title/tt0070903/fullcredits#cast, accessed January 25, 2013.

13 Hubbell has earlier pointed out that Roosevelt had made no effort to help Spain in 1937, provoking Katie to defend him on the grounds that "Congress was isolationist in '37."

14 On this point, see Richard Maltby, "Made for Each Other: The Melodrama of Hollywood and the House Committee on Un-American Activities, 1947," in Philip Davies and Brian Neve, eds, *Cinema, Politics and Society in America* (Manchester: Manchester University Press, 1981), 76–96.

15 Ceplair and Englund, *The Inquisition in Hollywood*, 282.

16 The actual text of the Waldorf Statement declared that "We will forthwith discharge or suspend without compensation those in our employ, and we will not re-employ any of the 10 until such time as he is acquitted or has purged himself of contempt and declares under oath that he is not a Communist." It also insisted that "We will not knowingly employ a Communist or a member of any party or group which advocates the overthrow of the government of the United States by force or by any illegal or unconstitutional methods." http://everything2.com/title/The+Waldorf+Statement, accessed January 26, 2013. On the Waldorf Statement and the beginning of the blacklist, see Ceplair and Englund, *The Inquisition in Hollywood*, 328–31.

17 On the formation of the committee, see Ceplair and Englund, *The Inquisition in Hollywood*, 275; Humphries, *Hollywood's Blacklists*, 88.

18 Humphrey Bogart, "I'm No Communist," *Photoplay* (March 1948), 53.

19 Ceplair and Englund, *The Inquisition in Hollywood*, 282.

20 Ibid., 281.

21 Ibid., 282.

22 Ibid., 282–3.

23 Ibid., 288.

24 Ibid., 276–7.

25 Ibid., 289.

26 Bogart, "I'm No Communist," 86. William Wyler, one of the founders of the CFA, was among the last to surrender, in 1953. See Humphries, *Hollywood Blacklists*, 150–1.

27 When Elia Kazan, who had "named names" to HUAC in 1952, received his honorary Oscar in March 1999, there were demonstrations outside the hall and a number of members of the audience at the Academy Awards ceremony pointedly refused to applaud. www.nytimes.com/1999/03/22/arts/amid-protests-elia-kazan-receives-his-oscar.html, accessed January 27, 2013.

28 Victor Navasky, "Has 'Guilty by Suspicion' Missed the Point?", *New York Times*, March 31, 1991, 9.

29 Ibid., 16.

30 See Navasky, *Naming Names*, ix.

31 The lawyer Felix Graff (Wanamaker) was based on a real lawyer, Martin Gang, who specialized in "clearing" individuals for the studios. Other victims of the blacklist associated with the film in addition to Wanamaker and Polonsky were Ileana Douglas, playing Zanuck's assistant (her grandparents were blacklisted) and Joan Scott, who appeared as a teacher (Scott was the widow of producer Adrian Scott, one of the original Hollywood Ten). Jeanne Hall, "The Benefits of Hindsight: Re-Visions of HUAC and the Film and Television Industries in *The Front* and *Guilty by Suspicion*," *Film Quarterly*, vol. 54, no. 2 (2001), 18.

32 Giglio, *Here's Looking at You*, 95.

33 Hall, "The Benefits of Hindsight," 16.

34 Faulk's story was recounted in the made-for-television film *Fear on Trial*, first broadcast by CBS in 1975.

35 Nicole Potter remarks of *Guilty by Suspicion* that "almost everybody seems to have been compromised by attending one meeting with a friend in the '30s." Potter, "Tales of the Red Menace," 32.

36 Polonsky quoted in Navasky, "Has 'Guilty by Suspicion' Missed the Point?" 16.

37 Navasky, "Has 'Guilty by Suspicion' Missed the Point?" 16.

38 Hall, "The Benefits of Hindsight," 25.

39 For the story of the making and suppression of *Salt of the Earth*, a film produced by blacklistees and dealing with a strike of Mexican-American

miners in New Mexico in 1951–2, see Herbert Biberman, *Salt of the Earth: The Story of a Film* (Boston: Beacon Press, 1965) and James J. Lorence, *The Suppression of "Salt of the Earth": How Hollywood, Big Labor and Politicians Blacklisted a Movie in Cold War America* (Albuquerque: University of New Mexico Press, 1999).

40 Hall, "The Benefits of Hindsight," 21.

41 Trumbo, as quoted in Navasky, *Naming Names*, 393.

42 Hall, "The Benefits of Hindsight," 26.

43 This sequence, drawn from the original Polonsky script, was based on an incident in which David Raksin, who had written the score for Polonsky's *Force of Evil* (1948), asked the writer/director if he could name him before HUAC since Polonsky himself had already been blacklisted. Navasky, "Has 'Guilty by Suspicion' Missed the Point?" 16.

44 Though Donald F. Crosby argues that McCarthy did not enjoy as much support within the Roman Catholic Church as earlier believed. Crosby, *God, Church, and Flag: Senator Joseph R. McCarthy and the Catholic Church, 1950–1957* (Chapel Hill: University of North Carolina Press, 2009; originally pub. 1978).

45 Robert J. Goldstein, *Political Repression in Modern America: 1870 to the Present* (Cambridge, Mass.: Schenkman, 1978), xvi.

46 See Murray Levin, *Political Hysteria in America: The Democratic Capacity for Repression* (New York: Basic Books, 1973), 4–5, 7; Robert Goldstein, *Political Repression in 19th Century Europe* (London: Croom Helm, 1983), xii.

47 Levin, *Political Hysteria in America*, 4–7 (quotation from 6).

48 Ibid., 5.

49 Richard Hofstadter, *The Paranoid Style in American Politics, and Other Essays* (New York: Knopf, 1965); David Brion Davis, *The Fear of Conspiracy: Images of Un-American Subversion from the Revolution to the Present* (Ithaca, NY: Cornell University Press, 1971).

50 Levin, *Political Hysteria in America*, 6 and 9 (quotations from 6).

51 Frank Donner, *Protectors of Privilege: Red Squads and Political Repression in Urban America* (Berkeley and Los Angeles: University of California Press, 1990).

52 Christensen, *Reel Politics*, 87.

53 Dorothy B. Jones, "Communism and the Movies: A Study of Film Content," in John Cogley, *Report on Blacklisting I: Movies* (New York: Fund for the Republic, 1956), 219, 221.

54 Murray Ross, "Labor Relations in Hollywood," *Annals of the American Academy of Political and Social Science*, vol. 254, The Motion Picture Industry (November 1947), 58–62, 6–7 (quotation from 6).

55 There are a number of more or less sensational books claiming to expose the relationship between Hollywood and the mafia. See, for example, Michael Munn, *The Hollywood Connection: The True Story of Organized Crime in*

Hollywood (New York: Robson Books, 1999) and Ted Schwarz, *Hollywood Confidential: How the Studios Beat the Mob at Their Own Game* (Lanham, MD: Taylor Publishing, 2007).

56 See Mike Nielsen and Gene Mailes, *Hollywood's Other Blacklist: Union Struggles in the Studio System* (London: BFI, 1995), 29–38.

57 Giglio, *Here's Looking at You*, 103.

58 Ross, "Labor Relations in Hollywood," 63–4: Gerald Horne, *Class Struggle in Hollywood, 1930–1950: Moguls, Mobsters, Stars, Reds, and Trade Unionists* (Austin: University of Texas Press, 2001), 3–4, 14–20, 153–222.

59 Horne, *Class Struggle in Hollywood*, 222.

Chapter 10

1 Seth Cagin and Philip Dray, *We Are Not Afraid: The Story of Goodman, Schwerner, and Chaney, and the Civil Rights Campaign for Mississippi* (New York: Nation Books, 2006), 1–14, 17–22, 26–7, 35–41, 44–6, 278–300. Also see William Bradford Huie, *Three Lives for Mississippi* (London: Heinemann, 1965), 156–90.

2 On June 21, 2005, 41 years to the day after the activists' murder, former Klansman Edgar Ray Killen was found guilty of their manslaughter by a biracial jury in Neshoba County, Mississippi. Neshoba County District Attorney Mark Duncan was quoted as saying that, in the light of this verdict, his county would at last escape its negative portrayal in *Mississippi Burning* and not "be known by a Hollywood movie anymore." http://edition.cnn.com/2005/LAW/06/21/mississippi.killings/, accessed April 5, 2013.

3 Gavin Smith "'Mississippi' Gambler: Alan Parker Rides Again," *Film Comment*, vol. 24, no. 6 (November 1988), 29.

4 Patrick Goldstein, "It's only a movie . . .," *Empire*, no. 1 (June/July 1989), 36.

5 Thomas Doherty, "*Mississippi Burning*," *Cineaste*, vol. 17, no. 2 (1989), 49; Thulani Davis, "Civil Rights and Wrongs," *American Film*, vol. 14, no. 3 (December 1988), 34–5.

6 John Salmond, "Alan Parker's *Mississippi Burning*," *Cinema Papers*, no. 73 (May 1989), 56.

7 The film does not, however, make a specific connection between this and the final prosecution of those involved in the killing of the three young men for depriving the victims of their civil rights (a Federal offense) instead of for murder (a crime against victims of state law). On the legal proceedings from 1965 to 1970, see Cagin and Dray, *We Are Not Afraid*, 441–52.

8 Toplin, *History by Hollywood*, 27; Cagin and Dray, *We Are Not Afraid*, 2.

9 Michael Yarrow, who had been born in Mississippi and arrived back in the state as an activist on the day Chaney, Goodman, and Schwerner were killed, recalled that Mississippi news suggested their disappearance was a hoax. Yarrow, "Burning Mississippi: Letters Home/Hollywood History," *Appalachian Journal*, vol. 17, no. 1 (Fall 1989), 53.

10 Parker based this scene "on the outtakes from the real incident." "A Cinematic lynching of the truth," *Empire*, no. 1 (June/July 1989), 36.

11 Sean French, "Parker's Brand: *Mississippi Burning*," *Sight and Sound*, vol. 58, no. 2 (Spring 1989), 132.

12 Barry McIlheney, "Hollywood History," *Empire*, no. 1 (June–July 1989), 82; Smith, "'Mississippi' Gambler," 29.

13 "Editorial," *Cineaste*, vol. 17, no. 2 (1989), 2.

14 "Editorial," *Cineaste*; Doherty, "*Mississippi Burning*," ibid., 49. At one point in the film, when Frank (Michael Rooker), a local racist, suggests Anderson goes back to his "commie, nigger-loving bosses up north," Anderson realistically observes that "you must not know my boss, Mr. Hoover . . . He's not too fond of commies."

15 "Editorial," *Cineaste*; Yarrow, "Burning Mississippi," 56.

16 Cagin and Dray, *We Are Not Afraid*, 393–400.

17 Salmond, "Alan Parker's *Mississippi Burning*," 57.

18 Jane Merkin, "New Movies–*Mississippi Burning*," *City Limits* [London] (4–11 May 1989), 20.

19 Toplin, *History by Hollywood*, 36; Smith, "'Mississippi' Gambler," 30; Goldstein, "It's only a movie . . .," 38.

20 "Editorial," *Cineaste*.

21 This particular verse deals with Noah condemning Canaan, the son of Noah's younger son Ham who has displeased him, to become the servant (in some translations slave) of one of Noah's other sons, Japhet. It needs considerable reinterpretation to transform into a justification of racism and segregation.

22 "I want the children up front," Parker insisted while shooting the rally sequence. "They have such extraordinary faces—I want people to see where the seeds of bigotry begin." Goldstein, "It's only a movie," 37.

23 Brian Case, "Alan Parker–Southern Discomfort," *Time Out* [London], no. 971 (March 29–April 5, 1989), 25.

24 This shot had its origins in a spontaneous gesture by Frances McDormand. Parker, seeing it and liking it, reshot it to include in the film. Davis, "Civil Rights and Wrongs," 38.

25 Case, "Alan Parker–Southern Discomfort," 24; Davis, "Civil Rights and Wrongs," 36; Smith, "'Mississippi' Gambler," 30.

26 See Eric Foner, *Reconstruction: America's Unfinished Revolution, 1863–1877* (New York: Harper and Row, 1988).

27 See, for example, Edward L. Ayers, *The Promise of the New South: Life After Reconstruction* (New York: Oxford University Press, 1992), 136, 146.

28 Lawrence Goodwyn, *Democratic Promise: The Populist Movement in America* (New York: Oxford University Press, 1976), 25–86, 162–264.

29 Goodwyn, *Democratic Promise*, 264–306. On Populism and African Americans, also see Charles Postel, *The Populist Vision* (New York: Oxford

University Press, 2007), 173–203; Gerald H. Gaither, *Blacks and the Populist Revolt: Ballots and Bigotry in the "New South"* (Montgomery: University of Alabama Press, 1977).

30 Goodwyn, *Democratic Promise*, 307–50, 387–533.

31 George Brown Tindall and David E. Shi, *America: A Narrative History* (New York: W. W. Norton, 1984), 474; J. Morgan Kousser, *The Shaping of Southern Politics: Suffrage Restriction and the Establishment of the One-Party South, 1880–1910* (New Haven: Yale University Press, 1974), 142–4, 159–65, 183–95.

32 Tindall and Shi, *America*, 475; Russell Korobkin, "The Politics of Disfranchisement in Georgia," *The Georgia Historical Quarterly*, vol. 74, no. 1 (Spring 1990), 20–58.

33 Case, "Alan Parker–Southern Discomfort," 23–4.

34 Davis, "Civil Rights and Wrongs," 35, 54; Goldstein, "It's only a movie . . .," 38.

35 "'Burning' heats up controversy in city spotlighted by film," *The Hollywood Reporter*, vol. 305, no. 45 (January 13, 1989), 28.

36 George Lardner, Jr., "On the Set: Dallas in Wonderland," *Washington Post*, May 19, 1991, http://web.archive.org/web/20000517172459/http://luna.cc.lehigh.edu/STONE:16:FRAME:X:41, accessed April 8, 2013.

37 Vincent Canby, "*JFK*: When Everything Amounts to Nothing," December 20, 1991, *New York Times*, www.nytimes.com/1991/12/20/movies/review-film-jfk-when-everything-amounts-to-nothing.html?pagewanted=all&src=pm, accessed April 8, 2013.

38 George F. Will, "*JFK*: Oliver Stone's Cartoon History a Three-hour Lie," *Seattle Post-Intelligencer*, December 26, 1991, A15.

39 Toplin, *History by Hollywood*, 72; Bernard Weinraub, "Valenti Calls *JFK* 'Hoax' and 'Smear,'" *New York Times*, April 2, 1992, http://www.nytimes.com/1992/04/02/movies/valenti-calls-jfk-hoax-and-smear.html, accessed April 8, 2013.

40 Norman Kagan, *The Cinema of Oliver Stone* (Oxford: Roundhouse, 1995), 13–15; Randy Roberts and David Welky, "A Sacred Mission: Oliver Stone and Vietnam," in Toplin, ed., *Oliver Stone's USA*, 66–70.

41 Kagan, *The Cinema of Oliver Stone*, 15–17; Roberts and Welky, "A Sacred Mission," 70–3.

42 Kagan, *The Cinema of Oliver Stone*, 17–18, 20, 28; Roberts and Welky, "A Sacred Mission," 74–5.

43 Roberts and Welky, "A Sacred Mission," 74; Rosenstone, "Oliver Stone as Historian," in Toplin, *Oliver Stone's USA*, 37.

44 Toplin, *History by Hollywood*, 49; Roberts and Welky, "A Sacred Mission," 83.

45 Roberts and Welky, "A Sacred Mission," 83.

46 Roberts and Welky, "A Sacred Mission," 83; Toplin, *History by Hollywood*, 49–50; Kagan, *The Cinema of Oliver Stone*, 183.

47 Toplin, *History by Hollywood*, 50–1. For Newman's view of the war, see John M. Newman, *JFK and Vietnam: Deception, Intrigue, and the Struggle for Power* (New York: Warner Books, 1992).

48 Kagan, *The Cinema of Oliver Stone*, 185; Toplin, *History by Hollywood*, 52.

49 The case provided the background to the rise of the rightwing military junta that ruled Greece, with US support, from 1967 to 1974.

50 Adam Barker, "Cries and Whispers," *Sight and Sound*, vol. 1, no. 10 (February 1992), 24.

51 The Kennedy record on civil rights is emphasized even further in the subsequent shot of a tearful black woman saying on television: "He did so much for this country, for colored people. Why? Why?"

52 Ron Briley, "Teaching *JFK*: Potential Dynamite in the Hands of Our Youth?," *Film and History*, vol. 28, nos. 1–2 (1998), 12; Nick Bryant, *The Bystander: John F. Kennedy and the Struggle for Black Equality* (New York: Basic Books, 2006), *passim*.

53 Alexander Cockburn, "John and Oliver's bogus adventure," *Sight and Sound*, vol. 1, no. 10 (February 1992), 23; Marcus Raskin, "*JFK* and the Culture of Violence," *American Historical Review*, vol. 97, no. 2 (April 1992), 493.

54 "Past Imperfect: History According to the Movies–A Conversation between Mark C. Carnes and Oliver Stone," *Cineaste*, vol. 22, no. 4 (March 1997), 36.

55 Rosenstone, *Visions of the Past*, 127.

56 For NSAM 263 and the Taylor-McNamara Report, see: http://history.state. gov/historicaldocuments/frus1961–63v04/d194; http://history.state.gov/ historicaldocuments/frus1961–63v04/d167; both accessed April 9, 2013. Stone's comments are in "Stone Responds–NSAM Argument," in Toplin, *Oliver Stone's USA*, 261–2.

57 For Stone's comments, see ibid., 262–3; for Sklar's, see Gary Crowdus, "Getting the Facts Straight," *Cineaste*, vol. 19, no. 1 (1992), 28–32. The text of NSAM 273 is at www.lbjlib.utexas.edu/johnson/archives.hom/nsams/nsam273. asp, accessed April 9, 2013.

58 Stanley Karnow, "*JFK*," in Carnes, *Past Imperfect*, 273.

59 Toplin, *History by Hollywood*, 58.

60 "I just hope," his wife shrewdly remarked in mid-1965, "that foreign problems do not keep mounting. They do not represent Lyndon's kind of presidency." Lady Bird Johnson, quoted in Eric F. Goldman, *The Tragedy of Lyndon Johnson* (London: Macdonald, 1969), 378.

61 Robert F. Kennedy, *Thirteen Days: A Memoir of the Cuban Missile Crisis* (New York: W. W. Norton, 1999), 38.

62 Karnow, "*JFK*," 270–1; Toplin, *History by Hollywood*, 54.

63 "Stone Responds–Jim Garrison," in Toplin, *Oliver Stone's USA*, 271, 275–7.

64 Stone, as quoted in William D. Romanowski, "Oliver Stone's *JFK*: Commercial Filmmaking, Cultural History, and Conflict," *Journal of Popular Film and Television*, vol. 21, no. 2 (Summer 1993), 67.

65 Ebert, "*JFK*."

66 Canby, "*JFK*: When Everything Amounts to Nothing" (compare Kenneth Turan, "*JFK*: Conspiracy in the Cross Hairs: Oliver Stone's Riveting, Controversial Saga of the Kennedy Assassination," *Los Angeles Times*, December 20, 1991); Kagan, *The Cinema of Oliver Stone*, 188.

67 Stone, as in Romanowski, "Oliver Stone's *JFK*," 67.

68 Canby, "*JFK*: When Everything Amounts to Nothing."

69 David M. Oshinsky, *A Conspiracy So Immense: The World of Joe McCarthy* (New York: Oxford University Press, 2005); Richard Hofstadter, "The Paranoid Style in American Politics," in Hofstadter, *The Paranoid Style in American Politics, and Other Essays* (New York: Knopf, 1965).

70 "Stone on Stone's Image," in Toplin, *Oliver Stone's USA*, 62.

71 Canby, "*JFK*: Where Everything Amounts to Nothing."

72 Gary Crowdus, "Clarifying the Conspiracy: An Interview with Oliver Stone," *Cineaste*, vol. 19, no. 1 (1992), 25.

73 Robert Burgoyne, *The Hollywood Historical Film* (Oxford: Blackwell, 2008), 130.

74 It is now available, in various versions, some with accompanying analysis, on *YouTube* and other internet sites.

75 Robert Burgoyne, *Film Nation*, 91.

76 Toplin, *History by Hollywood*, 63.

77 "Stone Responds-Questions About the Assassination of JFK," in Toplin, *Oliver Stone's USA*, 284.

78 Roger Ebert, "*JFK*," *Chicago Sun-Times*, December 20, 1991. Owen Gleiberman similarly commented on Kennedy's "head shooting off to the left (hence a second gunman aiming from the [grassy] knoll)." Gleiberman, "JFK (1991)," *Entertainment Weekly*, January 10, 1992.

79 Turan, "*JFK*: Conspiracy in the Cross Hairs." Rita Kempley sardonically noted that the cast "includes every liberal sympathizer in Hollywood except Jane Fonda." Kempley, "*JFK*," *Washington Post*, December 20, 1991.

80 Burgoyne, *The Hollywood Historical Film*, 141.

81 Gleiberman, "*JFK* (1991)."

82 "Stone Responds-Jim Garrison," in Toplin, *Oliver Stone's USA*, 274.

83 See, for example, Michael L. Kurtz, "Oliver Stone, *JFK* and History," in Toplin, *Oliver Stone's USA*, 169. For websites devoted to identifying such mistakes, see: www.jfk-online.com/jfk100menu.html; http://22november1963.org.uk/factual-errors-oliver-stone-movie-jfk; both accessed April 13, 2013.

84 Roy Grundman and Cynthia Lucia, "Gays, Women and an Abstinent Hero: The Sexual Politics of *JFK*," *Cineaste*, vol. 19, no. 1 (1992), 20–2; Desson Howe, "*JFK*," *Washington Post*, December 20, 1991.

85 "Stone Responds-Jim Garrison," in Toplin, *Oliver Stone's USA*, 274.

86 "Stone on Stone's Image," ibid., 40, 48.

87 Briley, "Teaching *JFK*," 11.

88 "Stone on Stone's Image," in Toplin, *Oliver Stone's USA*, 41, 45. See Oliver Stone and Zachary Sklar, *JFK: The Book of the Screenplay* (New York: Applause, 1992).

89 "Stone on Stone's Image," in Toplin, *Oliver Stone's USA*, 48.

90 Robert Brent Toplin, "Introduction," in Toplin, *Oliver Stone's USA*, 15–16.

91 Kurtz, "Oliver Stone, *JFK*, and History," in Toplin, *Oliver Stone's USA*, 174–5.

92 Toplin, "Introduction," in Toplin, *Oliver Stone's USA*, 21.

93 "Stone Responds-Stone on Kurtz" and "Stone Responds-Questions About the Assassination of JFK," both in Toplin, *Oliver Stone's USA*, 260, 284.

INDEX